R. Gupta's®

CLAT

Common Law Admission Test

Previous Years' Papers
(Solved)

For Undergraduate (UG) Programmes

by
RPH Editorial Board

2020
EDITION

Ramesh Publishing House, New Delhi

Published by

O.P. Gupta *for* Ramesh Publishing House

Admin. Office

12-H, New Daryaganj Road, Opp. Officers' Mess,
New Delhi-110002 ✆ 23261567, 23275224, 23275124

E-mail: info@rameshpublishinghouse.com
Website: www.rameshpublishinghouse.com

Showroom

- Balaji Market, Nai Sarak, Delhi-6 ✆ 23253720, 23282525
- 4457, Nai Sarak, Delhi-6, ✆ 23918938

Book Code: R-2071

ISBN: 978-81-942336-2-6

HSN Code : 49011010

CONTENTS

Previous Paper (Solved)

Common Law Admission Test (CLAT-UG)

Entrance Exam, 2019

Section-I : English Including Comprehension

Directions (Qs. No. 1-10): *From each set of sentences given below, choose the sentence that is grammatically correct.*

1. A. A few judges have cut short their vacation to clear a long pending cases
B. A few judges have cut short vacation to clear the long pending cases
C. A few judges has cut short its vacation to clear the long pending cases
D. A few judges have cut short their vacation to clear the long pending cases

2. A. Where's Hari? Here is he, right in front of us!
B. Where's Hari? Here he is, right in front of us!
C. Wheres' Hari? He is here, right in front of us!
D. Where's Hari? Is he here, right in front of us!

3. A. Customs officer's do not allow passenger to carry banned items into or out of the country.
B. Customs officers does not allow passengers to carry banned items into or out of country.
C. Customs officers do not allows passengers to carry banned items into or out of country.
D. Customs officers do not allow passengers to carry banned items into or out of the country.

4. A. Neither this nor that machine is working
B. Neither this nor that machine are working
C. Neither this and that machine is working
D. Neither this but that machine is working

5. A. I shall be doing a MBA online, and continue with my present job
B. I shall do a MBA online, and continue with my present job
C. I shall do an MBA online, and continue with my present job
D. I shall do an MBA online, but continuing with my present job

6. A. As soon as I boarded the train, I realized that I left my wallet at home
B. As soon as I boarded the train, I realize that I had left wallet at home
C. As soon as I board the train, I realized that I leave my wallet at home
D. As soon as I boarded the train, I realized that I had left my wallet at home

7. A. We can take either the morning flight nor the one in the afternoon.
B. We can take neither the morning flight or the one in the afternoon.
C. We can take either morning flight or the one in afternoon.
D. We can take either the morning flight or the one in the afternoon.

8. A. The management have promised that it will consider my appeal.
B. The management has promised that it will consider my appeal.
C. The management has promise that they will consider my appeal.
D. The management has promised that it will considered my appeal.

9. A. Tourists must follow the norms set upon the country they visit
B. Tourists must follow norms set by country they visit
C. Tourists must follow the norms set by the country they visit
D. Tourists must follow the norms set by the country they visits

10. A. An important file, along with two uniforms, are missing from the police station
B. A important file, along with two uniforms, is missed from the police station
C. An important files, along with two uniforms, are missing from the police station
D. An important file, along with two uniforms, is missing from the police station

Directions (Qs. No. 11-15): *In each of the questions given below, each sentence is labelled with a letter. From the given choices, choose the most logical order of sentences that constructs a coherent paragraph.*

11. (*a*) One of them copied and pasted large portions of the required text from a website.

(*b*) Before assigning the project to his students, the guide gave a presentation on plagiarism.
(*c*) The expulsion order that followed was not alarming.
(*d*) A few students did not pay much heed to the consequences of the illegal act.

A. (*c*)(*a*)(*b*)(*d*) B. (*d*)(*b*)(*c*)(*a*)
C. (*b*)(*a*)(*d*)(*c*) D. (*b*)(*d*)(*a*)(*c*)

12. (*a*) Goals are set, and relevant data is collected and analyzed.
(*b*) Strategies are made on the basis of the data and resources made available.
(*c*) There are various stages in framing a management-strategy, and its implementation.
(*d*) The strategies are implemented and monitored to ensure that the goals are achieved.

A. (*a*)(*b*)(*d*)(*c*) B. (*a*)(*c*)(*b*)(*d*)
C. (*c*)(*a*)(*b*)(*d*) D. (*c*)(*b*)(*a*)(*d*)

13. (*a*) Despite the awareness, some citizens fail to pay their taxes honestly.
(*b*) One of the factors that impacts our country's economy is income-tax.
(*c*) Awareness regarding this aspect of our economy is often made through the education system and media.
(*d*) Most of these defaulters not only get into trouble, but they also create additional work for the income-tax department.

A. (*a*)(*d*)(*b*)(*c*) B. (*c*)(*b*)(*a*)(*d*)
C. (*b*)(*c*)(*a*)(*d*) D. (*b*)(*d*)(*a*)(*c*)

14. (*a*) The responsible citizen helped to foil the plan of a hijack.
(*b*) The deep pockets of his leather jacket contained what had been feared!
(*c*) A person called up the airport and gave a message.
(*d*) All the passengers were carefully frisked, and one of them was asked to step aside.

A. (*b*)(*a*)(*d*)(*c*) B. (*c*)(*d*)(*b*)(*a*)
C. (*d*)(*a*)(*c*)(*b*) D. (*c*)(*d*)(*a*)(*b*)

15. (*a*) In the following years, more layers of snow add up to the existing mass.
(*b*) Consequently, the weight of the snow compresses and turns into solid ice.
(*c*) Most glaciers are found near the Poles.
(*d*) They begin to form when snow remains in the same area all year round.

A. (*a*)(*c*)(*b*)(*d*) B. (*c*)(*d*)(*b*)(*a*)
C. (*a*)(*b*)(*d*)(*c*) D. (*c*)(*d*)(*a*)(*b*)

Directions (Qs. No. 16-20): *Choose the correct meaning for each of the foreign language words and phrases given below.*

16. inter vivos
A. a transaction made for obtaining a legacy
B. an agreement to promote the welfare of one's country
C. a transaction made between living people
D. an agreement between warring nations

17. quantum ramifactus
A. the amount of damages suffered
B. the quality of goods supplied
C. the amount of relief given for damages caused
D. the weightage given to someone's suggestion

18. malus
A. mass B. harmless
C. harmful D. comforting

19. Volvo
A. I roll B. I run
C. I leap D. I jump

20. Charade
A. series B. charter
C. pretense D. spate

Directions (Qs. No. 21-25): *Choose the correctly spelled words in questions to fill in the blanks.*

21. Malti Ahuja is making a sincere effort to pay off her ....
A. crediter B. creditar
C. credittor D. creditor

22. It is our responsibility to leave a green and clean world for our ....
A. descendents B. decendants
C. descendants D. descendantes

23. The patient's death was the result of sheer .... on the part of the surgeon.
A. negligience B. negligence
C. negligennce D. neglegence

24. The scientist's biography is a blatant .... of facts.
A. misrepresentation B. misreprezentation
C. misrepresentetion D. misreprisentation

25. It was a .... to work with these scientists.
A. previlege B. priviledge
C. privilige D. privilege

Directions (Qs. No. 26-30): *Fill in the blank with the correct options.*

26. Son, ... ! Research the company before you apply for the job.
A. build castles in the air
B. hit the ceiling
C. get off on the wrong foot
D. hold your horses

27. Please, ... ! This is not the time to get anxious.
A. pull yourself together
B. pass the buck

C. bark up the wrong tree
D. go on a wild goose chase

28. In our company, we don't accept such carelessly done work. ....
A. So far so good.
B. Get your act together.
C. We'll cross the bridge when we come to it.
D. Your guess is as good as mine.

29. I can't work on this assignment anymore! I think I have ....
A. broken the ice
B. added insult to injury
C. chewed cud
D. bitten off more than I can chew

30. I'm a historian. I'm a .... in this seminar on robots!
A. drop in the bucket
B. fish out of water
C. fly in the ointment
D. fly on the wall

Directions (Qs. No. 31-40): *The questions in this section are based on what is stated or implied in the passage given below. For each question, choose the option that most accurately and completely answers the question.*

The words Invention and Innovation are closely linked, but they are not interchangeable. The inventor is a genius who uses his intellect, imagination, time and resources to create something that does not exist. But this invention may or may not be of utility to the masses. It is the enterprising innovator who uses various resources, skills and time to make the invention available for use. The innovator might use the invention as it is, modify it or even blend two or more inventions to make one marketable product. A great example is that of the iPhone which is a combination of various inventions.

If an invention is the result of countless trials and errors, so can be the case with an innovation. Not every attempt to make an invention is successful. Not every innovation sees the light of the day. Benjamin Franklin had the belief that success doesn't come without challenge, mistake, and in a few cases failure.

One of the world's most famous innovators, Steve Jobs says, "Sometimes when you innovate, you make mistakes. It is best to admit them quickly and get on with improving your other innovations."

Thus, inventors and innovators have to be intrepid enough to take risks; consider failures as stepping stones and not stumbling blocks.

Some inventions are the result of a keen observation or a simple discovery. The inventor of Velcro, also called the zipless zipper, is the Swiss engineer George de Mestral. He was hiking in the woods when he found burrs clinging to his clothes and his dog's fur. Back at home, he studied the burrs. He discovered that each burr was a collection of tiny hooks which made it cling on to another object. A few years later, he made and patented the strips of fabric that came to us as Velcro.

The world of inventions and innovations is a competitive one. But the race does not end here; it is also prevalent in the case of getting intellectual property rights. There have been inventors who failed to get a single patent while there have been some who managed to amass numerous patents in their lifetime. Thomas Edison had 1,093 patents to his credit!

We relate the telephone with Alexander Graham Bell. It is believed that around the same time, Antonio Meucci had also designed the telephone, but due to lack of resources and various hardships, he could not proceed with the patent of his invention. It is also believed that Elisha Gray had made a design for the telephone and applied for the patent at the U.S. patent office on the same day as Graham Bell did. By sheer chance, Graham's lawyer's turn to file the papers came first. Hence, Graham was granted the first patent for the telephone.

It is not easy, and at times almost impossible, for an inventor to be an innovator too. There are very few like Thomas Edison who graduated from being an incredible inventor to a successful manufacturer and businessman with brilliant marketing skills.

While innovations that have helped to enhance the quality of life are laudable, equally laudable are the inventions that laid the foundation of these very innovations.

31. The text in the passage can be best termed as:
A. narrative
B. descriptive
C. persuasive
D. expository

32. The main idea of the author is to:
A. highlight the difficulties faced by innovators.
B. focus on the hardships of patent-seekers.
C. compare innovators to inventors.
D. reveal the importance of inventors.

33. The author believes that:
A. innovators enhance the utility of inventions.
B. innovators face fewer challenges than inventors do.
C. every inventor has a patent for the invention.
D. invention is the same as innovation.

34. Benjamin Franklin and Steve Jobs, believe that:
A. there is no place for mistakes in the process of making an innovation.
B. making a mistake before finding success is not unusual.
C. failure is a permanent stumbling block.
D. all innovators have to go through failure.

35. Velcro can be best described as:
A. a highly-planned and deeply researched invention

B. the fruit of failure
C. the need of the hour
D. an accidental invention

36. It is believed that Graham Bell became the first patent holder of the telephone because of:
A. his ingenuity and good fortune.
B. the carelessness of Elisha's lawyer.
C. the clever trick played by his lawyer.
D. the biased officials in the patent office.

37. Which of the following is Untrue?
A. Inventors may not be innovators.
B. Innovators are not expected to be enterprising.
C. To get a patent, the applicant has to follow a legal process.
D. Intellectual property rights are not always easy to get.

38. Which of the following texts from the passage clearly indicates failure?
A. The world of inventions and innovations is a competitive one.
B. Not every innovation sees the light of the day.
C. Thus, inventors and innovators have to be intrepid enough to take risks.
D. None of the above

39. Which of these words can replace the word intrepid?
A. hasty B. intellectual
C. daring D. rich

40. Which of these words is the antonym of laudable?
A. praiseworthy
B. challenging
C. tiring
D. disgraceful

Section-II : General Knowledge and Current Affairs

41. The Chief Central Information Commissioner at present is:
A. Sudhir Bhargava B. R.K. Mathur
C. Sridhar Acharyulu D. Handu

42. India has recently set up the latest ISRO's Satellite Tracking and Data Reception Centre in:
A. Maldives B. Sri Lanka
C. Bhutan D. Nepal

43. The number of complaints with the Banking Ombudsman registered during 2018 increased by:
A. 10% B. 15%
C. 20% D. 25%

44. Which of the following formally quit from UNESCO recently?
A. USA B. China
C. Sweden D. India

45. The maximum punishment for a cyber-stalker imposed by an anti-terrorism court in Pakistan is:
A. 5 years B. 14 years
C. 10 years D. 24 years

46. In a major relief to micro, small and medium enterprises, the GST Council has recently increased the tax exemption limit per annum to:
A. 20 lakhs B. 30 lakhs
C. 40 lakhs D. 60 lakhs

47. Which of the following fruits got the Geographical Indication during October, 2018?
A. Shahi Litchi
B. Laxman Bhog Mango
C. Sirumalai Hill Banana
D. Mahabaleshwar Strawberry

48. The richest person in the world as per the details revealed in March, 2019 is:
A. Bill Gates B. Jeff Bezos
C. Amancio Ortega D. Bernard Arnault

49. The number of EB-5 visa applications, also known as 'cash for Green Card' visa to the U.S. has increased in the last two years by about:
A. 100% B. 200%
C. 300% D. 400%

50. India purchased surveillance aircrafts (AWACS) during 2016 from:
A. USA B. France
C. Russia D. Israel

51. The fastest train in India is:
A. Gatiman Express B. Shatabdi Express
C. Vande Bharat Express D. Rajdhani Express

52. The first humanoid police robot was introduced in the State of:
A. Karnataka B. Delhi
C. Gujarat D. Kerala

53. The world's first Diesel to Electric locomotive twin engine of 10,000 horse power was flagged off in:
A. USA B. China
C. India D. South Korea

54. The Headquarters of International Solar Alliance consisting of more than 121 countries is located in:
A. India B. South Africa
C. Malaysia D. China

55. The prestigious Seoul Peace Prize for 2018 was conferred on:

A. Kofi Annan B. Angela Merkel
C. Narendra Modi D. Putin

56. Which of the following countries during 2019 provided life time personal tax exemption to women with four children?
A. India B. Hungary
C. Norway D. Finland

57. In the 64th Film Fare Award, who won the best actress award?
A. Katrina Kapoor B. Priyanka Chopra
C. Deepika Padukone D. Alia Bhatt

58. Recently, the Government of India relaxed the Angel Tax Norms for Start-ups and enhanced the investment limit to:
A. ₹ 25 Crore B. ₹ 20 Crore
C. ₹ 15 Crore D. ₹ 30 Crore

59. India's first Chairperson of Lokpal is:
A. Justice Dipak Mishra
B. Justice Dilip Bhosale
C. Justice P.C. Ghose
D. Justice Thakur

60. In how many phases the 17th Lok Sabha elections were held in 2019?
A. Six B. Seven
C. Five D. Eight

61. How many States went to polls along with the 2019 Lok Sabha elections?
A. Three B. Four
C. Five D. Two

62. The National Common Mobility Card (NCMC), launched by the Central Government recently is also dubbed as:
A. One Nation One Card
B. Citizenship Card
C. Aadhar Card
D. Shopping Card

63. Which of the following cities bagged the Cleanest City Award for three consecutive years?
A. Mysore B. Ahmedabad
C. Chandigarh D. Indore

64. Who is known as the 'Father of Local Government in India'?
A. Lord Curzon B. Lord Mayo
C. Lord Wellesley D. Lord Ripon

65. Under which of the following missions, India has successfully tested its first-ever Anti-Satellite (A-SAT) Missile capability?
A. Mission Shakti B. Mission Agni
C. Mission Raftar D. Mission Sahas

66. Which Indian personality is the recipient of the Oxford University's Bodley Medal 2019?
A. Raghuram Rajan B. Amartya Sen
C. Manmohan Singh D. Shashi Tharoor

67. What is the name of the book containing English translation of the 100 year old classic Punjabi poem about Jallianwala Bagh massacre?
A. Drummer Hodge
B. Poems of the Jallianwala Bagh massacre
C. Poems about war
D. Khooni Vaisakhi

68. Which country has released a special stamp on Hindu epic Ramayana to commemorate the 70th anniversary of the diplomatic ties with India?
A. Indonesia B. Bangladesh
C. Sri Lanka D. India

69. Which day is observed as International Mother Earth Day?
A. April 20 B. April 21
C. April 23 D. April 22

70. Which state's Kandhamal Haldi (turmeric) received Geographical Indications (GI) tag recently?
A. Odisha B. Karnataka
C. Kerala D. Tamil Nadu

71. Which country's Navy department has signed first reliable communication link with the Indian Navy and Pacific Naval Commands under the COMCASA pact?
A. Sri Lanka B. Japan
C. Russia D. US

72. Name the script writer, who won the Deenanath Mangeshkar Lifetime Award 2019 recently.
A. Javed Akhtar B. Vishal Bhardwaj
C. Anurag Kashyap D. Salim Khan

73. Which space agency has recorded the first "marsquake" quake on the mars due to volcanic eruptions or land tides?
A. JAXA (Japan Aerospace Exploration Agency)
B. NASA (National Aeronautics and Space Administration)
C. ISRO (Indian Space Research Organisation)
D. Chines Space Agency

74. Name the third edition of bilateral maritime exercise between Australia and India that was held in Visakhapatnam.
A. Vajra Prahar B. Cobra Gold
C. Ausindex 19 D. Ausind 19

75. Holkhomang Haokip, who passed away recently, was a .... ?
A. Writer B. Producer
C. Football player D. Politician

76. Name the Howitzers guns inducted into Indian Army recently.
A. Dhanush
B. Panter
C. M102 howitzer
D. BL 9.2-inch howitzer

77. Who was the first Indian President to visit Croatia?
A. Abdul Kalam
B. Pratibha Patil
C. Pranab Mukherjee
D. Ram Nath Kovind

78. Which Island was notified as Island Protection Zone (IPZ) 2019 by Union Ministry of Environment, Forest and Climate Change recently?
A. Andaman and Nicobar Island
B. Kurumgad Island
C. Khanderi Island
D. Worli Island

79. Name the organization, which released the report on food crises titled 'Global Report on Food Crises' annually.
A. International Food Policy Research Institute (IFPRI)
B. Food and Agriculture Organization (FAO)
C. Food Corporation of India (FCI)
D. Food Security Information Network (FSIN)

80. Which is the happiest country as per the 2019 World Happiness Index?
A. Finland B. Denmark
C. Norway D. Sweden

81. The Headquarters of Asian Development Bank is situated in:
A. Manila, Philippines
B. Jakarta, Indonesia
C. Colombo, Sri Lanka
D. Honoi, Vietnam

82. The 'Golden Peacock' Award is given for excellence in:
A. Corporate Social Responsibility
B. Energy Savings
C. Literature
D. Corporate Governance

83. Which planet is known as Red Planet?
A. Venus B. Mercury
C. Mars D. Neptune

84. What is Psephology?
A. Statistical study of elections, voting, etc.
B. Study of rainfall pattern
C. Study of gene disorder
D. Study of female prisoners

85. The Global Teacher Award, 2019 was awarded to a teacher in:
A. South Korea B. Japan
C. Canada D. Kenya

86. Which state in India is the first State to achieve 100 percent sanitation coverage?
A. Andhra Pradesh B. Karnataka
C. Sikkim D. Manipur

87. The book titled 'God Save the Honourable Supreme Court' was authored by:
A. Soli Sorabjee B. Fali S. Nariman
C. K.K. Venugopal D. Justice Katju

88. The book titled 'Anita Gets Bail' was authored by:
A. Amitab Ghosh B. Kiran Bedi
C. Indira Jaisingh D. Arun Shourie

89. The first Indian Athlete to qualify for Olympics 2020 is:
A. K.T. Irfan B. Jinson Johnson
C. Tintu Lukka D. Sunita Rani

90. The South Asian nation that has won the SAFF Women's Championship for five times successively is:
A. Nepal B. India
C. Sri Lanka D. Bhutan

Section-III : Elementary Mathematics

91. The Municipality of a town increases water tax by 20% and water consumption decreased by 20%. Then the percentage of increase or decrease in the monthly expenditure is:
A. 4% increase B. 4% decrease
C. 5% increase D. 5% decrease

92. A child was born on 13th January, 1976 which was a Tuesday. What day of the week will be the child's birthday in the year 1986?
A. Sunday B. Friday
C. Saturday D. Monday

93. The perimeter of a rectangle is 60 cms. If its length is twice its breadth, then its area is:
A. 200 cm^2 B. 180 cm^2
C. 160 cm^2 D. 220 cm^2

94. A tree grows at the rate of 1/5th of its height annually. By how much height will it grow after 2 years, if its present height is 75 cms?
A. 108 cms
B. 90 cms
C. 144 cms
D. 112 cms

95. A train 600 meters long is running at a speed of 90 kms/hr. If it crosses a tunnel in one minute, then the length of the tunnel is:
A. 500 meters
B. 550 meters
C. 600 meters
D. 900 meters

96. A book seller sold a box of 10 pencils for ₹ 80 and incurred a loss. Had he sold it for ₹ 98, his gain would have been twice the loss he incurred earlier. The cost price of the box of pencils is:
A. ₹ 84 B. ₹ 86
C. ₹ 88 D. ₹ 90

97. In a 100 meters race, A beats B by 20 meters, B beats C by 5 meters. In the same race, A beats C by:
A. 26 meters B. 25 meters
C. 24 meters D. 22 meters

98. Beena got married 8 years ago. Today, her age is $1\frac{1}{4}$ times her age at the time of marriage. If her daughter's age is 1/10 times her age, then her daughter's age is:
A. 3 years B. 4 years
C. 5 years D. 2 years

99. A clock gains 2 minutes every hour. Then the angle traversed by the second hand in one minute is:
A. 360° B. 370°
C. 390° D. 372°

100. 80% of students of a class took Statistics and 45% took Mathematics. If each student took Statistics or Mathematics and 40 took both, the total number of students in the class was:
A. 160 B. 180
C. 200 D. 225

101. Kiran's brother is 5 years older to her. Her father was 30 years old when Kiran's sister was born, while her mother was 28 years old when Kiran was born. If Kiran's sister was 2 years old when her brother was born, what was the age of their father when Kiran's brother was born?
A. 32 B. 34
C. 37 D. 30

102. If Second Saturday and Sunday of every month is a holiday, then the total number of working days in a month of 31 days beginning with a Wednesday will be:
A. 23 B. 24
C. 25 D. 26

103. A mess contractor can either serve 450 students with the meal that he prepares or can cater to 270 cops with the same meal. If 300 students have already eaten in the mess, how many cops can be fed with the remaining meal?
A. 20 B. 45
C. 90 D. 180

104. A car driver increases the average speed of his car by 3 km/hr every hour. The total distance travelled in 7 hours if the distance covered in first hour was 30 km, is
A. 266 km B. 273 km
C. 280 km D. 287 km

105. A grocer mixes coffee powder of 2 types, one of which is priced at ₹ 60 and the other at ₹ 90. What should be the ratio of combining the two, to sell the blended mix coffee powder of the two types at ₹ 80?
A. 2 : 1 B. 2 : 3
C. 1 : 2 D. 3 : 2

106. The smallest number that should be subtracted from 2085, so that the new number is completely divisible by 23 is:
A. 9 B. 15
C. 20 D. 19

107. A tank is connected to three pipes – Pipe A, B and C. Pipe A can fill the tank in 6 hours, B can fill the tank in 8 hours and Pipe C can empty the full tank in 12 hours. How much time will it take to fill the tank completely if all three pipes are working together?
A. 4 hours
B. 4 hours 48 minutes
C. 5 hours
D. 5 hours 20 minutes

108. Naresh bought a bicycle each for his two sons, each bicycle priced at ₹ 3500. If the first bicycle is sold at a profit of 5%, the how much should the other bicycle be sold for, to gain a total of 20% on both?
A. 15% B. 10%
C. 25% D. 35%

109. An employee of an organization invests a total of ₹ 25,400 in two different schemes X and Y at a simple interest rate of 18% per annum and 10% per annum respectively. If a total of ₹ 6460 has been earned as simple interest in 2 years, what amount was invested in Scheme Y?
A. ₹ 8,625
B. ₹ 16,775
C. ₹ 12,240
D. ₹ 10,930

110. The difference between Simple Interest and Compound Interest on ₹ 500 for 1 year at 10% per annum, reckoned half yearly is:
A. ₹ 1 B. ₹ 1.25
C. ₹ 1.5 D. ₹ 2

Section-IV : Legal Aptitude

This section consists of fifty (50) questions. Each question consists of legal principle(s) (hereinafter referred to as 'principle') and facts. Such proposition may or may not be true in the real and legal sense, yet you have to conclusively assume them to be true for the purposes of this section. Principles have to be applied to the given facts to arrive at the most reasonable conclusion. Only one of the alternatives, i.e., (A), (B), (C), or (D) is the most reasonable conclusion. In other words, in answering the following questions, you must not rely on any principle except the principles that are given herein below for every question. Further you must not assume any facts other than those stated in the question. The objective of this section is to test your ability in legal aptitude, study of law, research aptitude and problem solving ability even if the 'most reasonable conclusion' arrived at may be absurd or unacceptable for any other reason.

111. Principle: Acceptance of proposal must be the exact mirror image of the proposal.

Facts: 'A' made a proposal to 'B' to sell a chair for ₹ 500. 'B' is desirous of buying the said chair for ₹ 400.

A. B has accepted the proposal of A.
B. B has not accepted the proposal of A.
C. It is not clear if B has accepted the proposal of A.
D. It is not clear whether A made a proposal to B.

112. Principle: An agreement with a boy below the age of eighteen years is not enforceable by law.

Facts: A man entered into an agreement with a girl of seventeen years of age.

A. The agreement is enforceable by law
B. The agreement is not enforceable by law
C. The agreement is enforceable by the girl
D. No inference can be drawn

113. Principle: Sale of liquor is illegal. All agreements relating to prohibited items do not exist in the eyes of law.

Facts: 'A' entered into an agreement with 'B' for the sale of liquor. 'A' failed to supply the agreed quantity of liquor to B.

A. B can bring a legal action against A
B. B cannot bring any legal action against A
C. A can bring a legal action against B
D. A and B can initiate appropriate legal proceeding against each other

114. Principle: The communication of a proposal is complete when it comes to the knowledge of the person to whom it is made.

Facts: 'A' sent a letter making a proposal to 'B' to purchase the house of B.

A. The communication of proposal is complete when A sent the letter
B. The communication of proposal is complete when B's wife received it
C. The communication of proposal is complete when B's wife handed over the letter to B
D. The communication of proposal is complete when B reads the letter

115. Principle: An agreement may be entered into orally, in writing, or by conduct.

Facts: 'A' went to the shop of 'B' and picked a tooth brush and gave a cheque of Rupees twenty to B and left the shop.

A. A entered into an agreement with B.
B. A did not enter into an agreement with B.
C. Payment of tooth brush cannot be made through a cheque.
D. A should have carried a currency note of Rupees twenty to make the payment.

116. Principle: Property consists of right to posses, right to use, right to alienate and right to exclude others. Sale is complete when property gets transferred from the seller to the buyer.

Facts: 'A' sold his car to 'B'. B requested A to keep the car in his care on behalf B for one month. A agreed.

A. Sale of car is complete
B. Sale of car is not complete
C. Sale will be completed when B keeps the car in his own care
D. Sale will be automatically completed after the expiry of one month

117. Principle: A person, who is usually mad, but occasionally not mad, may make a contract when he is not mad.

Facts: 'A' generally remains in the state of madness and rarely becomes capable of understanding anything.

A. A can make a contract
B. A can never make a contract
C. A can make a contract at any time whenever he pleases
D. A can make a contract only for his own benefit

118. Principle: An agreement without free consent can be enforced only at the option of the party whose consent was not free.

Facts: A obtains the consent of B to enter into an agreement by putting a gun on the head of B's girl friend.

A. B can enforce the agreement
B. B cannot enforce the agreement
C. A can enforce the agreement
D. Neither A nor B can enforce the agreement

119. Principle: Where one of the parties to a contract was in position to dominate the decision of the other party, the contract is enforceable only at the option of the party who was in a position to dominate decision of the other party.

Facts: A doctor asked his patient to make a payment of ₹ 10,00,000 (Ten Lac Only) for treatment of his fever. The patient paid an amount of ₹ 5,00,000 (Five Lac Only) and promised to pay the remaining amount after the treatment. After treatment the patient recovered from fever. The doctor demanded the remaining amount from the patient. The patient refused to pay.

A. The contract is enforceable against the doctor
B. The contract is enforceable against the patient
C. The contract is not enforceable
D. The contract is not enforceable against the patient

120. Principle: When, at the desire one person, any other person has done or abstained from doing something, such act or abstinence or promise is called a consideration for the promise.

Facts: X, the uncle of Y, made a promise to pay him an amount of ₹ 1,00,000 as reward if Y quits smoking and drinking within one year. Y quit smoking and drinking within six months.

A. Consideration has moved from the side of X
B. Consideration has moved from the side of Y
C. No consideration has moved from the side of Y
D. Quitting smoking and drinking cannot be a consideration

121. Principle: Law never enforces an impossible promise.

Facts: 'A' made a promise to 'B' to discover treasure by magic.

A. Law will enforce the promise
B. Law will not enforce the promise
C. Law will enforce the promise only at the option of A
D. Law will enforce the promise only at the option of B

122. Principle: When a person who has made a promise to another person to do something does not fulfill his promise, another person becomes entitled to receive, from the person who did not fulfill his promise, compensation in the form of money.

Facts: X made a promise to Y to repair his car engine. Y made the payment for repair. After the repair, Y went for a drive in the same car. While driving the car, Y met with an accident due to bursting of the tyre.

A. X will be entitled to receive compensation from Y in the form of money
B. Y will be entitled to receive compensation from X in the form of money
C. X will not be entitled to receive compensation
D. Y will not be entitled to receive compensation from X

123. Principle: Whoever takes away any movable thing from the land of any person without that person's consent is said to commit theft.

Facts: During his visit to the home of C, A asks B, the son of C, to accompany A to a forest. Neither A nor B inform C in this regard. B accompanies A to the forest.

A. A has committed theft
B. A has not committed theft
C. A has committed theft as soon as he entered the home of C
D. A has not committed theft till B did not accompany him

124. Principle: Nothing is an offence if it is done in good faith for the purpose of preventing or avoiding greater harm or damage to person or property.

Facts: A jumps into a swimming pool to save a boy from drowning. While pulling the boy from water A was hit by C. A left the boy in the water and attacked C. The boy died in the water.

A. A has not committed the offence of killing the boy
B. A has committed the offence of killing the boy
C. The boy has committed the offence of suicide
D. The boy has committed the offence of drowning

125. Principle: Causing of an effect partly by an act and partly by an omission is an offence.

Facts: A did not provide any food to his daughter D. He also confined D in a room. Consequently, D died.

A. A committed the offence of not providing food to D
B. A committed the offence of confining D
C. A committed the offence of killing D
D. A committed no offence

126. Principle: Nothing is an offence which is done in the exercise of the right of private defence. Nothing is an offence which is done in madness.

Facts: A, under the influence of madness, attempts to kill B. B to save his life kills A.

A. A has committed the offence of attempt to murder
B. A has committed an offence of being mad
C. B has committed an offence
D. B has not committed an offence

127. Principle: A man is guilty of not only for what he actually does but also for the consequences of his doing.

Facts: A wanted to kill the animal of B. He saw B standing with his animal and fired a gun shot at the animal. The gun shot killed B.

A. A is guilty of killing B
B. A is not guilty of killing B
C. B is guilty of standing with the animal
D. A did not know that the gun shot will kill B

128. Principle: Mere silence as to facts likely to affect the decision of a person to enter into a contract is not fraud.

Facts: A sells to B (A's daughter who is a minor) a horse which A knows to be unsound. A says nothing to B about the unsoundness of the horse.

A. A has committed fraud
B. A has committed no fraud
C. There cannot be a contract between a father and daughter
D. The daughter did not ask therefore the father did not tell, hence no fraud

129. Principle: Whoever attempts to commit the offence of cheating, commits an offence.

Facts: A with an intention to defraud B, obtains from him an amount of ₹ 500.

A. A has committed no offence
B. A has committed the offence of cheating
C. A has attempted to commit the offence of cheating
D. A has attempted to commit and has committed the offence of cheating

130. Principle: Whoever by words publishes any imputation concerning any person is said to defame that person.

Facts: During a marriage ceremony, A circulated a pamphlet saying sister of the bride 'S' is a thief, she has stolen the shoes of the bridegroom.

A. A defamed S
B. A did not defame S
C. A defamed the bridegroom
D. A defamed the bride

131. Principle: An employer is liable for an injury caused to an employee in the course of the employment.

Facts: 'A' and 'B' were working in a factory as unskilled labourers. A was carrying a basket of stones on his head. B was sitting on the ground. When A crossed B, all of a sudden a stone fell down from the basket and hit B on his head. B died instantaneously.

A. The employer will be liable
B. The employer will not be liable
C. A will be liable
D. Both employer and A will be liable

132. Principle: Damages the money recompense, as far as money can do, for the loss suffered by a person.

Facts: A, an Indian citizen, having a right to vote, was not allowed to cast his vote on the polling booth, by the returning officer. Name of A was mentioned in the voter's list. A has also reported at the polling booth in time. However, the candidate in whose favour A would have cast his vote won the election. A filed a suit claiming damages.

A. A will be entitled to damages
B. A will not be entitled to damages
C. A will be entitled to only nominal damages
D. A will be entitled to exemplary damages

133. Principle: When a party to a contract has refused to perform, or disabled himself from performing, his promise in its entirety, the other party shall not put an end to the contract.

Facts: A engaged B on April 12 to enter his service on June 1, but on May 11, A wrote to B that his services would not be needed. On May 22, B joined C for employment.

A. B cannot put the contract to an end
B. B can put the contract to an end
C. C can put his contract with B to an end
D. A must pay damages to B

134. Principle: Everyone shall be permitted to take advantage of his own wrong.

Facts: A legatee was heavily drunk and driving his car at a speed of 100 Km/per hour in a crowded market. All of a sudden his testator came on the road. There were other people on the road at that time. The car driven by legatee hit the testator and four other persons. All the five persons hit by the car died.

A. The legatee can take the benefit under the will
B. The legatee cannot take the benefit under the will
C. The legatee will be punished
D. The property of the testator will go to his heirs

135. Principle: Property can be transferred only by a living person to another living person.

Facts: 'A' transfers property of which he is the owner in favour of the unborn child of B.

A. Property has been transferred to the unborn child
B. Property has been transferred to B
C. Property has not been transferred to the unborn child
D. Property will be transferred to the unborn child after his birth

136. Principle: An interest created, dependent upon a condition fails, if the fulfilment of the condition is impossible.

Facts: A promises to pay ₹ 10 Lakh to B on condition that he shall marry A's daughter C. At the date on which A gave ₹ 10 Lac to B, C was dead.

A. B's interest fails
B. B's interest fails because of immorality
C. B's interest fails because of prohibition by law
D. B's interest does not fail

137. Principle: A condition must be complied with after the happening of the event to which such a condition is attached.

Facts: A promises to pay ₹ 5,000 to B on the condition that he shall marry with the consent of C, D and E. B marries without the consent of C, D and E, but obtains their consent after the marriage.

A. B has fulfilled the condition
B. B has not fulfilled the condition
C. The condition is illegal
D. B must divorce his wife

138. Principle: A condition must be complied in order to claim the benefit of an agreement.

Facts: A agrees to transfer a farm to B, if B shall not go to England within three years after the date of the agreement, his interest in the farm shall cease. B does not go to England within the term prescribed.

A. B's interest in the farm continues
B. B's interest in the farm does not continue
C. B has a fundamental right to go to England or not to go to England and hence the condition is illegal
D. The agreement between A and B is void

139. Principle: Existence of all the alleged facts is relevant whether they occurred at the same time and place or at different times and places.

Facts: A, a citizen of England, is accused of committing murder of B in India by taking part in a conspiracy hatched in England.

A. The facts that A accused of commission of murder and of conspiracy are relevant facts
B. Only the fact that A is accused of committing murder of B is relevant
C. Only the fact that A is accused of conspiracy hatched in England is relevant
D. A citizen of England cannot be tried in India

140. Principle: One who asserts must prove.

Facts: A desires a Court to give judgment that B, C and D shall be punished for a crime which A says B, C and D have committed.

A. A must prove that B, C and D were present at the place of crime
B. A must prove that B, C and D have committed the crime
C. B, C and D must prove that they have not committed the crime
D. Police must prove that B, C and D have committed the crime

141. Principle: Foreign judgment binds the parties and is conclusive unless it is obtained by fraud.

Facts: A obtains judgment from US court by producing fake documents.

A. New Suit can be filed in India on the same facts
B. Judgment can be enforced in US
C. Judgment can be enforced in India
D. New suit can not be filed in India on same facts

142. Principle: Decision of Court is Null and Void, if it is given by court which does not have jurisdiction over the subject matter.

Facts: A obtains decision from a court which did not have jurisdiction to deal with the subject matter.

A. Decision can be enforced because both the parties were present
B. Decision cannot be enforced because decision is null and void
C. Decision can be enforced because it is given a court
D. Decision can be enforced

143. Principle: Civil Suit can be filed where defendant resides or carries on business or where cause of action arises.

Facts: 'A' carries on business in Gurgaon, 'B' carries on Business in Mumbai. 'B' through his agent in Gurgaon purchases goods in Gurgaon and takes delivery through agent in Gurgaon. Where Civil Suit for payment of price can be filed by 'A'?

A. Gurgaon only where cause of action arises
B. At Mumbai where B carries on Business
C. At either of the places *i.e.*, Mumbai or Gurgaon
D. Anywhere in India

144. Principle: Civil Suit can be filed where defendant resides or carries on business or where cause of action arises.

Facts: An agreement is signed and executed in New Delhi between A and B for supply of goods wherein B is to supply goods to be delivered at New Delhi to client of A. A carries on business at Haryana and B carries on Business in UP. Civil suit by 'B' for payment of consideration can be filed against 'A' at

A. Only at New Delhi, where cause of action arises
B. Only at Haryana where 'A' carries on business
C. Only at UP where 'B' carries on business
D. At Haryana or at New Delhi

145. Principle: No court can execute the decisions unless it is having territorial jurisdiction over the property or the person against whom decision is to be executed. The Court which gave the decision can transfer the matter to the court which has the territorial jurisdiction over the person or property.

Facts: A decision is given by court at New Delhi on a contractual matter against X in a suit between X and Y. X is resident of Maharashtra and he has properties in Maharashtra and Gujarat.

A. New Delhi court can transfer the proceedings to Court at Maharashtra only
B. New Delhi court can execute the decision because it had the jurisdiction to decide the matter so it can execute also
C. New Delhi court can transfer the proceedings to court at Gujarat only
D. New Delhi court can transfer the proceedings to either of the courts *i.e.* Maharashtra or Gujarat

146. Principle: Nothing is an offence by reason of any harm it may cause to another person, if it is done in good faith and for the benefit of that person even without that person's consent.

Facts: A is attacked by a Lion and Lion drags him while he is crying for help. B, a passer by picks up A's gun in good faith and fires at Lion which injures A. B has never used the gun before.

A. B is liable for the injury because he knew that he can injure A as he has never used any gun before
B. B is not liable as he has done the act in good faith
C. B is liable because he has not taken A's consent before firing
D. B is liable because he has used A's gun without his consent

147. Principle: Nothing is an offence if it is done under intoxication and the person committing the offence was incapable to understand the nature of the Act. Intoxication should be without knowledge or against the will of the person.

Facts: A, B and C were having a party in Bar where A pursuaded B and C to take alcoholic drinks. On the persistent pursuation B and C also consumed alcohol along with A. B and C had never consumed alcohol before. After intoxication, there was some argument between B and C where C pushed B with full force causing serious injury to B.

A. C is liable
B. C is not liable because he was intoxicated
C. A is liable because A pursuaded them to consume alcohol whereas they had never consumed alcohol
D. A and C both are liable

148. Principle: Everyone has the right of private defence to defend his body and property by use of reasonable force unless that person had time to have recourse to protection of public authorities.

Facts: X receives information at 5.00 pm that Y along with few friends is planning to burn his crop at midnight which is ready to be harvested. He does not inform the village Police Station which was just one kilometer away. He gathers his family members and directs them to collect some weapons in the form of swords and lathis to protect his field/crop. At around 11.00 pm Y and his aides attack the crop and a severe fight ensues wherein Y is seriously injured.

A. X is not liable as he was exercising his right of private defence
B. X and his family are not liable for the injuries caused as they were exercising the right of private defence
C. X is liable
D. X and his family is liable as they have not informed the police

149. Principle: Anyone who induces or attempts to induce a voter to vote in a particular manner on the ground that the voter will face divine displeasure, shall be guilty of offence of interfering with free exercise of right to vote.

Facts: During election campaign period one candidate X told the voters that if they do not vote for her, voters will be cursed because the election candidate is the God's own child and those who do not vote for her, they will not be liked by God.

A. X has committed an offence

B. X has not committed an offence because she only narrated what she felt

C. X has not committed an offence because she has freedom of speech and expression

D. X has not committed an offence because she did not compel anyone to vote for her

150. Principle: Doing of an act which causes common injury, danger or annoyance to public or which is likely to cause such injury or annoyance is Public nuisance. A common nuisance is not excused because it causes some nuisance or advantage.

Facts: 'A' a farmer having large farmlands burns crop residue (stubble) on his fields after harvesting the crop to make the field ready for next crop as this is the easy, fast and convenient method of making the field ready for next crop. His farmlands are adjoining a densely inhabited residential area and people pass through the smoke while travelling on the road adjoining his farm-lands. The smoke caused by fire also enters the houses in the colony

A. A has not committed any offence since he does not cause any specific injury to any specific person

B. A has not committed any offence because he does not gain any advantage from persons living in the vicinity

C. A has committed public nuisance

D. A has not committed any offence because the alleged acts are done on the fields owned and used by him and acts are done without any intention to cause harm.

151. Principle: Death caused by rash or negligent act of a person is an offence.

Facts: X was driving his SUV car in a lonely road leading to a forest at 160 km per hour. Suddenly, someone appears from the forest on the road and in the resultant accident, the car hits the commuter causing his death.

A. X is not guilty of an offence as the accident has occurred on a lonely road

B. X is not guilty because there was no intention to kill the deceased

C. X is guilty of an offence death by rash or negligent act

D. X is not guilty because he was also injured in the accident

152. Principle: Whoever causes death by rash or negligent act commits an offence.

Facts: X is having a house on the roadside which is also having a street on the back of the house. He has a lawn on the back of his house where he has built a toilet. To prevent the intruders from entering his house, he got the fence charged with a high voltage live electric wire. Z was passing through the street at the backyard of the house of X and sat down to take rest near the fence. While getting up, his hands came in contact with the fence which was connected to high voltage electric wire causing his death.

A. X has not committed any offence because he has right to prevent trespass

B. X has committed an offence of causing death by rash and negligent act

C. X has committed no offence because he does not have any enmity with X

D. X has committed an offence of Murder

153. Principle: Killing is not murder, if it is committed in a sudden fight without pre-meditation in a heat of passion upon a sudden quarrel.

Facts: X and Y were buying liquor from a liquor shop at 7 pm. Y abused X and there was quarrel between them. X told Y that he will not spare him and Y shouted that his house is adjoining the shop only and if X had the guts, he can come anytime. X went back to his shop which was nearby, procured a knife and went to Y's residence at 9 pm and stabbed him to death.

A. X has committed murder

B. X has not committed an offence of murder since it was committed in sudden fight in a heat of passion

C. X has not committed murder of Y because he had no enimity with Y

D. X has committed no offence

154. Principle: Use of criminal force intentionally knowing that it would cause or is likely to cause injury or annoyance to the person against whom force is used, is an offence.

Facts: X, a renowned social worker who had launched a movement for liberation of women, pulls up a Muslim women's veil in public in good faith without her consent causing annoyance to her.

A. X is a renowned social worker and he has committed no offence because his motive was good

B. X acted in good faith to liberate her from clutches of tradition and has hence has committed no offence
C. X has done the act in public and not in secrecy therefore had not committed any offence
D. X has committed an offence by use of criminal force

155. Principle: Inducing any animal to move or to change its motion and thereby intentionally causing fear of injury or annoyance to others by such act, is an offence of use of criminal force.

Facts: X incites his dog to chase and run after his neighbour Y, to teach Y to stay away from him. The act is done without neighbour consent and against his will

A. X has committed no offence
B. X has committed no offence because no harm is caused to Y
C. X has committed no offence because his intention only to put fear in the mind of Y
D. X has committed an offence of use of criminal force

156. Principle: A spouse is not permitted to put in evidence in any court, any communication during marriage between the spouses without the consent of the person who made the communication.

Facts: X who is the wife of Y saw her husband (Y) coming out of the neighbour's house at 6.00 am in the morning. Y told his wife X that he has murdered the neighbour and handed over the jewellery of that neighbour to his wife.

A. X is allowed to appear as a witness in court to depose that her husband has told her that he committed a murder
B. X is not allowed to appear as a witness at all in any court
C. X is not allowed to appear as a witness to depose what was told by the husband to her, however, she can depose what she saw
D. X is an independent woman and she can do whatever she wants

157. Principle: Oral evidence must always be direct *i.e.*, of the person who says he saw the event and hearsay evidence is no evidence.

Facts: X was told by Y (whom X trusts) that Z has murdered A

A. Statement of X is admissible
B. Statement of X is not admissible because he has not seen Z murdering A
C. Statement of X is admissible because he trusts Y and Y never tells a lie
D. Statement of X is admissible because he is a renowned social activist and has a huge reputation to fight for the truth

158. Principle: Terms of any written contract can be proved by producing the written contract only and oral evidence is excluded.

Facts: A gives B receipt for money paid by B. Oral evidence is offered to prove payment.

A. Oral evidence to prove payment is allowed
B. Oral evidence to prove payment is not allowed
C. Oral evidence is always allowed to prove all facts
D. Oral evidence is generally disallowed

159. Principle: Employer is liable for the injury caused to the employee in the course of his employment.

Facts: X organized a party and hired a caterer. During the party, generator set went out of order and he requested one employee of caterer *i.e.* Y to bring the mechanic on his vehicle and promised to pay ₹ 1000 for the same to Y. Y met with an accident while going to fetch the mechanic and he seeks compensation.

A. X is liable as Y was working in the course of employment offered by X
B. X is not liable as Y is not his employee
C. X is liable because party was organized by him
D. Caterer is liable as Y is his employee

160. Principle: Master is liable for the acts of his servant done in the course of his duties.

Facts: X hired an employee Y in his construction business. Y was the property in-charge who received construction material and gave receipts for the material received by him. Z claimed payment for cement supplied to X which was duly received by Y. X denied the payment on the ground that he has only received half of the material and the balance was misutilized by the employee Y.

A. X is liable for the entire amount
B. X is liable for the part amount only *i.e.* for payment of the cost of half of the material
C. X is not liable for the misconduct/embezzlement of his employee
D. Z can claim the balance payment only from Y

Section-V : Logical Reasoning

161. If in English Alphabet 'e' and every alternate letter from 'e' onwards is written in Capitals, then how will sixth month from March will be coded:

A. SEPTEmbER B. SEptEMbEr
C. SepTeMber D. SEPtEmbER

162. If in a certain code, 'Clever' is written as 'XOVEVI', then 'Smart' would be written as:

A. HZNGI B. HNZIG
C. GHNGI D. GIHZN

163. Fill in the blank:

Q4RT, __________ , QRT6, QR7T, Q8RT

A. QTR7 B. QR5T
C. RQ9T D. TRQ6

164. Fill in the blank:

257, 291, ________, 365, 405

A. 313 B. 322
C. 327 D. 343

165. Manoj walks a distance of 5 meters towards North, then he turns to east and walks a distance of 10 meters. Then he turns to his right and covers a distance of 15 meters. He then turns to his left and covers a distance of 15 meters. Which direction is he facing now?

A. North B. East
C. West D. South

166. A man introduces a girl as the daughter of the sister of his father. How the girl is related to the man:

A. Daughter B. Niece
C. Grand daughter D. Cousin

Directions (Qs. No. 167-170): *Read the following information and choose the most appropriate option:*

P and Q are good in driving Motor cycle and Jeep. R and P are good in driving Jeep and Lorry. R, S and T are good in driving Motor Cycle and Lorry. T and R are good in driving Bus and Tempo. S and Q are good in driving Bus and Jeep.

167. Who is good in driving Motor cycle, Lorry and Tempo?

A. P B. Q
C. T D. S

168. Who is good in driving Motor Cycle, Jeep and Lorry but not bus?

A. R B. S
C. P D. T

169. Who is good in driving Tempo, Motor Cycle, Lorry but not Jeep?

A. S B. T
C. R D. Q

170. Who is good in driving all the vehicles?

A. R B. P
C. S D. T

171. In a bag there are some gold coins. In another bag there are 1/3rd extra gold coins as compared to first bag. If the difference in the number of gold coins in first and second bag is 5, then how many coins are there in the first bag?

A. 7 B. 9
C. 13 D. 15

Directions (Qs. No. 172 and 173): *Examine the following numbers and identify the next number.*

172. 53, 50, 45, 38, 29, _____

A. 11 B. 17
C. 18 D. 21

173. 20, 30, 42, 56, 72, ____

A. 82 B. 90
C. 92 D. 94

174. The words in the bottom row are related in the same way as the words in the top row. Fill in the blank.

Rose, Flower, Plant

Flat, House, ...

A. City B. Tent
C. Building D. Village

175. If Ocean: Waves, then Desert : ....

A. Water B. Sand
C. Brave D. Sand dunes

176. If $1 \times 7 = 8$, $2 \times 7 = 16$, $3 \times 7 = 24$, $4 \times 7 = 32$, then what is value of 9×7?

A. 63 B. 72
C. 81 D. 90

177. Find the odd one out:

Onlookers, Theatre goers, Queue, Spectators

A. Onlookers B. Theatre goers
C. Queue D. Spectators

178. Find the odd one out:

Heart, Lungs, Kidney, Skin, Liver

A. Skin B. Lungs
C. Heart D. Kidney

179. Find the odd-man out:

A. http://www.scholar.google.com
B. http://www.manupatra.com
C. http://www.lexisnexis.com
D. http://www.westlawindia.com

180. Find the odd one out:

Symphony, Orchestra, Guitar, Mob

A. Guitar B. Orchestra
C. Mob D. Symphony

Directions (Qs. No. 181-185): *Read the information given below to answer the questions.*

(*i*) Mohan's reading schedule consists of reading only subject on a given day of the week.

(*ii*) The subjects are Physics, Chemistry, Mathematics, Biology, and Social Science.

(*iii*) Monday to Saturday are reading days including one day only for play. Sunday is a complete holiday for Mohan.

(*iv*) Mathematics day is neither on the first day nor on the last day but earlier than the Chemistry day.

(*v*) Biology day is on the immediate next day of Chemistry day.

(*vi*) Physics day is on the immediate previous day of the play day.

(*vii*) Biology day and Social Science day have a gap of two days between them.

(*viii*) Social Science day is on the immediate next day of the play day.

181. Which of the following day is the play day?

A. Monday B. Tuesday
C. Wednesday D. Thursday

182. Physics day and Biology day have a gap of how many days between them?

A. One B. Two
C. Three D. Four

183. Which day is Social Science day?

A. Monday B. Tuesday
C. Wednesday D. Thursday

184. Which day is Mathematics day?

A. Monday B. Tuesday
C. Wednesday D. Thursday

185. Which of the following is the correct statement?

A. Biology day is after Chemistry day
B. Physics day is on Wednesday
C. Play day is on Monday
D. Chemistry day is earlier than Physics day

Directions (Qs. No. 186-190): *Read the information given below to answer the questions.*

A, B, C, D, E, F, G and H want to have a dinner on a round table and they have worked out the following seating arrangements.

(*a*) A will sit beside C.
(*b*) H will sit beside A.
(*c*) C will sit beside E.
(*d*) F will sit beside H.
(*e*) E will sit beside G.
(*f*) D will sit beside F.
(*g*) G will sit beside B.
(*h*) B will sit beside D.

186. Which of the following is wrong?

A. A will be to the immediate right of C
B. D will be to the immediate left of B
C. E will be to the immediate right of A
D. F will be to the immediate left of D

187. Which of the following is correct?

A. B will be to the immediate left of D
B. H will be to the immediate right of A
C. C will be to the immediate right of F
D. B will be to the immediate left of H

188. A and F will become neighbours if:

A. B agrees to change her sitting position
B. C agrees to change her sitting position
C. G agrees to change her sitting position
D. H agrees to change her sitting position

189. During sitting:

A. A will be directly facing C
B. B will be directly facing C
C. A will be directly facing B
D. B will be directly facing D

190. H will be sitting between:

A. C and B B. A and F
C. D and C D. E and G

Directions (Qs. No. 191-193): *Choose the set of three statements where the third statement can be logically derived from the preceding two.*

191. Statements:

1. Some students love reading.
2. Some adults do not love reading.
3. Some students are not adult.
4. Some students are adult.
5. No reading lover is an adult.
6. Some men do not love reading.

The set of statements is:

A. 1, 3, 4 B. 1, 5, 3
C. 1, 2, 4 D. 6, 2, 4

192. Statements:

1. All boys need books.
2. All girls need books.
3. Punjabis are girls.
4. Some Punjabis need book.
5. All boys are girls.
6. Some boys are Punjabis.

The set of statements is:

A. 5, 4, 1 B. 2, 5, 3
C. 6, 5, 3 D. 5, 2, 1

193. Statements:

1. All human beings need education.
2. All teachers need training.
3. Education is provided by the teachers.
4. X is a teacher.
5. X needs training.
6. Students are future of a nation.

The set of statements is:

A. 1, 2, 5 B. 2, 3, 4
C. 2, 4, 5 D. 4, 5, 6

Directions (Qs. No. 194-196): *Each of the following questions has a main statement followed by four statements: 1, 2, 3, 4. Choose the ordered pair of statements where the first statement implies the second, and the two statements are logically consistent with the main statement.*

194. Main statement: Only if the teaching standard is destroyed, will examination result be poor.

1. Examination result is poor.
2. Teaching standard is not destroyed.
3. Examination result is not poor.
4. Teaching standard is destroyed.

The ordered pair of statements is:

A. 2, 3 B. 2, 4
C. 1, 3 D. 1, 2

195. Main statement: The computer will not work if operating system fails.

1. Operating system fails.
2. Operating system does not fail.
3. The computer does not work.
4. The computer works.

The ordered pair of statements is:

A. 2, 1 B. 2, 3
C. 1, 4 D. 4, 2

196. Main statement: Either X or Y will take the only computer in the room.

1. X took the computer.
2. Y did not take the computer.
3. X did not take the computer.
4. Y took the computer.

The ordered pair of statements is:

A. 3, 1 B. 1, 3
C. 4, 3 D. 1, 2

197. 'All men are mortal and Victoria is a woman and hence Victoria is mortal'. This statement is:

A. Logically Valid B. Logically Invalid
C. Logically True D. Logically False

198. All men are chairs. John Doe is a man. In logical language, therefore:

A. John Doe is a chair
B. John Doe is a human being and therefore he cannot be a chair
C. A man cannot be a chair in any case
D. Chairs can be men

199. Identify the missing number:

1 and 3, 4 and 6, 7 and 9, ... and 12

A. 10 B. 11
C. 12 D. 13

200. Cobra: Snake :: Greyhound : ....

A. Eagle B. Black Mamba
C. Python D. Dog

ANSWERS

1	2	3	4	5	6	7	8	9	10
D	B	D	A	C	D	D	B	C	D
11	**12**	**13**	**14**	**15**	**16**	**17**	**18**	**19**	**20**
D	C	C	B	D	C	A	C	A	C
21	**22**	**23**	**24**	**25**	**26**	**27**	**28**	**29**	**30**
D	C	B	A	D	D	A	B	D	B
31	**32**	**33**	**34**	**35**	**36**	**37**	**38**	**39**	**40**
D	C	A	B	D	A	B	B	C	D
41	**42**	**43**	**44**	**45**	**46**	**47**	**48**	**49**	**50**
A	C	D	A	D	C	A	B	C	D
51	**52**	**53**	**54**	**55**	**56**	**57**	**58**	**59**	**60**
C	D	C	A	C	B	D	A	C	B
61	**62**	**63**	**64**	**65**	**66**	**67**	**68**	**69**	**70**
B	A	D	D	A	B	D	A	D	A
71	**72**	**73**	**74**	**75**	**76**	**77**	**78**	**79**	**80**
D	D	B	C	D	A	D	A	D	A

81	82	83	84	85	86	87	88	89	90
A	D	C	A	D	C	B	D	A	B
91	92	93	94	95	96	97	98	99	100
B	D	A	A	D	B	C	B	D	A
101	102	103	104	105	106	107	108	109	110
A	D	C	B	C	B	B	D	B	B
111	112	113	114	115	116	117	118	119	120
B	D	B	D	A	A	A	A	B	B
121	122	123	124	125	126	127	128	129	130
B	D	B	A	C	D	A	B	B	A
131	132	133	134	135	136	137	138	139	140
A	B	A	A	C	A	A	B	A	B
141	142	143	144	145	146	147	148	149	150
A	B	C	D	D	B	A	D	A	C
151	152	153	154	155	156	157	158	159	160
C	B	A	D	D	C	B	A	A	A
161	162	163	164	165	166	167	168	169	170
B	B	B	C	B	D	C	C	B	A
171	172	173	174	175	176	177	178	179	180
D	C	B	C	D	B	C	A	A	C
181	182	183	184	185	186	187	188	189	190
B	D	C	D	A	C	B	D	C	B
191	192	193	194	195	196	197	198	199	200
B	D	C	A	D	D	B	A	A	D

EXPLANATORY ANSWERS

41. **Central Information Commission** includes 1 Chief Information Commissioner (CIC) and not more than 10 Information Commissioners (IC) who are appointed by the President of India on the recommendations of a Committee. The first Chief Information Commissioner of India was Wajahat Habibullah. First woman Chief Information Commissioner was Deepak Sandhu. The present Chief Information Commissioner of India is Sudhir Bhargava.

46. In a major relief to micro, small and medium enterprises (MSMEs), the GST Council doubled the tax exemption limit to ₹ 40 lakh in annual revenue. The turnover limit for businesses availing of the GST composition scheme, which allows them to pay goods and services tax at a flat rate, was raised to ₹ 1.5 crore.

The move aims to allay the concerns of small traders.

For north-eastern and hilly states, the GST exemption limit has been doubled to ₹ 20 lakh. The decisions of the council came into effect from 1 April.

47. Bihar's Shahi litchi has received the geographical indication tag during October, 2018. The fruit is mostly grown in Muzaffarpur and its neighbouring districts of East Champaran, Vaishali, Samastipur and Begusarai. The tag, awarded by the India Patent Office, allows a state or a geographical region to lay an exclusive claim over a product, gives an assurance of quality, and is often used as a reason to increase product rates. A few other products with a geographical indication tag are Darjeeling tea, Mahabaleshwar strawberry, Jaipur blue pottery, Banarasi sarees and Tirupati laddus.

The fruit is the fourth product from Bihar, after Jardalu mango, Katarni rice and Magahi paan, to receive the status.

48. **Jeffrey Preston Bezos** is an American technology entrepreneur, investor, and philanthropist. He is the founder, chairman, CEO, and president of Amazon.com, Inc.

On July 27, 2017, Bezos momentarily became the world's wealthiest person when his estimated net worth increased to just over $90 billion.

His wealth surpassed $100 billion for the first time on November 24, 2017, and he was formally designated the wealthiest person in the world by *Forbes* on March 6, 2018, with a net worth of $112 billion.

The first centi-billionaire on the *Forbes* wealth index, he was named the "richest man in modern history" after his net worth increased to $150 billion in July, 2018.

In September 2018, *Forbes* described Bezos as "far richer than anyone else on the planet" as he added $1.8 billion to his worth when Amazon's market cap briefly reached $1 trillion. He is still the richest person on the planet.

51. **Vande Bharat Express,** also known as Train 18 is now the fastest train in India. It is an Indian semi-high speed intercity electric multiple unit.

India's first indigenously built engine-less train, meant for intra-day travel, can cut down travel time by 10 to 15 per cent compared to the Shatabdi. It is developed by Chennai-based Integral Coach Factory (ICF) at a cost of ₹ 100 crore.

The fully air-conditioned train offers better passenger comfort and safety, as all equipment are fixed under the carriage, so that more space is available on board.

Train 18 will replace the current Shatabdi Express. The train is capable of touching 200 kmph provided the other systems like tracks and signals support the speed.

52. The Kerala State Police claims to have created history by becoming one of the world's first and the very first police force in the country to induct humanoid robots.

Homeland security, forensic sciences, law and order are specific areas where robots are potentially used worldwide.

Kerala Police developed and introduced the humanoid robot called 'KP-Bot'.

KP-Bot is designed to provide round-the-clock service, involving public interface and front office administration and overcome human limitations to avoid, to the extent possible, human error.

However, it does not replace any human resources. Rather, it would act as the first contact point and a data collection tool to help improve the overall quality of service and performance levels.

'Duties' Assigned

The major 'duties' assigned to the KP-Bot are:

- Meet and greet officers through face recognition
- Meet and greet visitors, guide them to appropriate sections in the police headquarters
- Provide detailed and accurate information on procedures related to services verbally, supported by information displayed on the screen
- Collect information about visitors, to fix appointments and issue visitor IDs
- Create a case file on complaint/ petition as detailed by the visitor, and
- Allow officers to get connected to the robot though telepresence.

54. The **International Solar Alliance** (ISA) is an alliance of more than 122 countries initiated by India, most of them being **sunshine countries,** which lie either completely or partly between the Tropic of Cancer and the Tropic of Capricorn. The primary objective of the alliance is to work for efficient exploitation of solar energy to reduce dependence on fossil fuels. This initiative was first proposed by Indian Prime Minister Narendra Modi in a speech in November 2015 at Wembley Stadium, in which he referred to sunshine countries as *Suryaputra* ("sons of the Sun"). The alliance is a treaty-based inter-governmental organization. Countries that do not fall within the Tropics can join the alliance and enjoy all benefits as other members, with the exception of voting rights.

The initiative was launched by Prime Minister Narendra Modi at the India Africa Summit, and a meeting of member countries ahead of the 2015 United Nations Climate Change Conference in Paris in November 2015. The framework agreement of the International Solar Alliance opened for signatures in Marrakech, Morocco in November 2016, and 200 countries have joined.

It is headquartered in India. In January 2016, Narendra Modi, and the then French President François Hollande jointly laid the foundation stone of the ISA Headquarters and inaugurated the interim Secretariat at the National Institute of Solar Energy (NISE) in Gwal Pahari, Gurugram, India. The Indian government has dedicated five acres of land on the NISE campus for its future headquarters; it also has contributed ₹ 1.75 billion (US$25 million) to the fund to build a campus and for meeting expenditures for the first five years.

The alliance is also called International Agency for Solar Policy and Application (IASPA).

55. Prime Minister Narendra Modi was conferred the prestigious Seoul Peace Prize for 2018 for his contribution to International cooperation and fostering global economic growth. The award was presented to him by the Seoul Peace Prize Foundation at a grand ceremony. A short film on the life and achievements of Prime Minister Modi was also screened at the event.

Modi is the 14th recipient of the award and the past laureates included former UN Secretary General Kofi Annan, German Chancellor Angela Merkel and renowned international relief organizations like Doctors Without Borders and Oxfam.

The Seoul Peace Prize was established in 1990 to commemorate the success of the 24th Olympic Games held in Seoul. The award was established to crystalise

Korean people's yearning for peace on the Korean peninsula and in the rest of the world.

56. Hungary's Prime Minister Viktor Orban on February 10, 2019 announced new measures, under which increasing financial aid and subsidies will be provided to families that have more than three children.

The measures were announced by the Prime Minister during his "state of the nation" speech. They are meant to encourage women to have more children and to reverse Hungary's population decline.

Key Highlights:

- The Hungarian government has decided to provide a lifetime income tax exemption for women who give birth to at least four children.
- The government has also proposed the introduction of a subsidy worth 8,825 US dollars towards the purchase of a seven-seat vehicle for families with three or more children.
- It has also announced a seven-point plan to increase the fertility rate in the country.
- It has also promised to extend home loans to families with at least two children.
- Besides, a low-interest loan of 35,300 US dollars for women under the age of 40 who are marrying for the first time has also been proposed.
- The government has also decided to build 21,000 nurseries across the country in three years and provide grandparents with free childcare if they are raising their children's children.

59. Retired Supreme Court judge Pinaki Chandra Ghose was appointed as the first Lokpal of India by a committee consisting of Prime Minister Narendra Modi and Chief Justice of India Ranjan Gogoi and Loksabha speaker Sumitra Mahajan and Eminent Jurist Mukul Rohatgi on 17 March, 2019.

The Lokpal and Lokayuktas Act, 2013, commonly known as **The Lokpal Act,** is an anti-corruption Act of Indian Parliament in India which "seeks to provide for the establishment of the institution of Lokpal to inquire into allegations of corruption against certain important public functionaries including the Prime Minister, cabinet ministers, members of parliament, Group A officials of the Central Government and for matters connecting them".

60. The **2019 Indian general election** was held in seven phases from 11 April to 19 May, 2019 to constitute the 17th Lok Sabha. The votes were counted and result was declared on 23 May.

The Bharatiya Janata Party won 303 seats, further increasing its substantial majority and the BJP-led National Democratic Alliance won 353 seats. The Indian National Congress party won 52 seats, and the Congress-led United Progressive Alliance won 91. Other parties and their alliances won 98 seats. Indian National Congress again failed to secure the requisite 10% of the seats in the Lok Sabha and hence India remains without an official opposition party.

64. Lord Ripon is known as "Father of Local Self Government in India". Lord Ripon is known to have granted the Indians first taste of freedom by introducing the Local Self Government in 1882. His scheme of local self government developed the Munipal institutions which had been growing up in the country ever since India was occupied by the British Crown. He led a series of enactments in which larger powers of the Local self government were given to the rural and urban bodies and the elective people received some wider rights.

66. Nobel Prize-winning economist Amartya Sen has been awarded the prestigious Bodley Medal, the highest honour bestowed by the University of Oxford's world-famous Bodleian Libraries.

The Medal is awarded to individuals who have made outstanding contributions to the fields in which the Bodleian is active, including literature, culture, science and communication.

Amartya Sen is an Indian economist and philosopher, who since 1972 has taught and worked in India, the United Kingdom, and the United States. Sen has made contributions to welfare economics, social choice theory, economic and social justice, economic theories of famines, and indices of the measure of well-being of citizens of developing countries.

He is the Thomas W. Lamont University Professor at Harvard University and member of faculty at Harvard Law School. He is a Fellow and former Master of Trinity College, Cambridge and was awarded the Nobel Memorial Prize (also known as The Sveriges Riksbank Prize from the Royal Swedish Academy of Sciences) in Economic Sciences in 1998 and India's Bharat Ratna in 1999 for his work in welfare economics. In 2017, Sen was awarded the Johan Skytte Prize in Political Science for most valuable contribution to Political Science.

In 2004, Sen was ranked number 14 in BBC's poll of the Greatest Bengali of all time.

68. Indonesia released a special commemorative stamp on the theme of Ramayana to mark the 70th anniversary of diplomatic ties with India.

The stamp, designed by renowned Indonesian sculptor Padmashri Bapak Nyoman Nuart, features a scene from Hindu epic Ramayana in which Jatayu valiantly fought to save Sita.

India's Ambassador Pradeep Kumar Rawat and Indonesia's Deputy Foreign Minister Abdurrahman

Mohammad Fachir jointly presided over the inaugural event organised to flag off the 70th anniversary of establishment of diplomatic ties between the two countries.

Ambassador Rawat underscored the significant strides that both nations had made in their bilateral relations in the last 70 years with a high point being the elevation of the bilateral relationship to a Comprehensive Strategic Partnership in May, 2018 during the milestone visit of Prime Minister Modi.

Deputy Minister Fachir in his keynote address recalled the ancient cultural and civilizational bonds between India and Indonesia and called for promoting greater people to people exchanges in the 70th anniversary year.

69. **International Mother Earth Day** was established in 2009, by the General Assembly under Resolution A/RES/63/278. The Resolution was introduced by The Plurinational State of Bolivia and endorsed by over 50 member states. It recognizes that "the Earth and its ecosystems are our home" and that "it is necessary to promote harmony with nature and the Earth." The term Mother Earth is used because it "reflects the interdependence that exists among human beings, other living species and the planet we all inhabit". It is decided to designate April 22 as **International Mother Earth Day.**

72. Popular actor, producer and screen writer Salim Khan was awarded prestigious **Lifetime Deenanath Mangeskar Award, 2019.**

These awards are conferred to legends from the field of music, drama, art and social work. They were instituted in 2011 by Master Deenanath Mangeshkar Smruti Pratishthan in honour of music composer and singer Hridaynath Mangeskar. Lifetime achievement award carriers monetary award of ₹ 2 lakh and a memento.

Hridaynath Mangeskar was son of renowned musician Deenanath Mangeshkar and is younger brother of Indian music legends Lata Mangeshkar and Asha Bhosle.

The previous recipients of Lifetime achievement award include eminent personalities like Amitabh Bachchan, Hariprasad Chaurasia, AR Rahman etc.

82. **Golden Peacock Awards,** instituted by the **Institute of Directors (IoD),** India in 1991, are now regarded as a benchmark of Corporate Excellence worldwide. No other Business Award today receives the kind of recognition and adulation among peers, that Golden Peacock does.

Today, there are a large number of Business Awards globally. The purpose is to create a competition for raising overall performance standards and recognise the achievements of the best performing organisations.

Award winners are eligible to use the **Golden Peacock Awards Logo** with year on all printed and promotional materials, which evidences the highest accolade received by the organisation. The Award applications are assessed at three levels by Independent Assessors and finally by a Grand Jury.

All institutions whether public, private, non-profit, government, business, manufacturing and service sector are eligible to apply. Leadership Awards are determined through nomination. They provide not only world-wide recognition and prestige but also a competitive advantage in driving business in this turbulent global economy under Golden Peacock Award models.

89. National record holder K.T. Irfan became the first Indian from athletics to qualify for the next year's Olympics while finishing fourth in the 20 km event of the Asian Race Walking Championships in Nomi, Japan.

The 29-year-old Irfan clocked 1 hour 20 minutes and 57 seconds to better the Tokyo Olympics qualification standard of 1 hour 21 minutes.

No other Indian from athletics has so far qualified for Tokyo Olympics. Irfan, who has a personal best as well as national record of 1:20:21 which he did during his 10th place finish in 2012 Olympics, also qualified for this year's World Championships (September 27-October 6) in Doha, Qatar as he bettered the qualifying mark of 1:22:30.

The Kerala race walker had won the 20 km event in the National Open Race Walk Championships in Chennai with a time of 1:26:18.

He was one of the two Indian athletes who were expelled from the 2018 Gold Coast Commonwealth Games for not adhering to the 'no needle policy' of the Games. He was disqualified in the 20 km race walk event of the 2018 Asian Games after receiving his third warning for "loss of contact".

90. The **SAFF Women's Championship,** also called the South Asian Football Federation Women's Cup, is the main association football competition of the women's national football teams governed by the South Asian Football Federation (SAFF). Seven members currently compete in the tournament. Formerly, eight members competed, before the departure of Afghanistan from SAFF.

The current SAFF members are Bangladesh, Bhutan, India, Maldives, Nepal, Pakistan and Sri Lanka. It is held every two years.

So far India has won every edition, beating Nepal four times and Bangladesh once in the final.

India has clinched all five editions of SAFF championships.

91. Tax $\underset{\text{Initial}}{100} \xrightarrow[20\%\uparrow]{} \underset{\text{Final}}{120}$

Consumption $100 \xrightarrow[20\%\downarrow]{} 80$

Expenditure $\overline{10000} \longrightarrow \overline{9600}$

$$\% \text{ Expenditure } = \frac{10000-9600}{10000} \times 100$$
$$= \frac{400}{100}$$
= 4% decrease.

92. Given, 13th January 1976 → Tuesday
13th January 1986 → ?
No. of odd days 1600 (Y) + 375 (Y) + 13 (D)
= 0 + 93 leap year + 282 Non-leap year + 13
= (93 × 2) + (282 × 1) + 13
= 186 + 282 + 13
= 481
= 68 weeks + 5 odd days
∴ 5 odd days → Tuesday
Now, again
No. of odd days in 13th January, 1986
= 1600 (Y) + 385 (Y) + 13
= 0 + 96 leap years + 289 Non leap years + 13
= 96 × 2 + 289 × 1 + 13
= 192 + 289 + 13
= 494
= 70 weeks + 4 odd days
= 4 odd days
5 → Tuesday
4 → Monday
So on 13th January, 1986 it will be Monday.

93. Let the breadth of a rectangle (b) = x
Then, the length of a rectangle (l) = $2x$
Given that, perimeter of rectangle = 60 cms
$$2(l + b) = 60$$
$$2(2x + x) = 60$$
$$3x = 30$$
$$x = 10$$
∴ b = 10 cms
l = 20 cms
Area of rectangle = $l \times b$
= 20 × 10
= 200 cm^2.

94. Height of the tree after 2 years
$$= 75\left(1+\frac{1}{5}\right)^2$$
$$= 75\left(\frac{6}{5}\right)^2$$
$$= \frac{75 \times 6 \times 6}{5 \times 5}$$
= 108 cm.

95. Let the length of train = x meters
Given, speed of the train = 90 km/hr
$$= 90 \times \frac{5}{18} = 25 \text{ m/sec}$$
$$\because \quad \text{Speed} = \frac{\text{Distance}}{\text{Time}}$$
$$\frac{x+600}{60} = 25$$
$$x + 600 = 1500$$
x = 900 metres.

96. ∵ Cost price of the box is same
∴ Let CP of the box is ₹ x
$$2 \times \text{Loss} = \text{Profit}$$
$$2(x - 80) = (98 - x)$$
$$2x - 160 = 98 - x$$
$$3x = 258$$
$$x = 86$$
∴ The cost price of the box of pencils is ₹ 86.

97. ∵ A beats B by 20 metres
∴ A : B = 100 : 80 = 500 : 400
∵ B beats C by 5 metres
B : C = 100 : 95 = 400 : 380
∴ A : B : C = 500 : 400 : 380
= 100 : 80 : 76
∴ A beats C by 24 metres.

98. Let Reena's daughter age = x years
Then Reena age = $10x$ years
8 years ago Reena age = $(10x - 8)$ years
Today Reena age
$= \frac{5}{4}$ × Reena age 8 years ago
$$10x = \frac{5}{4} \times (10x - 8)$$
$$40x = 50x - 40$$
$$10x = 40$$
$$\therefore \quad x = 4$$
Hence, Reena's daughter age is 4 years.

99. ∵ Clock gains 2 minutes in every hour.
∴ 60 minutes of original clock
= 62 minutes of new clock
1 minute of original clock
$= \frac{62}{60}$ minutes of new clock
In, 1 minute second hand traversed = 360°
In, $\frac{62}{60}$ minutes, second hand traversed
$$= 360 \times \frac{62}{60} = 372°.$$

100. Number of students took both subject
= (80 + 45) – 100
= 125 – 100 = 25%

25% value = 40

100% value = $\frac{40}{25} \times 100$

= 160.

101. ∵ When Kiran's brother born then Kiran's sister age = 2 years and
At the time of Kiran's sister born her father age is 30 years
∴ At the time of Kiran's brother both her father age = 30 + 2 = 32 years.

102. Total Sunday in 31 days = 4 days
Second Saturday is also a Holiday
∴ Total Holiday = 4 + 1 = 5 days
Total working days = 31 − 5 = 26 days.

103. 450 × S = 270 × C

$$\frac{S}{C} = \frac{3}{5}$$

Let total meal = 450 × 3 = 1350 unit
Left meal = 1350 − 300 × 3
= 1350 − 900
= 450 unit
∴ No. of cops can be fed with the remaining meal

$$= \frac{450}{5} = 90.$$

104. We have 3, 6, 9, 12, ... this is an AP
d = 3 km/hr
a = 30 km
n = 7 hr

$$\text{Sum of an AP} = \frac{n}{2}[2a + (n-1)d]$$

$$= \frac{7}{2}[2 \times 30 + (7-1)3]$$

$$= \frac{7}{2}[60 + 18]$$

$$= \frac{7}{2} \times 78$$

= 7 × 39
= 273 km.

105. By allegation Rule,

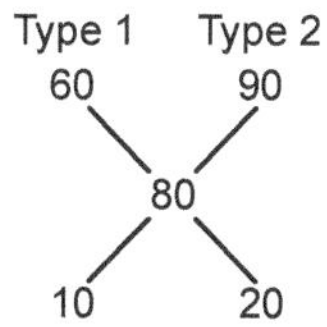

1 : 2

∴ Required ratio will be 1 : 2.

106. 23) 2085 (9
207
15
∴ We will substract 15.

107. Water filled in the tank in one hour

$$= \frac{1}{6} + \frac{1}{8} - \frac{1}{12}$$

$$= \frac{4+3-2}{24}$$

$$= \frac{5}{24}$$

$$\therefore \text{Required time} = \frac{24}{5}$$

= 4 hour 48 minutes.

108. Cost price of each bicycle = ₹ 3500
Let second bicycle sold at x% profit
Then, profit on first bicycle
= 3500 × 5% = 175
Profit on both the bicycle
= (3500 + 3500) × 20%

$$= 7000 \times \frac{20}{100}$$

= 1400

$$\therefore \quad 175 + 3500 \times \frac{x}{100} = 1400$$

175 + 35x = 1400
35x = 1225
x = 35%

109. Let amount invested in scheme 'Y' = x
Then amount invested in scheme 'X'
= 25,400 − x

$$\frac{(25400 - x) \times 2 \times 18}{100} + \frac{x \times 2 \times 10}{100} = 6460$$

914400 − 36x + 20x = 646000
−16x = −268400
x = 16775.

110. In half yearly,
t' = 2t = 2 years

$$r' = \frac{r}{2} = \frac{10}{2} = 5\%$$

We know that,
CI and SI difference for two years

$$= P\left(\frac{r}{100}\right)^2$$

$$= 500\left(\frac{5}{100}\right)^2$$

$$= 500 \times \frac{1}{20} \times \frac{1}{20}$$

= ₹ 1.25

161. $\underset{(5)}{e} \rightarrow$ odd place alphabet written in capital letter
even place alphabet written in small letter
Sixth month from March

$= \underset{19\ 5\ 16\ 20\ 5\ 13\ 2\ 5\ 18}{\text{S e p t e m b e r}}$

= SEptEMbEr

162. As, C l e v e r → (Opposite word in english Alphabet) → X O V E V I

Similarly, S m a r t → (Opposite word in english Alphabet) → [H N Z I G]

163. Number alternatively move forward and backward in +1 pattern.

164. 257 —(+34)→ 291 —(+36)→ [327] —(+38)→ 365 —(+40)→ 405

165.

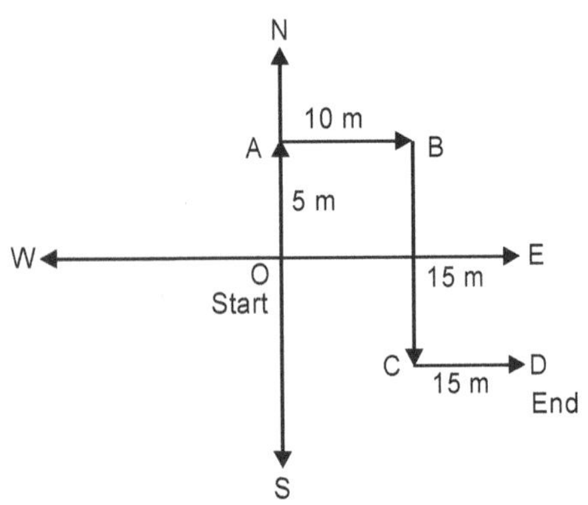

Manoj is facing in East direction.

166.

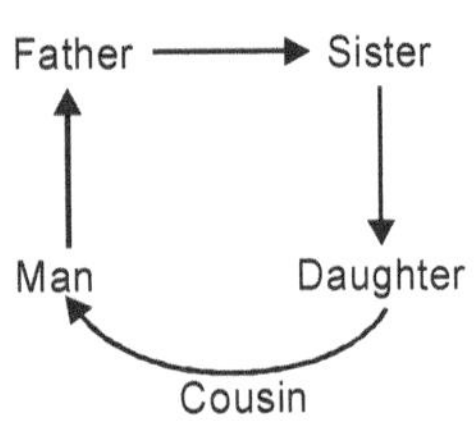

For 167-170.

	Motor Cycle	Jeep	Lorry	Bus	Tempo
P	✔	✔	✔	✘	✘
Q	✔	✔	✘	✔	✘
R	✔	✔	✔	✔	✔
S	✔	✔	✔	✔	✘
T	✔	✘	✔	✔	✔

171. Let the number of coins in the first bag is x

Then, No. of coins in the second bag = $\frac{4}{3}x$

According to question,

$$\frac{4}{3}x - x = 5$$

$$\frac{4x - 3x}{3} = 5$$

$$x = 15$$

∴ No. of coins in the first bag are 15.

172. 53 —(−3)→ 50 —(−5)→ 45 —(−7)→ 38 —(−9)→ 29 —(−11)→ [18]

173. 20 —(+10)→ 30 —(+12)→ 42 —(+14)→ 56 —(+16)→ 72 —(+18)→ [90]

176. As $1 \times 7 = 7 + 1 = 8$
$2 \times 7 = 14 + 2 = 16$
$3 \times 7 = 21 + 3 = 24$
$4 \times 7 = 28 + 4 = 32$
Similarly,
$9 \times 7 = 63 + 9 = 72$

For 181-185.

Subjects	**Day**
Physics	Monday
Play	Tuesday
Social Science	Wednesday
Mathematics	Thursday
Chemistry	Friday
Biology	Saturday

For 186-190.

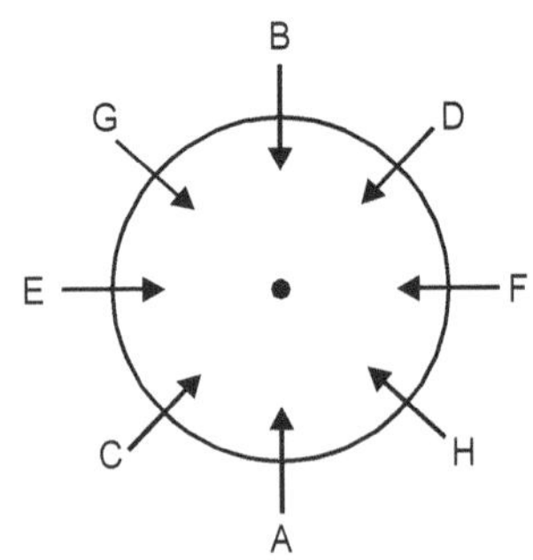

197. ∵ All men are mortal.
Victoria is a woman
∴ Victoria is mortal logically invalid because Victoria is a women not a man.

198. ∵ All men are chairs.
John Doe is a man
∴ John Doe is a chair.

199. 1 – 3 (+2) 4 – 6 (+2) 7 – 9 (+2) [10] – 12 (+2)

∴ Missing number is 10.

Previous Paper (Solved)

Common Law Admission Test (CLAT-UG)

Entrance Exam, 2018

Section-I : English Including Comprehension

Directions (Qs. No. 1-3): *In the paragraph below there are five sentences. In each sentence there are pairs of highlighted words (A, B). Select the most appropriate words to form correct sentences. Then from the options given select the correct option.*

1. Internationally high rise walls serve as street (A) **paintings** (B) **canvasses.** In Delhi and Gurgaon artists have (A) **earmarked** (B) **earmark** a district and after civic authority (A) **compliance** (B) **grant** transformed it into a throbbing art district. A walk through the (A) **instalment** (B) **installations** for public interaction is (A) **instituted** (B) **envisaged.** It is hoped that this will discourage defiling city's public places.

The correct sequence should be:

A. ABABB B. BABAB
C. BAABB D. ABABA

2. Pie charts are another extremely effective (A) **visual** (B) **graph** presentation of data. They show what proportions make up a whole. Each segment should be (A) **cleared** (B) **differentiated** by shading, cross – hatching or colour and should be (A) **labelled** (B) **articulated** horizontally. (A) **Initially** (B) **Conventionally,** the largest slice begins at the 12 O' clock position then slices are sequenced clockwise in (A) **descending** (B) **clarified** positions.

The correct sequence should be:

A. ABABA B. BBABA
C. BABBA D. BAABA

3. One of the predictable difficulties you can expect to (A) **encounter** (B) **counter** when you go to a different country to study or work is language. But difficulties may also result from (A) **culture** (B) **cultural** differences, which are often less (A) **conscious** (B) **obvious** at first and can be unexpected. A Dutch academic was one of the first persons to propose an (A) **influential** (B) **dire** theory of cultural (A) **diversity** (B) **division.**

The correct sequence should be:

A. ABABA B. ABBAA
C. AABBA D. ABABB

Directions (Qs. No. 4-6): *Identify the incorrect sentence/ sentences.*

4. (*a*) It is important to monitor the groups.
(*b*) Check that the instructions are clear, and tell the students to begin.
(*c*) Inefficient bus service are a hazard.
(*d*) Traffic in the city has reached unsustainable levels.

Code:

A. (*a*) B. (*b*)
C. (*c*) D. (*d*)

5. (*a*) The college has organized a science fare
(*b*) This is to notify that a leather wallet has been lost
(*c*) Shortly blood donation will begin a camp
(*d*) The agenda of the meeting is available on the website.

Code:

A. (*b*) B. (*c*)
C. (*d*) D. (*a*)

6. (*a*) It is vastly reading is significant
(*b*) Reading for pleasure is linked to parental support at an early age.
(*c*) We can read intensively and extensively.
(*d*) Basic literacy among the prison population is insignificant.

Code:

A. (*c*) B. (*d*)
C. (*b*) D. (*a*)

Directions (Qs. No. 7-12): *Fill up the blanks numbered (a) (b) (c) (d) (e) (f) in the passage given below with the most appropriate word from the options given for each blank.*

The main objective of art and (*a*) living is to develop (*b*) sensibilities and skills of healthful living besides providing a (*c*) ground for love of labour, (*d*) social attitudes and moral values so as to enable the child to be (*e*) to the ideas of others with humility and sincerity in thought, word and deed. Love for mankind and helping the needy would (*f*) at this stage and its culmination would be in terms of attainment of selfless service.

7. (*a*) is:

A. profitable B. promising
C. productive D. praise

8. (*b*) is:

A. nature B. healthy
C. aesthetic D. genuine

9. (*c*) is:

A. nurturing B. fruitful
C. attractive D. interesting

10. (*d*) is:

A. clear B. positive
C. growing D. negative

11. (*e*) is:

A. welcome B. clear
C. receptive D. illegal

12. (*f*) is:

A. disappear B. reveal
C. link D. germinate

Directions (Qs. No. 13 and 14): *Four alternative summaries are given in the text: Choose the option that best captures the essence of the text.*

13. Develop Critical Thinking

The way we see the world and relate to others is intrinsically connected to our own set of values that govern the way we decide to live. However, the influence of fashion, consumerism, pop culture, broken homes, social unrest, and the media is all-pervasive. For many people, teachers and students alike, this influence goes unquestioned. Critical thinking, if successfully taught at this level, becomes the antidote for individual and social illiteracy. For the authors, critical thinking should constitute an indivisible part of the overall educational process. Facione (1995) comments: 'Critical thinking lies at the root of civilisation. It is a cornerstone in the journey humankind is taking from beastly savagery to global sensitivity'.

Supporting the development of these skills involves reflective teaching and learning, which is highly complex and which some students may find difficult, or interpret as weakness on the part of the teacher. But in the long run, with patience on the part of the teacher, it will develop students who can view old or new material, from a variety of sources, through new eyes, using their skills to define their own stance and express it, often better in their second language, with an open-minded confidence.

A. The world view of the human being today is influenced by a lot of things. Critical thinking cannot be taught as it involves reflective teaching and could be misunderstood.
B. Critical thinking must be part of an individual's education but it is a difficult concept because it very often reflects a teacher as a dominating individual.
C. Critical thinking is an important aspect of an individual's literacy level and his social knowhow. It is part of civilization and eventually leads to global sensitivity. Students can look at information in a variety of ways.
D. Reflective teaching is another aspect of initial thinking and it could lead to individual and social illiteracy.

14. The construct of democracy rests on informed choice and governance on informed policy. Answers to critical questions are stranded in the arena of claims and counter claims. Measures of progress are simply not known or available. The debate to job creation is a mystery of sorts. The public are not aware that the Center and States spend crores on education, health and social services. Take education. Barely a few of Class V students can read a Class II text, the poor are switching to private schools and over 33% of million-plus schools do not maintain a feasible pupil teacher ratio.

A. Being informed is an important aspect of any democracy. This information is not available especially in the area of education, health and social services.
B. Answers are often given but they need to be deciphered accurately. Job clarity is available but sometimes it is a mystery. There is confusion about information.
C. Health and social services is clearly communicated but education remains an area of ignorance. Claims and counter claims create even more confusion.
D. Crores are spent on many areas of growth but there is no accountability for information. Parents are switching to private schools as the information on education is available there.

Directions (Qs. No. 15-19): *The word given in each of the sentences is used contextually. Pick the word from the alternatives given that is most inappropriate in the given context.*

15. VENERATE - We venerate aged priests and martyrs.

A. respect B. revere
C. spurn D. honor

16. PRUDENCE - Prudence and sacrifice help us in meeting the future.

A. caution B. reckless
C. foresight D. judgement

17. OSTENTATION - Ostentation in wealth and living styles can sometimes turn vulgar.

A. pageantry B. display
C. modesty D. flourish

18. DOCTRINE - A doctrine is often refined by reasoning.

A. offense B. dogma
C. precept D. principle

19. BENEVOLENCE : Every religion believes in the concept of benevolence.
A. generosity
B. malignity
C. liberality
D. benignity

Directions (Qs. No. 20 & 21): *Answer the question, based on the following information. Indicate which of the statements given with that particular question, is consistent with the information given in the passage below.*

A Holistic Viewpoint

It is now recognised by modern science that the universe at the subatomic level does not have solid material objects, but consists of only wavelike patterns which represent probabilities of interconnections between other interconnections, all of which together constitute an inseparable web of inter-relationships constituting the entire universe. Fritj of Capra therefore, views the universe not as "an assemblage of independent parts" but as "a dynamic web of inter-related events" in which each part of the web determines the structure of the whole. Geoffrey Chew views such inter-penetrating and interdependent relationships in the universe in terms of a "bootstrap" theory which implies that all forces in the universe are inseparably linked together, every part affects every other part, and the whole world is held together so to say, by bootstraps. David Bohm refers to a holographic concept which implies not only that every part is connected with every other part within the whole but also that, in a sense, each part contains the whole. This, according to David Bohm, recognises the "Undivided wholeness" of the entire universe instead of the classical idea of analysability of the world into separately and independently existent parts.

20. Choose the appropriate option:
A. there are many solid material objects in the universe
B. the entire universe has a web of inter-relationships
C. the universe comprises of a number of independent parts
D. these independent parts determine the structure of the web

21. Choose the appropriate option:
A. the holographic theory speaks of the exclusiveness of each part.
B. the world can be analysed into separate independent parts.
C. the classical idea recognizes the concept of wholeness.
D. the boot strap theory speaks of interdependent relationships

Directions (Qs. No. 22-24): *In the following sentence a part of the sentence is underlined. Beneath each sentence four different ways of paraphrasing the underlined part are indicated. Choose the best alternative among the four options.*

22. The police searched everywhere but they drew a blank.
A. upset
B. did not find any information
C. came to an end
D. drew a line

23. She was accused of being close-minded and intolerant.
A. did not agree
B. kept to herself
C. not open to new ideas
D. unwilling to discuss

24. Rehman likes to have a finger in every pie.
A. likes cooking
B. wants to do everything
C. object to everything
D. cannot take decisions

Directions (Qs. No. 25-27): *In the question below, a related phrase is followed by a group of words. Select the group of words that best expresses a relationship similar to the one expressed in the original phrase.*

25. At one's wits end
A. cannot say anything funny
B. not able to think logically
C. not able to work
D. clarity of thought

26. Gift of the gab
A. clever at work
B. flatter someone
C. promise blatantly
D. fluent at speaking

27. Die in harness
A. die while riding
B. die at the height of one's success
C. die with help
D. die when the work has been completed

Directions (Qs. No. 28 & 29): *Read the passage given below. Choose the best options for the Question.*

IOT has had an impact across all fields, be it industries, government, small or large businesses and even for Personal Consumption.

What is IOT (Internet of things) you might ask. It's been a growing topic of conversation for some time now. Put in the simplest term it means anything that has an on and off button and is connected to the internet for receiving, analyzing, storing or sending data. This could mean anything, from the watch that you wear to airplanes that can be controlled from a remote location. According to the analyst firm Gartner, by the year 2020 we'll have over 26 billion connected devices. That could mean people to people, people connected to things and things connected to things. The new rule of the future is going to be "Anything that can be connected will be connected". Take for example that when you set an alarm to wake up and that alarm goes off it not only wakes you up but also brews your coffee, sets the right temperature of water for your bath, puts on the television to bring you the latest updates from around the globe and all this before you even put a foot out of your bed. This is all done by simply getting the network of interconnected things/devices that have embedded sensors, network connectivity, software and necessary electronics that collect and exchange data.

To show how far we have come with technology and connectivity, we have smart watches such as Fitbit, Garmin to name a few that have changed the way we look at time. We have one device that not only tells us the time but also tracks the number of steps, calories and our heart rate. This watch is actually connected to our phone so with just one turn of the wrist one can tell who is calling or what messages have been received without having to dig through pockets or handbags.

IOT is making its presence felt in healthcare as well. Doctors can now remotely monitor and communicate with their patients and healthcare providers can benefit from this. Whether data comes from foetal monitors, electrocardiograms, temperature monitors or blood glucose levels, tracking this information is vital for some patients. Many of this requires follow up interaction with healthcare professionals. With smarter devices that deliver more valuable data it can reduce the need for direct patient - physician interaction.

Take for instance in the sporting field, minute chips are being attached to balls and bats which will transmit information of how fast the ball is travelling and a batsman's moves, the time, the angles, the pressure on the bat at different positions, data of the muscle stretch if he's hit a six so on and so forth. Formula one cars are also being fitted with these sensors which relays information on the minute moves being made by the driver. Chips are also being put into wearable devices of sportsmen to detect suboptimal action of any body parts to show signs of stress or strain which will help in the early detection of injuries and take preventive measures.

IOT has had an impact across all fields, be it industries, government, small or large business and even for personal consumption. IBM, Google, Intel, Microsoft and Cisco are some of the top players in the IOT spectrum.

With billions of devices connected security becomes a big issue. How can people make sure that their data is safe and secure? This is one of the major concerns in the IOT that becomes a hot topic. Another issue is with all these billions of devices sharing data companies will be faced with the problem of how to store, track, analyse and make vast sense of the information being generated. Companies are monitoring the network segment to identify anomalous traffic and to take action if necessary.

Now that we have a fair understanding of IOT let's see what impact it's had on the education sector. The only constant in our lives is change and learning. From the get go we learn, be it to the walk, talk or run. We adapt to the changing times and constantly learn from it. Education or learning as we know it in the broader sense is the most important of all and the one that decides which way we handle those changes to impact us and the world.

Today's world is fast paced and to keep up with this we need an infusion of speed with learning. From the classroom assignments, lectures, blackboards and chalk we have come a long way to what is now known as e-learning (electronic learning) or m-learning (mobile learning). With the GenNext it is imperative to provide the right kind of education.

The rise of technology and IOT allows schools to improve the safety of their campuses, keep track of resources and enhance access to information. It ensures data quality being the top priority but also facilitates development of content allowing teachers to use this technology to create smart lesson plans and ensuring the reach of this content to any corner of the world.

28. How is IOT a concept of connecting?
A. It is the internet in a different form.
B. It is the internet but connected to anything.
C. It is an analysing machine.
D. It is a data collection term.

29. It is said that we look at time differently now, why?
A. It is connected to different devices.
B. It is in a different format.
C. It is connected to the aeroplane.
D. It connects people.

30. IOT will help in simplifying patient - physician interaction because :
A. It helps reduce data.
B. Doctors can remotely connect to patients
C. It improves connectivity.
D. It is a simple process.

31. How will IOT work in the sporting field?
A. Through sport fields with chips.
B. Through special machine.
C. Through minute wearable chips which are connected.
D. Through special moves by the sportsmen.

32. Preventive measure is imperative because:
A. It can detect anything.
B. It identifies treatment needed.
C. It keeps them in touch.
D. It helps to identify stress and strain.

33. One of the major concerns of IOT is:
A. Security and privacy, data loss and tracking data
B. Only security and privacy.
C. Only data loss.
D. Only tracking data.

34. Technology and IOT has benefited education considerably because it has:

A. Helped in improving the lesson.
B. Helped keep track of all resources.
C. Helped teachers to track.
D. Helped with keeping up with the change in learning.

35. Teachers can use this data:
A. Only to teach with more resources.
B. Only to create a smart classroom.
C. Only to reach out to the world.
D. To teach with more resources, create a smart classroom and reach out to the world

36. Select a title that is most suitable for the passage
A. IOT curse or boon
B. IOT and our life tomorrow
C. IOT is changing the way we learn
D. IOT is all pervading

37. To conclude, IOT has an impact on:
A. Education, sports, medicine and our daily lives
B. Education, sports only
C. Education only
D. Education and medicine only

Direction (Qs. No. 38-40): *Choose the option closest to the Capitalized word.*

38. ANNIHILATE
A. devastate B. delay
C. investigate D. retaliate

39. FACILITATE
A. lend B. share
C. support D. serve

40. CAMPAIGN
A. lobby B. run
C. agree D. work

Section-II : General Knowledge and Current Affairs

41. Who wrote the memoir book "My Brief History"?
A. Dr. G. Madhavan Nair
B. Stephen Hawking
C. Angeline Merkel
D. Rosalind Franklin

42. What is the Motto of the Commonwealth Games 2018?
A. People, Place, Passion B. Share the Dream
C. Come out and play D. United by the moment

43. The 2024 Summer Olympics will be held in Paris, France for a third time. How many years before that, did the city host the Summer Olympics for the second time?
A. 100 Years B. 96 Years
C. 92 Years D. 88 Years

44. Who won the Men's Singles title in Australian Open 2018?
A. Dylan Alcott B. R. Nadal
C. Roger Federer D. Marin Cilic

45. In which election was the Electronic Voting Machines tried out on an experimental basis in India?
A. The 1982 Kerala Legislative Assembly Elections.
B. The Karnataka State for the 1984, Legislative Assembly Elections.
C. The UP State for the 1989, Lok Sabha Elections.
D. The 1987, Delhi Corporation Election in Karol Bagh constituency.

46. Recently a star, Icarus was seen by NASA's Hubble Space Telescope. What was the approximate time taken by Icarus' light to reach the Earth?
A. Nine billion years B. Ten million years
C. Seven trillion years D. One hundred years

47. Who won the first Gold Medal for India at the Commonwealth Games 2018?
A. Punam Yadav B. Mirabai Chanu
C. Jitu Rai D. Sanjita Chanu

48. Who is the first Indian to hold the post of Deputy Director General for Programmes at the World Health Organisation?
A. Rasha Omar B. Vijayalakshmi Pandit
C. Soumya Swaminathan D. Kiran Bedi

49. Who is the first female fighter pilot of India?
A. Punit Arora B. Avani Chaturvedi
C. Mitali Madhumita D. Priya Jhingan

50. The Reserve Bank of India issued the 100 rupee coin to mark the birth centenary of which Carnatic Music Legend?
A. Dr. Balamurali Krishna
B. Dr. M.S. Subbulakshmi
C. Muthuswami Deekshithar
D. Chembai Vaidynatha Bhagavathar

51. Which type of mango from Andhra Pradesh received a Geographical Indication (GI) Tag in 2017?
A. Alphonso B. Banganapalle
C. Totapuri D. Himsagar

52. The International Day of the Girl Child is observed by the UN on:
A. March 8 B. August 12
C. October 16 D. October 11

53. Where is the temple of Angkor Wat located?
A. Singapore B. Cambodia
C. Thailand D. Indonesia

54. Which one of the following States lifted the Santosh Trophy Football title 2018?
A. Kerala B. Punjab
C. Karnataka D. Uttar Pradesh

55. IRDA stands for:
A. Insurance Regulatory and Development Authority
B. International Resources Development Agency
C. Indian Roads Development Authority
D. Indian Rural Development Authority

56. The first Defence Minister of India was:
A. K.M. Cariappa B. V.K. Krishna Menon
C. Baldev Singh D. Kailash Nath Katju

57. Who is the legendary figure who won both a Nobel Prize and an Oscar?
A. Satyajit Ray
B. William Goldman
C. Gabriel Garcia Marquez
D. George Bernard Shaw

58. The discipline that deals with map making is known as:
A. Cryptography B. Carpology
C. Cartography D. Lithography

59. The prize established, based on a donation from the Sveriges Riksbank in memory of Alfred Nobel, is the:
A. Prize in Medicine
B. Prize in Economic Sciences
C. Peace Prize
D. Prize in Literature

60. What is the significance of May 13, 1952 with regard to Indian polity?
A. First sitting of the Lok Sabha
B. First sitting of the Rajya Sabha
C. First sitting of the Supreme Court of India
D. Formation of the Election Commission of India

61. Which among the following is the earliest literary work in Tamil language?
A. Manimegalai B. Silappadikaram
C. Thirukkural D. Tolkappiyam

62. Who has been appointed in 2018 as the Principal Scientific Advisor to the Government of India?
A. S.N. Joshi B. Rakesh Aggarwal
C. K Vijay Raghavan D. Vinod Kumar

63. Escape velocity of a rocket fired from the earth towards the moon is a velocity to get rid of the:
A. Centripetal force due to Earth's revolution
B. Earth's gravitational pull
C. Centripetal force due to Earth's rotation
D. Moons gravitational pull

64. From which animal is catgut usually made of?
A. Sheep B. Camel
C. Cat D. Rabbit

65. Who wrote the book *Der Ursprung der Familie, des Privateigenthums und des Staats/ The Origin of the Family, Private Property, and the State?*
A. Friedrich Engels
B. Lewis H. Morgan
C. Karl Marx
D. Friedrich Carl von *Savigny*

66. Name the part of the human body reclassified as an organ due to research conducted in the past decade.
A. Alimentary B. Mesentery
C. Epithelium D. Spleen

67. The World's first 'negative emissions' power plant has been built in:
A. Iceland B. Poland
C. Finland D. China

68. Which platform has been launched by the Union Government on the occasion of the 2018 International Women's Day?
A. Women Entrepreneurship Platform
B. Women Combat Platform
C. Women Power Platform
D. Women Literacy Platform

69. Who is the author of *'The Coalition Years 1996-2012'*?
A. Manmohan Singh B. Pratibha Patil
C. Sharad Pawar D. Pranab Mukherjee

70. What does 'NITI' in Niti Aayog stand for?
A. National Invitation to Invest in India
B. New India Transformation Initiative
C. National Institution for Transforming India
D. *Nayi India Turant India*

71. In commemoration of which of the following events, is May 1 celebrated in many places as the International Workers' Day?
A. The Haymarket affair, Chicago
B. Foundation Day of International Labour Organisation
C. Commencement of the First International Labour Conference
D. Concluding Day of the Russian Revolution

72. The National Social Security Board functioning under the Ministry of Labour and Employment is meant for recommending formulation of social security schemes for
A. Industrial workers
B. Women and Children
C. Government employees
D. Unorganised workers

73. The scarcity definition of economics is credited to:
A. Alfred Marshall B. Lionel Robbins
C. Adam Smith D. Dennis Robertson

74. Name the digital payment app introduced by Google in 2017 for India.
A. BHIM B. Tez
C. Citrus Pay D. MobiKwik

75. Which of the following countries runs bullet trains with the highest operational speed?
A. China B. Germany
C. South Korea D. USA

76. Who became the Chief Justice of the Federal Court of India on 14 August, 1947?
A. Maurice Gwyer
B. Patanjali Shastri
C. H.J. Kania
D. Srinivas Varadachariar

77. In which country outside India has the Energy Efficiency Services Limited, under the Ministry of Power, Government of India, launched the UJALA scheme in 2017?
A. Malaysia B. Srilanka
C. Indonesia D. Maldives

78. Which is thc organisation that initiatcs and prcscnts the National Film Awards in India?
A. Film and Television Institute of India
B. Central Board of Film Certification
C. Directorate of Film Festivals
D. Prasar Bharati

79. In 2017, eBay India was merged with which of the following Companies?
A. Flipkart B. Alibaba
C. Naaptol D. Snapdeal

80. The world's first fully Solar-powered Airport is
A. Cochin International Airport
B. Shanghai Pudong International Airport
C. Dubai International Airport
D. Singapore Changi Airport

81. The winner of the Jnanpith Award 2017 is
A. G. Sankara Kurup B. Shankha Ghosh
C. Raghuvir Chaudhari D. Krishna Sobti

82. What do the paintings of Ajanta caves primarily depict?
A. Ramayana B. Panchatantra
C. Jataka Tales D. Mahabharata

83. Which country joined as the eighth member of the South Asia Sub-regional Economic Cooperation (SASEC) in February 2017?
A. Myanmar B. Nepal
C. Bhutan D. Bangladesh

84. What is the theme of the 2018 World Wildlife Day?
A. Stop wildlife crime
B. Listen to the young voices
C. Big cats: predators under threat
D. The future of wildlife is in our hands

85. In which athletics event did Bob Beamon hold the world record for 23 years?
A. Triple Jump B. High Jump
C. Long Jump D. Steeple Chase

86. Which State government has come up with a Water ATM Policy in April 2018?
A. Haryana B. Maharashtra
C. Uttar Pradesh D. Madhya Pradesh

87. The military operation which annexed Hyderabad into the Indian Union was code - named as:
A. Operation Meghdoot B. Operation Polo
C. Operation Viraat D. Operation Vijay

88. Which of the following movies won the Best Movie Oscar Award 2018?
A. The Shape of Water B. Call Me by Your Name
C. Darkest Hour D. Dunkirk

89. Who is the first woman Defence Minister of Independent India?
A. Nirmala Sitharaman B. Indira Gandhi
C. Sushma Swaraj D. Sheela Dixit

90. What is the motto of the Supreme Court of India?
A. Satyameva Jayate
B. Dharmo Rakshati Rakshitah
C. Sarve Jana Sukhino Bhavanthu
D. Yato Dharmastato Jayah

Section-III : Logical Reasoning

91. Find the missing group in the sequence:
X7D, V11G, T13J, _____, P19P
A. Q15M
B. R17M
C. Q17L
D. R15M

92. Find the missing number in the sequence:
9, 3, ___, 1/3, 1/9
A. 2 B. 6
C. 1/2 D. 1

93. Which word does not belong with the others?
A. Flute B. Clarinet
C. Saxophone D. Violin

94. Find the next group of alphabets:
CFI, DHL, ILO, LPT, ________?
A. ORU B. RUW
C. OQT D. OSV

95. If "VOLKSWAGEN" is written as "UQKMRYZIDP" then "SWITZERLAND" is written as __________?

A. RVHSYDFPMOD B. TXJUAFSMBOE
C. RYHYVGQNZPE D. RYHVYGQNZPC

96. In an archery match, Suresh's team got more scores than Mahesh's team but not as many as Yogesh's team. Yogesh's team got more scores than Mukesh's team. Mukesh's team got less score than Mahesh's team.

Which team is in second place in the descending order of scores?

A. Yogesh's team B. Mukesh's team
C. Suresh's team D. Mahesh's team

97. Choose the word that is not a necessary part of the underlined word.
Movie
A. Scene B. Video
C. Duration D. Dialogue

98. The doctor is a person who looks after the sick people and prescribes medicines so that the patient recovers fast. In order to become a doctor, a person has to study medicine. Doctors lead a hard life. Their life is very busy. They get up early in the morning and go to the hospital. They work without taking a break. They always remain polite so that patients feel comfortable with them. Since doctors work so hard we must realise their value.

Based on the above paragraph, who among the following is/are doctor(s)?

(*i*) Kumar Sharma wakes up early in the morning everyday and treats everyone with patience. He usually gives emergency aid to the persons who are injured in accidents.
(*ii*) Rakesh studied medicine in Russia and practiced medicine there for 2 years. Later, stopped medical practice and turned into some business.
(*iii*) Shalini works in Apollo Hospitals. She always remains polite so that patients feel comfortable. She is a specialist in providing quality care for the cancer patients.

A. All are doctors
B. Rakesh and Shalini are the doctors
C. Kumar Sharma and Rakesh are doctors
D. Only Rakesh is a doctor

Directions (Qs. 99-103): *Read the passage given below and answer the Question.*

Ten friends attended a marriage, five of them Venkat, Manohar, Ravi, Prasanth and Tilak are sitting in a row facing North and other five friends Vidya, Maya, Divya, Keerthi and Anu are sitting in a row facing south not exactly in the same order. Each friend in a row is facing exactly one from the other row. One of them is using a Skoda Car. Manohar sits opposite to his friend who is using a Ford Car and sits at one of the extremes. The friend who uses a Honda car, is not Ravi who sits second to the right of Manohar. Venkat sits exactly in the middle of Ravi and the friend who uses a Nissan car is not Manohar. Keerthi does not sit at the extreme end but uses a Tata car and sits opposite the friend who uses a Fiat Car. The one who uses a Maruthi car sits opposite to the friend who is to the immediate left of Keerthi. The friend who uses a Toyota Car but not Anu, sits opposite Prasanth. Tilak does not sit at any of the extremes, but sits opposite the friend who uses a Chevrolet car, and is sitting adjacent to Divya and the friend who uses a Mahindra car. Vidya neither uses Chevrolet nor Toyota cars.

99. Who uses the Mahindra Car?
A. Venkat B. Anu
C. Vidya D. Divya

100. Keerthi is how many places away from the one who uses the Ford car?
A. One B. Three
C. Four D. Two

101. Who sits third to the left of the one who uses the Chevrolet?
A. Anu B. Maya
C. Divya D. Vidya

102. Which one does not belong to the group?
A. Maruthi B. Skoda
C. Honda D. Mahindra

103. Which is the car used by Maya?
A. Toyota B. Chevrolet
C. Mahindra D. Ford

104. In a queue, I am the last person while my friend is seventh from the front. If the person exactly between me and my friend is on the 23rd position from the front, what is my position in the queue?
A. 37 B. 36
C. 38 D. 39

Directions (Qs. No. 105 & 106): *Read the statement and on the basis of that, choose the most appropriate course of action(s) given below the statement.*

105. **Statement:** Most of those who study in premier Medical colleges in India migrate to developed nations for better prospects in their professional pursuits.

Courses of Action:

I. All the students joining these colleges should be asked to sign a bond at the time of admission to the effect that they will remain in India at least for ten years after they complete their medical education.

II. All those students who desire to settle in the developed nations should be asked to pay the entire cost of their education which the government subsidised.

A. Only I follows B. Only II follows
C. Both I and II follow D. Neither I nor II follows

106. **Statement:** Official data show more people died on Indian roads in 2016 than in 2015; UP and Tamil Nadu accounted for the largest numbers of fatalities.

Courses of Action:

I. Government should make a policy regulating the manufacturing of automobiles for private use.
II. Government should take steps to create awareness among the public about road safety.
III. Accidents can be avoided if the Government takes steps to make good roads.
IV. To eliminate accidents completely the Government should impose stringent punishments for traffic violations.

A. Only II and IV follow
B. Only II follows
C. Only III and IV follow
D. Only IV follows

Directions (Qs. No. 107 & 108): *Read the statements and presume that whatever statements given are true. On the basis of that, choose the most appropriate conclusion(s) given below.*

107. **Statements** : Some rats are cows.
All cows are animals.
Conclusions : I. All rats are animals
II. Some animals are rats

A. Only Conclusion I follows
B. Only Conclusion II follows
C. Both Conclusions I and II follow
D. Neither Conclusion I nor Conclusion II follows.

108. **Statements** : All the students are young.
All the teens are young.
Some men are teens.
Conclusions : I. Some students are teens.
II. Some young are students.
III. Some young are men.

A. Only (I) follows
B. Only (II) and (III) follow
C. Only (I) and (II) follow
D. Only (I) and (III) follow

109. 'X' started walking towards the west, after travelling 5 kilometres turned exactly to his right and walked 3 kms. Then he decided to walk exactly to his left. On reaching 2 kilometres, he heard a voice and walked back. Then he noticed that, his friend 'Y' was walking towards him from his right side. In which direction is 'Y' walking?

A. East B. West
C. North D. South

110. If 'DECEMBER' is 'AUGUST', 'MARCH' is 'MAY', 'SEPTEMBER' is 'SEPTEMBER' and 'OCTOBER' is 'JULY', then 'JUNE' is?

A. February B. April
C. January D. November

Directions (Qs. No. 111 & 112): *Read the information below and answer the Question.*

A neurosurgeon, an orthopaedist, a plastic surgeon and an ophthalmologist visited the patient after a surgery.
The time of each visit is mentioned below:
Neurosurgeon at 7:45
Orthopaedist 8:30
Plastic surgeon 9:15
Ophthalmologist 9:50
Each time mentioned above may be either A.M. or P.M.

111. If the ophthalmologist generally goes for his rounds before the surgeons, but not unless any other doctor does, and the neurosurgeon is not the last to go for his rounds, what is the correct sequence of their visit?

A. Orthopaedist, Neurosurgeon, Plastic surgeon, Ophthalmologist
B. Neurosurgeon, Orthopaedist, Plastic surgeon, Ophthalmologist
C. Orthopaedist, Ophthalmologist, Neuro-surgeon, Plastic surgeon
D. Ophthalmologist, Orthopaedist, Neuro-surgeon, Plastic surgeon

112. Who were the doctors to visit the patient in the evening?

A. Neurosurgeon and Plastic surgeon
B. Plastic surgeon, Ophthalmologist and Neurosurgeon
C. Orthopaedist and Neurosurgeon
D. Ophthalmologist, Orthopaedist and Plastic surgeon

113. Samantha is your father's mother's grandson's daughter. Therefore, Samantha is your

A. niece B. sister
C. uncle D. brother

114. Look at this series: 7, 10, 8, 11, 9, 12, ...
What number should come next?

A. 7 B. 10
C. 12 D. 13

115. In an interview for selection of two District Judges, four candidates, P, Q, R and S were shortlisted. All of them had 10 years standing as Lawyers. Who among them are most suitable?

I. P – Very academic not much interested in litigation practice, very honest and impatient.
II. Q – A patient listener, average in academics, thorough with Laws and sharp.
III. R – Jovial, patient, good academic records and actively involved in politics.
IV. S – Shrewd, quick tempered, punctual and published several Legal articles

A. P and Q B. Q and S
C. R and S D. P and S

116. Find the odd one out.
A. Bat B. Vulture
C. Eagle D. Owl

Directions (Qs. No. 117 & 118): *Read the information below and answer the Question.*

On the farewell day five best friends, namely, Vishal, Anirudh, Gaurav, Mansi and Sapna, clicked their photo, facing the photographer who is on the west. They were standing as per the following conditions:

(*i*) Sapna stands to the right of Mansi and Gaurav
(*ii*) Gaurav stands to the left of Vishal and Sapna
(*iii*) Mansi stands between Vishal and Anirudh
(*iv*) There are two people between Anirudh and Gaurav

117. Who will be standing at the 2nd position from the right in the photograph?
A. Vishal B. Mansi
C. Gaurav D. Anirudh

118. Who stands to the left of Anirudh?
A. Sapna B. Gaurav
C. Mansi D. Vishal

119. Find the equivalent for '?'
Sphygmomanometer : Blood Pressure :: Pyrometer : ?
A. Temperature B. Blood Flow
C. Urine Flow D. Atmospheric Pressure

120. From morning 11 O' clock to Evening 7 O' clock, how many times the hour hand and minutes hand will overlap each other?
A. 9 B. 8
C. 7 D. 6

121. Find the odd one out
A. Police station B. Railway station
C. Supermarket D. Airport

Direction (Qs. No. 122 and 123): *Read the following carefully and answer the question given below.*

122. Although women now constitute 30 percent of the global industrial force, legal hurdles and traditional barriers still hinder the vast majority of women in their efforts to achieve parity with men.
The paragraph best supports the statement:
A. The Author claims that Feminism rules.
B. Equality of men and women is still a myth.
C. Women should surpass men in all the fields.
D. The Author claims that women have to take more efforts.

123. If TEACHER is coded as CAHEETR and STUDENT is coded as DUETNST, then what is the code for SUCCESS?
A. CECSUSS B. CCEUSSS
C. SCUSCES D. UCSECSS

Directions (Qs. No. 124-129): *Read the following and answer the Question.*

Chetan invited five of his friends, namely Ritwik, Avantika, Darshan, Parul and Shweta to his birthday party. Each of the five friends gifted Chetan a different article – a jacket, a watch, a shirt, a video game and a headphone. As a return gift, Chetan gifted each of them a different article – goggles, a bag, a pen, a mobile case and a diary. The following is additional information about the gifts given by the friends and the return gifts they received.

(*i*) Avantika gifted the shirt but did not receive a bag in return.
(*ii*) Shweta did not gift the headphone but received the mobile case in return.
(*iii*) Neither Ritwik nor Darshan gifted the jacket but the person who did gift it, received the goggles in return.
(*iv*) The person who gifted the video game received a diary or a bag.
(*v*) Darshan did not gift a watch but received a pen in return.
(*vi*) Neither Shweta gifted a video game nor did Ritwik received a diary in return.

124. Who gifted the watch?
A. Shweta B. Darshan
C. Ritwik D. Parul

125. Who received goggles as a return gift?
A. Avantika B. Ritwik
C. Parul D. Darshan

126. Which among the following combination is correct?
A. Avantika – Bag
B. Ritwik – Video Game
C. Ritwik – Diary
D. Parul – Watch

127. Who gifted the headphones?
A. Shweta B. Ritwik
C. Darshan D. Parul

128. Which among the following combination is correct?
A. Avantika – Diary
B. Headphones – Diary
C. Ritwik – Goggles
D. Watch – Bag

129. The one who received the bag in return, gifted which among the following items?
A. Watch B. Video game
C. Headphones D. Jackets

Direction: *Examine the following expressions/activities/ processes, and arrange them in the most logical sequence.*

130. 1. Design, 2. Need,
3. Launching, 4. Research,
5. Testing, 6. Identify
A. 4, 1, 6, 2, 3, 5 B. 2, 6, 4, 1, 5, 3
C. 3, 5, 4, 1, 6, 2 D. 2, 4, 1, 5, 6, 3

Section-IV : Elementary Mathematics (Numerical Ability)

131. The value of the expression

$$\frac{\left(1\frac{29}{36}+4\frac{1}{8}\times 1\frac{7}{11}\right)\div\left(5\frac{1}{9}-7\frac{7}{8}\div 9\frac{9}{20}\right)}{3\frac{1}{5}\div\frac{9}{2}\text{ of }5\frac{1}{3}}$$ is

A. $\frac{2}{15}$ B. 2

C. $7\frac{1}{2}$ D. 15

132. The fractions $\frac{42}{491}, \frac{30}{313}$ and $\frac{35}{367}$ are arranged in ascending order of magnitude as:

A. $\frac{35}{367}, \frac{30}{313}, \frac{42}{491}$ B. $\frac{42}{491}, \frac{35}{367}, \frac{30}{313}$

C. $\frac{30}{313}, \frac{35}{367}, \frac{42}{491}$ D. $\frac{42}{491}, \frac{30}{313}, \frac{35}{367}$

133. Let x be the greatest number of 4 digits, which when divided by 15, 20 and 28 leaves in each case the remainder 2. The sum of digits of x is:

A. 19 B. 21

C. 23 D. 25

134. A student was asked to simplify the expression: $\frac{0.1216\times 0.105\times 0.0002}{0.625\times 0.08512\times 0.039\times 0.16}$ his answer was $\frac{1}{65}$. What is the difference between his answer and the correct answer?

A. $\frac{1}{65}$ B. $\frac{1}{130}$

C. $\frac{1}{26}$ D. $\frac{1}{13}$

135. When 13511, 13903 and 14589 are divided by the greatest number 'n', the remainder in each case is 'm'. The value of $(n + m)$ is:

A. 183 B. 182

C. 181 D. 179

136. ABCD is a quadrilateral in which measures of angle D and angle C are 60 degree, and 100 degree respectively. If the internal bisectors of angle A and angle B meet at P, then measure of angle APB is:

A. 80° B. 90°

C. 100° D. 110°

137. Suman saves 10% of her monthly salary. Now her expenditure increases by 30% and savings increases by 50%. The present increase in her salary is:

A. 25% B. 30%

C. 32% D. 40%

138. A sum amounts to ₹ 9680 in 2 years and to ₹ 10648 in 3 years respectively at compound interest. What will be the amount if the same sum is invested for $1\frac{2}{5}$ years at the same rate of compound interest?

A. ₹ 9025 B. ₹ 9152

C. ₹ 9215 D. ₹ 9251

139. The marked price of an article is 20% more than the cost price. If the article is sold at a discount of 15% on its marked price, then the gain percent is:

A. 5 B. $4\frac{1}{2}$

C. $2\frac{1}{2}$ D. 2

140. Reshma sells an article to Rekha at 37.5% profit, Rekha sells it to Madhu at $9\frac{1}{11}$% profit. Again Madhu sells it to Mitu at 25% loss. If Mitu pays ₹ 342 for the article, then what is the cost price of the article to Reshma?

A. ₹ 304 B. ₹ 266.50

C. ₹ 380 D. ₹ 384.75

141. The number of children in a camp is x and their average weight is 20 kg. If 5 children each weighing 12 kg, join the camp or if 10 children each weighing 21 kg leave the camp, the average weight in both the cases remain the same. The value of x is:

A. 18 B. 16

C. 15 D. 14

142. In a 120 litre of solution of acid and water, acid is 75%. A person takes out 20 litres of this solution and added 16.2 litres of acid and 3.8 litres of water in the remaining solution. What is the percentage of water in the final solution?

A. 22 B. 24

C. 25 D. 28

143. Twelve men and 5 women can complete a work in 2 days whereas 4 men and 3 women can complete the same work in 5 days. In how many days can 8 men complete the work?

A. 3 B. 4

C. 5 D. 6

144. a and b are inversely proportional to each other and are positive. If a increases by 100%, then b decreases by:

A. 50% B. 75%

C. 100% D. 200%

145. Four pipes A, B, C and D can fill a tank with water in 15, 20, 30 and 60 hours respectively. Pipe A is opened at 4 a.m., B at 5 a.m., C at 6 a.m. and D at 7 a.m. When is the tank filled up completely?

A. 9:30 a.m. B. 10:00 a.m.
C. 10:30 a.m. D. 11:00 a.m.

146. If a person travels at a speed of 40 km/h he will reach his destination on time. He covered half the journey in $\frac{2}{3}$ of the time. At what speed (in km/h) should he travel to cover the remaining journey to reach the destination on time?

A. 48 B. 50
C. 60 D. 72

147. The parallel sides of a trapezium shaped field are 25 m and 10 m and non parallel sides are 14 m and 13 m. What is the area (in m^2) of the field?

A. 204 B. 196
C. 156 D. 144

148. $x^2(a-b) + a^2(b-x) + b^2(x-a)$ is factored as:

A. $(a-b)(x-a)(x-b)$ B. $(a-b)(x-a)(x+b)$
C. $(b-a)(x+a)(x-b)$ D. $(a+b)(x-a)(x+b)$

149. Three fair dice are thrown simultaneously. What is the probability that the sum of numbers on their tops, is at least 6?

A. $\frac{5}{108}$ B. $\frac{1}{24}$
C. $\frac{103}{108}$ D. $\frac{17}{18}$

150. Six dice are stacked on the floor as shown in the figure below. On each dice, the sum of numbers on opposite faces is 7, *i.e.,* if 1 is written on one face then 6 is written on the face opposite it and so on.

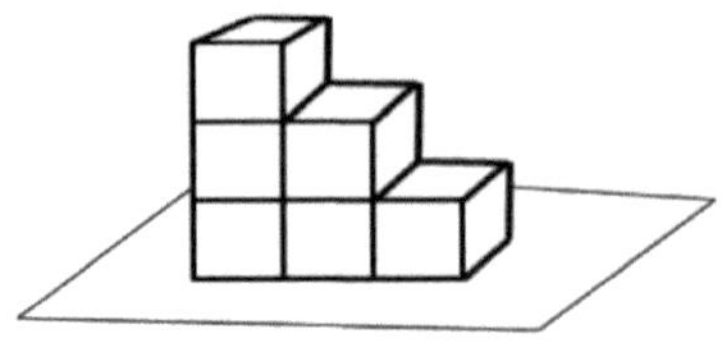

What is the maximum possible sum of numbers on the 21 visible faces?

A. 88 B. 89
C. 96 D. 147

Section-V : Legal Aptitude

151. Article 51-A on Fundamental Duties was inserted into the Constitution of India through the:

A. 41st Constitution (Amendment) Act, 1976
B. 44th Constitution (Amendment) Act, 1978
C. 40th Constitution (Amendment) Act, 1976
D. 42nd Constitution (Amendment) Act, 1976

152. The highest law officer in India is the:

A. Attorney General
B. Advocate General
C. Solicitor General
D. Chief Justice of the Supreme Court of India

153. How many languages are there in the Eighth Schedule of the Constitution of India?

A. 21 B. 22
C. 19 D. 18

154. A Panchayat Samiti at the block level in India is only a/an:

A. Administrative authority
B. Co-ordinating and Supervisory authority
C. Consultative Committee
D. Advisory body

155. Which of the following is NOT a fundamental duty as per the provisions of the Constitution of India?

A. To uphold and protect the sovereignty, unity and integrity of India
B. To join the Defence Forces of India
C. To defend the country and render national service when called upon to do so
D. To value and preserve the rich heritage of our composite culture

156. The Right to Education Act, 2009 (RTE) provides for free and compulsory education to:

A. All illiterate children of India
B. All citizens of India
C. Children aged between 6 and 14 years
D. All children up to the age of 10 years

157. The question below consists of two statements, one labelled as 'Assertion' (A) and another as 'Reason' (R). Examine these two statements carefully and select the answers to these items from the codes given below.

Assertion (A) : It is the legal and constitutional duty of the State to provide legal aid to the poor.

Reason (R) : No one should be denied justice by reason of his poverty.

Codes:

A. Both A and R are individually true and R is the correct explanation to A
B. Both A and R are individually true but R is not the correct explanation to A
C. A is true but R is false
D. A is false but R is true

158. Which was the law introduced by Sir William Bentinck to prohibit the practice of Sati?
A. Bengal Sati Regulation, 1829
B. U.P. Sati Prohibition Act, 1828
C. Indian Sati Prohibition Act, 1827
D. Rajasthan Sati (Prevention) Act, 1830

159. **Legal Principle:** Nothing is an 'offence', if committed by a child below seven years of age.

Fact Situation: Adil, aged six years, is a student of class one. He placed his sharpened pencil on the bench with its pointed end up when his classmate Ajay stood up to answer a question from the teacher. Ajay gets hurt when he sits on the pencil and Adil and his friends have a good laugh. Ajay's father, on seeing his son injured when he returns home, wants action against Adil.

Which of the following statements is the most appropriate in relation to the legal principle stated above?
A. Adil has committed an 'offence'.
B. Adil has not committed any 'offence'.
C. Childish pranks cannot be investigated by the police.
D. The class teacher must be arrested.

160. **Legal Principle:** The doctrine of basic structure in Constitutional jurisprudence means that the Constitution of India has certain basic features that cannot be taken away through amendments by the Parliament. The power of judicial review is a part of the basic structure and it helps the constitutional Courts to determine whether an amendment is against the basic structure or not.

Fact Situation: Parliament proposes an amendment to limit the power of appeal against conviction for the offence of Sedition, to be exercised only by the Supreme Court of India.

Which of the following statements is the most appropriate in relation to the legal principle stated above?
A. The proposed amendment is against the doctrine of basic structure.
B. The proposed amendment is unconnected to the doctrine of basic structure.
C. The proposed amendment can be reviewed and struck down by the Constitutional Courts.
D. The proposed amendment is beyond the power of the Parliament.

161. Who among the following was the first Chairman of the Constituent Assembly in India?
A. Dr. Rajendra Prasad
B. Dr. Sachchidananda Sinha
C. Harendra Coomar Mookerjee
D. Dr. B.R. Ambedkar

162. **Legal Principle:** It is an offence to obstruct a public servant in the due discharge of his duty. Right of private defence is available to protect one's person and property.

Fact Situation: Sidhu comes to the rescue of his uncle who is sought to be taken into a car by some men. In the process, he causes injury to some of them. Later, it turns out that the men were police persons in plain clothes trying to enforce a warrant against his uncle.

Which of the following statements is the most appropriate in relation to the legal principle stated above?
A. Sidhu has committed the offence of obstructing a public servant in due discharge of his duty.
B. Sidhu has not committed an offence since he did not know that the men were from the police.
C. Sidhu's uncle has resisted arrest and should be proceeded against.
D. Sidhu should not have tried to help his uncle without ascertaining the fact

163. **Legal Principle:** An employer is liable for the act of his servant performed during the course of employment.

Fact Situation: While working as a driver for Verma, Alok sometimes used to earn some side income by carrying parcels for others in Verma's car without his knowledge or permission. While going to pick Verma from the airport one day, Alok stopped to deliver a parcel he was carrying with him. While he was delivering the parcel, which unknown to him was one of contraband goods, the police arrested Alok.

Which of the following statements is the most appropriate in relation to the legal principle stated above?
A. Verma is liable for the act of Alok since he is Verma's driver.
B. Verma is liable for the act of Alok since he had gone to pick Verma from the airport.
C. Verma is not liable for the act of Alok since Alok himself did not know that he was carrying contraband goods.
D. Verma is not liable for the act of Alok since carrying the parcel was not in the course of his employment.

164. Which law introduced the system of dyarchy in India during the British reign?
A. The Government of India Act, 1858
B. The Government of India Act, 1909
C. The Government of India Act, 1919
D. The Government of India Act, 1935

165. **Legal Principle:** The Latin maxim nemo bis punitur pro eodem delictomeans that nobody can be punished twice for the same offence.

Fact Situation: Sajan, a petty thief, is caught and thrashed thoroughly by the people before being handed over to the police. Sajan pleads before the magistrate that since he was already thrashed by the people he should not be again punished by the State.

Which of the following statements is the most appropriate in relation to the legal principle stated above?

A. Sajan is right since nobody should be punished for the same offence twice.

B. Thrashing given by the people does not amount to legal punishment and so Sajan can be punished by the State.

C. Giving a good thrashing to the thief is the best form of punishment to prevent future theft.

D. The Magistrate should take into consideration the thrashing received by Sajan while fixing his punishment.

166. Legal Principle: The Latin maxim *qui facit per alium, facit per se* means that he who acts through another, acts himself.

Fact Situation: Heema requests her minor sister Harika to purchase a bag for her from the local shop. Harika purchases the bag on credit telling the shop keeper that her sister will pay for it. Afterwards, Heema refuses to pay for the bag.

Which of the following statements is the most appropriate in relation to the legal principle stated above?

A. Since Heema has not purchased the bag herself she is not liable to pay for it.

B. Harika being a minor the shop keeper should not have sold the bag to her.

C. Since she purchased the bag through her sister, Heema is liable to pay for it.

D. Harika being a minor should not have been entrusted by Heema for the purchase of the bag.

167. Legal Principle: Negligence is the absence of care by one party which results in some damage to another. Damage is an essential ingredient to constitute a tort of negligence.

Fact Situation: Mistry left his ladder on the public road while unloading it from a truck when he went to open the shutters of his shop. Saini who was riding his motorcycle had to swerve hard to avoid hitting the ladder as he came with speed on the road. Saini fell down but was miraculously not injured.

Which of the following statements is the most appropriate in relation to the legal principle stated above?

A. Mistry is not liable for the tort of negligence since Saini was not injured though he fell down.

B. Mistry is liable for the tort of negligence since Saini fell down due to the presence of the ladder.

C. Mistry is not liable for the tort of negligence since Saini was speeding on the road.

D. Mistry is liable for the tort of negligence since he was careless in leaving the ladder on the road.

168. Legal Principle: Every partner is liable alone and jointly with other partners for the debts of a partnership firm incurred for the business. Every partner is an agent of every other partner while being a principal in his own right in the business of the partnership.

Fact Situation: Varun is a partner in a firm with Chinmoy and Jaffar. Jaffar purchases a car for his personal purpose and obtains credit for the same in the name of the partnership behind the back of the other partners. He fails to pay the due amount on the expiry of the period of credit.

Which of the following statements is the most appropriate in relation to the legal principle stated above?

A. Varun, Chinmoy and Jaffar are liable to pay for the car since they are partners and the credit was obtained in the name of the firm.

B. Varun and Chinmoy are not liable to pay for the car since Jaffar purchased it for his personal purpose.

C. Varun, Chinmoy and Jaffar are liable as partners for all credit obtained in the name of the firm even if it is for the personal purpose of a partner.

D. Jaffar can use the credit of the firm to make purchases even for personal purposes since he is a partner in the partnership.

169. Legal Principle: Parents are not liable for wrongs committed by their children unless they provide the opportunity for such wrongful acts to be committed by their children.

Fact Situation: Sunil, a minor, takes the keys to his father's car from the table top where his father keeps it, drives the car on the public road and hits a pedestrian who gets injured.

Which of the following statements is the most appropriate in relation to the legal principle stated above?

A. Since Sunil took the car without his father's permission, his father is not liable for Sunil's act resulting in the accident.

B. Sunil's father is liable for the conduct of Sunil resulting in the accident since he left the car keys where his son could easily take it without permission.

C. Accidents happen despite utmost care and hence neither Sunil nor his father is liable in the instant case.

D. Sunil's father is not liable since he had kept his car locked and securely deposited its keys without negligence on his table top.

170. Legal Principle: No remedy lies in law where an injury is caused to a person without any infringement of his legal right.

Fact Situation: Ashutosh started a tuition Centre right next to the one being run for the past twenty years by Gulshan. After Ashutosh started his Centre, a large number of students shifted from Gulshan's tuition Centre to Ashutosh's Centre forcing Gulshan to close down his establishment suffering huge losses. Can Gulshan initiate legal action against Ashutosh?

Which of the following statements is the most appropriate in relation to the legal principle stated above?

A. Ashutosh must compensate Gulshan for his loss consequent to the start of the new tuition Centre.
B. Gulshan cannot blame Ashutosh if he cannot retain his students.
C. Ashutosh has not violated any legal right of Gulshan, though students shifted to Ashutosh's Centre and though Gulshan suffered loss, after he shut down his tuition Centre.
D. Gulshan should have improved his quality with lower fees to retain his students in the light of competition brought in by Ashutosh.

171. Legal Principle: Article 20(3) of the Constitution of India states that no person accused of any offence shall be compelled to be a witness against himself.

Fact Situation: Ubaid refuses to give a sample of his blood after he is stopped by the police for driving over the speed limit. The police suspect him to be driving under the influence of alcohol, which is prohibited under the law.

Which of the following statements is the most appropriate in relation to the legal principle stated above?

A. Ubaid is protected by Article 20(3) in his refusal to give a blood sample.
B. Ubaid is not protected by Article 20(3) as he was under the influence of alcohol.
C. Ubaid is not protected by Article 20(3) in his refusal to give a blood sample since he is not accused of any offence yet.
D. Refusal to give a blood sample is a crime and Ubaid must be punished for the same.

172. The law which provides special powers to the Armed Forces in India is popularly known as:

A. AFSPA
B. POTA
C. TADA
D. SARFAESI

173. Legal Principle: The law states that a food business operator must be registered with or licensed by the Food Safety and Standards Authority of India (FSSAI) to run a food business.

Fact Situation: Kavita's neighbours suffer food poisoning after consuming sweets gifted by her on the occasion of a celebration at her home. Kavita does not have a registration or license from the FSSAI.

Which of the following statements is the most appropriate in relation to the legal principle stated above?

A. Kavita is in violation of the law since she does not have a FSSAI registration or license.
B. Kavita is not in violation of the law since she did not make the sweets she gave by way of gift.
C. Law does not apply in cases like this where transactions happen between neighbours.
D. Kavita need not take a license or register with FSSAI since she is not running a food business.

174. Legal Principle: An agreement entered into by way of a wager/bet is unenforceable in law.

Fact Situation: Thomas is very good at predicting outcomes of cricket matches. Raja and Hoja give him rupees thousand each to enable him to bet with others about the outcome of a cricket match. Thomas wins rupees three lakh after betting three thousand rupees.

Which of the following statements is the most appropriate in relation to the legal principle stated above?

A. Thomas must share rupees three lakh with Raja and Hoja equally.
B. Thomas must return rupees thousand each to Raja and Hoja.
C. Thomas need not share the three lakh with Raja and Hoja since it is the outcome of an unenforceable agreement.
D. If Thomas does not pay them rupees two lakh each, Raja and Hoja can sue him to recover their share.

175. Legal Principle: *'Audi alteram partem'* is a Latin phrase which means 'hear the other side'. It is the principle that no person should be judged without a fair hearing.

Fact Situation: Sanjay, in Delhi, is accused of theft and brought before the Court. The magistrate discovers that Sanjay is mute.

Which of the following statements is the most appropriate in relation to the legal principle stated above?

A. The principle is not applicable to Sanjay since he is mute.

B. The principle is applicable to Sanjay even though he cannot speak since he can be asked to write down his defence.
C. The Magistrate has to take all measures to understand what Sanjay has to convey about the accusation against him.
D. Since it is a Latin principle it is not applicable in India.

176. Legal Principle: An essential condition in a contract for sale of goods is that the seller has title over the goods sold.

Fact Situation: Ranjan pays rupees two thousand and buys a watch from Mohit who runs a watch showroom and a repair shop. Jatin sees the watch with Ranjan and tells him that it is his watch and was only given to Mohit for repairs. If what Jatin says is true.

Which of the following statements is the most appropriate in relation to the legal principle stated above?
A. Ranjan is now the owner of the watch since he paid rupees two thousand for it.
B. Ranjan is not the owner of the watch since Mohit did not have a title to it.
C. Mohit must pay Jatin rupees two thousand since he sold Jatin's watch.
D. Mohit is the owner of the watch since he sold it to Ranjan.

177. Legal Principle: The insurer agrees to pay no more than the actual amount of the loss.

Fact Situation: Sunny insures his car worth rupees five lakh with X, an insurance company, for its value. He again insures the same car with Y, another insurance company, on the same terms. There is an accident and the car suffers a total loss. In his separate suits against X and Y, if Sunny recovers rupees five lakh from X, how much can he recover from Y?

Which of the following statements is the most appropriate in relation to the legal principle stated above?
A. Sunny can recover rupees five lakhs from Y.
B. Sunny cannot recover any amount from Y.
C. Sunny must pay Y, the rupees five lakhs he received from X.
D. Sunny cannot insure his car with both X and Y at the same time.

178. Legal Principle: When there is an infringement of the legal right of a person, he gets a right to sue the wrongdoer for remedy irrespective of any actual loss caused.

Fact Situation: Saroj is prevented from voting at an election. The candidate she intended to vote for, wins the election.

Which of the following statements is the most appropriate in relation to the legal principle stated above?
A. Saroj's legal right has been violated and she can sue the persons who prevented her from voting
B. Since Saroj's candidate has won the election, her rights are not violated and she cannot sue.
C. Since Saroj is not the candidate, her rights are not violated if she is prevented from voting.
D. This principle is not at all applicable in this case.

179. Which of the following is the oldest law code in India?
A. Hammurabi's code
B. Prasarsmriti
C. Manusmriti
D. Naradasmriti

180. Legal Principle: A product cannot be sold in shops to consumers after its date of expiry.

Fact Situation: Lata, while shopping, notices that the milk packets on the shelves are due for expiry on that day. She objects to this to the shopkeeper, saying that since she was there to buy milk for the next day, keeping the milk on its date of expiry was against the law.

Which of the following statements is the most appropriate in relation to the legal principle stated above?
A. Lata is right and the shopkeeper should take the milk packets off his shelves.
B. The shopkeeper should not sell the milk packets after the date of expiry is over.
C. The shopkeeper must remove the milk packets from the shelves and keep it refrigerated.
D. Milk is not a product and hence the principle is not applicable in this case.

181. Legal Principle: Nuisance is the unlawful interference with a person's enjoyment of his land or some rights over or in connection with it.

Fact Situation: Ashok, in his nineties, is hard of hearing and plays the radio very loudly throughout the day and on a daily basis. Raju, his neighbour, complaints that he cannot listen to his favourite TV show in his home due to the radio of Ashok.

Which of the following statements is the most appropriate in relation to the legal principle stated above?
A. Listening to the radio is Ashok's freedom.
B. Ashok is creating nuisance to his neighbour by playing the radio loud perpetually and disturbing Raju in being able to listen to the TV in his home.
C. Raju is creating nuisance by complaining about Ashok's enjoyment of hearing his radio.
D. Raju should appreciate that Ashok is aged and hard of hearing.

182. Legal Principle: Agreements in restraint of trade are void and unenforceable.

Fact Situation: Manu has been working as a blacksmith in his village for many decades. Somu has been undergoing training with him for the past three years. After his training is over, Somu enters into an agreement with Manu that he will not start a competing business in the same village while Manu is alive.

Which of the following statements is the most appropriate in relation to the legal principle stated above?

A. This agreement is void and unenforceable since it is a restraint on trade.
B. This agreement is valid and enforceable since Manu is Somu's teacher.
C. This agreement is valid but not enforceable after Manu's death.
D. This agreement is valid and enforceable since it is to protect Manu's interest in consideration for teaching Somu to be a blacksmith.

183. What does FIR stand for under the Criminal Law?

A. Forensic Investigation Report
B. First Investigation Report
C. First Information Report
D. Formal Interrogation Record

184. Under which of the following enactments, is the use of mobile phone while driving made punishable?

A. The Information Technology Act
B. The Indian Penal Code
C. The Motor Vehicles Act
D. The Criminal Procedure Code

185. Legal Principle: A person is liable to compensate others for harm caused by the escape of any inherently dangerous material that he keeps on his land.

Fact Situation: Ankit lights a bonfire in his courtyard to warm himself up during a cold winter evening. A strong wind suddenly blows some sparks from the fire, on to his neighbour's house which catches fire and gets completely destroyed.

Which of the following statements is the most appropriate in relation to the legal principle stated above?

A. Ankit's neighbour is liable to Ankit for distress caused by keeping a house that catches fire so quickly.
B. Ankit is not liable because nobody could foresee that the sudden wind will blow the sparks to cause a fire.
C. Ankit's neighbour cannot make Ankit liable for the loss of his house since it was an accidental fire that destroyed it.
D. Ankit is liable to compensate because the fire escaped from his premises to burn down his neighbour's house.

186. Legal Principle: A characteristic feature of partnerships is the principle of mutual agency, *i.e.,* every partner is an agent for every other partner and will hence be able to bind them by his act, within the business of partnership.

Fact Situation: Ram and Shyam are partners of M/s R & S Trading Company which trades in rice varieties. Ram agrees to purchase ten tons of rice from Govind. Ram dies after the rice is delivered to the premises of M/s R & S Trading Company but before the payment of price is made. Is the agreement binding on Shyam?

Which of the following statements is the most appropriate in relation to the legal principle stated above?

A. Being partners, Ram's agreement to purchase rice for their partnership, is not binding on Shyam.
B. Since Ram is no more, the agreement is not binding on Shyam.
C. Being partners, Ram's agreement to purchase rice for their partnership, is binding on Shyam.
D. The agreement is binding on Ram and not on Shyam since the rice is delivered only to M/s R & S Trading Company and not to Shyam.

187. Who is an Ombudsman?

A. A judicial officer designated to receive complaints against the violation of rights of citizens.
B. An official who is charged with representing the interests of the public by investigating and addressing complaints of maladministration or a violation of rights.
C. An elected representative of the people to investigate and address the complaints of maladministration or a violation of rights.
D. A specially designated police officer assigned with the power to investigate and address the complaints of maladministration or a violation of rights.

188. Which authority in India notified the guidelines for the protection of persons assisting accident victims on Indian roads based on the Supreme Court direction?

A. Ministry of Surface Transport, Govt. of India
B. Ministry of Social Justice, Govt. of India
C. Ministry of Road Transport and Highways, Govt. of India
D. National Human Rights Commission

189. Article 1 of a legal instrument reads: "All human beings are born free and equal in dignity and rights. They are endowed with reason and conscience and should act towards one another in a spirit of brotherhood".

Which is the legal instrument being referred to above?
A. National Human Rights Act, 1995
B. Constitution of India, 1951
C. Universal Declaration of Human Rights, 1948
D. Philadelphia Declaration, 1944

Directions (Qs. No. 190-193): *Examine the Statement and Conclusions given below and choose a suitable answer from the options given:*

190. Statement: It is a fundamental duty, which is unenforceable in a Court of Law that every citizen shall renounce practices derogatory to the dignity of women.

Conclusions:
1. Reservation of seats for women in employment is violative of the principle stated.
2. Asking a lady inappropriate questions about her personal life is violative of the principle stated.

A. Only Conclusion 1 follows.
B. Only Conclusion 2 follows.
C. Conclusions 1 and 2 follow.
D. Neither Conclusion 1 nor 2 follows.

191. Statement: A punishment is the imposition of an undesirable or unpleasant outcome upon a group or individual, meted out by an authority.

Conclusions:
1. Eye for an eye and tooth for a tooth is an example of punishment.
2. Imposition of fine on someone who inflicted bodily injury on another is justified by the statement.

A. Only Conclusion 1 follows.
B. Only Conclusion 2 follows.
C. Conclusions 1 and 2 follow.
D. Neither Conclusion 1 nor 2 follows.

192. Statement: Necessity knows no law.

Conclusions:
1. The act of a captain throwing some cargo into the ocean to save the ship from sinking is justified by the principle.
2. The act of a man out of poverty and starvation stealing some food from a hotel is justified by the principle.
3. The act of a tourist killing a tiger when it was attacking a villager is justified by the principle.

A. Only Conclusion 1 follows.
B. Only Conclusion 2 follows.
C. Only Conclusion 1 and 3 follow.
D. All Conclusions follow.

193. Statements:
1. Justice delayed is justice denied. Justice hurried is justice buried.
2. More than 3 crore cases are pending in the Indian Courts.

Conclusions:
1. People are not getting justice in India.
2. Disposal of cases by 'Fast track courts' results in injustice.
3. Cases must be disposed off within a reasonable time.

A. Only Conclusion 1 follows.
B. Only Conclusion 2 follows.
C. Only Conclusion 3 follows.
D. No Conclusion follows.

194. Legal Principle: One of the principles of 'Natural Justice' states that, "No person shall be a judge in his own cause".

Facts: A, a driver of B, a Branch Manager of ABC Bank was caught, suspecting theft, in the bank premises. The Bank management instituted an enquiry and made B the enquiry officer.

Which of the following statements is correct?
A. As B is a Bank Manager and not a judge, this principle is inapplicable.
B. Since the suspected theft was in the bank premises, the manager is the only competent person to enquire. Hence, the principle is not applicable.
C. Since B is the employer of A, B should not be conducting the enquiry on the basis of the given principle.
D. The principle will be applicable, only if the theft committed by A was in relation to the car.

195. Legal Principle: Justice should not only be done, but also seen to be done.

Facts: L, an honest Lawyer had 200 shares in Company X. Later, L was elevated to the High Court as a Judge and had to deal with Company matters. A dispute between Company X and its creditors came before L for decision.

Which among the following proposition is true?
A. L, as an honest person will definitely judge the matter on the merits only. So, the principle cannot apply.
B. A judge cannot excuse himself from taking up a case posted before him by the Court Registry.
C. L should refrain from hearing the matter as he holds shares of the Company X.
D. Since, L has only 200 shares he has no substantial interest in the company and hence can decide the matter.

196. Legal Principle: A person who keeps hazardous substances in his premises, is responsible for the fault if that substance escapes in any manner and causes damage.

Facts: A, an industrialist stored 1000 litres of liquid ammonia in a tank in his premises for his industrial use. There was a leakage from the tank due to which there was ammonia vapour in the surroundings. Many workers in other industries as well as his own industry and some members from the public suffered serious health hazards. Examine the liability of A, if any.

A. A may be liable for the injury sustained by his workers only and not others.
B. A is liable as he is responsible for the injury caused by the leakage of ammonia from his premises.
C. A is not liable because there was no fault on his part for the escape of the dangerous substance.
D. A is not liable because he did not expect a leakage from the tank.

197. Legal Principle: In the law of evidence, a person missing for long and not heard of, for over seven years is presumed to have died.

Facts: A, B and C are children of F and M. At the age of 20, A went out in search of a job and was not contacting the family. All attempts to trace A by the family failed. Eight years after the death of the parents, B and C entered into a partition and took equal share in the property of F and M. One year after this, A returned home with his wife and two children and claimed his share in the property. Whether A's claim is legally sustainable?

A. Since A was not heard of, for more than eight years, the legal presumption of death will apply and hence, he cannot claim a share in the property.
B. It was A's duty to be in touch with the family at least once in a year. The failure of this duty will disentitle him from claiming property.
C. A will succeed because he is a legitimate son of F and M.
D. B and C are legally bound to give 1/3rd share of the property to A.

198. Legal Principle: 'Gift' means transfer of certain existing property made voluntarily and without consideration, by a donor, to a donee, and accepted by or on behalf of the donee during the lifetime of the donor.

Facts: Amit executed a gift deed for property 'X' in favour of Sooraj, who happened to be Amit's loyal servant's son settled in the U.S. Two months thereafter, Amit died without leaving a will regarding his assets. Amit's children initiated steps to partition his entire property, including property 'X' among themselves. At that time, Sooraj came to India, and learning about the gift, claimed the property 'X'.

A. Sooraj can legally get the property 'X', as soon as he gets to know about the gift.
B. Sooraj cannot legally claim the property 'X' because, the children of Amit have already initiated steps for partition.
C. Sooraj can claim the property 'X', because, his acceptance of the gift is implicit by his conduct of claiming the property as soon as he came to know about the gift.
D. Sooraj apparently did not comply with the essential requirements of a gift and hence, the entire property including property 'X', can be partitioned among the children of Amit.

199. The right to information under the Right to Information Act, 2005 is a:

A. Legal Right B. Fundamental Right
C. Human Right D. Constitutional Right

200. The primary legislation relating to organ donation and transplantation, aimed at regulation of removal, storage and transplantation of human organs for therapeutic purposes and for prevention of commercial dealings in human organs in India, namely, the Transplantation of Human Organs Act, was passed in the year

A. 1994 B. 1998
C. 2004 D. 2014

ANSWERS

1	2	3	4	5	6	7	8	9	10
C	A	B	C	C	A	C	C	A	B
11	**12**	**13**	**14**	**15**	**16**	**17**	**18**	**19**	**20**
C	D	C	A	C	B	C	A	B	B
21	**22**	**23**	**24**	**25**	**26**	**27**	**28**	**29**	**30**
D	B	C	B	B	D	B	B	A	B
31	**32**	**33**	**34**	**35**	**36**	**37**	**38**	**39**	**40**
C	D	A	D	D	B	A	A	C	A
41	**42**	**43**	**44**	**45**	**46**	**47**	**48**	**49**	**50**
B	B	A	C	A	A	B	C	B	B
51	**52**	**53**	**54**	**55**	**56**	**57**	**58**	**59**	**60**
B	D	B	A	A	C	D	C	B	B

61	62	63	64	65	66	67	68	69	70
D	C	B	A	A	B	A	A	D	C
71	72	73	74	75	76	77	78	79	80
A	D	B	B	A	C	A	C	A	A
81	82	83	84	85	86	87	88	89	90
D	C	A	C	C	A	B	A	B	D
91	92	93	94	95	96	97	98	99	100
B	A	D	A	D	C	D	D	C	B
101	102	103	104	105	106	107	108	109	110
B	D	A	D	B	B	B	B	C	B
111	112	113	114	115	116	117	118	119	120
C	A	A	B	B	A	A	C	A	C
121	122	123	124	125	126	127	128	129	130
A	B	B	A	C	B	C	A	B	B
131	132	133	134	135	136	137	138	139	140
D	B	C	B	A	A	C	B	D	A
141	142	143	144	145	146	147	148	149	150
C	B	B	A	D	C	B	A	C	B
151	152	153	154	155	156	157	158	159	160
D	A	A	B	B	C	A	A	B	C
161	162	163	164	165	166	167	168	169	170
B	B	D	C	B	C	B	B	B	C
171	172	173	174	175	176	177	178	179	180
C	A	D	C	C	B	B	A	C	B
181	182	183	184	185	186	187	188	189	190
B	A	C	C	D	C	B	C	C	B
191	192	193	194	195	196	197	198	199	200
C	C	C	C	C	B	A	D	A	A

EXPLANATORY ANSWERS

41. **My Brief History** is a memoir published in 2013 by the English physicist Stephen Hawking. *My Brief History* recounts Stephen Hawking's improbable journey, from his post-war London boyhood to his years of international acclaim and celebrity.

Writing with humility and humour, Hawking opens up about the challenges that confronted him following his diagnosis of ALS aged twenty-one. Tracing his development as a thinker, he explains how the prospect of an early death urged him onward through numerous intellectual breakthroughs, and talks about the genesis of his masterpiece *A Brief History of Time*—one of the iconic books of the twentieth century.

42. The **2018 Commonwealth Games** was **XXI Commonwealth Games** that were held on the Gold Coast, Queensland, Australia. It was the fifth time Australia had hosted the Commonwealth Games and the first time a major multi-sport event achieved gender equality by having an equal number of events for males and female athletes.

The official motto for the 2018 Commonwealth Games was "Share the Dream". It was chosen to highlight the dreams and experience at the games that were shared by participants of the games, ranging from athletes to volunteers and the host country Australia to the world including the Commonwealth nations.

43. The **2024 Summer Olympics** will be held in Paris. Having previously hosted both the 1900 and 1924 Summer Olympics, Paris will become only the second city to host the Olympic Games three times, after London (1908, 1948 and 2012).

44. Swiss tennis player Roger Federer (World No. 2) has retained his Men's Singles title by winning 2018 Australian Open. It was Federer's 20th Grand Slam singles title and record-equalling sixth Australian Open men's singles title.

45. The Electronic Voting Machine is the end product of considerable experience and extensive trials at elections in different parts of India under the guidance of the

Election Commission of India. These machines were used for the first time during the General Election to the Kerala Legislative Assembly held in May, 1982. To start with, Electronic Voting Machines were used in 50 polling stations of Parur Assembly Constituency in Kerala.

46. Nasa's Hubble Space Telescope has discovered the farthest individual star ever seen - an enormous blue stellar body nicknamed Icarus located over halfway across the universe. The star, harboured in a very distant spiral galaxy, is so far away that its light has taken nine billion years to reach Earth. It appears to us as it did when the universe was about 30 per cent of its current age.

48. The World Health Organization (WHO) appointed Soumya Swaminathan one of two deputy directors general, the first time such a post has been ever created within the organisation. The position is also the highest post held by an Indian in the WHO. Dr. Swaminathan is currently the Director General of the Indian Council of Medical Research (ICMR).

49. **Avani Chaturvedi** is one of the first female fighter pilots of India. She is from Satna district in Madhya Pradesh. She was declared as the first combat pilot along with two of her cohort, Mohana Singh, and Bhawana Kanth. The trio was inducted into the Indian Air Force fighter squadron in June 2016.

50. The Centre is all set to roll out ₹ 100 coins for the first time in the country. The Ministry of Finance issued a notification regarding the introduction of ₹ 100 coins to commemorate the birth centenary of AIADMK founder Dr. MG Ramachandaran and renowned Carnatic singer Dr. MS Subbulakshmi.

The Reserve Bank of India will also issue new ₹ 5 and ₹ 10 coins to honour the former Tamil Nadu chief minister and the Bharat Ratna-winning singer.

51. The Banganapalle mango has received the geographical indication (GI) tag, making Andhra Pradesh the owner of the variety that originates in its Kurnool district.

The Banganapalle mango is one the most preferred varieties of the fruit in both Andhra Pradesh and Telangana. The application for the GI tag was made in 2011, prior to the bifurcation of Andhra Pradesh in 2014 to create Telangana.

52. Since 2012, 11 October has been marked as the International Day of the Girl child. The day aims to highlight and address the needs and challenges girls face, while promoting girls' empowerment and the fulfillment of their human rights.

53. Temple of Angkor Wat located in Cambodia. Angkor is one of the most important archaeological sites in South-East Asia. It was originally constructed as a Hindu temple dedicated to the god *Vishnu* for the *Khmer* Empire, gradually transforming into a Buddhist temple towards the end of the 12th century.

54. Kerala emerged as champions of the 72nd Santosh Trophy 2018 after winning the final over 10-man Bengal. The **Santosh Trophy** is an association football knock-out competition contested by the regional state associations and government institutions under the All India Football Federation (AIFF), the sport's governing body in India.

55. The **Insurance Regulatory and Development Authority of India** (IRDAI) is an autonomous, statutory body tasked with regulating and promoting the insurance and re-insurance industries in India. It was constituted by the Insurance Regulatory and Development Authority Act, 1999, an Act of Parliament passed by the Government of India. The agency's headquarters are in Hyderabad.

57. **George Bernard Shaw** was an Irish playwright, critic, polemicist, and political activist. His influence on Western theatre, culture and politics extended from the 1880s to his death and beyond. He wrote more than sixty plays, including major works such as *Man and Superman* (1902), *Pygmalion* (1912) and *Saint Joan* (1923). Shaw became the leading dramatist of his generation, and in 1925 was awarded the Nobel Prize in Literature.

He became the first person to have been awarded both a Nobel Prize and an Oscar.

58. **Cartography** is the practice of making maps as well as the study of maps.

The International Cartographic Association defines cartography as the discipline dealing with the conception, production, dissemination and study of maps. Cartography is also about representation - the map.

59. The **Nobel Memorial Prize in Economic Sciences** is an award for outstanding contributions to the field of economics, and generally regarded as the most prestigious award for that field.

The prize was established in 1968 by a donation from Sweden's central bank, the Swedish National Bank, on the bank's 300th anniversary.

Since 1901, the Nobel Prize has been honoring men and women from all corners of the globe for outstanding achievements in physics, chemistry, physiology or medicine, literature, and for work in peace. The foundations for the prize were laid in 1895 when Alfred Nobel wrote his last will, leaving much of his wealth to the establishment of the Nobel Prize.

60. The Rajya Sabha, the Upper House of the Parliament of India had its first sitting on May 13, 1952.

61. The **Tholkappiyam** is a work on the grammar of the Tamil language and the earliest extant work of Tamil literature and linguistics. It deals with the Tamil language. Having three sections, the first two deal with language (linguistics) and the third about the subject matters referred to in Tamil literature, the behaviour of the Tamils. Each section has been divided into nine chapters.

64. **Catgut** is a type of cord that is prepared from the natural fibre found in the walls of animal intestines. Catgut makers usually use sheep or goat intestines, but occasionally use the intestines of cattle, hogs, horses, mules, or donkeys. Despite the name, catgut manufacturers do not use cat intestines.

65. **The Origin of the Family, Private Property, and the State** is an 1884 historical materialist treatise by Friedrich Engels. It is partially based on notes by Karl Marx to Lewis H. Morgan's book Ancient Society (1877). The book is an early anthropological work and is regarded as one of the first major works on family economics.

66. Mesentery is a new organ has been discovered hiding in plain sight inside the human body. It was previously thought to be just a few fragmented structures in the digestive system.

In general, a fold of tissue that attaches organs to the body wall. The word mesentery usually refers to the small bowel mesentery, which anchors the small intestines to the back of the abdominal wall. Blood vessels, nerves, and lymphatics branch through the mesentery to supply the intestine.

67. After opening the world's first commercial Direct Air Capture (DAC) plant designed to pull CO_2 out of the air, Swiss company Climeworks join forces with a geothermal power plant in Iceland to create the world's first "negative emission" power plant.

68. NITI Aayog launched the Women Entrepreneurship Platform (WEP), on the occasion of International Women's Day 8 March 2018. The initiative is aimed at building an ecosystem for women across India to realize their entrepreneurial aspirations, scale-up innovative initiatives and chalk-out sustainable, long-term strategies for their businesses.

The platform aspires to substantially increase the number of women entrepreneurs who will create and empower a dynamic New India. These aspirations are manifest in the three pillars on which WEP is built: *Ichha Shakti* (motivating aspiring entrepreneurs to start their enterprise), *Gyaan Shakti* (providing knowledge and ecosystem support to women entrepreneurs to help them foster entrepreneurship) & *Karma Shakti* (providing hands-on support to entrepreneurs in setting-up and scaling up businesses).

69. "The Coalition Years 1996-2012" book is written by former president of India Pranab Mukherjee.

The Coalition Years begins its journey in 1996 and explores the highs and lows that characterized sixteen years of one of the most tumultuous periods in the nation's political history. It is an insightful account of the larger governance phenomenon in India—coalition politics—as seen through the eyes of one of the chief architects of the post-Congress era of Indian politics.

70. The **NITI Aayog** also **National Institution for Transforming India,** is a policy think tank of the Government of India, established with the aim to achieve Sustainable Development Goals and to enhance cooperative federalism by fostering the involvement of State Governments of India in the economic policy-making process using a bottom-up approach.

NITI Aayog aims to build strong States that will come together to build a strong India. To build knowledge systems for the States and the Centre.

71. International Workers' Day was officially recognized in 1889 at the first International Socialist Congress in Paris to commemorate the Haymarket Affair—a bloody confrontation between striking union workers and Chicago police in 1886.

72. The main responsibility of the Labour and Employment Ministry is to protect and safeguard the interests of workers in general and those who constitute the poor, deprived and disadvantage sections of the society, in particular, with due regard to creating a healthy work environment for higher production and productivity and to develop and coordinate vocational skill training and employment services. Government's attention is also focused on promotion of welfare and providing social security to the labour force both in organized and unorganized sectors, in tandem with the process of liberalization. These objectives are sought to be achieved through enactment and implementation of various labour laws, which regulate the terms and conditions of service and employment of workers.

73. **Lionel Robbins** was a British economist. Robbins gave his own definition of economics in his book "An Essay on the Nature and Significance of Economic Science" published in 1932. Lionel Robbins has given scarcity definition of economics in these words, "Economics is a Science that studies human behaviour as a relationship between **limited resources and unlimited wants** which have **alternative uses".**

74. Google has launched its new **digital payment app 'Tez'** for India. The app is probably going to feature a digital wallet where customers can store money and has been integrated with India's Unified Payments Interface (UPI) to allow for money transfers at no cost, and an easy checkout system. It's likewise said to support credit cards and third-party wallets like Paytm and Mobikwik.

77. India's zero-subsidy UJALA (Unnat Jyoti by Affordable Lighting for All) Scheme was launched in Melaka State of Malaysia by Efficiency Services Limited (EESL), under Union Ministry of Power. It highlights success of Indian model UJALA scheme to promote efficient lighting, using efficient equipment to... reduce electricity bills and preserve environment at global level.

78. The **Directorate of Film Festivals** in India is an organisation that initiates and presents the International Film Festival of India, the National Film Awards and the Indian Panorama. Although the Directorate helps appoint members of the jury panels each year, it has no input on which films are selected for consideration and which films ultimately win awards at the various functions it initiates.

80. The Cochin International Airport in Kerala is setting example for the rest of the world by contributing towards the environment. It is the first ever fully solar powered airport with an inauguration dedicated solar plant.

81. Eminent Hindi Litterateur Krishna Sobti (92) was awarded the 53rd Jnanpith Award for the year 2017 for her path-breaking contribution to Indian literature.

She is known for experimenting with new writing styles and creating bold and daring characters in her stories. Her language is highly influenced by the intermingling of Hindi, Urdu and Punjabi cultures.

82. The Ajanta Caves are one of the oldest UNESCO World Heritage Sites in India. The carvings and paintings at Ajanta date back to the beginning of the era of classical Indian art.

The Ajanta caves are home to paintings and sculptures that depict heavy influence of Buddhist philosophy and religious teachings of the Buddha. Various incidents from the life of Gautam Buddha and the Jataka Tales are represented and recreated on the walls of these caves. Scenes from the royal court of the respective eras are also painted.

84. World Wildlife Day is an opportunity to celebrate the many beautiful and varied forms of wild fauna and flora and to raise awareness of the multitude of benefits that conservation provides to people. The World Wildlife Day (WWD) is observed every year on March 3 to raise awareness about our planet's flora and fauna. World Wildlife Day will be celebrated in 2018 under the theme "Big cats: predators under threat".

Big cats are among the most widely recognized and admired animals across the globe. However, today these charismatic predators are facing many and varied threats, which are mostly caused by human activities.

86. Haryana government comes up with Water ATM Policy to provide clean drinking water at public places.

Under this policy, public places such as bus-stands, railway parks, bus stops, parking areas and markets would be identified. Functioning of water ATMs would be ensured in three ways.

87. **Operation Polo** is the code name of the Hyderabad "police action" in September 1948, by the newly independent India against the Hyderabad State. It was a military operation in which the Indian Armed Forces invaded the Nizam-ruled princely state, annexing it into the Indian Union.

88. "The Shape of Water" won Oscars for best picture and directing at the 2018 Academy Awards. ***The Shape of Water*** is a 2017 American romantic dark-fantasy drama film directed by Guillermo del Toro and written by del Toro and Vanessa Taylor.

90. The **Supreme Court of India** is the highest judicial forum and final court of appeal under the Constitution of India, the highest constitutional court, with the power of constitutional review. Consisting of the Chief Justice of India and 30 sanctioned other judges, it has extensive powers in the form of original, appellate and advisory jurisdictions.

The motto of the Supreme Court of India is *"Yato Dharmastato Jayah"*.

91.

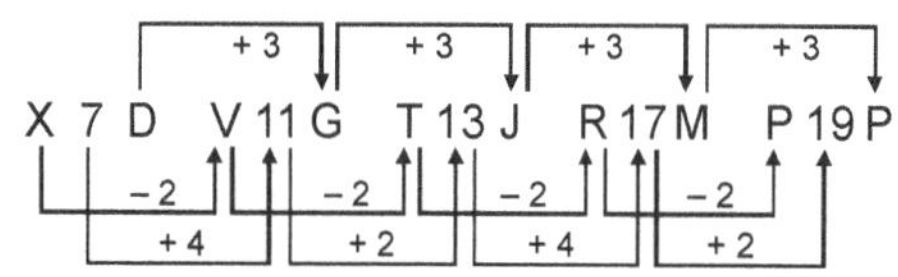

Hence, R17M will come at the place of missing space.

92.

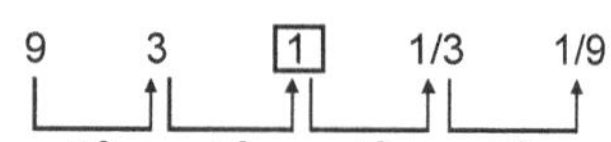

Hence, 1 will come at the missing place.

94.

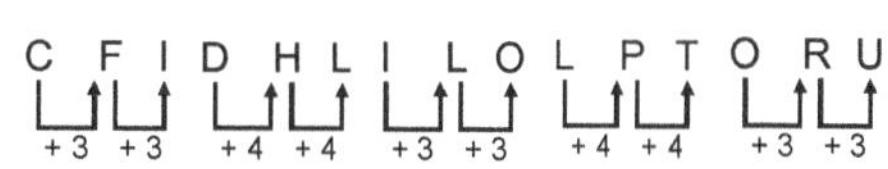

Hence, ORU will come at the next group of alphabets.

95. V O L K S W A G E N is written as

−1 2 −1 2 −1 2 −1 2 −1 2

U Q K M R Y Z I D P

S W I T Z E R L A N D is written as

−1 2 −1 2 −1 2 −1 2 −1 2 −1

R Y H V Y G Q N Z P C

96. Yogesh's team : ____________________

Suresh's team : ________________

Mahesh's team : ____________

Mukesh' team : _____

∴ Suresh' team is in second place in the descending order of scores.

114. 7 10 8 11 9 12 [10] 13

(+1, +1, +1 above: 10 → 11, 11 → 12, 12 → 13; +1, +1, +1 below: 7 → 8, 8 → 9, 9 → 10)

Hence, next number should be 10.

123. TEACHER is coded as CAHEETR

[First middle letter then left letter then right, then left, then right....repeat]

and STUDENT is written as DUETNST

[First middle letter then left, then right]

Similarly, SUCCESS is written as CCEUSSS

[First middle letter then left letter, then right letter on son on].

For Qs. No. 124-129:

Avantika	Shirt	a diary
Shweta	Watch	Mobile case
Parul	Jacket	Goggles
Darshan	Headphone	a pen
Ritwik	Video game	a bag

124. Shweta gifted the watch.

125. Parul received goggles as a return gift.

126. Ritwik–Video game combination is correct.

127. Darshan gifted the headphone.

128. Avantika–Diary combination is correct.

129. Ritwik received a bag in return and gifted videogame to Chetan.

131. $$\frac{\left(\frac{65}{36}+\frac{33}{8}\times\frac{18}{11}\right)\div\left(\frac{46}{9}-\frac{63}{8}\div\frac{189}{20}\right)}{\frac{16}{5}\div\frac{9}{2}\text{ of }\frac{16}{3}}$$

$$=\frac{\left(\frac{65}{36}+\frac{27}{4}\right)\div\left(\frac{46}{9}-\frac{63}{8}\times\frac{20}{189}\right)}{\frac{16}{5}\div 24}$$

$$=\frac{\left(\frac{308}{36}\right)\div\left(\frac{77}{18}\right)}{\frac{16}{5}\times\frac{1}{24}}$$

$$=\frac{\frac{308}{36}\times\frac{18}{77}}{\left(\frac{2}{15}\right)}$$

$$=\frac{(2)}{\left(\frac{2}{15}\right)}=(15).$$

132. $\frac{42}{492},\frac{39}{313},\frac{35}{367}$

$$\frac{42}{492}=0.085$$

$$\frac{39}{313}=0.125$$

$$\frac{35}{367}=0.095$$

Hence, Ascending order are

$$\frac{42}{492},\frac{35}{367},\frac{39}{313}.$$

133. LCM (15, 20, 28) = 420

We know 4-digit greatest number = 9999

4-digit greatest number divided by 420 leaves remainder will be,

```
420 ) 9999 ( 23
      840
      ----
      1599
      1260
      ----
       339
```

Number = 9999 – 339 + 2

= 9660 + 2

= 9662

Sum of digit = 9 + 6 + 6 + 2 = 23.

134. Correct answer is:

$$=\frac{0.1216\times0.105\times0.0002}{0.625\times0.08512\times0.039\times0.16\times10}$$

$$=\frac{1216\times105\times2\times100}{625\times8512\times39\times16}$$

$$=\frac{1}{130}$$

$$\text{Difference}=\frac{1}{65}-\frac{1}{130}$$

$$=\frac{2-1}{130}=\frac{1}{130}.$$

135. n = The greatest number, when divided to the number 13511, 13903 and 14589 leaves equal remainder 'm'

$$n = \text{HCF}(|13511 - 13903|, |13903 - 14589|, |14589 - 13511|)$$

$$n = \text{HCF}(392, 686, 1078)$$

$$n = 98$$

$$\text{Remainder } m = 13511 \div 98$$

$$m = 85$$

So, $$m + n = 98 + 85 = 183.$$

136. Let $\angle APB = x°$

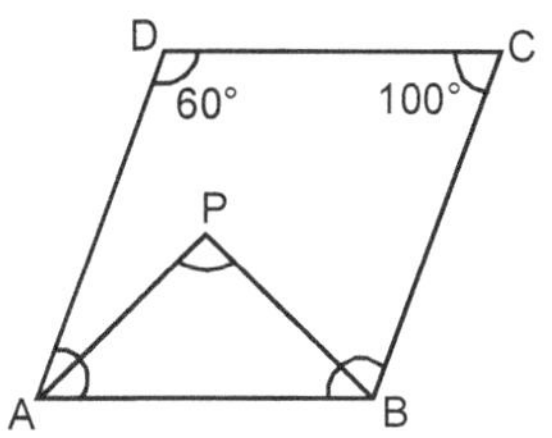

We know,

$$\angle A + \angle B + \angle C + \angle D = 360°$$

$$\angle A + \angle B = 200$$

$$\frac{\angle A + \angle B}{2} = 100°$$

In ΔAPB, $$\frac{\angle A}{2} + \frac{\angle B}{2} + x° = 180°$$

$$\frac{\angle A + \angle B}{2} + x° = 180°$$

$$x° = 180° - 100°$$

$$x° = 80°.$$

137. Let Suman's Salary is ₹ 100

According to question,

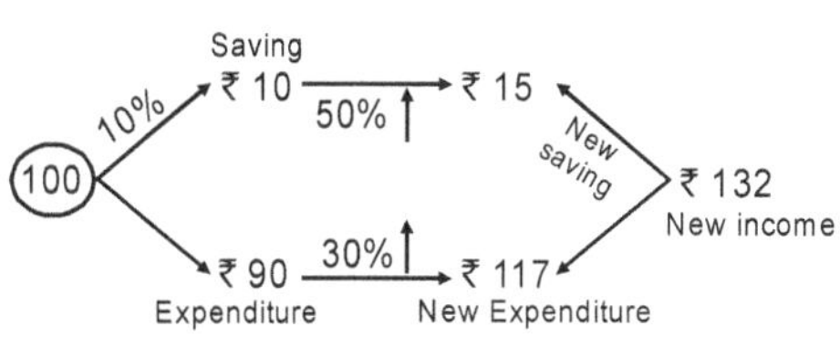

$$\text{Income increase} = \frac{132 - 100}{100} \times 100 = 32\%.$$

138. Let the Sum = ₹ x and rate = $r\%$

According to question,

$$9680 = x\left(1 + \frac{r}{100}\right)^2 \quad ...(i)$$

$$10648 = x\left(1 + \frac{r}{100}\right)^3 \quad ...(ii)$$

$$\frac{\text{equation } (ii)}{\text{equation } (i)}$$

$$\left(1 + \frac{r}{100}\right) = \frac{10648}{9680}$$

$$\left(\frac{100 + r}{100}\right) = \frac{10648}{9680}$$

$$100 + r = 110$$

$$r = 10\%$$

Put in equation (i)

$$9680 = x\left(1 + \frac{10}{100}\right)^2$$

$$9680 = x \times \left(\frac{11}{10}\right)^2$$

$$x = 8000$$

So, Amount after $1\frac{2}{5}$ years

$$A = 8000\left(1 + \frac{10}{100}\right)^1 \left(1 + \frac{\frac{2}{5} \times 10}{100}\right)$$

$$A = 8000\left(\frac{11}{10}\right) \times \left(\frac{26}{25}\right)$$

$$A = ₹\ 9152.$$

139. Let the CP of article = ₹ 100

M.P. of article = ₹ 120 (20% of CP)

S.P. of article = ₹ 102 (15% discount)

$$\%\text{ gain} = \frac{102 - 100}{100} \times 100 = 2\%.$$

140. Let the C.P. of article = ₹ x

$$37.5\% = \frac{3}{8},$$

$$9\frac{1}{11}\% = \frac{1}{11},$$

$$25\% = \frac{1}{4}$$

According to question,

$$342 = x\left(1+\frac{3}{8}\right)\left(1+\frac{1}{11}\right)\left(1-\frac{1}{4}\right)$$

$$342 = x \times \frac{11}{8} \times \frac{12}{11} \times \frac{3}{4}$$

$$x = \frac{342 \times 8}{9}$$

$x =$ ₹ 304.

141. Sum of weight of children = $20x$

According to question,

$$\therefore \quad \frac{20x + 5 \times 12}{x+5} = \frac{20x - 21 \times 10}{x-5}$$

$$\therefore \quad \frac{20x + 60}{x+5} = \frac{20x - 210}{x-10}$$

$20x^2 - 200x + 60x - 600$

$= 20x^2 + 100x - 210x - 1050$

$-140x - 600 = -110x - 1050$

$-30x = -450$

$x = 15.$

142. In the solution acid : water

= 75% : 25%

= 3 : 1

Acid in the solution = $120 \times \frac{3}{4} = 90$

Water in the solution = $120 \times \frac{1}{4} = 30$

Acid and Water in Remaining solution

Acid = $100 \times \frac{3}{4} = 75$

Water = $100 \times \frac{1}{4} = 25$

Acid quantity in the final solution

= 75 + 16.2

= 91.2

Water quantity in the final solution

= 25 + 3.8

= 28.8

% Water in the solution

$$= \frac{28.8}{(91.2 + 28.8)} \times 100$$

$$= \frac{2880}{120} = 24\%.$$

143. $\because$ (12M + 5W) × 2 = (4M + 3W) × 5

24M + 10W = 20M + 15W

4M = 5W

$$W = \frac{4}{5}M$$

Let 8 men can complete the work in x days

then, $\left(12M + 5 \times \frac{4}{5}M\right) \times 2 = 8M \times x$

16M × 2 = 8M × x

x = 4 days.

144. Given that $a \propto \frac{1}{b}$

i.e., $a = \frac{k}{b} \Rightarrow b = \frac{k}{a}$

Let in the starting 'a' = x

$$b = \frac{k}{x}$$

$$b' = \frac{k}{2x} \quad [\because a \text{ increase } 100\%]$$

$$b \text{ decrease by} = \frac{\frac{k}{x} - \frac{k}{2x}}{\frac{k}{x}} \times 100$$

$$= \frac{100}{2} = 50\%.$$

145. 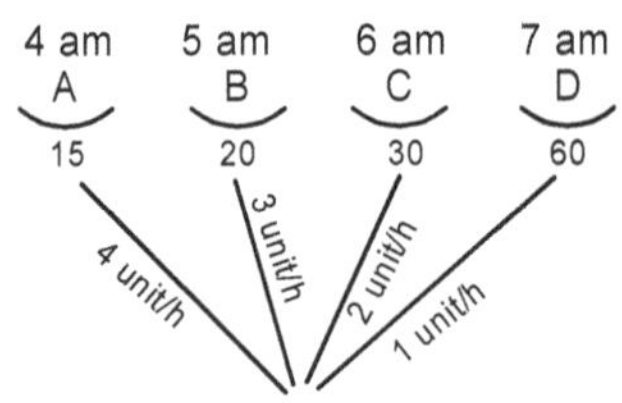

LCM (15, 20, 30, 60) = 60 unit

Let capacity of tank = 60 unit

At 7 am water filled in the tank

= 4 × 3 + 3 × 2 + 2

= 2 unit

Rest capacity of the tank

= [60 – 20]

= 40 unit

Now at 7 am all the four pipes are working

Now, time taken to fill remaining part of the tank

$$= \frac{40}{(4+3+2+1)}$$

= 4 hour

Time at which tank is full

= 7 am + 4 h

= 11:00 am.

146. Let the time taken to reach the destination

= t hour, and

The speed to covered the half journey

= x km/h

Total distance of the journey = $40t$ km

Half distance of the journey = $20t$ km

$$t_1 + t_2 = t$$

$$\frac{2}{3}t + \frac{20t}{x} = t$$

$$\frac{20}{x} = 1 - \frac{2}{3}$$

$$\frac{20}{x} = \frac{1}{3}$$

$$x = 60 \text{ km/h}.$$

147. In ΔAPD,

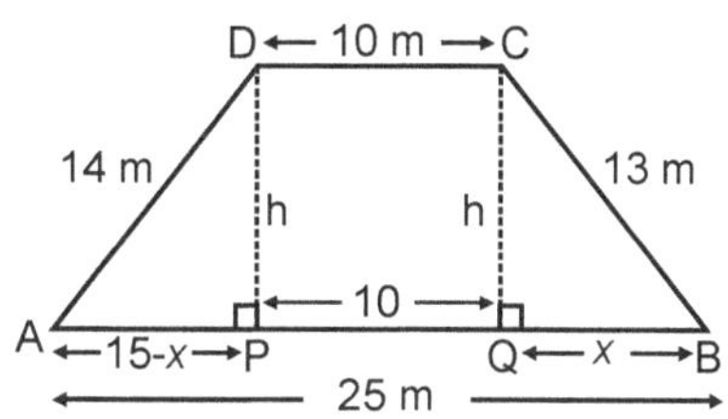

$$(h)^2 = (14)^2 - (15 - x)^2$$

$$(h)^2 = 196 - 225 - x^2 + 30x$$

$$h^2 = -29 + 30x - x^2 \quad ...(i)$$

In ΔBQC,

$$h^2 = (13)^2 - x^2$$

$$h^2 = 169 - x^2 \quad ...(ii)$$

Equations (i) and (ii),

$$-29 + 30x - x^2 = 169 - x^2$$

$$30x = 198$$

$$x = 6.6$$

In ΔBQC, $h^2 = 169 - x^2$

$$h^2 = 169 - 43.56$$

$$h^2 = 125.44$$

$$h = 11.2 \text{ m}$$

∵ Area of Trapezium

$= \frac{1}{2}$(sum of parallel side) × height

$$= \frac{1}{2}(10 + 25) \times 11.2$$

$$= \frac{35 \times 11.2}{2}$$

$$= \frac{392}{2}$$

$= 196$ m^2.

148. $x^2 (a - b) + a^2 (b - x) + b^2 (x - a)$

$= x^2a - x^2b + a^2b - a^2x + b^2x - b^2a$

$= x^2(a - b) - x(a^2 - b^2) + ab(a - b)$

$= (a - b) [x^2 - x(a + b) + ab]$

$= (a - b) [x^2 - xa - xb + ab]$

$= (a - b) [x(x - a) - b(x - a)]$

$= (a - b) (x - a) (x - b)$.

149. Total outcomes = 6 × 6 × 6

= 216

Probability to get the sum on the '6'

Favourable case

= (1, 2, 3) (1, 3, 2) (2, 1, 3) (2, 3, 1) (3, 1, 2) (3, 2, 1) (1, 1, 4), (4, 1, 1), (4, 4, 1) (2, 2, 2)

= (10)

$$\text{Probability} = \frac{10}{216}$$

$$= \frac{5}{108}$$

Probability to get the sum at least

$$6 \text{ on the top} = 1 - \frac{5}{108}$$

$$= \frac{103}{108}.$$

150. Number of dice

5 face visible = 1

4 face visible = 2

3 face visible = 2

2 face visible = 1

Maximum possible sum of numbers

= 1(6 + 5 + 4 + 3 + 2) + 2(6 + 5 + 2 + 4) + 2(6 + 1 + 5) + (6 + 1)

= 1(20) + 2 × 17 + 24 + 7

= 20 + 34 + 28 + 7 = 89.

Previous Paper (Solved)

Common Law Admission Test (CLAT-UG)

Entrance Exam, 2017

Section-I : English Including Comprehension

Directions (Qs. No. 1-10): *Fill in the blanks by choosing the most appropriate option.*

1. Would anybody ___ a mother have risked her life for the baby?

A. but B. however
C. than D. rather

2. You have played a great role, for ___ your help I possibly would have landed myself into a problem.

A. although B. without
C. after D. despite

3. The doctor advised him to go ___ several medical tests.

A. through B. into
C. under D. about

4. If they want to succeed, they ___ have to work very hard.

A. ought B. will
C. must D. should

5. She stood ______ Amit, but could not utter a single word for quite so me time.

A. before B. to
C. about D. for

6. Kanak is endowed _______ many great qualities.

A. in B. by
C. with D. of

7. The minister flew ______ the flooded areas in a helicopter.

A. in B. about
C. over D. along

8. The passengers were very happy _______ the friendly and warm treatment.

A. to B. from
C. about D. by

9. We shall fail _______ we are industrious.

A. though B. unless
C. until D. whether

10. Sunita decided to set ______ some time every day for prayers.

A. aside B. in
C. up D. on

Directions (Qs. No. 11-15): *Read the given passage carefully and choose the most appropriate option to the questions given below.*

The World Trade Organisation (WTO) was created in the early 1990s as a component of the Uruguay Round negotiation. However, it could have been negotiated as part of the Tokyo Round of the 1970s, since negotiation was an attempt at a 'constitutional reform' of the General Agreement on Tariffs and Trade (GATT). Or it could have been put off to the future, as the US government wanted. What factors led to the creation of the WTO in the early 1990s?

One factor was the pattern of multilateral bargaining that developed late in the Uruguay Round. Like all complex international agreements, the WTO was a product of a series of trade-offs between principal actors and groups. For the United States, which did not want a new organization, the disputed settlement part of the WTO package achieved its longstanding goal of a more effective and more legal dispute settlement system. For the Europeans, who by the 1990s had come to view GATT dispute settlement less in political terms add more as a regime of legal obligations, the WTO package was acceptable as a means to discipline the resort to unilateral measures by the United States. Countries like Canada and other middle and smaller trading partners were attracted by the expansion of a rule-based system and by the symbolic value of a trade organization, both of which inherently support the weak against the strong. The developing countries were attracted due to the provisions banning unilateral measures. Finally, and perhaps most important, many countries at the Uruguay Round came to put a higher priority on the export gains than on the import losses that the negotiation would produce, and they came to associate the WTO and a rule-based system with those gains. This reasoning–replicated in many countries–was contained in U.S. Ambassador Kantor's defence of the WTO, and it announced to a recognition that international trade and its benefits cannot be enjoyed unless trading nations accept the discipline of a negotiated rule-based environment.

A second factor in the creation of the WTO was pressure from lawyers and the legal process. The dispute settlement system of the WTO was seen as a victory of legalists but the matter went deeper than that. The GATT, and the WTO, are contract organizations based on rules, and it is inevitable that an organization creating a further rule will in turn be influenced by legal process. Robert Hudee has written of the 'momentum of legal development', but what is this precisely? Legal development can be defined as promotion of the technical legal values of consistency, clarity (or certainty) and effectiveness; these are values that those responsible for administering any legal system will seek to maximize. As it played out in the WTO, consistency meant integrating under one roof the whole lot of separate agreements signed under GATT auspices; clarity meant removing ambiguities about the powers of contracting parties to make certain decisions or to undertake waivers; and effectiveness meant eliminating exceptions arising out of grandfather-rights and resolving defects in dispute settlement procedures and institutional provisions. Concern for these values is inherent in any rule-based system of co-operation, since without these value rules would be meaningless in the first place, therefore, create their own incentive for fulfilment.

The moment of legal development has occurred in other institutions besides the GATT, most notably in the European Union (EU). Over the past two decades the European Court of Justice (ECJ) has consistently rendered decisions that have expanded incrementally the EU's internal market, in which the doctrine of 'mutual recognition' handed down in Cassis de Dijon case in 1979 was a key turning point. The court is now widely recognized as a major player in European integration, even though arguably such a strong role was not originally envisaged in the Treaty of Rome, which initiated the current European Union.

One means the Court used to expand integration was the 'teleological method of interpretation', whereby the actions of member states were evaluated against 'the accomplishment of the most elementary goals set forth in the Preamble to the (Rome) treaty'. The teleological method represents an effort to keep current policies consistent with slated goals, and it is analogous to the effort in GATT to keep contracting party trade practices consistent with slated rules. In both cases legal concerns and procedures are an independent force for further co-operation.

In the large part the WTO was an exercise in consolidation. In the context of a trade negotiation that created a near revolutionary expansion of international trade rules, the formation of the WTO was a deeply conservative act needed to ensure that the benefits of the new rules would not be lost. The WTO was all about institutional structure and dispute settlement: these are the concerns of conservatives and not revolutionaries, that is why lawyers and legalists took the lead on these issues. The WTO codified the GATT institutional practice that had developed by custom over three decades, and it incorporated a new dispute settlement system that was necessary to keep both old and new rules from becoming a sham. Both the international structure and the dispute settlement system were necessary to preserve and enhance the integrity of the multilateral trade regime that had been built incrementally from the 1940s to the 1990s.

11. In the method of interpretation of the European Court of Justice:

A. Current policies need to be consistent with stated goals.

B. Actions against member states needed to be evaluated against the said community goals.

C. Contracting party trade practices need to be consistent with stated rules.

D. Enunciation of the most elementary community goals needed to be emphasized.

12. What would be the closest reason why WTO was not formed in 1970s?

A. The Tokyo Round negotiations was an attempt at constitutional reform.

B. The US government did not like it.

C. Lawyers did not work for the dispute settlement system.

D. Important players did not find it in their best interest to do so.

13. The most likely reason for the acceptance of the WTO package by nations was that:

A. They recognized the need for a rule-based environment to protect the benefits of increased trade.

B. Its rule-based system leads to export gains.

C. It has the means to prevent the US from taking unilateral measures.

D. It settles disputes more legally and more effectively.

14. According to the passage, WTO promoted the technical legal values partly through.

A. Rules that create their own incentive for fulfilment.

B. Ambiguities about the powers of contracting parties to make certain decisions.

C. Integrating under one roof the agreements signed under GATT.

D. Grandfather-rights exceptions and defects in dispute settlement procedures.

15. In the statement '... it amounted to a recognition that international trade and its benefits cannot be enjoyed unless trading nations accept the discipline of a negotiated rule-based environment', it refers to:

A. The higher priority on export gains placed by many countries at the Uruguay Round.

B. The export gains many countries came to associate with a rule-based system.

C. Ambassador Kantor's defence of the WTO.

D. The provision of a rule-based system by the WTO.

Directions (Qs. No. 16-20): *In each of the following sentences, some part of the sentence or the entire sentence is underlined. Beneath each sentence, you will find four ways of phrasing the underlined part. Choose the most appropriate option given in each of the sentences given below that is the best version than the underlined part of the sentence.*

16. Two valence states of uranium, one with a deficit of four electrons and the other one with a deficit of six occurs in nature and contributes to the diversity of uranium's behaviour.

A. the other with a deficit of six, occur in Nature and contribute

B. one with six occurs in Nature and contributes

C. the other with a deficit of six, occurs in Nature and contributes

D. the other one a deficit of six, occur in Nature and contribute

17. Initiative and referendum, is a procedure that allows voters to propose and pass laws as well as to repeal them.

A. will allow laws on be proposed, passed, as well as repealed by voters

B. allows voters to propose, pass and to repeal laws

C. will allow voter to propose, pass, as well as to repeal laws.

D. allows voters to propose to pass, and repeal laws

18. Plausible though it sounds, the weakness of the hypothesis is that it does not incorporate all relevant facts.

A. the weakness of the hypothesis which sounds plausible.

B. even though it sounds plausible, the weakness of the hypothesis

C. though plausible, the hypothesis' weakness

D. though the hypothesis sounds plausible, its weakness

19. During her lecture, the speaker tried to clarify directional terms, for not everyone in attendance was knowledgeable that winds are designed by the direction from which they come.

A. For everyone in attendance did not know.

B. For not everyone attending knew.

C. With everyone in attendance not knowing.

D. With everyone attending not knowledgeable.

20. Many of them chiselled from solid rock centuries ago the mountainous regions are dotted with hundreds of monasteries:

A. chiselled from solid rock centuries ago, the mountainous regions are dotted with many hundreds of monasteries.

B. The mountainous regions are dotted with hundreds of monasteries, many of which are chiselled from solid rock centuries ago.

C. The mountainous regions are dotted with hundreds of monasteries, many of them chiselled from solid rock centuries ago.

D. Hundreds of monasteries, many of them chiselled from solid rock centuries ago, are dotting the mountainous regions.

Directions (Qs. No. 21-30): *Choose the correct spellings in questions given below.*

21. A. Renumaration B. Remunaration
C. Remuneration D. Renumeration

22. A. Gallows B. Ghellows
C. Gellows D. Ghallows

23. A. Blashphemy B. Blasphemy
C. Blasphamy D. Bleshphemy

24. A. Accomedation B. Accomadation
C. Accommedation D. Accommodation

25. A. Hypothecation B. Hyphothecation
C. Hypthacation D. Hypathecation

26. A. Anulment B. Annulmant
C. Annulment D. Annulement

27. A. Interrogation B. Interagation
C. Interogation D. Interogetion

28. A. Gratetious B. Gratuitus
C. Gratuitous D. Gratitious

29. A. Moretorium B. Moratorium
C. Moratarium D. Maratorium

30. A. Abeyence B. Abhayence
C. Abheyance D. Abeyance

Direction (Qs. No. 31-40): *In each of the following sentences four words or phrases are underlined. If there is any mistake with regard to grammar or usage, it is in the underlined part only. Identify the incorrect part.*

31. The Most (A)/ difficult job is to bend (B)/ and then lifting (C)/ the weight. (D)

A. D B. B
C. C D. A

32. He gave me (A)/ a ticket so that (B)/ I may visit (C)/ the book fair. (D)

A. A B. B
C. D D. C

33. Our boss always (A)/ asks us to pay (B)/ full (C)/ attention to the work at hand. (D)

A. B B. D
C. C D. A

34. Evidently (A)/ our product is the most (B)/ unique in (C)/ the market. (D)

A. B B. C
C. A D. D

35. After being finished (A)/ the (B)/ last chapter of the book, return it (C)/ to me. (D)
A. B B. A
C. D D. C

36. The hope (A)/ to go through (B)/ the book today I have (C)/ almost read (D)/ half of it.
A. B B. C
C. D D. A

37. On listening (A)/ to the confession of love (B)/ she blushed until (C)/ she was purple. (D)
A. A B. C
C. B D. D

38. Since (A)/ I have forgotten (B)/ all the equations I will have (C)/ to start from the scratch. (D)
A. C B. D
C. A D. B

39. Five gallons of (A)/ petrol are (B)/ not enough (C)/ to cover the distance. (D)
A. D B. B
C. A D. C

40. The officer asked that (A)/ the report (B)/ be submitted (C)/ immediately. (D)
A. D B. C
C. B D. A

Section-II : General Knowledge and Current Affairs

41. As on 31st January 2016, the highest number of law colleges were present in:
A. Andhra Pradesh B. Maharashtra
C. Uttar Pradesh D. Madhya Pradesh

42. India's third largest trading partner during 2016 is:
A. U.A.E B. Saudi Arabia
C. Dubai D. Kuwait

43. The first country to have announced euthanasia of a child is:
A. Norway B. Belgium
C. Denmark D. Finland

44. The Hubble telescope of NASA is located in:
A. NASA headquarters B. Iceland
C. Space D. Canada

45. During 2017, which SAARC country has notified the Right to Information Act?
A. Bhutan B. Afghanistan
C. Sri Lanka D. Nepal

46. Among the following M.L.As, who was disqualified by the Governor during January 2017 under Article 192 of the Constitution for undertaking government contracts?
A. Srinivas Prasad of Karnataka
B. Uma Shankar Singh of Bihar
C. Jayalalithaa of Tamil Nadu
D. P.C. George of Kerala

47. Which country offered asylum seekers 1,200 Euros to leave by withdrawing their application for protection?
A. Denmark B. Germany
C. Italy D. France

48. NASA rediscovered India's lunar spacecraft that was lost in the space during the past eight years known as:
A. Chandrayaan–I B. Chandrayaan–II
C. Mangalayaan–I D. Mangalayaan–II

49. Among the following, who has won the maximum number of titles?
A. Saina Nehwal B. Gopichand
C. P.V. Sindhu D. Srikant

50. The first country in the world to have begun shutting down the entire Frequency Modulation (FM) radio network to be replaced by Digital Audio Broadcasting is:
A. United States of America
B. China
C. Switzerland
D. Norway

51. 'Scorpion kick' is a phrase used in:
A. Kung Fu B. Kabaddi
C. Kalari Fight D. Kick Boxing

52. Solar Impulse–2 is:
A. Solar powered ship
B. Hybrid airplane
C. Solar powered airplane that completed the first around the world
D. Impact of climate change for overall increase of 2°C a year

53. 'World's longest all women Non-stop flight' from New Delhi to San Francisco covering 14,500 kms was operated by:
A. Jet Airways B. Air India
C. American Airlines D. United Airlines

54. Prithvi Defence Vehicle is:
A. The name of a newly developed tank
B. The name of an amphibious Naval vessel
C. The name of a single seated aircraft developed by HAL
D. The name of India's Nuclear Intercepter Missile

55. Till the end of 2016, the total number of UNESCO's World Heritage Sites in India is:

A. 18 B. 35
C. 21 D. 42

56. How many billionaires India has lost since demonetization on November 8, 2016?
A. Eighteen B. Two
C. Eight D. Eleven

57. The Happiness Index Department or a Wing has been established in the states of:
A. Madhya Pradesh and Tamil Nadu
B. Andhra Pradesh and Madhya Pradesh
C. Madhya Pradesh and Goa
D. Andhra Pradesh and Sikkim

58. Among the following who was crowned as 'Miss Supernational' during 2016?
A. Shilpa Shetty B. Srinidhi Shetty
C. Alia Bhatt D. Aishwarya Rai

59. World's longest rail tunnel is about:
A. 32 kms. B. 47 kms.
C. 57 kms. D. 23 kms.

60. The 2016 Nobel Peace Prize was won by the President of:
A. South Africa
B. Columbia
C. Sri Lanka
D. United States of America

61. Who has been selected for 2016 BC Roy Award?
A. Dr. P. Raghu Ram B. Dr. Jagat Ram
C. Dr. N. Bhaskaran D. Dr. J. Rajendra

62. The top destination for domestic tourists in India for the past three consecutive years has been:
A. Tamil Nadu B. Rajasthan
C. Kerala D. Odisha

63. Among the following professors of Indian origin who has received Knighthood for the work as a co-inventor of next generation DNA Sequencing called Solexa Sequencing is?
A. Satyendra Nath Bose
B. Shankar Balasubramanian
C. Mehnad Saha
D. P.C. Mahalanobis

64. Japan is threatening to drag India to W.T.O on issues relating to the export of its:
A. Steel B. Tea
C. Small ships D. Electronic goods

65. Which of the following individuals was called a 'deceptive actor' by China's Foreign Ministry during March 2017?
A. Sirisena B. Narendra Modi
C. Donald Trump D. Dalai Lama

66. The world's first artificial intelligence lawyer, a robot, is named as:
A. Ross B. Boss
C. Watson D. IBM-LaBrain

67. Which court has stayed the execution of death sentence of Kulbhushan Jadhav in May 2017?
A. International Court of Justice
B. Supreme Court of India
C. International Criminal Court
D. Supreme Court of Pakistan

68. India emerged as ___________ largest holder of the U.S. Government Securities at the end of 2016:
A. Twenty fourth B. Twelfth
C. Twenty eighth D. Fifteenth

69. Juno is the name of a:
A. Solar powered space craft
B. Hydrogen fuelled space craft
C. Hydrogen fuelled submarine
D. Atomic powered submarine

70. The Union Cabinet has recently approved the setting up of a Permanent Tribunal for resolving:
A. Complaints from three services
B. Inter-state water disputes
C. Inter-state boundary disputes
D. Election disputes

71. Donald Trump is _____________ President of the United States.
A. 46th B. 44th
C. 43rd D. 45th

72. The World Bank had cut India's GDP growth for 2016–2017 to:
A. 8% B. 7.6%
C. 7% D. 8.6%

73. According to the Survey Report released by Transparency International during March 2017 on India, the most corrupt are:
A. Business executives B. Police
C. Government officials D. Local Councillors

74. Highest number of open prisons in India as on 2015 are in:
A. Kerala B. Maharashtra
C. Rajasthan D. Tamil Nadu

75. The first Commercial Court and Commercial Disputes Resolution Centre was inaugurated at:
A. Ahmedabad, Gujarat
B. Mumbai, Maharashtra
C. Visakhapatnam, Andhra Pradesh
D. Raipur, Chattisgarh

76. The Japanese Prime Minister who offered 'sincere and everlasting condolences' to the people of the United States for killing more than 2,400 soldiers in the attack on Pearl harbour was:

A. Shinzo Abe B. Juniciro Koizumi
C. Hayato Ikeda D. Kakuei Tanaka

77. The first statue of a woman in Parliament Square in England is that of:
A. Millicent Fawcett B. Mother Theresa
C. Margaret Thatcher D. Queen Elizabeth–II

78. COIN, a software programme developed by J. P. Morgan supports:
A. Bitcoin
B. Interpreting commercial documents
C. Financial accounting
D. Robotic surgery

79. The first elected civilian President in Myanmar is:
A. Aung San B. Htin Kyaw
C. Khin Ayi D. Aung San Suu Kyi

80. The bowler who has claimed the fastest 250 wickets in Cricket test matches is:
A. Rangana Herath B. Dennis Lillee
C. Anil Kumble D. Ravichandran Ashwin

81. Which of the following country enacted a law during August 2016 providing for the right to register the marriages of Hindus?
A. Iran B. Afghanistan
C. Saudi Arabia D. Pakistan

82. India's voting rights at the International Monetary Fund increased from 2.3% to:
A. 2.8% B. 2.4%
C. 2.6% D. 2.5%

83. In terms of steel production in the world during 2015–2016, India stood at:
A. Fourth B. Third
C. Fifth D. Second

84. Which country 3D–Printed a home of 37 sq.mts?
A. Spain B. Russia
C. South Korea D. Taiwan

85. Immediately before Antonio Guterres was appointed the U.N. Secretary General in October 2016, he was:
A. United Nations High Commissioner for Refugees
B. The Prime Minister of Portuguese
C. Commissioner General of UNRWA
D. United Nations High Commissioner for Human Rights

86. Volvo has launched the world's largest bus that can carry up to:
A. 300 passengers B. 260 passengers
C. 320 passengers D. 150 passengers

87. With the development of Terahertz (THz) transmitter, it is expected to be faster than 5G mobile networks by:
A. Ten times B. Four times
C. Five times D. Two times

88. Which shoe company in the United States of America has won an IPR dispute against China recently for using their logo?
A. Nike B. Adidas
C. Reebok D. New Balance

89. Name the President elect of France who is likely to take the oath on 14 May 2017.
A. Marine Le Pen B. Emmanuel Macron
C. Francois Fillon D. Francois Holland

90. Who called the immigration the 'Trojan horse of Terrorism'?
A. Angela Merkel, Chancellor of Germany
B. Theresa May, Prime Minister of U.K.
C. Donald Trump, President of the U.S.
D. Viktor Orban, Prime Minister of Hungary

Section-III : Elementary Mathematics (Numerical Ability)

91. 'A' and 'B' complete a work in 12 days, 'B' and 'C' in 8 days and 'C' and 'A' in 16 days. 'A' left after working for 3 days. In how many days more will 'B' and 'C' finish the remaining work?
A. $3\frac{3}{4}$ B. $4\frac{3}{4}$
C. $6\frac{5}{6}$ D. $7\frac{3}{4}$

92. A man rows to a place 45 kms distant and back in 12 hours. He realises that he can row 5 kms downstream in the same time as 3 kms against the stream. The velocity of the stream is:
A. 4 kms/hr B. 1.5 kms/hr
C. 1 km/hr D. 2 kms/hr

93. The Banker's discount on a sum of money for 18 months is ₹ 600 and the true discount on the same sum for 3 years is ₹ 750/. The rate percentage is:
A. 12% B. 20%
C. 10% D. 15%

94. A piece of cloth costs rupees 75. If the piece is four meters longer and each meter costs rupees 5 less, the cost remains unchanged. What is the length of the piece?
A. 10 meters B. 12 meters
C. 6 meters D. 8 meters

95. Taps 'A' and 'B' can fill a tank in 37½ minutes and 45 minutes respectively. Both taps are opened and after some time tap 'B' is turned off. The tank is filled completely in exactly 30 minutes, if tap 'B' is turned off after:

A. 12 minutes B. 15 minutes
C. 9 minutes D. 10 minutes

96. A trader sells rice at a profit of 20% and uses weights which are 10% less than the correct weight. The total gain earned by him is:

A. $33\frac{1}{3}\%$ B. 35%
C. $22\frac{2}{9}\%$ D. 30%

97. The difference between simple interest and compound interest at the same rate for rupees 5,000 for two years is rupees 98. The rate of interest is:

A. 12% B. 14%
C. 10½% D. 10%

98. The average weight of three men 'X', 'Y' and 'Z' is 75 kgs. Another man 'A' joins the group and the average weight now becomes 80 kgs. If another person 'B' whose weight is 5 kgs more than 'A' replaces 'X', then the average weight of 'Y', 'Z', 'A' and 'B' will be 85 kgs. What is the weight of 'X'?

A. 78 kgs. B. 84 kgs.
C. 82 kgs. D. 80 kgs.

99. In an office, 1/3 of the workers are men, 1/2 of the men are married and 1/3 of the married men have children. If 3/4 of the women are married and 2/3 of the 2/3 of the married women have children, then the part of workers without children are:

A. $\frac{5}{18}$ B. $\frac{4}{9}$
C. $\frac{17}{36}$ D. $\frac{11}{18}$

100. There are two urns. One contains two white balls and four red balls, the other contains three white and nine red balls. All balls are of the same shape and size. From each urn, one ball is drawn. What is the probability of getting both the balls of the same colour?

A. $\frac{1}{12}$ B. $\frac{7}{12}$
C. $\frac{1}{2}$ D. $\frac{1}{24}$

101. A can do a piece of work in 8 days and B alone can do the same work in 10 days. A and B agreed to do the work together for ₹ 720. With the help of C, they finished the work in 4 days. How much C is to be paid?

A. ₹ 80 B. ₹ 70
C. ₹ 82 D. ₹ 72

102. A vessel contains a mixture of milk and water in the ratio of 5 : 3 respectively. How much of the mixture must be siphoned off and replaced with water, so that the mixture may be half milk and half water?

A. $\frac{1}{5}$ B. $\frac{1}{4}$
C. $\frac{1}{3}$ D. $\frac{1}{7}$

103. Age of father 10 years ago was three times the age of his son. After 10 years, father's age is twice that of his son. The ratio of their present ages is:

A. 7 : 3 B. 7 : 4
C. 11 : 7 D. 9 : 5

104. Gold and copper are as heavy as water by 19 and 9 times respectively. The ratio in which these two metals be mixed so that the mixture is 17 times as heavy as water is:

A. 4 : 1 B. 3 : 2
C. 2 : 3 D. 3 : 4

105. Two men and seven boys can do a work in 14 days. Three men and eight boys can do the same work in 11 days. Further eight men and six boys can do three times the amount of this work in:

A. 18 days B. 21 days
C. 30 days D. 24 days

106. A train 'X' leaves station 'A' at 3 p.m. and reaches station 'B' at 4.30 p.m., while another train 'Y' leaves station 'B' at 3.00 p.m. and reaches station 'A' at 4.00 p.m. These two trains cross each other at:

A. 3.36 p.m. B. 3.30 p.m.
C. 3.20 p.m. D. 3.40 p.m.

107. Keerthi's father gave him some money to buy books. He spent half of the money equally to buy books and entertaining his friends. Whatever amount left with him, he deposited half in his savings account and gave ₹ 5 to a poor person as charity. Finally, Keerthi was left with ₹ 20 which he returned to his father. What amount did his father give him initially?

A. ₹ 160 B. ₹ 120
C. ₹ 100 D. ₹ 200

108. Praveen has ₹ 4,662 in the form of 2, 5 and 10 rupee notes. If these notes are in the ratio of 3 : 5 : 8, the number of five rupees notes with him is:

A. 336 B. 250
C. 210 D. 84

109. A boat travels upstream from A to B and back from B to A in 5 hours. The speed of the boat in still water is 8 km/hour and the speed of the current is 4 km/hour. Then, the distance from A to B is:

A. 9 kms. B. 10 kms.
C. 15 kms. D. 12 kms.

110. A clock was set correct at 12 O'clock. It loses 10 minutes per hour. What will be the angle between the hour and minute hands of the clock after one hour?

A. 85° B. 105°
C. 75° D. 90°

Section-IV : Legal Aptitude

Directions (Qs. No. 111-145): *These questions consists of legal proposition(s)/ principle(s) (hereinafter referred to as 'principle') and facts. Such principles may or may not be true in the real and legal sense, yet you have to conclusively assume them to be true for the purposes of this Section. In other words, in answering these questions, you must not rely on any principle except the principles those are given herein below for every question. Further, you must not assume any facts other than those stated in the question. The objective of this section is to test your interest towards study of law, research aptitude and problem solving ability, even if the 'most reasonable conclusion' arrived at may be absurd or unacceptable for any other reason. It is not the objective of this section to test your knowledge of law. Therefore, to answer a question, principle is to be applied to the given facts and to choose the most appropriate option.*

111. Principle: According to law, a person is deemed to have attained the age of majority when he completes the age of 18 years, except in the case of a person where a guardian of a minor's person or property has been appointed under the Guardians and Wards Act, 1890 or where the superintendence of a minor's property is assumed by a Court of Wards. Indian law expressly forbids a minor from entering into a contract. Hence, any contract entered into by a minor is void-a-binitio regardless of whether the other party was aware of his minority or not. Further, though a minor is not competent to contract, nothing in the Contract Act prevents him from making the other party bound to the minor.

Facts: Lal executed a promissory note in favour of Gurudutt, aged 16 years stating that he would pay Gurudutt a sum of ₹ 2 Lakhs when he attains the age of majority. On attaining the age of 18, Gurudutt demanded the amount from Lal, who refused to pay. Gurudutt wants to take legal action against Lal. Identify the most appropriate legal position from the following:

A. Gurudutt should not have entered into a contract with Lal when he was a minor.

B. Lal was not aware of the fact that Gurudutt was a minor.

C. Lal argues that as per the Guardians and Wards Act, 1890, Gurudutt can claim the money only after he attains the age of 21.

D. A promissory note duly executed in favour of a minor is not void and can be sued upon by him, because he though incompetent to contract, may yet accept a benefit.

112. Principle: In criminal law, misappropriation is the intentional, illegal use of the property or funds of another person for one's own use or other unauthorized purpose, particularly by a public official, a trustee of a trust, an executor or administrator of a dead person's estate or by any person with a responsibility to care for and protect another's assets. Embezzlement is misappropriation when the funds involved have been lawfully entrusted to the embezzler. On the contrary, theft is the illegal taking of another person's property or services without that person's permission or consent with the intent to deprive the rightful owner of it.

Facts: A went for swimming at the Municipal Swimming Pool. A handed over all his valuables, including some cash to X, the guard on duty for safe custody, as notified by the Municipality. After swimming for an hour, A came out and searched for X. He found another guard on duty and that guard informed A that X had gone home after completing his shift and did not hand over anything to be given to A. A registered a complaint with the police. X was traced but he told the police that he sold all the valuables and the entire cash was used for drinking liquor. What offence, if any, was/were committed by X?

A. If at all X is liable, it is for criminal misappropriation only.

B. X is liable for criminal misappropriation and embezzlement.

C. X is not guilty of criminal misappropriation as he did not make any personal gain out of those items with him.

D. X is liable for theft as he took A's property without X's permission.

113. Principle: Every agreement, by which any party is restricted absolutely from enforcing his right in respect of any contract, by the usual legal proceedings in the ordinary Tribunals, is void to that extent. The law also provides that nobody can confer jurisdiction to a civil court by an agreement between parties.

Facts: A and B entered into a valid contract for rendering certain service. A clause in the contract was that in case of any dispute arose out of the contract; it shall be referred to for Arbitration only. Is the contract valid?

A. Arbitrator cannot be termed as an ordinary Tribunal. Hence, the agreement is void and would be unenforceable.

B. The parties were trying to confer jurisdiction to some authority to decide a dispute and hence the clause would be invalid.

C. The contract is valid but the clause regarding Arbitration is void.

D. Arbitration is also a valid dispute settlement machinery recognized by law and hence the entire contract is valid.

114. Principle: Every agreement, of which the object or consideration is opposed to public policy, is void. An agreement which has the tendency to injure public interest or public welfare is one against public policy. What constitutes an injury to public interest or public welfare would depend upon the times and the circumstances.

Facts: 'A' promises to obtain for 'B' an employment in the public service, and 'B' promises to pay rupees 5,00,000/ to 'A'.

A. The agreement is valid, as it is a contract between two parties with their free consent.
B. The agreement is void because rupees 5,00,000 is excessive.
C. The agreement is void, as the object and consideration for it is opposed to public policy.
D. The agreement is valid, as it is with consideration for public service.

115. Principle: According to the law of trade unions in India, no suit or other legal proceeding shall be maintainable in any civil court against any registered trade union or any officer or member thereof in respect of any act done in contemplation or in furtherance of a trade dispute.

Facts: Soloman, the Secretary of a registered Trade Union took a loan from a Bank for the higher education of his daughter. Soon after completing the course she was married to an NRI Engineer. Solomon did not repay the loan. The Bank demanded the payments from Soloman and warned him that the Bank will take suitable legal action against him. Identify the legal position in this regard.

A. The Bank can file a suit for recovery of the loan amount against Soloman as he took the loan for a personal purpose and in such case no immunity will work.
B. The Bank cannot initiate any action against Soloman as he is the Secretary of a Registered Trade Union.
C. The Bank can recover the loan amount from the Trade Union as Soloman is the Secretary of the Union.
D. As Soloman did not use the loan amount for his use and hence, no action can be initiated against him.

116. Principle: When a person who has made a promise to another person to do something does not fulfill his promise, the other person becomes entitled to receive, from the person who did not fulfill his promise, compensation in the form of money.

Facts: 'X' made a promise to 'Y' to repair his car engine. 'Y' made the payment for repair. After the repair, 'Y' went for a drive in the same car. While driving the car, 'Y' met with an accident due to bursting of a tyre.

A. 'X' will not be entitled to receive compensation.
B. 'Y' will not be entitled to receive compensation from 'X'.
C. 'X' will be entitled to receive compensation from 'Y' in the form of money.
D. 'Y' will be entitled to receive compensation from 'X' in the form of money.

117. Principle: An agreement, the terms of which are not certain, or capable of being made certain, is void.

Facts: Sunder agreed to take Bhola's penthouse on rent for three years at the rate of rupees 12,00,000/per annum provided the house was put to thorough repairs and the living rooms were decorated according to contemporary style.

A. It is voidable contract at the option of Bhola.
B. There is a valid contract because there is an offer from Sunder and acceptance from Bhola
C. There is a valid contract because all the terms of contract are certain and not vague as the rent is fixed by both of them and the term 'present style' only can be interpreted to mean the latest style.
D. There is no valid contract because it has vague and uncertain terms, as the term 'present style' may mean one thing to Sunder and another to Bhola.

118. Principle: According to Sec. 2 of the Industrial Disputes Act, 1947, 'Industrial dispute means any dispute or difference between employers and employers or between employers and workmen or between workmen and workmen, which is connected with the employment or non-employment or the terms of employment or with the conditions of labour of any person'.

Facts: The employees of DK Enterprises met the management and requested half a day leave to allow them to celebrate a lunar eclipse, which was going to happen two days later. The management refused the request. Does this situation amount to an 'industrial dispute'?

A. No as declaring holidays is a prerogative of the employer. So no industrial dispute.
B. No as Lunar eclipse is unconnected with employment.
C. As the difference of opinion between the employees and employer is on declaration of holiday it amounts to an issue connected with employment or with the terms of employment and hence, an industrial dispute.
D. Yes, because there is some difference of opinion it would be an industrial dispute.

119. Principle: When a person falsifies something with the intent to deceive another person or entity is forgery and is a criminal act. Changing or adding the signature on a document, deleting it, using or possessing the false writing is also considered forgery. In the case of writing to fall under the definition, the material included must have been fabricated or altered significantly in order to represent something it is actually not.

Facts: John was a publisher of ancient books and papers. In one of his books on the World Wars, he gave photograph of some letters written by famous historic personalities. A researcher in history noted that in the pictures of some of the letters printed in the book, John had added some words or sentences in his own handwriting to give completeness to the sentences, so that the readers will get a clear picture of the writer's intention. The researcher challenges the originality of those pictures and claims that the book containing the forged letters should be banned. Examine the validity of the researcher's demand.

A. The additions were made to give clarity to the original document and did not in any sense change the contents of the documents and hence there is no forgery as alleged by the researcher.
B. As forgery amounts to adding or deleting anything from an original document, the demand of the researcher is valid.
C. The additions in the letters were made by the publisher in his own handwriting would have made material alteration to the original meaning and hence amounted to forgery.
D. Allowing forged publications to be circulated among the public is as good as committing fraud on the public, so the publication should be banned.

120. Principle: A violation of a legal right of someone, whether results in a legal injury or not, gives rise to an action in tort for compensation. At the same time, an action by someone, which results in some loss or damage to somebody else is not actionable, if there is no violation of a right of that somebody.

Facts: AB Coaching Centre was a popular CLAT coaching academy with several good trainers. A lot of aspirants used to attend its coaching classes from all over and was making good profit. This was going on for the past several years. During a session, T, one of the very good and popular trainers of ABCC, had some difference of opinion with the owner of ABCC and left the coaching centre. In August 2016, T started another Entrance Coaching Centre closer to ABCC which resulted in a substantial drop in its students and huge financial loss. The owner of ABCC wants to file a case against T for the loss sustained by ABCC. What do you think is the right legal position?

A. T will be liable to compensate the loss to ABCC.
B. T started the new coaching centre near ABCC intentionally, and shall be liable to compensate the loss of ABCC.
C. 'T' should have consulted ABCC before starting his coaching centre.
D. T has not violated any of ABCC's legal right though they sustained some financial loss, and not legally bound to compensate ABCC.

121. Principle: Section 34 of Indian Penal Code provides that 'When a criminal act is done by several persons in furtherance of the common intention of all, each of such persons is liable for that act in the same manner as if it were done by him alone.'

Facts: Three vagabonds, Sanju, Dilbag and Sushil decided to commit burglary. In the night, Sushil opened the lock and they broke into a rich man's house when the entire family was on a pilgrimage. Sanju had gone to that house earlier in connection with some cleaning job. There was only a servant lady in the house. Hearing some sounds from the master bed room, the servant switched on the lights and went up to the room from where she heard the sound. Noticing that the servant was going to cry for help, Sanju grabbed her and covered her mouth with his hands and dragged her into the nearby room. The other two were collecting whatever they could from the room. When they were ready to go out of the house, they looked for Sanju and found him committing rape on the servant. They all left the house and the servant reported the matter to the police and identified Sanju. Subsequently, all three were arrested in connection with the offences of house breaking, burglary and rape. Identify the legal liability of the three.

A. Only Sanju will be liable for rape as he was the one who actually committed the offence.
B. All three are liable for all the offences as there was common intention to commit the crimes.
C. Only Dilbag and Sushil are liable for burglary in looting the house, and all three will be liable for housebreaking and rape as they did not stop Sanju from committing the offence and hence were accomplice to the offence.
D. Sanju will be liable only for housebreaking and rape as he did not participate in the burglary.

122. Principle: An offer made by one party when accepted by another makes it a contract.

Transactions:

1. P offered to sell his house for ₹ 20 lakhs to R; R told P that he was interested to buy a house for 15 lakhs only.
2. C was looking for a house for not more than 25 lakhs; P informed C that his house was available for 20 lakhs.

3. K wanted to buy some old furniture; L told K that he would sell his furniture for ₹ 10,000.
4. R advertised to sell his old car for a price of ₹ Three lakhs; S found the advertisement and offered to buy it for ₹ 2 lakhs 50 thousand; R agrees to sell it to S.

Which among the above is actually a contract?

A. Situation 3 only is a contract
B. Situations 1 and 2 are contracts
C. Situation 4 only is a contract
D. Situations 2 and 4 are contracts

123. Principle: Where one of the parties to a contract was in a position to dominate the decision of the other party, the contract is enforceable only at the option of the party who was in a position to dominate the decision of the other party.

Facts: A doctor asked his patient to make a payment of rupees Ten Lakh for treatment of his fever. The patient paid an amount of rupees Five Lakh and promised to pay the remaining amount after the treatment. After treatment the patient recovered from fever. The doctor demanded the remaining amount from the patient. The patient refused to pay.

A. The contract is enforceable against the patient by the doctor.
B. The contract is enforceable against the doctor.
C. The contract is not enforceable without the consent of the patient.
D. The contract is not enforceable as doctor was in dominating position.

124. Principle: According to law, a person who find goods belonging to another and takes them into his custody, is subject to the same responsibility as a bailee. Bailee is a person or party to whom goods are delivered for a purpose, such as custody or repair, without transfer of ownership. The finder of the goods legally can sell the goods found by him under certain circumstances including the situation that the owner refuses to pay the lawful charges of the finder.

Facts: P, a college student, while coming out of a Cricket stadium found a necklace, studded with apparently precious diamonds. P kept it for two days thinking that the owner would notify it in a local newspaper. Since he did not notice any such notification, P published a small classified advertisement in a local newspaper. In two days' time, P was contacted by a film actor claiming that it was her Necklace and requested P to return it to her. P told her that she should compensate him for the advertisement charges then only he would return it otherwise he will sell it and make good his expenses. The film star told P that she had advertised in a national newspaper about her lost Necklace which was lost somewhere in the Cricket Stadium. The advertisement was published for three consecutive days incurring a large expenditure for her. Mentioning all this she refuses to pay P and claims the Necklace back. Which among the following is the most appropriate answer to this?

A. As it was wrong on the part of P to bargain over a property belonging to a celebrity and he should have accepted some gift which might have been given by the film star and returned the Necklace instead of threatening her that he would sell it.
B. As the film star had notified in the newspaper, P ought to have read it and contacted her instead of publishing another notification. So he cannot claim any compensation.
C. P was requesting the film star for the actual expenditure incurred by him before returning the Necklace. This request is legally sustainable.
D. The film star was right in refusing P, as she did not offer any reward for anyone who would return the Necklace.

125. Principle: The Constitution of India guarantees certain fundamental rights to its citizens. The Constitution also provides that these rights cannot be taken away by state even by a law. For violation of this, the person adversely affected by the law may approach the High Court or the Supreme Court for the issuance of an appropriate writ. One of these rights includes the freedom to form association that implies the right to join an association or not to join such an association.

Facts: Owing to some industrial disturbances created by XATU, one of the several trade unions in AB Chemicals (Pvt) Ltd., the Company issued a circular to all its employees that as far as possible the employees may disassociate with XATU. Navin is an employee of AB Chemicals and the current General Secretary of XATU. Aggrieved by this circular, which affected the fundamental rights of his and other members of the Union, approaches the High Court of the state for a relief. Identify the most reasonable legal proposition.

A. Circular issued by a Company amounts to law in the constitutional sense and hence the High Court can issue a writ as pleaded for by Navin.
B. The circular interferes with the freedom guaranteed by the Constitution and hence the High Court can issue an appropriate writ.
C. The prohibition against any imposition of restriction against a fundamental right is not applicable to anybody other than the state and hence Navin will not get any relief from the High Court.
D. The Company's circular is illegal and has to be quashed by the Court.

126. Principle: Contract is a written or spoken agreement, with specific terms between two or more persons or entities in which there is a promise to do something in return for a valuable benefit known as consideration. Such an agreement is intended to be enforceable by law. A unilateral contract is one in which there is a promise to pay or give other consideration in return for actual performance.

Facts: A Toilet Soap Manufacturing Company in India in order to promote the sale of their product, published an advertisement in all the Newspapers on January 1, 2017 that the Company has kept a model ignition key of an Audi A3 Car. The advertisement also stated that whoever gets the said key before December 31, 2017 from a soap bar will be gifted with the Audi A3 Car. Mr. Martin, a foreigner who came to India as a Tourist who was staying in a Hotel found a Key similar to same Car Ignition Key. Mr. Martin brought this matter to the notice of the Hotel Manager. The Manager informed Mr. Martin about the Company's advertisement on January 1, 2017. Mr. Martin wants to claim the Car. Will he succeed?

A. No. The Soap Company has not entered into a contract with Mr. Martin as he was not in India on January 1, 2017 when the advertisement was published.
B. Mr. Martin obtained the Key before the stipulated date from the Soap Bar. So he is covered by the offer of the Soap Company and can claim the car.
C. No. Actual intention of the Company was to promote the sale of the Soap.
D. The Hotel Manager who could legally claim the Car as he was the one actually purchased the soap for the use in the Hotel.

127. Principle: Penal laws provide that whoever voluntarily has carnal intercourse against the order of nature with any man or woman, shall be punished for rape.

Facts: A Police Officer found a man engaged in carnal intercourse with an animal. The Police Officer arrested the man and produced him before the Court.

A. Court will not punish the police officer.
B. Court will punish the police officer.
C. Court will not punish the man for rape.
D. Court will punish the man for rape.

128. Principle: Acceptance of a proposal must be absolute and unqualified.

Facts: 'A' made a proposal to sell his motorcycle to 'B' for rupees 25,000/. 'B' agreed to buy it for rupees 24,000. 'A' sold his motorcycle to 'C' for 26,000 the next day. 'B' sues 'A' for damages.

A. 'B' will get the difference of rupees 1,000 only
B. 'B' will not get any damages from 'A'
C. 'B' will get damages from 'A'
D. 'B' can proceed against 'C'

129. Principle: It is a case of fraud where a party to a contract knows or believes a fact to be true, but conceals it actively from the other party with a view to induce that person to enter into the contract.

Facts: While taking a life insurance policy, in reply to questions by the insurance company during the inquiry into his proposal, Zameer deliberately concealed the fact of his medical treatment for a serious ailment, which he had undergone only a few weeks ago.

A. The concealment of fact by Zameer amounted to fraud.
B. The act of Zameer amounted to innocent misrepresentation.
C. The act of Zameer did not amount to any misrepresentation.
D. The act of Zameer did not amount to fraud, as disclosing the fact would have resulted in exposure of his privacy.

130. Principle: There are legal provisions to give authority to a person to use necessary force against an assailant or wrong-doer for the purpose of protecting one's own body and property as also another's body and property when immediate aid from the state machinery is not readily available; and in so doing he is not answerable in law for his deeds.

Facts: X, a rich man was taking his morning walk. Due to the threat of robbers in the locality, he was carrying his pistol also. From the opposite direction, another person was coming with a ferocious looking dog. All of a sudden, the dog which was on a chain held by the owner, started barking at X. The owner of the dog called the dog to be calm. They crossed each other without any problem. But suddenly, the dog started barking again from a distance. X immediately took out his pistol. By seeing the pistol the dog stopped barking and started walking with the owner. However, X shot at the dog which died instantly. The owner of the dog files a complaint against X, which in due course reached the Magistrate Court. X pleads the right of private defence. Decide,

A. There was no imminent danger to X as the dog stopped barking and was walking with the owner. Hence, shooting it amounted to excessive use of the right of private defence and hence liable for killing the dog.
B. The right of private defence is available to persons against assailants or wrong-doers only and a dog does not fall in this category.
C. Shooting a fierce dog is not to be brought under the criminal law. So the case should be dismissed.
D. As there was no guarantee that the dog would not bark again, shooting it was a precautionary measure and hence within the right available to X under law.

131. **Principle:** Under the Employees Compensation Act, 1923, an employer is liable to pay compensation to his workmen for injuries sustained by them by an accident arising out of and in the course of employment.

Facts: M, the Manager of SRK Industries asked his secretary S to submit a report at the Government Labour Office. 'S' submitted the report as directed. On his way back S met one of his class mates. He then decided to have a cup of tea together on a way side restaurant. Some time later, 'S' got a message from his office to report back as it was long time since he left the office. 'S' rushed back on his Motor Cycle. On his way back a Truck which was coming from a side road hit 'S'. He was admitted in a nearby hospital with multiple injuries. He claims compensation under the Employees Compensation Act from his employer.

A. The Employer is liable to pay compensation as the accident took place arising out of and in the course of employment.
B. The Employer is not liable as the truck driver was negligent.
C. The Employer is not liable as he was admitted in a private hospital and not a Government Hospital.
D. The Employer is liable as S had to rush back to the office, because of the message from the office.

132. **Principle:** When a person falsifies something with the intent to deceive another person or entity is forgery and is a criminal act. Changing or adding the signature on a document, deleting it, using or possessing the false writing is also considered forgery. In the case of writing/painting to fall under the definition, the material included must have been fabricated or altered significantly in order to represent something it is actually not.

Facts: David made a living travelling from city to city, selling paintings that he claimed were done by great artists. Since the artists' signatures were in place, many people fell for them and purchased the paintings. One of these artists saw three of his alleged paintings in a City gallery containing his name. He knew these were not his works and he complained to the police. Police traced David and initiated legal proceedings. Is David guilty of any offence?

A. There is no point in taking legal action against David as the signature has not done any alteration to the art work.
B. David is guilty of forgery as the addition of the signature was with an intention to make people believe that those were the paintings of the great artists.
C. Those who buy the art pieces from David ought to have been careful in checking it and ensuring that they were originals before purchasing it.
D. David is not guilty of any offence as he was selling the art pieces for his living.

133. **Principle:** If a party to a contract agrees to it under undue influence of any other party then the party under the undue influence may refuse to perform in accordance with the agreement.

Facts: A, a rich youngster became a member of a religious group and soon he was appointed by P the head of the group as his personal secretary. As per the rules of the group, all officials and staff of the group were supposed to stay in the group's official premises itself. Some days later, A was asked by P to execute a Gift deed in favour of P, in which it was mentioned that all immovable properties in his name are being gifted to P. A was unwilling to execute the deed, but he was forcefully restrained by P and his body guards in P's office and made A sign the gift deed. Soon after this A left the group and refused to hand over the property as agreed to in the gift deed. Is A's action valid?

A. As Gift is also a contract, the consent of A was not obtained by P while executing the deed.
B. It is illegal for religious groups acquire property from its members.
C. A executed the deed, under compulsion and undue influence, and was right in withdrawing from the contract.
D. As the gift deed was executed by A, he cannot refuse.

134. **Principle:** Whoever takes away with him any minor less than sixteen years of age if a male, or less than eighteen years of age if a female, out of the custody of parents of such minor without the consent of such parents, is said to commit no offence.

Facts: 'A', a man, took away a girl below sixteen years to Mumbai without informing the parents of the girl.

A. 'A' committed no offence against the parents of the girl.
B. 'A' committed no offence against the girl as well as her parents.
C. 'A' committed an offence against the girl.
D. 'A' committed an offence against the girl as well as her parents.

135. **Principle:** Nothing is an offence which is done in the exercise of the right of private defence.

Facts: 'A', under the influence of madness, attempts to kill 'B'. 'B' to save his life kills 'A'.

A. 'B' has committed an offence.
B. 'A' has not committed an offence because he was mad.
C. 'B' has not committed any offence.
D. 'A' has committed the offence of attempt to murder.

136. Principle: Negligence is actionable in law. In simple terms, negligence is the failure to take proper care over something.

Facts: A, a doctor, conducted a hysterectomy sincerely on B and left a small cotton swab inside the abdomen. As a consequence of which B developed some medical problems and had to undergo another surgery. Is A liable?

A. A is not liable as he did not foresee any consequences at the time of surgery.
B. As only a small swab was left in the abdomen, there was no negligence.
C. A is liable for the negligence as he failed to take proper care during the surgery.
D. Liability for negligence does not arise here as A performed the operation sincerely.

137. Principle: When a person interferes with peaceful possession of another person without the permission of the person in possession of those premises, commits trespass to land.

Facts: 'T' just walked over the land of 'P' to reach his house as it was a short cut. 'P' had displayed a notice that it is not a thoroughfare. 'P' did not cause any damage to the land.

A. 'T' has not committed any trespass on the land of 'P'.
B. 'T' has violated privacy of 'P'
C. 'T' has committed trespass to land
D. 'T' has created nuisance for 'P'

138. Principle: A contract would be invalid and unlawful, if the contract is for an immoral or illegal purpose.

Facts: P, was a young and helpless widow, living on the pavement. R, a neighbour gave her a house, registered in her name, on the condition that she should allow R to keep his smuggled goods and drugs in her house. After the registration was done, according to the condition in the contract, R's agents went to keep some packets in her house, she refused. R told her the condition under which the house was given to her. She still refused. Is P justified in her action?

A. As R was making the contract for illegal activities, P's stand is valid in law.
B. R can take back the house by cancelling the transfer deed.
C. P is right as she did not like smuggled goods to be kept in her house.
D. P is not justified as she did not have the right to deny R's request.

139. Principle: When a person consented to an act to be done by another, he cannot claim any damages resulting from doing that act, provided the act done is the same for which consent is given.

Facts: 'P' submitted a written consent to a surgeon 'S' for undergoing a surgical operation for removal of appendicitis. The surgeon while doing surgery also removed the gall bladder of 'A'.

A. 'P' is required to pay expenses for surgery for Appendicitis but not for gall bladder
B. 'P' is not bound to pay expenses of the surgery
C. 'P' can claim damages from 'S'
D. 'P' cannot claim damages from 'S'

140. Principle: A master shall be liable for the fraudulent acts of his servants committed in the course of employment. However, the master and third parties must exercise reasonable care in this regard.

Facts: Rahul was a door to door salesman with United Manufacturing Company (the Company). The Company was manufacturing Water Purifiers. Rahul, along with the Company's products, used to carry Water Purifiers manufactured by his Cousin in a local Industrial Estate. He used to sell the local product at a lower rate giving the impression to the buyers that he is offering a discount on the Company's product. The Company Management detected the fraudulent activity of Rahul and dismissed him from service. Rahul still continued to carry on with his activity of selling the local product pretending that he was still a salesman of the Company. Several customers got cheated in this process. The fraud was noticed by the Company when the customers began to complain about the product. The customers demanded the Company to compensate their loss.

A. The Company is liable to compensate all the customers as it did not inform the public about Rahul's fraudulent conduct and the subsequent dismissal.
B. The liability rests with the local manufacturer as it was a defective product.
C. The Company is not liable as Rahul was dismissed by the Company.
D. The Company is liable to the customers who purchased the local product from Rahul only till he remained as a salesman of the Company.

141. Principle: A person is said to do a thing fraudulently, if he does that thing with intent to defraud, but not otherwise.

Facts: 'A' occasionally hands over his ATM card to 'B' to withdraw money for 'A'. On one occasion 'B' without the knowledge of 'A', uses 'A's ATM card to find out the balance in 'A's account, but does not withdraw any money.

A. 'B' has not committed the act fraudulently
B. 'B' has committed the act fraudulently
C. 'B' has committed misappropriation
D. 'B' has committed breach of faith

142. Principle: Assault is causing bodily injury to another person by use of physical force.

Facts: Rustum while entering into compartment of a train raised his fist in anger towards a person Sheetal, just in front of him in the row, to get way to enter into the train first, but did not hit him. Rustum has:

A. Insulted Sheetal
B. Rightly showed his anger
C. Committed an assault on Sheetal
D. Not committed an assault on Sheetal

143. Principle: Ownership in property consists of right to possess, right to use, right to alienate and right to exclude others. Sale is complete when property gets transferred from the seller to the buyer on sale.

Facts: 'A' sold his car to 'B'. After this, 'B' requested 'A' to keep the car in his care on behalf 'B' for one month. 'A' agreed.

A. Sale will be automatically completed after the expiry of one month
B. Sale will be completed when 'B' will take the delivery of the car.
C. Sale of car is not complete
D. Sale of car is complete.

144. Principle: When a person makes such a statement which lowers other person's reputation in the estimation of other persons, is liable for committing defamation.

Facts: 'A' writes a letter to 'B' in which he uses abusive language against 'B' and also states that 'B' is a dishonest person. 'A' put the letter in a sealed envelope and delivered it to 'B'.

A. 'A' has committed defamation
B. 'A' has not committed moral wrong
C. 'A' has not committed defamation
D. 'A' has committed a moral wrong

145. Principle: The concept of natural justice is against bias and for the right to a fair hearing. While the term natural justice is often retained as a general concept, and it has largely been replaced and extended by the general 'duty to act fairly'.

Fact: 'X', a male employee of a company was dismissed by the employer just on the basis of a complaint by 'Y', a female employee of the company that 'X' was trying to be too friendly with her and often requested her to accompany him to the canteen. Is the dismissal of 'X' valid?

A. No, because the employer did not give a chance to 'X' to explain his side, thereby violated the principles of natural justice.
B. Yes, moral law is antique and therefore, not applicable in modern times, therefore the termination is valid and no violations of the principles of natural justice occurred.
C. Yes, because men are not supposed to behave improperly with women and hence there is no violation of any principles of law.
D. No, because in the modern times this type of behaviour is common.

Directions (Qs. No. 146-160): *Legal phrases are followed by four meanings. Choose the most appropriate option:*

146. In pari delicto:

A. Where the petitioner is at fault
B. Where both parties to a dispute are equally at fault
C. Where the lawyer is at fault
D. Where the judge is at fault

147. Turpis arbiter' means:

A. Inefficient lawyer
B. Corrupt judge
C. Inefficient judge
D. Corrupt prosecutor

148. Caveat venditor:

A. Manufacturer beware
B. Buyer beware
C. Seller beware
D. Transporter beware

149. 'Animus possidendi' means:

A. Intent to contract
B. Intention to harm
C. Intention to return
D. Intention to possess

150. Malus animus:

A. Bad intention
B. Animal farm
C. Good intention
D. Physical force

151. Lex loci:

A. Italian laws
B. Domestic laws
C. Latin regulations
D. Law of a place

152. Per incuriam:

A. Mistaken decision
B. Supremacy of law
C. Mistaken identity
D. Supremacy of the Constitution

153. 'Sine die' means:

A. Adjourned for the day and scheduled to meet next day again.
B. Adjourned for the day and meet after one week.
C. Adjourned without fixing any date for the next meeting.
D. Adjourned for the day and meet after one month.

154. Bona vacantia:

A. Vacant land.
B. Order of the court for eviction.
C. Goods that have no owner.
D. Vacant building.

155. 'Jus Gentium' means:

A. Global administrative law
B. Law of Societies
C. Law among Nations
D. Global justice

156. Pari passu:
A. On an unequal status
B. Supremacy of law
C. Diverse nature
D. On equal footing

157. 'Punctum Temporis' means:
A. Temporary position
B. Point of time
C. Functional authority
D. Timely assistance

158. Autrefois convict:
A. Formerly convicted
B. Doubtful conviction
C. Failed prosecution
D. To be convicted

159. Lis pendens:
A. Facts of case proved
B. Decided case
C. Pending suit
D. No legal issues involved

160. Faux pas:
A. Passage of time
B. Cheating
C. Pausing for a while
D. Tactless mistake

Section-V : Logical Reasoning

Directions (Qs. No. 161-163): *Read the following information carefully and choose the appropriate option in the questions given below.*

(*i*) There is a group of five persons—A, B, C, D and E.
(*ii*) One of them is a Singer, one is a Dancer, one is a Painter, one is a Teacher and one is a Doctor.
(*iii*) Three of them—A, C and Doctor prefer rice to chapatti and two of them—B and the Painter prefer chapatti to rice.
(*iv*) The Teacher, D and A are friends to one another but two of these prefer chapatti to rice.
(*v*) The Singer is C's brother.

161. Who is a Teacher?
A. C B. E
C. D D. B

162. Who is a Dancer?
A. C B. E
C. D D. A

163. Who is a Singer?
A. B B. C
C. A D. D

Directions (Qs. No. 164-166): *Read the following information carefully and choose the most appropriate option in the questions given below.*

(*i*) Six flats on a floor in two rows facing North and South are allotted to P, Q, R, S, T and U.
(*ii*) Q gets a North-facing flat and is not next to S.
(*iii*) S and U get diagonally opposite flats.
(*iv*) R, next to U gets a South-facing flat and T gets a North-facing flat.

164. If the flats of T and P are interchanged, who's flat will be next to that of U?
A. Q B. T
C. R D. P

165. Whose flat is between Q and S?
A. P B. U
C. R D. T

166. Which of the following combination gets South-facing flats?
A. U, R, P B. data inadequate
C. Q, T, S D. U, P, T

Directions (Qs. No. 167 and 168): *Which alternative applies to the following Statement or Assumptions? Choose the most appropriate option.*

167. 'There is no man that is not naturally good' is equivalent to the proposition:
A. All men are naturally good.
B. Some men are not naturally good.
C. No men are good.
D. Some men are naturally good.

168. 'Only ignorant people believe in witchcraft' is equivalent to:
A. All persons who believe in witchcraft are ignorant.
B. No ignorant persons are those who do not believe in witchcraft.
C. There is no link between ignorance and witchcraft.
D. Some ignorant persons are not those who believe in witchcraft.

Directions (Qs. No. 169 and 170): *Find the odd one out from the following:*

169. A. Open secret B. Exact estimate
C. Clearly visible D. Only choice

170. A. Campaign B. Crusade
C. Expedition D. Cruise

Directions (Qs. No. 171-200): *Choose the most appropriate option for each of the following questions.*

171. A person who renounces religious or political belief or principle is called:

A. apostate B. Antiquarian
C. Apostle D. Ascetic

172. wave: crest as ________ : peak.

A. River B. land
C. Water D. Mountain

173. When Ravi saw Ramesh, he recalled, 'He is the son of the father of my daughter'. Who is Ramesh?

A. Brother-in-law B. Cousin
C. Brother D. Uncle

174. How many times from 4 pm to 10 pm, the hands of a clock are at right angles?

A. 6 B. 10
C. 9 D. 11

175. There were twelve dozens of chocolates with a shopkeeper. Ten chocolates were distributed by the shopkeeper to the children of his colony. The shopkeeper then added two more dozens of chocolates in his stock. If the shopkeeper divided the total chocolates equally in two different packets, then how many chocolates were there in each packet?

A. 152 B. 89
C. 158 D. 79

176. Two ladies and two men are playing bridge and seated at North, East, South and West of a table. No lady is facing East. Persons sitting opposite to each other are not of the same sex. One man is facing South. Which direction are the ladies facing to?

A. East and West. B. South and East.
C. None of these. D. North and West.

177. Mare is to Horse as:

A. Sow is to Boar B. Pony is to Donkey
C. Geese is to Duck D. Deer is to Buck

178. A man walks 1 km. towards East and then he turns to South and walks 5 kms. Again he turns to East and walks 2 kms. After this he turns to North and walks 9 kms. Now, how far is he from his starting point?

A. 5 kms. B. 4 kms.
C. 9 kms. D. 10 kms.

179. In a military secret service map, South-East is shown as North, North-East as West and so on. What will West become?

A. South-East B. North-East
C. South-West D. North-West

180. No parrots are black.
All crows are black.
From the above premises which one of the following conclusions is true?

A. No conclusion can be drawn.
B. No crows are parrots.
C. Some parrots are not crows.
D. Some crows are not parrots.

181. Identify the statement which cannot be accepted:

A. Almost one third of the human body is made up of water
B. The earth revolves around the sun in 366 days
C. Odyssey is an ancient epic
D. Human race will become extinct sooner or later

182. Sunil's school bus is facing North when it reaches his school. After starting from Sunil's house, it turned right twice and then left before reaching the school. What direction the bus was facing when it left the bus stop in front of Sunil's house?

A. East B. South
C. North D. West

183. Crumb : Bread is as

A. Water : Vessel
B. Splinter : Wood
C. Inch : Unit
D. Powder : Face

184. If South-East becomes North, North-East becomes West and so on, what will West become?

A. East B. North-West
C. North D. South-East

185. What is meant by 'Alliteration'?

A. Act of literary modification.
B. Acts of an environmentally conscious person.
C. The occurrence of the same letter or sound at the beginning of adjacent or closely connected words.
D. Words which sound alike but have different meanings.

186. _______ is a hater of knowledge and learning.

A. Moroccan B. Mystique
C. Misogynist D. Misologist

187. In a company, 60% workers are males. If the number of female workers in the company is 800, what is the number of male workers in the company?

A. 1600 B. 1200
C. 1400 D. 1900

188. Coding and decoding 9: 72 : : 8 : ?

A. 18 B. 43
C. 64 D. 34

189. The birthday of Ms. Y was celebrated six days before Ms. X, who was born on 4th October 1999. The independence day of that year fell on Sunday. On which day did Ms. Y celebrate her birthday, if it was not a leap year?

A. Wednesday B. Sunday
C. Tuesday D. Monday

190. Vaishnavi prefers Economics to Maths, English to Social science, and Political Science to History. If she prefers Maths to History, and Social science to Maths, which is Vaishnavi's least preferred subject?
A. Economics B. Maths
C. Social science D. History

191. Ravi was showing a photograph to his friend, Gopi. Pointing at a boy in the photograph, Ravi said: 'The boy sitting at the left is the son of the wife of the only son of the grand-mother of my younger brother'. What is the relation between the boy in the photograph and Ravi?
A. Brothers
B. Ravi's brother-in-law
C. First Cousins
D. Nephew and uncle

192. If in a certain code, the word MILITARY is written as 12324567, then in the same code, the word TAIL will be written as:
A. 5432 B. 2345
C. 4523 D. 3254

193. 'Some of the valuable books are seldom read', means:
A. All the valuable books are read.
B. Some of the valuable books are not read.
C. All the valuable books are not read.
D. Some of the valuable books are read.

194. If 27th March, 2011 was Sunday, what was the day on 27th June, 2011?
A. Sunday B. Saturday
C. Monday D. Tuesday

195. If in a code language, 'ABANDON' is written as 'aramoim'. 'BORE' is written as 'rits' and 'BASIL' is written as 'rabut', then what is the original word for the code: 'bituo'?
A. SOLID B. NASIA
C. SOMAD D. SOFIA

196. A girl introduced a boy as the son of the daughter of the father of her uncle. The boy is girl's:
A. Son-in-law B. Son
C. Uncle D. Brother

197. In the series of alphabets given below, which is the missing alphabet series?
AX, DU, GR, ____, ML
A. JN B. JO
C. IK D. HQ

198. John wants to go the university. He starts from his house which is in the East and comes to a crossing. The road to his left ends in a theatre, straight ahead is the hospital. In which direction is the University?
A. West B. East
C. South D. North

199. Pointing to a girl in the photograph, Ram said, 'Her mother's brother is the only son of my mother's father'. How is the girl's mother related to Ram?
A. Aunt B. Sister
C. Grandmother D. Mother

200. Pointing to a photograph, Prakash said, 'She is the daughter of my grand-father's only son' How is Prakash related to the girl in the photograph?
A. Brother B. Cousin
C. Father D. Uncle

ANSWERS

1	2	3	4	5	6	7	8	9	10
A	B	A	B	A	C	C	C	B	A
11	**12**	**13**	**14**	**15**	**16**	**17**	**18**	**19**	**20**
B	D	A	C	B	C	B	D	B	C
21	**22**	**23**	**24**	**25**	**26**	**27**	**28**	**29**	**30**
C	A	B	D	A	C	A	C	B	D
31	**32**	**33**	**34**	**35**	**36**	**37**	**38**	**39**	**40**
C	D	B	A	D	C	D	B	B	B
41	**42**	**43**	**44**	**45**	**46**	**47**	**48**	**49**	**50**
C	A	B	C	C	B	B	A	A	D
51	**52**	**53**	**54**	**55**	**56**	**57**	**58**	**59**	**60**
B	C	B	D	B	D	B	B	C	B
61	**62**	**63**	**64**	**65**	**66**	**67**	**68**	**69**	**70**
A	A	B	A	D	A	A	B	A	B
71	**72**	**73**	**74**	**75**	**76**	**77**	**78**	**79**	**80**
D	C	B	C	D	A	A	B	B	D

81	82	83	84	85	86	87	88	89	90
D	C	B	B	A	A	A	D	B	D
91	**92**	**93**	**94**	**95**	**96**	**97**	**98**	**99**	**100**
B	D	B	C	C	A	B	D	D	B
101	**102**	**103**	**104**	**105**	**106**	**107**	**108**	**109**	**110**
D	A	A	A	B	A	C	C	C	A
111	**112**	**113**	**114**	**115**	**116**	**117**	**118**	**119**	**120**
D	B	D	C	A	B	D	C	A	D
121	**122**	**123**	**124**	**125**	**126**	**127**	**128**	**129**	**130**
A	C	A	C	C	B	C	B	A	A
131	**132**	**133**	**134**	**135**	**136**	**137**	**138**	**139**	**140**
A	B	C	B	C	C	C	A	C	A
141	**142**	**143**	**144**	**145**	**146**	**147**	**148**	**149**	**150**
A	D	D	C	A	B	B	C	D	A
151	**152**	**153**	**154**	**155**	**156**	**157**	**158**	**159**	**160**
D	A	C	C	C	D	B	A	C	D
161	**162**	**163**	**164**	**165**	**166**	**167**	**168**	**169**	**170**
A	C	C	C	D	A	A	A	C	D
171	**172**	**173**	**174**	**175**	**176**	**177**	**178**	**179**	**180**
A	D	A	D	D	D	A	A	A	B
181	**182**	**183**	**184**	**185**	**186**	**187**	**188**	**189**	**190**
A	D	B	D	C	D	B	C	C	D
191	**192**	**193**	**194**	**195**	**196**	**197**	**198**	**199**	**200**
A	C	B	C	A	D	B	D	A	A

EXPLANATORY ANSWERS

91. (A + B)'s 1 day work = $\frac{1}{12}$

(B + C)'s 1 day work = $\frac{1}{8}$

(C + A)'s 1 day work = $\frac{1}{16}$

2(A + B + C)'s 1 day work

$$= \frac{1}{12}+\frac{1}{8}+\frac{1}{16}$$

$$= \frac{4+6+3}{48}=\frac{13}{48}$$

(A + B + C)'s 1 day work = $\frac{13}{96}$

(A + B + C)'s 3 days work

$$= \frac{13}{96}\times 3=\frac{13}{32}$$

Remaining work = $1-\frac{13}{32}=\frac{19}{32}$

$\frac{1}{8}$ part (B + C) can do in 1 day

1 part (B + C) can do in 8 day

$\frac{31}{32}$ part (B + C) can do in $8\times\frac{19}{32}=\frac{19}{4}$

$$= 4\frac{3}{4}\text{ days}$$

Hence (B + C) can do whole work in $4\frac{3}{4}$ days.

92. In downstream time taken for 5 km = x hours

In upstream time taken for 3 km = x hours

In downstream speed of current = $\frac{5}{x}$ km/hr

In upstream speed of current = $\frac{3}{x}$ km/hr

$$\frac{45}{(5/x)}+\frac{45}{(3/x)} = 12$$

$$\Rightarrow \quad \frac{x}{5}+\frac{x}{3} = \frac{12}{45}$$

$$\Rightarrow \quad \frac{3x+5x}{15} = \frac{4}{15}$$

$\Rightarrow \quad 8x = 4$

$\Rightarrow \quad x = \frac{1}{2}$

Speed of the boat in downstream

$= \frac{5}{1/2} = 10$ km/hr

Speed of the boat in upstream

$= \frac{3}{1/2} = 6$ km/hr

$\therefore$ Speed of the current

$= \frac{1}{2}(10-6)$

$= \frac{4}{2} = 2$ km/hr.

93. BD for $\frac{3}{2}$ years = ₹ 600

BD for 3 years = $600 \times \frac{2}{3} \times 3$ = ₹ 1200

TD for 3 years = ₹ 750

Hence, Sum = $\frac{1200 \times 750}{1200 - 750}$

$= \frac{1200 \times 750}{450}$ = ₹ 2000

Rate = $\frac{1200 \times 100}{2000 \times 3} = 20\%$.

94. Let length of the cloth = x m

Cost of 1 m cloth = ₹ $\frac{75}{x}$

According to the question,

$(x+4)\left(\frac{75}{x} - 5\right) = 75$

$\Rightarrow \quad (x + 4)(75 - 5x) = 75x$

$\Rightarrow \quad 75x + 300 - 5x^2 - 20x = 75x$

$\Rightarrow \quad 5x^2 + 20x - 300 = 0$

$\Rightarrow \quad x^2 + 4x - 60 = 0$

$\Rightarrow \quad x^2 + 10x - 6x - 60 = 0$

$\Rightarrow \quad x(x + 10) - 6(x + 10) = 0$

$\Rightarrow \quad (x + 10)(x - 6) = 0$

$\Rightarrow \quad x = 6$

Hence, the length of the cloth = 6 m.

95. (A + B)'s 1 minute work = $\left(\frac{2}{75} + \frac{1}{45}\right)$

$= \frac{6+5}{225} = \frac{11}{225}$

Let pipe B is closed after x minute

(A + B)'s x minute work = $\frac{11x}{225}$

A's (30 – x) minute work = $\frac{2}{75}(30 - x)$

$\therefore \quad \frac{11x}{225} + \frac{2(30-x)}{75} = 1$

$\Rightarrow \quad 11x + 6(30 - x) = 225$

$\Rightarrow \quad 5x = 45$

$\Rightarrow \quad x = 9$

Hence, pipe B is closed after 9 minutes.

97. $\frac{5000 \times r \times 2}{100} = 100r$

$A = 5000\left(1 + \frac{r}{100}\right)^2$

$= 5000 \frac{(100+r)^2}{100 \times 100}$

$= \frac{(100+r)^2}{2}$

C.I. = $\frac{(100+r)^2}{2} - 5000$

$= \frac{10000 + r^2 + 200r - 10000}{2}$

C.I. – S.I. = $\frac{r^2 + 200r}{2} - 100r$

$\Rightarrow \quad 98 = \frac{r^2 + 200r - 200r}{2}$

$\Rightarrow \quad 196 = r^2$

$r = 14\%$.

98. Total weight of XYZ = 75 × 3 = 225 kg

Total weight of AXYZ = 80 × 4 = 320 kg

$\therefore$ Weight of A = 320 – 225

= 95 kg

Weight of B = 95 + 5 = 100 kg

Total weight of YBAZ = 85 × 4 = 340 kg

Total weight of ABXYZ = 195 + 225

= 420 kg

$\therefore$ Weight of X = 420 – 340

= 80 kg

99. Let number of workers = x

Number of men = $\frac{1}{3}$ of $x = \frac{x}{3}$

Number of married men

$$= \frac{1}{2} \text{ of } \frac{x}{3} = \frac{x}{6}$$

Number of men those have children

$$= \frac{1}{3} \text{ of } \frac{x}{6} = \frac{x}{18}$$

$$\text{Number of women } = x - \frac{x}{3} = \frac{2x}{3}$$

Number of married women

$$= \frac{3}{4} \text{ of } \frac{2x}{3}$$

$$= \frac{3}{4} \times \frac{2x}{3} = \frac{x}{2}$$

Number of women those have children

$$= \frac{2}{3} \text{ of } \frac{x}{2} = \frac{x}{3}$$

$$\text{Now, } \quad x - \left(\frac{x}{18} + \frac{x}{3}\right) = x - \left(\frac{x+6x}{18}\right)$$

$$= x - \frac{7x}{18}$$

$$= \frac{18x - 7x}{18} = \frac{11x}{18}$$

Hence, the part of workers without children

$$= \frac{11}{18}.$$

100. In the first Urn

Number of white balls = 2

Number of red balls = 4

$$\text{Probability of white ball } = \frac{2}{6} = \frac{1}{3}$$

In the 2nd Urn

Number of white balls = 3

Number of red balls = 9

$$\text{Probability of white ball } = \frac{3}{12} = \frac{1}{4}$$

$$\text{Required probability } = \frac{1}{3} + \frac{1}{4} = \frac{4+3}{12}$$

$$= \frac{7}{12}.$$

101. $\text{A's 1 day work} = \frac{1}{8}$

$$\text{B's 1 day work} = \frac{1}{10}$$

$$\text{(A + B + C)'s 1 day work} = \frac{1}{4}$$

$$\text{C's 1 day work} = \frac{1}{4} - \left(\frac{1}{8} + \frac{1}{10}\right)$$

$$= \frac{1}{4} - \left(\frac{5+4}{40}\right)$$

$$= \frac{1}{4} - \frac{9}{40}$$

$$= \frac{10-9}{40} = \frac{1}{40}$$

$$\text{A : B : C} = \frac{1}{8} : \frac{1}{10} : \frac{1}{40}$$

$$= 5 : 4 : 1$$

$$\text{C's share} = \frac{1}{10} \times 720 = ₹\ 72.$$

103. Let the present age of father = x years

and the present age of son = y years

According to the question,

10 years ago,

$x - 10 = 3(y - 10)$

$\Rightarrow \quad x - 10 = 3y - 30$

$\Rightarrow \quad x - 3y = -20$ ...(*i*)

After 10 years:

$x + 10 = 2(y + 10)$

$\Rightarrow \quad x + 10 = 2y + 20$

$\Rightarrow \quad x - 2y = 10$ ...(*ii*)

From (*i*) and (*ii*)

$$\begin{array}{r} x - 3y = -20 \\ x - 2y = 10 \\ - \quad + \quad - \\ \hline -y = -30 \end{array}$$

$\therefore \quad y = 30$

Putting the value of y in (*i*)

$x - 3 \times 30 = -20$

$\Rightarrow \quad x = 90 - 20 = 70$

The ratio of their present ages

$$= \frac{70}{30} = 7 : 3$$

Putting the value of b in (*i*), then we get,

$$2m = \frac{1}{14} - 7 \times \frac{1}{154}$$

$$= \frac{1}{14} - \frac{1}{22}$$

$$= \frac{11-7}{154} = \frac{4}{154}$$

$$m = \frac{4}{154 \times 2} = \frac{1}{77}$$

Now, $8m = 8 \times \frac{1}{77} = \frac{8}{77}$

$$6b = 6 \times \frac{1}{154} = \frac{3}{77}$$

$(8m + 6b)$'s 1 day work

$$= \frac{8}{77} + \frac{3}{77} = \frac{11}{77}$$

They can do whole work

$$= \frac{77}{11} = 7 \text{ days}$$

3 times work, they can do in 7 × 3 days
= 21 days.

104. Mixing 1 gram gold with x gram copper we get $(x + 1)$ gram metal

1G = 19W, 1C = 9W

1g gold + xg copper = $(x + 1)$g metal

$\Rightarrow$ 19W + 9xW = $(1 + x) \times$ 17W

$\Rightarrow$ 19W + 9xW = 17W + 17xW

$\Rightarrow$ 2W = 8xW

$\Rightarrow$ $x = \frac{2W}{8W} = \frac{1}{4}$

Hence, ratio of gold and copper

$$= 1 : \frac{1}{4} = 4 : 1.$$

105. $(2m + 7b)$'s 1 day work $= \frac{1}{14}$ ...(*i*)

$(3m + 8b)$'s 1 day work $= \frac{1}{11}$ ...(*ii*)

Equation (*i*) multiply by 3 and (*ii*) multiply by 2

$$6m + 21b = \frac{3}{14}$$

$$6m + 16b = \frac{2}{11}$$

$$- \quad - \quad -$$

$$5b = \frac{3}{14} - \frac{2}{11}$$

$$= \frac{33 - 28}{154} = \frac{5}{154}$$

$$b = \frac{5}{154 \times 5} = \frac{1}{154}$$

From equation (*i*) $2 \times m + 7 \times \frac{1}{154} = \frac{1}{14}$

$$2m + \frac{1}{22} = \frac{1}{14}$$

$$2m = \frac{1}{14} - \frac{1}{22} = \frac{11 - 7}{154} = \frac{4}{154} = \frac{2}{77}$$

$$m = \frac{1}{77}$$

$$(8m + 6b) = 8 \times \frac{1}{77} + 6 \times \frac{1}{154}$$

$$= \frac{22}{154} = \frac{11}{77} = \frac{1}{7}$$

$\frac{1}{7}$ work is done by 8 men and 6 boys = 1 day

whole work is done by 8 men and 6 boys = 7 days

Three times work is done by 8 men and 6 boys
= 7 × 3 = 21 days.

106. Let distance between Station A and Station B = x km.

Time taken by train $x = \frac{3}{2}$ hours

Time taken by train y = 1 hour

$\therefore$ Speed of $x = x \times \frac{2}{3}$ km/hr

and speed of $y = x \times 1$ km/hr

Let both trains meet after y hours

$$\frac{2xy}{3} + xy = x$$

$\Rightarrow$ $\frac{2xy + 3xy}{3} = x$

$\Rightarrow$ $5xy = 3x$

$\Rightarrow$ $5y = 3$

$\Rightarrow$ $y = \frac{3}{5}$ hours

$$= \frac{3}{5} \times 60 = 36 \text{ minutes}$$

Hence, these two trains cross each other at 3.36 p.m.

107. Let Keerthi's father gave him = ₹ x

Money spent = ₹$\frac{x}{2}$

Remaining money = $x - \frac{x}{2} = \frac{x}{2}$

Deposited in saving account

$$= \frac{1}{2} \text{ of } \frac{x}{2} = \frac{x}{4}$$

Poor person = ₹ 5

$$x = \frac{x}{2} + \frac{x}{4} + 5 + 20$$

$$\Rightarrow \quad x = \frac{x}{2} + \frac{x}{4} + 25$$

$$\Rightarrow \quad x = \frac{2x + x + 100}{4}$$

$$\Rightarrow \quad 4x - 3x = 100$$

$$\Rightarrow \quad x = ₹\ 100$$

Hence, Keerthi's father gave him ₹ 100 initially.

108. Let notes of ₹ 2, ₹ 5 and ₹ 10 are $3x$, $5x$ and $8x$

Then, $(3x \times 2) + (5x \times 5) + (8x \times 10)$

$$= 4662$$

$$\Rightarrow \quad 6x + 25x + 80x = 4662$$

$$\Rightarrow \quad 111x = 4662$$

$$\Rightarrow \quad x = \frac{4662}{111} = 42$$

Hence, number of ₹ 5 notes

$$= 5 \times 42 = 210.$$

109. Let the distance between A to B = x km

$$\frac{x}{8+4} + \frac{x}{8-4} = 5$$

$$\Rightarrow \quad \frac{x}{12} + \frac{x}{4} = 5$$

$$\Rightarrow \quad \frac{x+3x}{12} = 5$$

$$\Rightarrow \quad 4x = 60$$

$$\Rightarrow \quad x = 15$$

Hence, the distance between A to B

$$= 15 \text{ km}.$$

For Qs. No. 164-166:

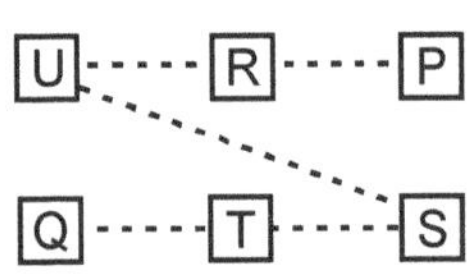

164. Since, P and T interchanged their flats, then R will next to the U.

165. T's flat between Q and S.

166. U, R and P get South-facing flat.

167. All men are naturally good.

168. All persons who believe in witchcraft are ignorant.

169. Clearly visible.

170. Cruise.

171. A person who renounces religion or political belief or principle is called *apostate.*

172. Wave : Crest as Mountain : peak

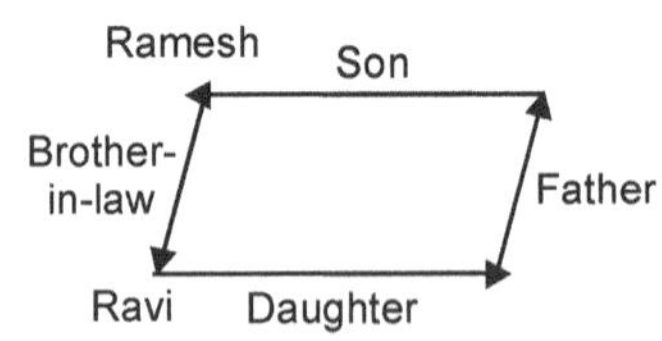

173. Hence, Ramesh is brother-in-law.

174. In 1 hour the hands of a clock make 2 times right angles.

∴ The hands of a clock between 4 pm to 10 pm make 11 times right angles.

175. Total no. of chocolates

$$= 12 \times 12 + 2 \times 12$$

$$= 144 + 24 = 168$$

$$168 \div 2 = 84$$

But 84 is not in option.

Hence, option (D) is correct.

176.

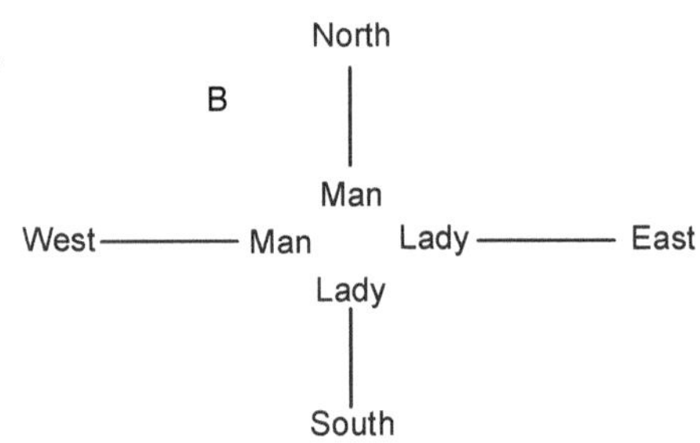

Hence, ladies are facing in North and West direction.

177.

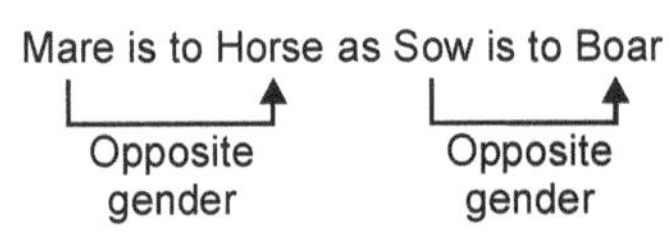

178.

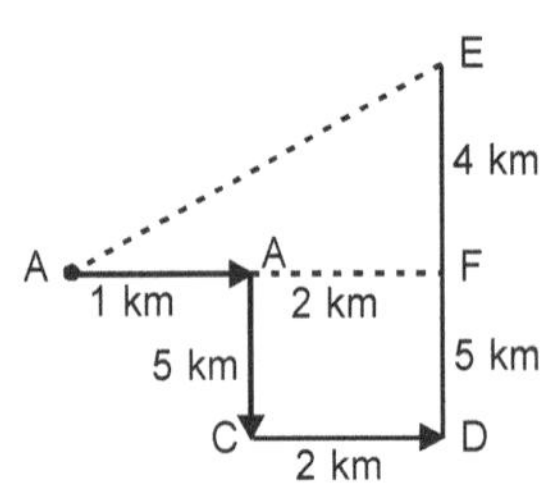

$$(AE)^2 = (AF)^2 + (EF)^2$$

$$= (3)^2 + (4)^2 = 9 + 16 = 25$$

$$\Rightarrow \quad AE = 5 \text{ km}$$

He is 5 km away from the starting point.

180. No parrots are black

All crows are black

Hence, no crows are parrots is true.

187. Let total number of workers in the company = x

According to the question,

$$40\% \text{ of } x = 800$$

$$\Rightarrow \quad \frac{40}{100} \times x = 800$$

$$\Rightarrow \quad x = \frac{800 \times 100}{40} = 2000$$

Number of males in the company

$$= 2000 - 800 = 1200.$$

188. Coding and decoding 9 : 72 :: 8 : x

$$9 \times x = 72 \times 8$$

$$\Rightarrow \quad x = \frac{72 \times 8}{9} = 64$$

$\therefore$ 9 : 72 : : 8 : 64.

192. Given,

M I L I T A R Y
↓ ↓ ↓ ↓ ↓ ↓ ↓ ↓
1 2 3 2 4 5 6 7

Similarly,

T A I L
↓ ↓ ↓ ↓
4 5 2 3

Hence, TAIL will be written as 4523.

194. Since, 27th March, 2011 was Sunday

$\therefore$ 27th June 2011 = 4 + 30 + 31 + 27 = 92 days

92 ÷ 7 = 13 Sundays

remainder = 1

Hence, 27th June, 2011 was Monday.

195. A B A N D O N is written as
↓ ↓ ↓ ↓ ↓ ↓ ↓
a r a m o i m

B O R E is written as
↓ ↓ ↓ ↓
r i t s

and B A S I L is written as
↓ ↓ ↓ ↓ ↓
r a b u t

S O L I D
↓ ↓ ↓ ↓ ↓
b i t u o

Hence, the original word for the code bituo is SOLID.

196.

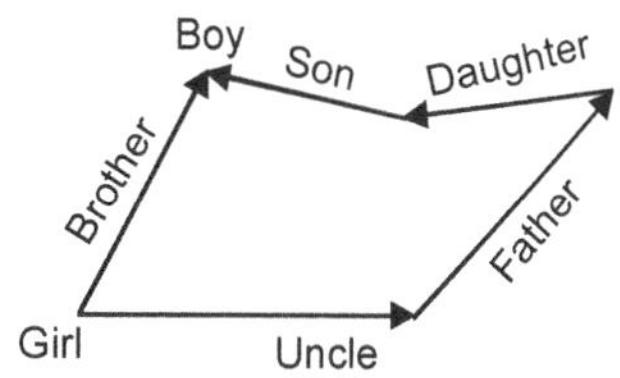

Hence, the boy is girl's brother.

197.

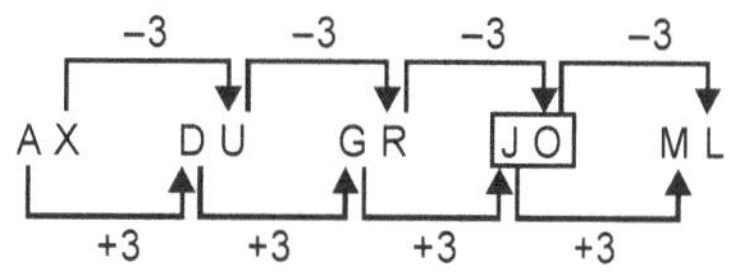

Hence, JO will come at the missing place.

198.

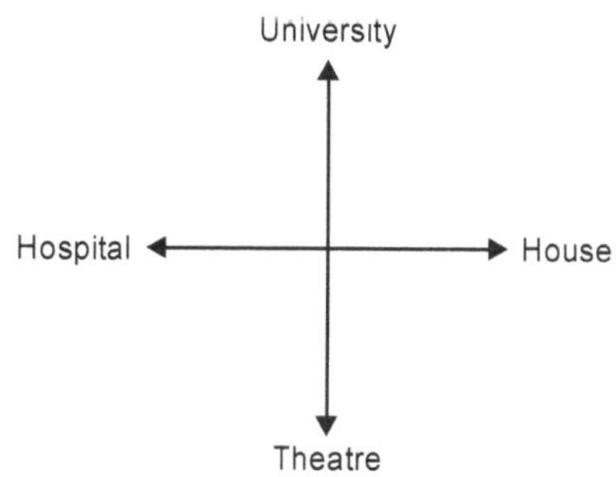

Hence, University is in the North direction.

Previous Paper (Solved)

Common Law Admission Test (CLAT-UG)

Entrance Exam, 2016

Section-I : English Including Comprehension

Directions (Qs. No. 1 to 10) : *Fill in the blanks by choosing the most appropriate option:*

1. The method and practice of teaching is called ....
A. philately B. pedagogy
C. training D. paediatrics

2. I like reading journals .... novels.
A. most than B. more than
C. the best D. the less than

3. There isn't .... water in the overhead tank.
A. little B. some
C. any D. lot of

4. A thief does not .... the door.
A. knock B. knock at
C. knock on D. knock to

5. They always give the available seats to .... comes.
A. whoever B. whichever
C. whom D. whomever

6. A fire broke .... in the neighbourhood.
A. out B. away
C. off D. from

7. Professor Ahmed .... teaching us .... August, 2012.
A. had been, since B. has been, since
C. was, for D. has been, for

8. It's unfortunate that he died .... cancer.
A. by B. from
C. of D. with

9. There is a lot of work .... hand. Let's cancel .... picnic .
A. on, a B. in, a
C. in, the D. upon, the

10. If you promise .... angry with me, I'll tell you what I broke.
A. not get B. not getting
C. get not D. not to get

Directions (Qs. No. 11 to 15) : *Complete the sentences with the correct options:*

11. I can't bear .... late.
A. been B. being
C. to D. be

12. Mani, along with his friends, ... for basket ball practice every morning.
A. goes B. are going
C. go D. were going

13. Her parents have arrived .... the airport.
A. at B. in
C. to D. on

14. I have never come .... any one as rude as him.
A. at B. across
C. to D. around

15. They returned home .... a taxi.
A. on B. with
C. from D. in

Directions (Qs. No. 16 to 20) : *Choose the correct spellings in questions given below:*

16. A. deceeve B. decieve
C. diecieve D. deceive

17. A. collaborat B. colaborate
C. collaborrate D. collaborate

18. A. sacrilegious B. saereligious
C. sacrilegious D. sacribegous

19. A. berrister B. berister
C. barisster D. barrister

20. A. integrity B. intigerity
C. integerety D. integerity

Directions (Qs. No. 21 to 24) : *Choose the most appropriate option for each of the following questions:*

21. "Amicus curiae" means:
A. One of the judges of the court
B. One among the expert witnesses in a case
C. A friend of the court
D. One among the parties to the dispute

22. "Ab initio" means:
A. in defence of a comment
B. from the beginning

C. in continuation with
D. in connection with the future

23. "To bury the hatchet" means:
A. to hide some treasure
B. to end a feud with an enemy
C. to cremate carcass of an animal
D. to plant grass in the field

24. "Faux pas" means:
A. expected to happen
B. social blunder
C. fake identity
D. false

Directions (Qs. No. 25 to 28): *Choose the correct option for each of the following questions:*

25. A. Please stop interfering with my romantic life.
B. Please stop interfering into my romantic life.
C. Please stop interfering for my romantic life.
D. Please stop interfering in my romantic life.

26. A. The Titanic did not reach it's destination.
B. The Titanic did not reach her destination.
C. The Titanic did not reach their destination.
D. The Titanic did not reach his destination.

27. A. Your grammar is very good but you need to work on managing your pronunciation.
B. Your grammar is very good, but you need to work on modifying your pronunciation.
C. Your grammar is very good, but you need to work on correcting your pronunciation.
D. Your grammar is very good, but you need to work on repairing your pronunciation.

28. A. The Film Star climbed off the car and smiled at the people.
B. The Film Star come out of the car and smiled at the people.
C. The Film Star got out of the car and smiled at the people.
D. The Film Star got off the car and smiled at the people.

Directions (Qs. No. 29 & 30): *Complete the proverb, in the following questions:*

29. .... waters run ....
A. Hot, fast B. Muddy, slow
C. Stagnant, leisurely D. Still, deep

30. When .... is bliss, it is .... to be wise.
A. ignorance, folly B. knowledge, better
C. romance, boring D. bachelorhood, single

Directions (Qs. No. 31 to 40): *Read the given passage carefully and answer the questions given after the passage:*

1. Often, we passionately pursue matters that in the future appear to be contradictory to our real intention or nature; and triumph is followed by remorse or regret. There are numerous examples of such a trend in the annals of history and contemporary life.
2. Alfred Nobel was the son of Immanuel Nobel, an inventor who experimented extensively with explosives. Alfred too carried out research and experiments with a large range of chemicals; he found new methods to blast rocks for the construction of roads and bridges; he was engaged in the development of technology and different weapons; his life revolved around rockets and cannons and gun powder. The ingenuity of the scientist brought him enough wealth to buy the Bofors armament plant in Sweden.
3. Paradoxically, Nobel's life was a busy one yet he was lonely; and as he grew older, he began suffering from guilt of having invented the dynamite that was being used for destructive purposes. He set aside a huge part of his wealth to institute Nobel Prizes. Besides honouring men and women for their extraordinary achievements in physics, chemistry, medicine and literature, he wished to honour people who worked for the promotion of peace.
4. It's strange that the very man whose name was closely connected with explosives and inventions that helped in waging wars willed a large part of his earnings for the people who work for the promotion of peace and the benefit of mankind. The Nobel Peace Prize is intended for a person who has accomplished the best work for fraternity among nations, for abolition or reduction of war and for promotion of peace.
5. Another example that comes to one's mind is that of Albert Einstein. In 1939, fearing that the Nazis would win the race to build the world's first atomic bomb, Einstein urged President Franklin D Roosevelt to launch an American programme on nuclear research. The matter was considered and a project called the Manhattan Project was initiated. The project involved intense nuclear research the construction of the world's first atomic bomb. All this while, Einstein had the impression that the bomb would be used to protect the world from the Nazis. But in 1945, when Hiroshima was bombed to end World War II, Einstein was deeply grieved and he regretted his endorsement of the need for nuclear research.
6. He also stated that had he known that the Germans would be unsuccessful in making the atomic bomb, he would have probably never recommended making one. In 1947, Einstein began working for the cause of disarmament. But, Einstein's name still continues to be linked with the bomb.

Man's fluctuating thoughts, changing opinions, varying opportunities keep the mind in a state of flux. Hence, the paradox of life: it's certain that nothing is certain in life.

31. The Manhattan Project was initiated ....
A. in honour of Einstein
B. to carry out nuclear research
C. to protect the Nazis
D. to bomb Hiroshima

32. In paragraph 4, the word 'accomplished' means ....
A. made an effort to do something
B. won awards
C. worked hard
D. completed successfully

33. In the fifth paragraph, the word 'endorsement' means
A. making a promise to do something
B. expressing one's regret
C. expressing one's opposition
D. expressing one's approval or support

34. Working with arms and ammunition helped Alfred to amass ....
A. wealth B. enemies
C. popularity D. intelligence

35. The paradox, 'it's certain that nothing is certain in life', indicates the writer's
A. persuasive nature
B. scientific mind
C. hatred for scientists
D. analytical mind

36. Immanuel's interest in dynamites influenced Alfred's inclination for working ....
A. with explosives
B. for humanity
C. with contradiction
D. for the Nobel Peace Prize

37. One of the paradoxes in Alfred's life was that he was ....
A. lonely yet rich
B. occupied yet lonely
C. intelligent yet lonely
D. hard working but a failure

38. The passage is ....
A. an argumentative essay
B. a process essay
C. an expository essay
D. a descriptive essay

39. Einstein had the impression that the Germans would ....
A. be unsuccessful in making the atomic bomb.
B. bomb Hiroshima.
C. be successful in making the world's first atomic bomb.
D. work for humanity.

40. Alfred established the Nobel Prizes to ....
A. use his wealth for hard working people.
B. honour only those people who are intelligent.
C. remind people of his achievements.
D. ease his guilt and promote work for the betterment of mankind.

Section-II : General Knowledge and Current Affairs

Directions (Qs. No. 41 to 50) : *Choose the most appropriate option:*

41. The Parliament of which country became first Parliament in the world to run entirely on Solar Power?
A. Pakistan B. India
C. Japan D. UK

42. Name the country that has six Deputy Prime Ministers.
A. Nigeria B. Nicaragua
C. Nepal D. Maldives

43. In case the President of India wants to resign, he shall address his resignation to the:
A. Vice-President
B. Chief Election Commissioner
C. Prime Minister
D. Chief Justice of India

44. Punjabi has become the .... most common language in the Parliament of Canada.
A. second B. fourth
C. fifth D. third

45. In April 2016, The Duke and Duchess of Cambridge visited India. Their names are:
A. Prince William and Kate Middleton
B. Prince Charles and Cathy
C. Prince Robert and Kateler
D. Prince Hillery and Victoria

46. The Rajya Sabha in April, 2016 passed two Bills, which had already been passed by the Lok Sabha earlier, repealing certain outdated/old laws. The Bills intended to repeal:
A. 315 laws B. 1053 laws
C. 153 laws D. 513 laws

47. In case of death of both the President and Vice-President of India, who shall act as the President of India?
A. Attorney General of India
B. Prime Minister
C. Chief Justice of India
D. The Parliament will nominate from among its Members

48. Mars is also known as the:
A. Blue Planet B. Red Planet
C. Brown Planet D. Green Planet

49. Who is the President of Sri Lanka?
A. K. Sripavan B. Ranil Wickramasinghe
C. Jayavardane D. Maithripala Sirisena

50. Which State has the largest number of foreign students in India?
A. Maharashtra B. Uttar Pradesh
C. Karnataka D. Haryana

51. The largest diaspora in the world is from:
A. South Africa B. Mexico
C. China D. India

52. Which State of India was declared in January, 2016 as the "first organic farming State of India"?
A. Haryana B. Punjab
C. Kerala D. Sikkim

53. The country which cloned a buffalo calf first is:
A. Denmark B. U.S.A.
C. Sweden D. India

54. Who was the Constitutional Advisor to the Constituent Assembly in framing the Indian Constitution?
A. Sir B.N. Rau
B. Dr. Rajendra Prasad
C. Pandit Jawaharlal Nehru
D. Dr. B.R. Ambedkar

55. The Constitution (One Hundredth Amendment) Act, 2015 was enacted to give effect to:
A. the transfer of certain territories by India to Bangladesh and transfer of certain territories from Bangladesh to India
B. the acquiring of territories by India from Bangladesh.
C. National Judicial Appointment Commission
D. transfer of certain territories by India to Bangladesh.

56. Which State has become the first State to introduce compulsory gender education at the graduate level?
A. Punjab B. Kerala
C. Telangana D. Andhra Pradesh

57. "Beyond the Lines - An Autobiography" is authored by:
A. Mr. Arun Shourie B. Mr. Kuldip Nayar
C. Justice Krishna Iyer D. Mr. Soli Sarab Ji

58. India signed the "Paris Agreement on Climate Change" in April, 2016 at:
A. Geneva B. Paris
C. New York D. New Delhi

59. Prime Minister, Mr. Narendra Modi, in March, 2016, launched an ambitious programme "Setu Bharatam". The programme is aimed at:
A. Making all National Highway railway level crossing free by 2019.
B. Linking all major cities and towns by rail, air and road by 2019.
C. Providing travel concession to senior citizens throughout India.
D. Providing travel concession to women and children throughout India.

60. In an attempt to curb black money, the Government has made PAN mandatory for all financial transactions exceeding Rupees:
A. 2 lakhs B. 1 lakh
C. 3 lakhs D. 4 lakhs

61. Who is the Chairperson of National Human Rights Commission?
A. Justice Balakrishnan B. Justice B.S. Chauhan
C. Justice D.K. Jain D. Justice H.L. Dattu

62. Which day is celebrated as "World Consumer Rights Day"?
A. 15th March B. 5th June
C. 5th September D. 15th July

63. Who was conferred the Rajiv Gandhi Khel Ratna award during August, 2015?
A. Dhoni B. Saina Nehwal
C. Sania Mirza D. Virat Kohli

64. .... is the fastest planet to revolve around the Sun.
A. Jupiter B. Mars
C. Mercury D. Venus

65. The highest peace time gallantry award Ashok Chakra was awarded posthumously during 2016 to:
A. Mohan Nath Goswami
B. Mahendra Singh
C. Rajesh Atra
D. Jagdish Chand

66. The maximum number of 'Smokeless Villages' are found in the State of:
A. Rajasthan B. Punjab
C. Telangana D. Karnataka

67. Who is the Chairman of National Green Tribunal?
A. Justice R.C. Lahoti
B. Justice Bhandhari
C. Justice Swatanter Kumar
D. Justice Balakrishna Reddy

68. Parliament of India consists of:
A. Council of States
B. President, House of the People and Council of States
C. House of the People and Council of States
D. House of the People

69. Which country is the first developed nation to default on debt of IMF?
A. Japan B. UK
C. Greece D. USA

70. The direction to hold floor test to prove majority in the Legislative Assembly of Uttarakhand, to be held on 10th May, 2016 has been given on 6th May, 2016, by:
A. The Governor of Uttarakhand
B. The Supreme Court of India
C. The High Court of Uttarakhand
D. The President of India

71. In January, 2016, at the first stage, the Union Ministry of Urban Development unveiled the list of .... cities for smart cities mission out of 98 shortlisted cities:
A. 20 B. 25
C. 15 D. 30

72. The "Paris Agreement" was adopted in the twenty first session of Conference of Parties in the month of:
A. February, 2016 B. November, 2015
C. December, 2015 D. January, 2016

73. Who has scored the fastest century in a Test Cricket match?
A. Brendon McCullum, New Zealand
B. AB de Villiers, South Africa
C. Misbah Ul Haq, Pakistan
D. Vivian Richards, West Indies

74. Who has written the book "Indomitable Spirit"?
A. Justice Krishna Iyer B. Sh. Narendra Modi
C. Dr. A.P.J. Abdul Kalam D. Ms. Arundhati Roy

75. In which of the following States/Union Territories, the Election Commission has decided to hold election in a single phase on May 16, 2016?
A. Kerala, Tamil Nadu and Pondicherry
B. West Bengal, Kerala and Tamil Nadu
C. West Bengal, Kerala and Assam
D. Assam, Kerala and Pondicherry

76. Country's first 'visually-challenged friendly' railway station is:
A. Tirupathi B. Varanasi
C. New Delhi D. Mysuru

77. Power to summon the Houses of the Parliament is vested with:
A. President
B. Vice-President
C. Prime Minister
D. Speaker and Vice-President

78. Who is the Union Finance Minister of India?
A. Mr. Rajnath Singh
B. Mr. Arun Jaitly
C. Mr. Sushma Swaraj
D. Mr. D.V. Sadananda Gowda

79. The Currency of Thailand is:
A. Peseta B. Baht
C. Rupee D. Ringgit

80. Who is the author of "Crime & Punishment?"
A. Harold Joseph Laski B. Karl Marx
C. Fyodor Dostoevsky D. Geoffrey Chaucer

81. At the Asian Indoor Athletics Championships held at Doha in February, 2016, who among women won the gold medal in Long Jump?
A. Olga Rypakova of Kazakhstan
B. Mayooka Johny of India
C. Irina Ektova of Kazakhstan
D. Prajusha of India

82. Name the Indian Gymnast who has become the first female Indian Gymnast to qualify for the Olympics.
A. Bisweshwari Nandi B. Anjubala
C. Rupinder Kaur D. Dipa Karmakar

83. In 2015, Prime Minister Mr. Narendra Modi launched a new campaign, "Start up India, Stand up India". The campaign is aimed at:
A. Promoting Swatch Bharat
B. Promoting bank financing for start ups and offer incentives to boost entrepreneurship and job creation.
C. Promoting free education to all children below the age of 14 years and assuring them jobs after obtaining higher education.
D. Making India Digital

84. Under the Constitution of India the official language of the Union is:
A. Hindi in Devanagari Script
B. English and Hindi
C. Hindi
D. English

85. How many Indian Universities/Institutes figure among the top 200 in BRICS rankings?
A. 26 B. 16
C. 6 D. 20

86. Which organization has the motto 'Be Prepared'?
A. National Cadet Corps
B. National Service Scheme
C. National Disaster Management Authority
D. Boys' Scout

87. Who was crowned as the winner of Femina Miss India 2016 and who will represent India at the Miss World pageant?
A. Pankhuri Gidwani
B. Sushruthi Krishna

C. Sushobita Kapoor
D. Priyadarshini Chatterjee

88. Who lit the torch from the sun's rays reflected in a parabolic mirror during the Olympic flame lighting ceremony for the Rio 2016 Olympic Games at the site of ancient Olympia in Greece on 22nd April, 2016?
A. Ronaldo
B. Katerina Lehou
C. Joanie Laureh aka Chyna
D. Katerina Kaif

89. A Japanese Maglev, which is the fastest passenger train in the world, has broken its own record in 2015. The train reached .... kmph in the test run.
A. 603 B. 503
C. 453 D. 403

90. Who is the Chairperson of NITI Aayog?
A. Ms. Sushma Swaraj
B. Ms. Sushmita Mahajan
C. Sh. Narendra Modi
D. Sh. Arun Jaitly

Section-III : Elementary Mathematics (Numerical Ability)

Directions (Qs. No. 91 to 110) : *Choose the most appropriate option:*

91. A shop gives 15% discount on the purchase of a T.V. If paid for in cash immediately, a further discount of 12% is given. If the marked price is ₹ 15,000, what is the price of the T.V. if cash purchase is made?
A. ₹ 11,475 B. ₹ 11,220
C. ₹ 12,750 D. ₹ 10,950

92. The traffic lights at three different signal points change after every 45 seconds, 75 seconds and 90 seconds respectively. If all change simultaneously at 7:20:15 hours, then they will change again simultaneously at
A. 7:27:50 hours B. 7:27:45 hours
C. 7:28:00 hours D. 7:27:30 hours

93. A train which is moving at an average speed of 40 kmph, reaches its destination on time. When its average speed reduces to 35 kmph, then it reaches its destination 15 minutes late. The distance travelled by the train is:
A. 30 kms B. 40 kms
C. 70 kms D. 80 kms

94. The angles between the hands of a clock when the time is 4:25 am is:
A. 14½ degrees B. 12½ degrees
C. 17½ degrees D. 13½ degrees

95. A circular park, 42 m in diameter, has a path 3.5 m wide running around it on the outside. Find the cost of gravelling the path at ₹ 4 per m^2.
A. ₹ 2002 B. ₹ 1652
C. ₹ 1672 D. ₹ 2048

96. If the product of zeroes of the polynomial $ax^2 - 6x - 6$ is 4, find the value of 'a'
A. $-\frac{1}{2}$ B. $\frac{3}{2}$
C. $-\frac{3}{2}$ D. $\frac{1}{2}$

97. 60 kg of an alloy X is mixed with 100 kg of an alloy Y. If alloy X has lead and tin in the ratio of 3:2 and alloy Y has tin and copper in the ratio of 1:4, then the amount of tin in the new alloy is
A. 53 kgs. B. 80 kgs.
C. 44 kgs. D. 36 kgs.

98. If a boy is standing at the top of the tower and another boy is at the ground at some distance from the foot of the tower, then the angle of elevation and depression between the boys when both look at each other will be:
A. Equal
B. Cannot be predicted for relation
C. Angle of depression will be greater
D. Angle of elevation will be greater

99. Two consecutive even positive integers, sum of the squares of which is 1060 are:
A. 16 and 18 B. 12 and 14
C. 22 and 24 D. 20 and 22

100. A man buys ₹ 20 shares paying 9% dividend. The man expects to have an interest of 12% on his money. The market value of each share is:
A. ₹ 12 B. ₹ 15
C. ₹ 21 D. ₹ 18

101. What is the sum of all the natural numbers from 1 to 100?
A. 5000 B. 5050
C. 6000 D. 5052

102. The angle subtended by the Minor segment of a circle at the center is .... the angle subtended by the Major segment at the center of the circle.
A. greater than B. lesser than
C. not related to D. equal to

103. 12 defective pens are accidentally mixed with 132 good ones. It is not possible to just look at a pen and tell whether or not it is defective. One pen is taken out at random from this lot. Determine the probability that the pen taken out is a good one.

A. $\frac{11}{12}$ B. $\frac{10}{12}$

C. $\frac{7}{12}$ D. $\frac{9}{12}$

104. A man earns ₹ 20 on the first day and spends ₹ 15 on the next day. He again earns ₹ 20 on the third day and spends ₹ 15 on the fourth day. If he continues to save in this way, how soon will he have ₹ 60 in hand?

A. on 12th day

B. on 24th day

C. on 17th day

D. on 27th day

105. A library has an average of 510 visitors on Sundays and 240 on other days. What is the average number of visitors per day in the month of June beginning with a Sunday?

A. 250 B. 280

C. 276 D. 285

106. A patient in a hospital is given soup daily in a cylindrical bowl of diameter 7 cm. If the bowl is filled with soup to a height of 4 cm, how much soup the hospital has to prepare daily to serve 250 patients?

A. 40 litres B. 38.5 litres

C. 38 litres D. 39.5 litres

107. The number of 'three digit numbers' which are multiples of 9 are:

A. 101 B. 99

C. 100 D. 98

108. The value of a machine depreciates every year at the rate of 10% on its value at the beginning of that year. If the present value of the machine is ₹ 729, its worth three years ago was:

A. ₹ 1000 B. ₹ 750.87

C. ₹ 800 D. ₹ 947.70

109. The mean of 72 items was found to be 63. If two of the items were misrecorded as 27 and 9 instead of 72 and 90 respectively, find the correct mean.

A. 64.25 B. 64.75

C. 63.25 D. 65.75

110. A part of monthly hostel charges is fixed and the remaining depends on the number of days one has taken food in the mess. When a student A takes food for 20 days, she has to pay ₹ 1000 as hostel charges whereas a student B, who takes food for 26 days, pays ₹ 1180 as hostel charges. Find the fixed charges and the cost of food per day.

A. 200, 20 B. 400, 40

C. 300, 30 D. 400, 30

Section-IV : Legal Aptitude

Directions (Qs. No. 111 to 145) : *Follow the instructions carefully and choose the most appropriate option:*

The question numbers 111-145 in this section consist of legal proposition(s)/principle(s) (hereinafter referred to as 'principle') and facts. Such principles may or may not be true in the real and legal sense, yet you have to conclusively assume them to be true for the purposes of this Section. In other words, in answering the following questions, you must not rely on any principle except the principles those are given herein below for every question. Further, you must not assume any facts other than those stated in the question. The objective of this section is to test your interest towards study of law, research aptitude and problem solving ability, event if the "most reasonable conclusion" arrived at may be absurd or unacceptable for any other reason.

To answer a question, the given principle is to be applied to the given facts so as to arrive at most reasonable conclusion. Only one of the options, *i.e.*, (A), (B), (C), or (D) is the most reasonable conclusion.

111. Principle: Letters or words not describing quality of things can be registered as a trade mark.

Facts: Ram made an application for registration of alphabet 'B' written in a fancy style as trademark to be applied on packets and cartons of shoes manufactured by him.

A. The alphabet 'B' cannot be registered as trademark because it is an English letter.

B. The alphabet 'B' can be registered as trademark because it describes the quality of things.

C. The alphabet 'B' can be registered as trademark.

D. The alphabet 'B' cannot be registered as trademark because it belongs to humanity.

112. Principle: Existence of all the alleged facts is relevant, whether they occurred at the same time and place or at different times and places.

Facts: 'A', a citizen of England, is accused of committing murder of 'B' in India by taking part in a conspiracy hatched in England.

A. Only the fact that 'A' is accused of conspiracy hatched in England is relevant.

B. Only the fact that 'A' citizen of England is accused of committing murder of 'B' in India is relevant.

C. The facts that 'A' citizen of England is accused of commission of murder in India and of conspiracy hatched in England are relevant facts.

D. 'A' citizen of England cannot be tried in India.

113. Principle: Nothing is an offence, which is done by accident or misfortune, and without any criminal intention or knowledge in the doing of a lawful act in a lawful manner by lawful means and with proper care and caution.

Facts: 'A' takes up a gun, not knowing whether it is loaded or not, points it playfully at 'B' and pulls the trigger. Consequently, 'B' falls dead.

A. B's death is accidental, as 'A' did not have the knowledge that the gun is loaded.
B. B's death is accidental, as 'A' had no intention to kill 'B'.
C. B's death is accidental, as 'A' was just pointing the gun playfully at 'B'.
D. B's death is not accidental, as there was want of proper care and caution on the part of 'A'.

114. Principle: A condition to a contract can also be complied with after the happening of the event to which such a condition is attached.

Facts: 'A' promises to pay ₹ 5000 to 'B' on the condition that he shall marry with the consent of 'C', 'D' and 'E'. 'B' marries without the consent of 'C', 'D' and 'E', but obtains their consent after the marriage.

A. 'B' has not fulfilled the condition.
B. 'B' has fulfilled the condition.
C. 'B's marriage is not valid.
D. The condition is illegal.

115. Principles:

- A person is said to abet the doing of a thing when he instigates any other person to do that thing.
- Mere acquiescence, however, does not amount to instigation.

Facts: 'A' says to 'B': I am going to kill 'C'. And, 'B' replies: "Do as you wish and take the consequences"; whereafter 'A' kills 'C'.

A. 'B' is jointly liable with 'A' for killing 'C'.
B. 'B' has not abetted 'A' to kill 'C'.
C. 'B' has abetted 'A' by conspiracy.
D. 'B' abetted 'A' to kill 'C'.

116. Principle: Defamation is the publication of a statement which tends to lower reputation of a person in the estimation of other members of the society generally.

Facts: 'A' writes a highly offensive and derogatory letter about 'B', and sends it directly to 'B' in a sealed cover.

A. 'A' is liable to 'B' for defamation, as the letter is highly offensive and derogatory and is directly sent to 'B'.
B. 'A' is liable to 'B' for defamation, as the letter is highly offensive and derogatory.
C. 'A' is liable to 'B' for defamation, as it has hurt his (B's) self-esteem.
D. 'A' is not liable to 'B' for defamation, since there is no publication to any other person in whose estimation the reputation of 'B' could be brought down.

117. Principle: Where a person lawfully does anything for another person, or delivers anything to him, not intending to do so or to provide gratuitously, and such other person takes the benefit of that; the latter is bound to compensate the former for something done or thing provided, or to restore, the thing so delivered.

Facts: Trader 'A' delivers certain eatables at B's house by mistake. 'B' consumed the eatables without asking anything. Which of the following derivations is correct?

A. 'B' is bound to pay 'A' for the eatables.
B. 'B' is not bound to pay 'A' for the eatables.
C. 'B' can be made liable to pay for the eatables, only if 'A' establishes an express contract between 'A' and 'B'.
D. It is the discretion of 'B' to make payment to 'A'.

118. Principle: Law never enforces an impossible promise.

Facts: 'A' made a promise to 'B' to discover treasure by magic.

A. Law will not enforce the promise
B. Law will enforce the promise only at the option of 'B'.
C. Law will enforce the promise.
D. Law will enforce the promise only at the option of 'A'.

119. Principle: Intentional application of force to another person is actionable in law.

Facts: 'P' and 'D' are unknown to each other. When 'P' is about to sit on a chair, 'D' intentionally pulls it away as a result of which 'P' falls on to the floor and is injured.

A. 'D' is not liable as such jokes are common in the society.
B. 'D' is not liable as 'P' is not seriously injured.
C. 'D' is liable as the intentionally caused injury to P.
D. 'D' is not liable as the injury is not directly caused.

120. Principle: Mere silence as to facts likely to affect the decision of a person to enter into a contract is not fraud.

Facts: 'A' sells to 'B' (A's daughter who is minor) a horse which 'A' knows to be unsound. 'A' says nothing to 'B' about the unsoundness of the horse.

A. 'B' can take plea of fraud because she is minor.
B. 'A' has committed fraud.
C. There cannot be a contract between a father and daughter.
D. 'A' has not committed fraud.

121. Principle: A person is said to have committed assault when an apprehension is caused in the mind of a person that he is about to use physical force against his body.

Facts: 'A' abuses 'B' while he was sitting in a moving train, by aggressively shaking his fists when 'B' was standing on the railway platform at a distance.

A. 'A' has caused fear of assault in the mind of 'B'.
B. 'A' has committed assault against 'B'.
C. 'A' has not committed assault against 'B'.
D. 'A' has caused apprehension of assault in the mind of 'B'.

122. Principle: Consent is a good defence in a civil action for tort but the act should be the same for which consent was given.

Facts: 'B' was formally invited by 'A' to his house. 'B' after sitting for some time in drawing room, moved to the bed room of the house. 'A' sued 'B' for trespass.

A. 'B' has offended 'A' by moving to bed room.
B. 'B' has interfered with privacy of 'A'
C. 'B' has committed trespass as there was no consent of 'A' for entry in the Bed room.
D. 'B' has committed no trespass as he entered the house with 'A's consent.

123. Principle: Copyright law protects only work. 'Work' means cinematographic film but does not include performance by an actor in a cinematographic film.

Facts: Alia Bhatt acted in a movie.

A. The acting of Alia Bhatt can be protected as film producer's work.
B. The acting of Alia Bhatt can be protected under copyright law as professional work.
C. The acting of Alia Bhatt cannot be protected under copyright law.
D. The acting of Alia Bhatt can be protected under copyright law only as an artistic work.

124. Principle: A person, who is usually of unsound mind, but occasionally normal, may make a contract when he is not of unsound mind.

Facts: 'A' generally remains in the state of unsound mind and rarely becomes capable of understanding the things.

A. 'A' can make a contract at any time whenever he pleases.
B. 'A' can make a contract only for his own benefit.
C. 'A' can make a contract when normal.
D. 'A' can never make a contract.

125. Principles:

- A servant is one who is employed to do some work for his employer (master). He is engaged under a contract of service. He works directly under the control and directions of his master.
- In general, the master is vicariously liable for those torts (wrongful acts) of his servant which are done by the servant in the course of his employment.

Facts: 'M' appointed 'D' exclusively for the purpose of driving his tourist vehicle. 'M' also appointed 'C' exclusively for the purpose of performing the work of a conductor for the tourist vehicle. During one trip, at the end of the journey, 'C', while 'D' was not on the driver's seat, and apparently for the purpose of turning the vehicle in the right direction for the next journey, drove it through the street at high speed, and negligently injured 'P'.

A. 'M' could not be made liable for the act of 'C', as his (C's) act of driving the vehicle was not in the course of his employment.
B. 'M' could be made liable for the act of 'C', as his (C's) act of driving the vehicle was within his scope of employment.
C. 'M' could be made liable for the act of 'C', as 'C' was employed under a contract of service.
D. 'M' is not liable as he was not present at the time of accident.

126. Principle: In cases where there is an infringement of legal right even without any actual loss or damage, the person whose right is infringed has a cause of action.

Facts: 'P' was wrongfully prevented by the Returning Officer from exercising his vote in an assembly election. However, the candidate for whom he wanted to caste his vote won the election. Still, he ('P') brought an action claiming damages. Which of the following derivations is correct?

A. 'P' would succeed in his action, as it is mandatory to cast vote.
B. 'P' would not succeed in his action, as the candidate for whom he wanted to give his vote won the election.
C. 'P' would not succeed in his action, as he did not suffer any loss in that election.
D. 'P' would succeed in his action, as he was wrongfully prevented from exercising his legal right of voting in that election.

127. Principle: Sale of liquor is illegal. All agreements relating to prohibited items do not exist in the eyes of law.

Facts: 'A' entered into an agreement with 'B' for the sale of liquor. 'A' failed to supply the agreed quantity of liquor to 'B'.

A. 'B' cannot bring any legal action against 'A'.
B. 'A' and 'B' can initiate appropriate legal proceeding against each other.
C. 'A' can bring a legal action against 'B'.
D. 'B' can bring a legal action against 'B'.

128. Principle: The communication of a proposal is complete when it comes to the knowledge of the person to whom it is made.

Facts: 'A' sent a letter making a proposal to 'B' to purchase the house of 'B'.

A. The communication of proposal is complete when B's wife handed over the letter to 'B'.
B. The communication of proposal is complete when B's wife received it.
C. The communication of proposal is complete when 'B' reads the letter.
D. The communication of proposal is complete when A sent the letter.

129. Principle: Killing is not murder if the offender, whilst deprived of the power of self-control by intense and sudden provocation, causes the death of the person who gave the provocation.

Facts: 'A', a man found his girl friend sleeping, in her own bed room, with another man named 'B'. 'A' did not do anything but went to his home, picked a gun and cartridges, returned to the girl friend's bed room with loaded gun but found the place empty. After fifteen days he saw his girl friend dining in a restaurant. Without waiting for even a second, 'A' fired five bullets at his girl friend who died on the spot.

A. 'A' could have killed both 'B' and his girl friend.
B. 'A' did not kill his girl friend under intense and sudden provocation.
C. 'A' could have killed 'B' instead of his girl friend.
D. 'A' killed his girl friend under intense and sudden provocation.

130. Principle: Whoever does not arrest the killer and report the matter to the concerned authorities commits an offence.

Facts: 'A', a woman, sees 'B', another woman, killing a third woman 'C'. 'A' neither attempted to arrest 'B' nor informed the concerned authorities.

A. 'B' has not committed an offence.
B. 'A' has not committed an offence.
C. 'B' has committed an offence.
D. 'A' has committed an offence.

131. Principles:

- An independent contractor is one who is employed to do some work of his employer. He is engaged under a contract for services. He undertakes to produce a given result, and in the actual execution of the work, he is not under the direct control or following directions of his employer. He may use his own discretion in execution of the work assigned.
- In general, an employer is not liable for the torts (wrongful acts) of his independent contractor. But, the employer may be held liable if he directs him to do some careless acts.

Facts: Ramesh hired a taxi-cab to go to Delhi Airport. As he started late from his home, he kept on urging the taxi-driver to drive at a high speed and driver followed the directions; and ultimately due to high speed an accident took place causing injuries to a person.

A. Ramesh would not be held liable for damages because the driver was an independent contractor and not his servant.
B. Ramesh would not be liable as car was not owned by him.
C. Ramesh would be held liable for damages as he exercised the control by giving directions to the driver.
D. Ramesh would not be held liable for damages because Ramesh did not know the consequences of such rash driving.

132. Principle: Whoever by words or writing conveys to others any imputation concerning any person's reputation is said to defame that person.

Facts: During a marriage ceremony, 'A' circulated a pamphlet saying that 'S', sister of the bride, is a thief, she has stolen the shoes of the bridegroom.

A. 'A' has defamed 'S'.
B. 'A' has defamed the bridegroom.
C. 'A' defamed the bride.
D. 'A' did not defame 'S' as he never intended it.

133. Principle: One who dishonestly misappropriates or converts to his own use or sells any movable property belonging to another, is guilty of the offence of misappropriation.

Facts: 'A' takes property belonging to 'Z' out of Z's possession, in good faith, believing when he takes it, that the property belongs to himself. Subsequently, 'A', on discovering his mistake, without disclosing the actual facts, dishonestly sells the property to a stranger.

A. 'A' is not guilty because when he took the property, he believed in good faith that it belonged to him.
B. 'A' is guilty of an offence of misappropriation.
C. 'A' may be guilty of theft but not for misappropriation.
D. 'A' is not guilty as the property can be recovered from the stranger.

134. Principle: Whoever takes away any moveable thing from the land of any person without that person's consent, he is said to have committed theft.

Facts: During his visit to the house of 'C', 'A' asked 'B', the son of 'C', to accompany 'A' to the forest. Neither 'A' nor 'B' informed 'C' in this regard. 'B' accompanied 'A' to the forest.

A. 'A' has not committed theft.
B. 'A' has not committed theft till 'B' did not accompany him.

C. 'A' has committed theft.
D. 'A' has committed theft as soon as he entered the house of 'C'.

135. Principle: False imprisonment is a tort (wrong) which means the total restraint of a person's liberty without lawful justification.

Facts: A part of a public road had been closed for spectators of a boat race. 'P' wanted to enter but he was prevented by 'D' and other policemen because he had not paid the admission fee. 'P' was able to enter the enclosure by other means but was unable to go where he wanted to go. The policemen refused access to where he wanted to go but allowed him to remain where he was or to go back. 'P' remained within the enclosure and refused to leave. Subsequently, 'P' sued 'D' for false imprisonment.

A. It was a case of false imprisonment, but 'D' could not be made liable for it.
B. 'D' could not be made liable for false imprisonment, as he did not totally restrict P's movements.
C. 'D' could be made liable for false imprisonment, as he did restrict P's movements.
D. 'D' could not be made liable for false imprisonment, as he has not touched him.

136. Principle: Import means bringing some consignment into India from a foreign country.

Facts: A consignment from Sri Lanka entered the territorial waters of India. However, this consignment never crossed the Indian custom barrier nor did it enter into the stream of commerce in India.

A. The consignment was not imported into India.
B. The consignment will only be imported into India when it crosses the Indian custom barrier.
C. The consignment was imported into India.
D. The consignment will only be imported into India when it enters into the stream of commerce in India.

137. Principle: Nothing is an offence which is done by a child under twelve years of age, who has not attained sufficient maturity of understanding to judge the nature and consequences of his conduct on that occasion.

Facts: Himesh, 11 years old boy, picks up a gold ring worth ₹ 5000/- lying on a table in his friend's house and immediately sells it for ₹ 2000/-, and misappropriates the money.

A. Himesh would be protected under the principle stated above because he is below 12 years of age.
B. Himesh would not be protected under the principle stated above because his acts show that he was sufficiently mature to understand the nature and consequences of his conduct.
C. Himesh would be protected under the principle stated above because his acts show that he was not sufficiently mature to understand the nature and consequences of his conduct.
D. Himesh would not be protected under the principle stated above because, irrespective of the age, stealing is an offence.

138. Principle:

1. Wagering agreements are void.
2. Collateral agreements to wagering contracts are valid.

Facts: XYZ Bank lends ₹ 40,000 to Sabu in order to enable him to award as prize to Randeep who is the winner of horse race. Later Sabu refuses to pay the prize stating that horse racing is wagering agreement. Can XYZ Bank recover money from Sabu?

A. No, as it is a wagering contract.
B. Bank can recover money from Sabu so that payment of prize money can be made to Randeep.
C. Yes, as it is only a collateral agreement to horse racing and therefore the bank can recover the money from Sabu.
D. Horse racing is illegal and therefore XYZ Bank cannot recover anything from Sabu.

139. Principle: An agreement without free consent can be enforced only at the option of the party whose consent was not free.

Facts: A obtains the consent of 'B' to enter into an agreement by putting a gun on the head of B's girl friend.

A. 'B' can enforce the agreement.
B. 'A' can enforce the agreement.
C. 'B' cannot enforce the agreement.
D. Neither 'A' nor 'B' can enforce the agreement.

140. Principle: Acceptance of proposal must be the exact mirror image of the proposal.

Facts: 'A' made a proposal to 'B' to sell a chair for ₹ 500. 'B' expressed his desire to buy the said chair for ₹ 400.

A. 'B' has not accepted the proposal of 'A'.
B. It is not clear whether 'B' has accepted the proposal of 'A' or not.
C. 'B' has accepted the proposal of 'A'.
D. It is not clear whether A made a proposal to 'B'.

141. Principle: There are certain acts which, though harmful, are not wrongful in law; therefore, do not give legal right to bring action in law, to the person who suffers from such acts.

Facts: 'Prakash' has a rice mill. His neighbour, Shanti, sets up another rice mill and offers a tough competition to Prakash. As a consequence, Prakash's profits fall down. He brings a suit against Shanti for damages.

A. Prakash can succeed in his claim as it is a case of actual damages.
B. Prakash cannot succeed in his claim for damages, as it is a case of damage without infringement of any legal right.
C. Prakash can succeed in his claim for damages, as it is a case of damage as a result of infringement of his legal right.
D. Prakash may succeed in his claim for damages, as it is a case of loss to his business.

142. Principle: Consent is a good defence for civil action in tort. But consent must include both knowledge of risk and assumption of risk, i.e., readiness to bear harm.

Facts: A lady passenger was aware that the driver of the cab, in which she opted to travel was little intoxicated. The cab met with an accident and lady got injured.
A. Lady can refuse to pay the fare as she had suffered injuries.
B. Lady is entitled to claim compensation as she only knew about risk and there was no assumption of risk.
C. Lady is not entitled to claim compensation as she had knowledge of the risk.
D. Driver can take the plea that he was lightly intoxicated.

143. Principle: An agreement may be entered into orally or in writing, or by conduct.

Facts: 'A' went to the shop of 'B' and picked a toothbrush and gave a cheque of Rupees twenty to 'B' and left the shop.
A. 'A' should have carried a currency note of Rupees twenty to make the payment.
B. There was an agreement between 'A' and 'B'.
C. Payment of toothbrush cannot be made through a cheque.
D. 'A' did not enter into an agreement with 'B'.

144. Principle: Causing of an effect partly by an act and partly by an omission is an offence.

Facts: 'A' confined her daughter 'D' in a room. 'A' also did not provide any food to her daughter 'D'. Consequently, 'D' died of starvation.
A. 'A' committed the offence of causing death of 'D'.
B. 'A' committed the offence of confining 'D'.
C. 'A' committed the offence of not providing food to 'D'.
D. 'A' committed no offence.

145. Principle: Law does not penalise for wrongs which are of trivial nature.

Facts: In the course of a discussion, 'A' threw a file of papers at the table which touched the hands of 'B'.
A. 'A' is liable for insulting 'B'.
B. 'A' is not liable for his act, as it was of trivial nature.
C. 'A' is liable for his act, as the file touched 'B's hand.
D. 'A' is liable for his act, as it assaulted 'B'.

Directions (Qs. No. 146 to 160) : *Choose the most appropriate option:*

146. Under the Constitution of India 'Right to Pollution Free Environment' has emerged as a fundamental right from the right to:
A. Freedom of movement under Article 19
B. Equality under Article 14
C. Life and personal liberty under Article 21
D. Conserve culture under Article 29.

147. 'alibi' means a plea by an accused person that he:
A. was present elsewhere.
B. remained in judicial custody.
C. underwent preventive detention.
D. was facing trial.

148. 'obiter dicta' means:
A. Basis of judicial decision.
B. Judgment of a court in the case before it.
C. An opinion given by the court not necessary for the decision.
D. Direction by a judge.

149. If an authority is holding information about another in a 'fiduciary capacity', the information under the Right to Information Act, 2005 may not be obtainable. 'Fiduciary relationship' is based on:
A. Authority B. Trust
C. Law D. Contract

150. Under the Constitution of India restriction on freedom of religion cannot be placed on the ground of:
A. Morality B. Social justice
C. Health D. Public order

151. As per law the minimum age for the marriage of a boy and a girl in India is:
A. 21 years in both cases
B. 18 years and 21 years respectively
C. 21 years and 18 years respectively
D. 18 years in both cases

152. Which among the following was described by Dr. B.R. Ambedkar as the "heart and soul of the Constitution of India"?
A. Freedom of Religion
B. Right to Constitutional Remedies
C. Right to equality
D. Right to move throughout the territory of India

153. The Supreme Court of India has struck down the Constitution (Ninety-ninth Amendment) Act, 2014 as unconstitutional. It is related to :

A. Land Exchange between India and Bangladesh
B. National Judicial Appointment Commission
C. Religious Rights
D. Jallikattu (Bull Fighting)

154. 'lis pendens' means:
A. Awaited information. B. On the basis of evidence.
C. Decision awaited. D. A pending suit.

155. Which one of the following is not a Directive Principle of State Policy under Part IV of the Constitution of India?
A. Provision for just and humane conditions of work and maternity relief.
B. Organisation of village panchayats.
C. Promotion of adult education.
D. Promotion of international peace and security.

156. 'persona non grata' means:
A. Non-performance of promise.
B. Non-person.
C. An unacceptable person.
D. Ungrateful person.

157. The object of which one of the following writs is to prevent a person to hold public office which he is not legally entitled to hold?
A. Mandamus B. Quo warranto
C. Certiorari D. Prohibition

158. Which Indian State has prescribed minimum educational qualification for candidates contesting panchayat polls?
A. Gujarat
B. Kerala
C. Haryana
D. Punjab

159. Which among the following does not belong to the 'right to freedom of religion'?
A. Freedom from payment of taxes for promotion of any particular religion.
B. Freedom from attending religious instruction or religious worship in certain educational institutions.
C. Freedom of conscience and free profession, practice and propagation of religion.
D. Freedom of speech and expression

160. 'audi alteram partem' means:
A. Not connected to facts.
B. Following the substantive law.
C. A transferee cannot retransfer.
D. Giving opportunity of hearing of the other side.

Section-V : Logical Reasoning

Directions (Qs. No. 161 to 163): *Read the following information carefully and choose the most appropriate option:*

A and B are good in driving bus and car. C and A are good in driving car and scooter. C, D and E are good in driving scooter and tractor. E and C are good in driving scooter and auto-rickshaw. D and B are good in driving bus and tractor.

161. Who is good in driving scooter, tractor and auto-rickshaw but not good in driving car?
A. A B. D
C. C D. E

162. Who is good in driving tractor, scooter, car and auto-rickshaw but not bus?
A. C B. B
C. D D. A

163. Who is good in driving scooter, tractor and bus?
A. C B. B
C. A D. D

Directions (Qs. No. 164 to 166): *Read the following information carefully and choose the most appropriate option:*

In each question, there is a statement and two assumptions numbered as I and II. Read the statement and find which of the given assumptions is implicit:

A. If Assumption I is implicit.
B. If Assumption II is implicit.
C. If neither Assumption I nor Assumption II is implicit.
D. If both Assumption I and Assumption II are implicit.

164. Statement: The next meeting of the executive board of a company will be held after six months.

Assumptions:
I. Existing executive board will be dissolved before six months
II. The company will remain in function after six months.
A. Assumption II is implicit.
B. Assumption I is implicit.
C. Both Assumption I and Assumption II are implicit.
D. Neither Assumption I nor Assumption II is implicit.

165. Statement: To attend a convocation ceremony scheduled to be held on Thursday at GM University, Chennai, Mr. X left for Chennai on Tuesday by train.

Assumptions:
I. Mr. X may reach home on Saturday
II. Mr. X may reach the University on Wednesday
A. Assumption II is implicit.
B. Neither Assumption I nor Assumption II is implicit.

C. Assumption I is implicit.
D. Both Assumption I and Assumption II are implicit.

166. **Statement:** In the State of Zuminisia, people prefer to travel by X airline instead of Y airline, as X airline has advanced German security system and 99% on time operations.

Assumptions:

I. Airline X with advanced German security system and record on time operation is perceived better than airline Y.

II. Had advanced German security system and on time performance record of Y airline been implemented, it would have been preferred over airline X.

A. Neither Assumption I nor Assumption II is implicit.
B. Assumption II is implicit.
C. Assumption I is implicit.
D. Both Assumption I and Assumption II are implicit.

Directions (Qs. No. 167 and 168): *Read the following information carefully and choose the most appropriate option:*

In a joint family, A, B, C, D, E and F are the members. B is the son of C. A and C are husband and wife. C is not the mother of B. E is the brother of C. D is the daughter of A and F is the brother of B.

167. Who is the mother of B?

A. E B. F
C. D D. A

168. Which of the following is a pair of females in the family?

A. DF B. AE
C. AD D. BD

Directions (Qs. No. 169 and 170): *Read the following information carefully and choose the most appropriate option:*

In each of the questions, two statements are numbered as I and II. There may be a cause and effect relationship between the two statements. The statements may be the effect of the same cause or an independent cause. The statements may be independent causes without having any relationship. Read both the statements and mark your answer as:

A. If statement I is the cause and statement II is its effect.
B. If statement II is the cause and statement I is its effect.
C. If both statements I and II are independent causes.
D. If both statements I and II are effects of independent causes.

169. **Statement I:** The Government, by legislation has decided to make all public information available to general public.

Statement II: Before passing of legislation, general public did not have access to public information.

A. Statement II is the cause and statement I is its effect.
B. Both statements I and II are independent causes.
C. Statement I is the cause and statement II is its effect.
D. Both statements I and II are effects of independent causes.

170. **Statement I:** In last two years, there is a considerable reduction in cancellation of flights due to fog in North India.

Statement II: In last two years, there is a considerable improvement in passenger amenities on all airports of North India.

A. Both statements I and II are effects of independent causes.
B. Statement I is the cause and statement II is its effect.
C. Statement II is the cause and statement I is its effect.
D. Both statements I and II are independent causes.

Directions (Qs. No. 171 to 200): *Choose the most appropriate option:*

171. Which word in the following group DOES NOT belong to the others?

PROSPER, EXCITE, THRIVE, FLOURISH

A. Excite B. Flourish
C. Thrive D. Prosper

172. If it is true that 'Religious fundamentalism is dangerous to the society', then which one of the following statements can also be true?

A. Religious pluralism is dangerous to the society.
B. Belief in any religion is dangerous to the society.
C. Religion without reason is dangerous to the society.
D. Disrespect for other religions is dangerous to the society.

173. Examine the series and identify the missing number:

46, 44, 40, 38, 34, ...

A. 30 B. 32
C. 28 D. 26

174. In a class, student X has 8th position from the top and 84th from the bottom. How many students are there in the class?

A. 88 B. 96
C. 98 D. 91

175. Four statements are given below. Group two of them in such a way that one is logically incorrect and the other is verifiable as a matter of fact

(*a*) The Sun does not rise in the East.
(*b*) A straight line is the shortest distance between any two points.
(*c*) Every circle has a centre.
(*d*) The maximum duration of a total solar eclipse is about 7.5 minutes.

A. [a, c] B. [c, d]
C. [a, d] D. [a, b]

176. Find the odd one out from the following group.
WINDSHIELD, SPARK PLUG, CLUTCH PEDAL, CAR, ENGINE

A. Car B. Spark Plug
C. Engine D. Windshield

177. Choose the pair of words from the options that best represents a similar relationship as the one expressed in the following pair of words.
WAITER : RESTAURANT

A. Driver : Car B. Teacher : School
C. Author : Book D. Actor : Acting

178. If it is true that 'Good governance implies law and order in society' then identify the statement which has to be accepted along with the given statement?

A. An able government very effectively uses laws to promote peace.
B. A strong government uses force to impose laws.
C. Law is indispensable for the society.
D. A healthy society is governed by maximum number of laws.

179. Who among the following is the odd one in the following group of persons?
Chief Justice of India, Attorney General of India, Solicitor General, Advocate General

A. Solicitor General.
B. Advocate General.
C. Attorney General of India.
D. Chief Justice of India.

180. If it is false that 'Men always pray to God', then which one of the following statements is true?

A. Men seldom pray to God.
B. Men always pray to God.
C. All men pray to God.
D. Some men pray to God.

181. There is some relationship between the figures given in the series. Find out the missing one from the alternatives given below.

A.  B. 

C.  D. 

182. In a bag, there are some diamonds. In another bag, there are one fourth the number more than the number of diamonds in the first bag. If the difference in the number of diamonds in the first and second bag is 3, how many diamonds are there in the first bag?

A. 12 B. 10
C. 8 D. 16

183. Mr. X, the President of a club arrived in a meeting at 10 minutes to 1230 hrs. Mr. X came earlier by 20 minutes than the other participating members in the meeting, who arrived late by 30 minutes. At what time was the meeting scheduled?

A. 1220 hrs B. 1210 hrs
C. 1250 hrs D. 1240 hrs

184. If Oceans are Deserts, then Waves are:

A. Sand Dunes B. Ripples
C. Powerful D. Water

185. Identify the statement which cannot be true.

A. Snow is white.
B. Black body radiation is a physical phenomenon.
C. Every natural number has a successor.
D. All bachelors are faithful to their wives.

186. In certain code MAIL is written as ZNVY then how will FILM be written in that code?

A. MLIF B. NORY
C. XLMP D. SVYZ

187. You are given a 60-inch long ribbon, and you are instructed to cut 601-inch long strips out of this ribbon. The time taken to cut one strip is one second. So how long will it take to cut 60 strips?

A. 1 minute and 1 second
B. 1 minute
C. 59 seconds
D. 30 seconds

188. From among the given options, identify the statement which means the same as the statement 'The dual nature of light is an enigma'.

A. Light has distinct properties which makes it unique.
B. Light is mysterious.
C. Two contradictory descriptions of light presuppose a third description.
D. The nature of light is an enigma.

189. Identify the argument which cannot be accepted.

A. All wives are married. Therefore, all married people are wives.
B. All unmarried women are spinsters. Therefore, all spinsters are women.
C. All equilateral triangles are equiangular. Therefore, all equiangular triangles are equilateral.
D. All rainy days are wet days. Therefore, all wet days are rainy days.

190. Geeta is twice the present age of Seema. If age of Seema is 20 years now, how many years ago Geeta was three times Seema's age?

A. 8 B. 12
C. 9 D. 10

191. This question consists of a related pair of words, followed by four pairs of words. Choose the pair that best represents a similar relationship as the one expressed in the given pair of words:

SANDERLING : BIRD

A. Water : Fish
B. Frog : Toad
C. Cat : Mare
D. Mastiff : Dog

192. An old woman decided to divide her gold among her daughter and daughters-in-law. She first kept exactly half of the gold for her daughter. Then she divided the rest of her gold among her daughters-in-law. The eldest one got 26 grams more than the youngest daughter-in-law. The middle one got twice as the youngest one. If the eldest daughter-in-law got 66 grams of gold, how much was received by the daughter?

A. 172 grams B. 186 grams
C. 194 grams D. 192 grams

193. Assume that both premises, 'No innocent person should be punished' and 'Socrates in innocent' are true. Then which one of the following options is necessarily true?

A. It is not proper to punish Socrates.
B. Socrates should not be punished.
C. Socrates is not punished.
D. Socrates may not be punished.

194. If it is false that 'There is at least one octogenarian in the room', then which one of the following is probable?

A. One person in the room is not an octogenarian.
B. No one in the room is an octogenarian.
C. All those who are in the room are octogenarians.
D. Some people in the room are not octogenarians.

195. A 2100 member team consisting of Team Leaders and Athletes is attending a National Athletic Meet. For every 20 Athletes, there is one Team Leader. How many Team Leaders would be there in the team?

A. 105 B. 110
C. 95 D. 100

196. If it is true that 'All humans are imperfect', then which one of the following is necessarily true?

A. Every human is imperfect.
B. No humans are imperfect.
C. All imperfect beings are humans.
D. Some humans are not imperfect.

197. Identify the statement which cannot be false.

A. All radii of any given circle are of equal length.
B. Water evaporates at 100°C.
C. Democracy is the best form of government.
D. Myopia is a congenital disorder.

198. If it is false that 'Animals are seldom aggressive', then which one of the following statements conveys the same meaning?

A. All animals are always aggressive.
B. All animals are aggressive.
C. Sometimes animals are aggressive.
D. At least one animal is aggressive.

199. Examine the following numbers and identify the next number:

45; 43; 40; 36; 31; 25; ....

A. 17 B. 23
C. 29 D. 18

200. A, B, C and D have got some money with them. If A gives 8 rupees to B, B will have as much as C has and A will have 3 rupees less than what C has. Also if A takes 6 rupees from C, A will have twice as much money as D. If B and D together have 50 rupees, how much money does A and B have respectively?

A. 40, 27 B. 29, 32
C. 32, 29 D. 27, 40

ANSWERS

1	2	3	4	5	6	7	8	9	10
B	B	C	B	A	A	B	C	C	D
11	**12**	**13**	**14**	**15**	**16**	**17**	**18**	**19**	**20**
B	A	A	B	D	D	D	A	D	A
21	**22**	**23**	**24**	**25**	**26**	**27**	**28**	**29**	**30**
C	B	B	B	D	B	C	C	D	A
31	**32**	**33**	**34**	**35**	**36**	**37**	**38**	**39**	**40**
B	D	D	A	D	A	B	D	C	D
41	**42**	**43**	**44**	**45**	**46**	**47**	**48**	**49**	**50**
A	C	A	D	A	B	C	B	D	C

51	52	53	54	55	56	57	58	59	60
D	D	D	A	A	C	B	C	A	A
61	**62**	**63**	**64**	**65**	**66**	**67**	**68**	**69**	**70**
D	A	C	C	A	D	C	B	C	B
71	**72**	**73**	**74**	**75**	**76**	**77**	**78**	**79**	**80**
A	C	A	C	A	D	A	B	B	C
81	**82**	**83**	**84**	**85**	**86**	**87**	**88**	**89**	**90**
B	D	B	A	B	D	D	B	A	C
91	**92**	**93**	**94**	**95**	**96**	**97**	**98**	**99**	**100**
B	B	C	C	A	C	C	A	C	B
101	**102**	**103**	**104**	**105**	**106**	**107**	**108**	**109**	**110**
B	B	A	C	D	B	C	A	B	D
111	**112**	**113**	**114**	**115**	**116**	**117**	**118**	**119**	**120**
C	C	D	B	D	D	A	A	C	D
121	**122**	**123**	**124**	**125**	**126**	**127**	**128**	**129**	**130**
C	C	C	C	A	D	A	C	B	D
131	**132**	**133**	**134**	**135**	**136**	**137**	**138**	**139**	**140**
C	A	B	A	B	C	B	C	A	A
141	**142**	**143**	**144**	**145**	**146**	**147**	**148**	**149**	**150**
B	B	B	A	B	C	A	C	B	B
151	**152**	**153**	**154**	**155**	**156**	**157**	**158**	**159**	**160**
C	B	B	D	C	C	B	C	D	D
161	**162**	**163**	**164**	**165**	**166**	**167**	**168**	**169**	**170**
D	A	D	A	A	C	D	C	A	A
171	**172**	**173**	**174**	**175**	**176**	**177**	**178**	**179**	**180**
A	D	B	D	C	A	B	A	D	A
181	**182**	**183**	**184**	**185**	**186**	**187**	**188**	**189**	**190**
C	A	B	A	D	D	C	D	A	D
191	**192**	**193**	**194**	**195**	**196**	**197**	**198**	**199**	**200**
D	B	B	B	D	A	A	C	D	A

EXPLANATORY ANSWERS

91. Marked price of the T.V. = ₹ 15000

$$\text{Discount} = \frac{15}{100} \times 15000$$

$$= ₹\ 2250$$

$$\text{Selling price} = 15000 - 2250$$

$$= ₹\ 12750$$

$$\text{Further discount} = \frac{12}{100} \times 12750$$

$$= 255 \times 6$$

$$= 1530$$

Hence, the price of the T.V.

$$= ₹\ 12750 - 1530$$

$$= ₹\ 11220$$

92. L.C.M of 45, 75 and 90

3	45, 75, 90
5	15, 25, 30
3	3, 5, 6
	1, 5, 2

L.C.M. = 3 × 5 × 3 × 5 × 2 = 450

450 seconds = 7 minutes and 30 seconds.

Hence, they will change again simultaneously at 7:27:45 hours.

93. Let the distance = x km

According to the question,

$$\frac{x}{35} - \frac{x}{40} = \frac{15}{60}$$

$\Rightarrow \quad \frac{8x-7x}{280} = \frac{1}{4}$

$\Rightarrow \quad \frac{x}{280} = \frac{1}{4}$

$\Rightarrow \quad 4x = 280$

$\Rightarrow \quad x = 70$ km

Hence, the distance travelled by the train is 70 kms.

94. Given time = 4 : 25 am.

$\because$ When the minute-hand is ahead of the hour-hand, the angle between the two hands at M minutes past H hour is given by

$$\text{Angle} = 30\left(\frac{M}{5}-H\right)-\frac{M}{2} \text{ degrees}$$

$$= 30\left(\frac{25}{5}-4\right)-\frac{25}{2}$$

$$= 30\left(\frac{25-20}{5}\right)-\frac{25}{2}$$

$$= 30\times\frac{5}{5}-\frac{25}{2}$$

$$= 30-\frac{25}{2}=\frac{60-25}{2}=\frac{35}{2}$$

$$= 17\frac{1}{2} \text{ degrees.}$$

95. Area of the path $= \pi(R^2 - r^2)$

$= \pi(R + r)(R - r)$

$= \pi(24.5 + 21)(24.5 - 21)$

$= \frac{22}{7}\times 45.5\times 3.5$

$= 22 \times 45.5 \times .5$ m^2

Cost of gravelling the path 1 m^2 = ₹ 4

$\therefore$ Cost of gravelling the path $22 \times 45.5 \times .5$ m^2

$= ₹ \frac{22\times 455\times 5}{10\times 10}\times 4$

$= ₹\ 22 \times 91 = ₹\ 2002$

96. $\because$ The product of polynomial $ax^2 - 6x - 6 = 4$

$\Rightarrow$ Product of roots $= \frac{c}{a}$

$\Rightarrow \quad 4 = -\frac{6}{a}$

$\Rightarrow \quad 4a = -6$

$\Rightarrow \quad a = -\frac{6}{4}=-\frac{3}{2}$

Hence, the value of $a = -\frac{3}{2}$

97. Amount of tin in alloy X $= \frac{2}{5}\times 60 = 24$ kg

Amount of tin in alloy Y $= \frac{1}{5}\times 100 = 20$ kg

Hence the amount of tin in new alloy

$= 24 + 20 = 44$ kg.

98.

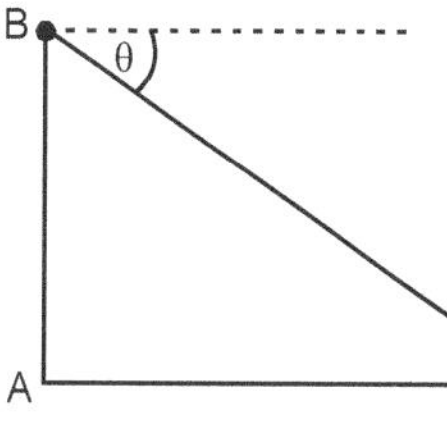

Angle of elevation and depression between the boys when both look at each other will be equal.

99. Let two consecutive even positive integers are x and $(x + 2)$

According to the question,

$x^2 + (x + 2)^2 = 1060$

$\Rightarrow \quad x^2 + x^2 + 4x + 4 = 1060$

$\Rightarrow \quad 2x^2 + 4x - 1056 = 0$

$\Rightarrow \quad x^2 + 2x - 528 = 0$

$\Rightarrow \quad x^2 + 24x - 22x - 528 = 0$

$\Rightarrow \quad x(x + 24) - 22(x + 24) = 0$

$\Rightarrow \quad (x + 24)(x - 22) = 0$

$x = 22$ or -24 which is not possible.

Hence, required numbers are 22 and 24.

100. Dividend on one share

$= 20\times\frac{9}{100} = ₹\frac{9}{5}$

When the dividend ₹ 12 then investment

= ₹ 100

When the dividend ₹ $\frac{9}{5}$ then investment

$= \frac{100}{12}\times\frac{9}{5} = ₹\ 15$

Hence, the market value of each share = ₹ 15

101. Sum of n natural numbers

$= \frac{n(n+1)}{2}$

$= \frac{100(100+1)}{2} = 50 \times 101$

$= 5050$

Hence, the sum of all the natural numbers from 1 to 100 = 5050.

102. The angle subtended by the minor segment of a circle at the centre is less than the angle subtended by the major segment at the centre of the circle.

103. Required probability = $\frac{132}{144} = \frac{11}{12}$

104. 2nd 4th 6th 8th 10th 12th 14th 16th 17th

5 + 5 + 5 + 5 + 5 + 5 + 5 + 5 + 20

= 40 + 20 = 60

Hence, on 17th day he will have ₹ 60 in hand.

105. 30 − 5 = 25

No. of Sundays = 5

No. of visitors on Sundays = 510 × 5

= 2550

No. of visitors on other days = 25 × 240

= 6000

Hence, total no. of visitors in the library in June month = 2550 + 6000 = 8550

∴ Average no. of visitors per day

$$= \frac{8550}{30} = 285$$

106. Volume of cylinder = $\pi r^2 h$

$$= \frac{22}{7} \times \frac{7}{2} \times \frac{7}{2} \times 4 = 154 \text{ cm}^3$$

Required amount of Soup = 154 × 250

= 38500 cm^3

= 38.5 litres.

107. Number of three digit number which are multiples of 9

12, 13, 14, ... 111

nth term = $a + (n - 1)d$

$\Rightarrow$ 111 = 12 + $(n - 1) \times 1$

= 12 + n − 1 = n + 11

$\Rightarrow$ n = 111 − 11 = 100

Hence, the number of three digit numbers which are multiples of 9 are 100.

108. The worth three years ago

$$= \frac{P}{\left(1-\frac{R}{100}\right)^n} = \frac{729}{\left(1-\frac{10}{100}\right)^3}$$

$$= \frac{729}{\left(\frac{9}{10}\right)^3} = 729 \times \frac{10 \times 10 \times 10}{9 \times 9 \times 9}$$

= 1000

Hence, value of the machine 3 years ago was ₹ 1000.

109. Total no. of 72 items = 72 × 63 = 4536

Increased number = (72 + 90) − (27 + 9)

= 162 − 36 = 126

New total no. = 4536 + 126 = 4662

New mean = $\frac{4662}{72} = 64.75$

110. Let fixed charge = ₹ x and cost of food per day = ₹ y

According to the question,

$x + 20y = 1000$ ...(*i*)

$x + 26y = 1180$ ...(*ii*)

Subtracting (*i*) from (*ii*) then we get

$y = 30$ and $x = 400$

Hence, fixed charge = ₹ 400 and cost of food per day = ₹ 30.

Previous Paper (Solved)

Common Law Admission Test (CLAT-UG)

Entrance Exam, 2015

Section-I : English Including Comprehension

Directions (Qs. No. 1 to 3) : *In the question, there are five sentences. Each sentence has pairs of words/phrases that are italicized and highlighted. From the italicized and highlighted word(s)/phrase(s), select the most appropriate word(s)/phrase(s) to form correct sentences. Then, from the options given, choose the best one.*

1. The ***further (A) / farther (B)*** he pushed himself, the more disillusioned he grew.

For the crowd it was more of a ***historical (A) / historic (B)*** event; for their leader it was just another day.

The old has a healthy ***distrust (A) / mistrust (B)*** for all new technology.

The film is based on a ***worthy (A) / true (B)*** story.

She coughed ***discreetly (A) / discretely (B)*** to announce her presence.

A. BABAB B. ABBBA
C. BAABA D. BBAAB

2. ***Regrettably (A) / Regretfully (B)*** I have to decline your invitation. The critics ***censored (A) / censured (B)*** the new movie because of its social unacceptability.

He was ***besides (A) / beside (B)*** himself with range when I told him what I had done.

Anita had a beautiful ***broach (A) / brooch (B)*** on the lapel of her jacket.

He has the same capacity as an adult to ***consent (A) / assent (B)*** to surgical treatment.

A. BABBA B. BBAAB
C. ABBBA D. BABAB

3. The prisoner's ***interment (A) / internment (B)*** came to an end with his early release.

She managed to bite back the ***ironic (A) / caustic (B)*** retort on the tip of her tongue.

Jeans that ***flair (A) / flare (B)*** at the bottom are in fashion these days.

They heard the bells ***peeling (A) / pealing (B)*** far and wide.

The students ***baited (A) / bated (B)*** the instructor with irrelevant questions.

A. BBABB B. ABBBB
C. BABBA D. BBBBA

Directions (Qs. No. 4 to 6) : *Identify the incorrect sentence/ sentences.*

4. (*a*) I want to do an MBA before going into business.
(*b*) Priti's husband has been on active service for three months.
(*c*) The horse suddenly broke into a buckle.
(*d*) I need to file an insurance claim.

A. (*b*) and (*a*) B. (*c*) only
C. (*b*) and (*c*) D. (*b*), (*c*) and (*d*)

5. (*a*) I must run fast to catch up with him
(*b*) The newly released book is enjoying a popular run.
(*c*) The doctor is on a hospital round.
(*d*) You can't run over him like that.

A. (*a*) and (*c*) B. (*d*) only
C. (*a*), (*c*) and (*d*) D. (*a*) only

6. (*a*) The letter was posted to the address.
(*b*) Your stand is beyond all reasons.
(*c*) How do you deal with friend who doesn't listen to a reason?
(*d*) My wife runs profitable business in this suburb.

A. (*a*) only B. (*d*) only
C. (*b*) and (*c*) D. (*c*) and (*d*)

Directions (Qs. No. 7 to 12) : *Fill up the blanks, numbered 7, 8, 9, 10, 11 and 12 in the passage given below with the most appropriate word from the options given for each blank.*

"Between the year 1946 and the year 1995, I did not file any income tax returns." With that **...(7)...** statement, Soubhik embarked on an account of his encounter with the Income Tax Department. "I originally owed ₹ 20,000 in unpaid taxes. With **...(8)...** and **...(9)...**, the 20,000 became 60,000. The Income Tax Department then went into action, and I learned first-hand just how much power the Tax Department wields. Royalties and trust funds can be **...(10)...**; automobiles may be **...(11)...**, and auctioned off. Nothing belongs to the **...(12)...** until the case is settled."

7. A. devious B. blunt
C. tactful D. pretentious

8. A. interest B. taxes
C. principal D. returns

9. A. sanctions B. refunds
C. fees D. fines

10. A. closed B. detached
C. attached D. impounded

11. A. smashed B. seized
C. dismantled D. frozen

12. A. purchaser B. victim
C. investor D. offender

Directions (Qs. No. 13 and 14): *Four alternative summaries are given the text. Choose the option that best captures the essence of the text.*

13. Some decisions will be fairly obvious—"no-brainers". Your bank account is low, but you have a two-week vacation coming up and you want to get away to some place warm to relax with your family. Will you accept your in-laws, offer of free use of their Florida beachfront condo? Sure. You like your employer and feel ready to move forward in your career. Will you step in for your boss for three weeks while she attends a professional development course? Of course.

1. Some decisions are obvious under certain circumstances. You may, for example, readily accept a relative's offer of free holiday accommodation. Or step in for your boss when she is away.
2. Some decisions are no-brainers. You need not think when making them. Examples are condo offers from in-laws and job offers from bosses when your bank account is low or boss is away.
3. Easy decisions are called "no-brainers" because they do not require any cerebral activity. Examples such as accepting free holiday accommodation abound in our lives.
4. Accepting an offer from in-laws when you are short on funds and want a holiday is a no-brainer. Another no-brainer is taking the boss's job when she is away.

A. 1 B. 2
C. 3 D. 4

14. Physically, inertia is a feeling that you just can't move; mentally, it is a sluggish mind. Even if you try to be sensitive, if your mind is sluggish, you just don't feel anything intensely. You may even see a tragedy enacted in front of your eyes and not be able to respond meaningfully. You may see one person exploiting another, one group persecuting another, and not be able to get angry. Your energy is frozen. You are not deliberately refusing to act; you just don't have the capacity.

1. Inertia makes your body and mind sluggish. They become insensitive to tragedies, exploitation, and persecution because it freezes your energy and decapacitates it.
2. When you have inertia you don't act although you see one person exploiting another or one group persecuting another. You don't get angry because you are incapable.
3. Inertia is of two types—physical and mental. Physical inertia restricts bodily movements. Mental inertia prevents response to events enacted in front of your eyes.
4. Physical inertia stops your body from moving; mental inertia freezes your energy and stops your mind from responding meaningfully to events, even tragedies, in front of you.

A. 1 B. 2
C. 3 D. 4

Directions (Qs. No. 15 to 19): *For the word a contextual sentence is given. Pick the word from the alternatives given that is most inappropriate in the given context.*

15. SPECIOUS: A specious argument is not simply a false one but one that has the ring of truth.
A. Deceitful B. Fallacious
C. Credible D. Deceptive

16. OBVIATE: The new mass transit system may obviate the need for the use of personal cars.
A. Prevent B. Forestall
C. Preclude D. Bolster

17. DISUSE: Some words fall into disuse as technology makes objects obsolete.
A. Prevalent B. Discarded
C. Obliterated D. Unfashionable

18. PARSIMONIOUS: The evidence was constructed from every parsimonious scraps of information.
A. Prevalent B. Penurious
C. Thrifty D. Altruistic

19. FACETIOUS: When I suggested that war is a method of controlling population, my father remarked that I was being facetious.
A. Jovian B. Jovial
C. Jocular D. Joking

Directions (Qs. No. 20 and 21) : *Answer the question based on the following information. Indicate which of the statements given with that particular question consistent with the description of unreasonable man in the passage below.*

Unreasonableness is a tendency to do socially permissible things at the wrong time. The unreasonable man is the sort of person who comes to confide in you when you are busy. He serenades his beloved when she is ill. He asks a man who has just lost money by paying a bill for a friend to pay a bill for him. He invites a friend to go for a ride just after the friend has finished a long car trip. He is eager to offer services which are not wanted, but which cannot be politely refused. If he is present at an arbitration, he stirs up dissension between the two parties, who were really anxious to agree. Such is the unreasonable man.

20. The unreasonable man tends to:
A. entertain women
B. be a successful arbitrator when dissenting parties are anxious to agree
C. be helpful when solicited
D. tell a long story to people who have heard it many times before

21. The unreasonable man tends to:
A. bring a higher bidder to a salesman who has just closed a deal
B. disclose confidential information to others
C. sing the praise of the bride when he goes to a wedding
D. sleep late and rise early

Directions (Qs. No. 22 to 24) : *In the following sentence, a part of the sentence is underlined. Beneath each sentence, four different ways of paraphrasing the underlined part are indicated. Choose the best alternative among the four options.*

22. The management can still hire freely <u>but cannot scold freely</u>.
A. cannot scold at will
B. cannot give umbrage
C. cannot take decision to scold
D. cannot scold willfully

23. This government has given subsidies to the Navratnas but there is <u>no telling whether the subsequent one will do</u>.
A. whether the subsequent government will do so
B. if the government to follow will accept the policy
C. if the government to follow will adhere to the policy
D. no telling whether the subsequent one will do so

24. The Romanians may be restive under Soviet direction but <u>they are tied to Moscow by ideological and military links</u>.
A. they are close to Moscow from ideological and military perspective
B. they are preparing for a greater revolution
C. secretly they rather enjoy the prestige of being protected by the mighty soviets
D. there is nothing they can do about it

Directions (Qs. No. 25 to 27): *In the question, a related pair of words or phrases is followed by a pair of words or phrases. Select the pair that best expresses a relationship similar to the one expressed in the original pair.*

25. Dulcet : Raucous
A. Sweet : Song
B. Crazy : Insane
C. Palliative : Exacerbating
D. Theory : Practical

26. Malapropism : Words
A. Anachronism : Time
B. Ellipsis : Sentence
C. Jinjanthropism : Apes
D. Catechism : Religion

27. Peel : Peal
A. Coat : Rind
B. Laugh : Bell
C. Rain : Reign
D. Brain : Cranium

Directions (Questions 28 to 37) : *In view of the passage given below. Choose the best option for question.*

When talks come to how India has done for itself in 50 years of Independence, the world has nothing but praise for our success in remaining a democracy. On other fronts, the applause is less loud. In absolute terms, India has not done too badly, of course, life expectancy has increased. So has literacy. Industry, which was barely a fledging, has grown tremendously. And as far as agriculture is concerned, India has been transformed from a country perpetually on the edge of starvation into a success story held up for others to emulate. But these are competitive times when change is rapid, and to walk slowly when the rest of the world is running is almost as bad as standing still on walking backwards.

Compared with large chunks of what was then the developing world South Korea, Singapore, Malaysia, Thailand, Indonesia, China and what was till lately a separate Hong Kong–India has fared abysmally. It began with a far better infrastructure than most of these countries had. It suffered hardly or not at all during the Second World War. It had advantages like an English speaking elite, quality scientific manpower (including a Nobel laureate and others who could be ranked among the world's best) and excellent business acumen. Yet, today, when countries are ranked according to their global competitiveness, it is tiny Singapore that figures at the top. Hong Kong is an export powerhouse. So is Taiwan. If a symbol were needed of how far we have fallen back, note that while Korean Cielos are sold in India, no one is South Korea is rushing to buy an Indian car. The reasons list themselves. Topmost is economic isolationism.

The government discouraged imports and encouraged self-sufficiency. Whatever the aim was, the result was the creation of a totally inefficient industry that failed to keep pace with global trends and, therefore, became absolutely uncompetitive. Only when the trade gates were opened a little did this become apparent. The years since then have been spent in merely trying to catch up. That the government actually sheltered its industrialists from foreign competition is a little strange. For in all other respects, it operated under the conviction that businessmen were little more than crooks how were to be prevented from entering the most important areas of the economy, how were to be hamstrung in as many ways as possible, how were to be tolerated in the same way as an inexcisable wart. The high expropriatory rates taxation, the licensing laws, the reservation of whole swathes of industry for the public sector, and the granting of monopolies to the public sector firms were the principle manifestations of this attitude. The government forgot that before wealth could be distributed, it had to be created.

The government forgot that itself could not create, but only squander wealth. Some of the manifestations of the old attitude have changed. Tax rates have fallen. Licensing has been all but abolished. And the gates of global trade have been opened wide. But most of these changes were first by circumstances partly by the foreign exchange bankruptcy of 1991 and the recognition that the government could no longer muster the funds of support the public sector, leave alone expand it. Whether the attitude of the government itself, or that of more than handful of ministers, has changed, is open to question. In many other ways, however, the government has not changed one with. Business still has to negotiate a welter of negotiations. Transparency is still a longer way off. And there is no exit policy. In defending the existing policy, politicians betray an inability to see beyond their noses. A no-exit policy for labour is equivalent to a no-entry policy for new business. If one industry is not allowed to retrench labour, other industries will think a hundred times before employing new labour. In other ways too, the government hurts industries.

Public sector monopolies like the department of telecommunications and Videsh Sanchar Nigam Ltd. make it possible for Indian business to operate only at a cost several times that of their counterparts abroad. The infrastructure is in a shambles partly because it is unable to formulate a sufficiently remunerative policy for private business, and partly because it does not have the stomach to change market rates for services. After a burst of activity in the early nineties, the government is dragging its feet. At the rate it is going, it will be another fifty years before the government realizes that a pro-business policy is the best pro-people policy. By then of course, the world would have moved even farther ahead.

28. The writer's attitude towards the Government is........
A. critical B. ironical
C. sarcastic D. derisive

29. The writer is surprised at the Government's attitude towards its industrialists because.....
A. the government did not need to protect its industrialists.
B. the issue of competition was non-existent.
C. the government looked upon its industrialists as crooks.
D. the attitude was a conundrum.

30. The Government was compelled to open the economy due to...........
A. pressure from international market.
B. pressure from domestic market.
C. foreign change bankruptcy and paucity of funds with the government.
D. All of the above

31. The writer ends the passage on a note of.......
A. cautious optimism B. pessimism
C. optimism D. pragmatism

32. According to the writer India should have performed better than the other Asian nations because...........
A. it had adequate infrastructure
B. it had better infrastructure
C. it had better politicians who could take the required decisions
D. All of the above

33. India was in better condition than the other Asian nations because..........
A. it did not face the ravages of the Second World Wat.
B. it had an English speaking populace and good business sense.
C. it had enough wealth through its exports.
D. Both A and B above

34. The major reason for India's poor performance is.............
A. economic isolationism
B. economic mismanagement
C. inefficient industry
D. All of these

35. One of the factors of the government's projectionist policy was..........
A. encouragement of imports
B. discouragement of imports
C. encouragement of exports
D. discouragement of exports

36. The example of the Korean Cielo has been presented to highlight.............
A. India's lack of stature in the international market.
B. India's poor performance in the international market.
C. India's lack of creditability in the international market.
D. India's disrepute in the international market.

37. According to the writer........
A. India's politicians are myopic in their vision of the country's requirements.
B. India's politicians are busy lining their pockets.
C. India's politicians are not conversant with the needs of the present scenario.
D. All of the above

Directions (Qs. No. 38 to 40) : *Choose the option closest in meaning to the Capitalized word.*

38. GRANDIOSE
A. imposing B. unpretentious
C. boring D. lanky

39. SPRY
A. doubtful B. nimble
C. prognosticate D. leave

40. FUDGE
A. to sweeten B. smear
C. irritate D. falsify

Section-II : General Knowledge and Current Affairs

41. Attukal Pongal festival, which is figured in Guinness Book of World Records is celebrated in...........
A. Tamil Nadu B. Kerala
C. Telangana D. Goa

42. In February 2015, which Indian Cricket legend has been inducted into the ICC Hall of Fame?
A. Rahul Dravid
B. Anil Kumble
C. Sachin Tendulkar
D. Mohammad Azharuddin

43. Which of the following Acts formally introduced the principle of elections for the first time?
A. The Indian Councils Act, 1909
B. Government of India Act, 1919
C. The Government of India Act, 1935
D. India's Independence Act, 1947

44. IRCTC has recently launched a new service called 'RuPay prepaid cards' which will enable passengers to book their tickets, do shopping and pay service bills online. This service was launched in collaboration with which bank?
A. Union Bank of India
B. State Bank of India
C. ICICI Bank
D. Bharatiya Mahila Bank

45. Garuda Shakti III is the military exercise between India and which country?
A. Nepal B. Russia
C. Indonesia D. China

46. Match List-I with List-II and select the best option using the code given below the lists:

List-I (Organization/Centers)	***List-II (Locations)***
1. High Altitude Warfare School	(*a*) Chennai
2. Indian Air force Training center	(*b*) Gulmarg
3. National Defense College	(*c*) New Delhi
4. Institute of National Integration	(*d*) Pune

A. 1-(*b*), 2-(*a*), 3-(*c*), 4-(*d*)
B. 1-(*a*), 2-(*b*), 3-(*c*), 4-(*d*)
C. 1-(*a*), 2-(*b*), 3-(*d*), 4-(*c*)
D. 1-(*b*), 2-(*a*), 3-(*d*), 4-(*c*)

47. Name India's Beyond Visual Range (BVR) Air-to-Air missile which was successfully test fired on 19 March 2015 from a Sukhoi-30 fighter aircraft?
A. Astra B. K-100
C. Mitra D. Tejas

48. The ISRO has developed a "Flood Hazard Atlas" by mapping flood prone and vulnerable areas in which state?
A. Kerala B. Maharashtra
C. Assam D. Tripura

49. Which South East Asian country has recently banned surrogacy service to end its flourishing rent-a-womb industry?
A. Singapore B. Laos
C. Thailand D. Vietnam

50. Which of the following is the oldest share market in India?
A. Bombay B. Madras
C. Calcutta D. Delhi

51. The name of new Andhra Pradesh Capital is likely to be.........
A. Amaravathi B. Badrachala
C. Krishna Nagar D. Varshavathi

52. The Ufa city, where annual BRICS summit-2015 is scheduled to be held is in which country?
A. China B. Russia
C. South Africa D. Brazil

53. The "Ease of Doing Business Index" is prepared and published by..........
A. World Trade Organisation
B. World Bank Group
C. United Nations
D. European Union

54. Prime Minister Modi has launched the "Give It Up" campaign for voluntarily giving up.......
A. Use of tobacco products
B. LPG subsidy
C. Use of incandescent bulbs
D. Use of plastics

55. Which one of the following Railway Zones and the corresponding Headquarter pairs is not correctly matched?

A. North Eastern Railway: Gorakhpur
B. South Eastern Railway: Bhubaneswar
C. Eastern Railway: Kolkata
D. South East Central Railway: Bilaspur

56. Which among the following is the world's largest e-commerce company?
A. Amazon B. eBay
C. Alibaba D. Flipkart

57. Which committee was constituted by RBI to review governance of boards of banks in India?
A. P J Nayak Committee
B. H R Khan Committee
C. Harsh Vardhan Committee
D. K Subramanian Committee

58. The recently announced Paramparagat Krishi Vikas Yojana aims to boost....... ?
A. Organic Farming B. Drip Irrigation
C. Horticulture crops D. Vegetable production

59. The winner of 2015 Malaysian Grand Prix is .... ?
A. Sebastian Vettel B. Kimi Raikkonen
C. Lewis Hamilton D. Jenson Button

60. Which one of the following is essentially a solo dance nowadays performed in group as well?
A. Kuchipudi B. Kathak
C. Manipuri D. Mohiniattam

61. Who among the following was the author of Rajtarangini, commonly regarded as the first genuine history of India written by an Indian?
A. Banbhatta B. Ravikirti
C. Pushpananda D. Kalhana

62. Name the golfer who won the Indian Open title on 22 February 2015.
A. SSP Chowrasia B. Anirban Lahiri
C. Siddikur Rahman D. Daniel Chopra

63. Which space agency has successfully launched the world's first all electric satellites in March, 2015?
A. Russia Federal Space Agency
B. China National Space Administration
C. SpaceX
D. European Space Agency

64. Among the following 18th century Indian rulers has been called 'Plato of his tribe'?
A. Sawai Jai Singh B. Badam Singh
C. Suraj Mal D. Guru Gobind Singh

65. Bhalchandra Nemade who has been selected for the 50th Jnanpith Award for 2014, on 6 February 2015, is a famous writer in which language?
A. Marathi B. Odiya
C. Malayalam D. Urdu

66. A Snickometer is associated with which sports?
A. Tennis B. Cricket
C. Hockey D. Football

67. Which of the following is incorrect option?
A. Within the Arctic and Antarctic Circles there is at least one day in the year during which the sun does not set and at least one day on which it never rises.
B. At the North Pole there is darkness for half the year.
C. At the summer solstice, the sun shines vertically over the Tropic of Capricorn.
D. The sun shines vertically over the Equator twice in the year.

68. What is the correct sequence of the following movements in chronological order?
1. Civil Disobedience Movement
2. Khilafat Movement
3. Home Rule Movement
4. Quit India Movement
A. 1, 2, 3, 4 B. 4, 3, 2, 1
C. 3, 2, 1, 4 D. 2, 4, 1, 3

69. Recently, which country became the first member country to the UN Framework Convention on Climate Change (UNFCCC) to submit its action plan on Intended Nationally Determined Contribution (INDC)?
A. India B. Switzerland
C. Australia D. Singapore

70. Lysosomes, which are known as suicide bags, are produced by which organelle?
A. Mitochondria B. Golgi body
C. Ribosome D. Peroxisome

71. Which is the single policy rate to unambiguously signal the stance of monetary policy as recently recommended by RBI?
A. PLR B. Repo
C. Bank D. CLR

72. Which city has become India's first fully WiFi-enabled metro city on 5 February 2015?
A. Mumbai B. Kolkata
C. Chennai D. Delhi

73. Who among the following is India's first chief of Cyber Security?
A. B. J. Srinath
B. Gulshan Rai
C. A. S. Kamble
D. Amardeep S. Chawla

74. Which one of the following is the online grievances monitoring portals launched by union government for Indians living abroad?

A. Madad B. Sankalp
C. Mythri D. Rakshan

75. Which of the following is a Direct Tax?
A. Excise duty B. Sales tax
C. Income tax D. None of the above

76. Indian Space Research Organisation was recently conferred 'Space Pioneer Award' by the National Space Society (NSS) of which country over the historic feat on successfully sending an orbit to Martian atmosphere in its very first attempt?
A. France B. European Union
C. China D. USA

77. Recently in which country did Indian Prime Minister Narendra Modi inaugurate the first of the eight Coastal Surveillance Radar Systems (CSRS) being set up by India?
A. Mauritius B. Maldives
C. Sri Lanka D. Seychelles

78. Greece and Turkey are working to resolve their dispute over sovereignty and related rights in the area of which sea?
A. Black Sea
B. Sea of Marma
C. Aegean Sea
D. Mediterranean Sea

79. Name the Indian industrialist on whose 175th birth anniversary, Union government launched the commemorative stamp on 6 January 2015?
A. G D Birla
B. T V Sundaram Iyengar
C. Kasturbhai Lalbhai
D. Jamsetji Nusserwanji Tata

80. Which one of the following pairs is not correctly matched?
A. Kunal Bahl & Rohit Bansal – Snapdeal
B. Sachin Bansal & Binny Bansal – Red Bus
C. Deepinder Goyal & Pankaj Chaddah – Zomato
D. Bhavish Aggarwal & Ankit Bhati – Ola Cab

81. Which state is to host the 36th National Games in 2016?
A. Karnataka B. Goa
C. Tamil Nadu D. Telangana

82. Project Varsha, India's new naval base under construction is near which of the following cities?
A. Kochi B. Karwar
C. Visakhapatnam D. Chennai

83. Young Indian shuttler K. Srikanth on 15 March 2015 won which of the following major badminton championship?
A. China Grand Prix Gold
B. Australian Grand Prix Gold
C. Swiss Grand Prix Gold
D. Indonesian Grand Prix Gold

84. What is the name given to the dedicated TV channel for farmers that was announced in the Union Budget for 2014-15 and ₹ 100 crore was set aside for its establishment?
A. Kisan
B. Farmers Show
C. Krishi Channel
D. None of the above

85. The "Friends for Life" – an elephant conservation project has been launched by World Wide Fund for Nature India and.......
A. Aditya Birla Group
B. Muthoot Group
C. Manapuram Group
D. Reliance Ltd.

86. The National Industrial Corridor (NIC) that was proposed to be established in the Union Budget of 2014-15, will have its headquarters at which city?
A. Pune B. Bhubaneswar
C. Bangalore D. Hyderabad

87. President Pranab Mukherjee on 6 January 2015 signed the ordinance to amend Citizenship Act, 1955. Which of the statements in this regard is/are right?
I. The ordinance exempts Person of Indian Origin (PIO) from appearing before the local police station on every visit.
II. It replaced the clause that says foreigners marrying Indians must continuously stay in the country for a period of six months before they get an Indian citizenship.
A. I only B. II only
C. Both I and II D. Neither I nor II

88. Name the renowned Indian ecologist who has been chosen for the prestigious 2015 Tyler Prize for Environmental Achievement on 23 March 2015?
A. M S Swaminathan
B. Kasthuri Rangan
C. Jayaram Ramesh
D. Madhav Gadgil

89. How much Foreign Direct Investment (FDI) in country's defence sector was proposed in the Union Budget 2014-15 presented on 10 July 2014?
A. 51% B. 49%
C. 29% D. 10%

90. The protein CA-125 (Cancer Antigen-125) is used as biomarker for detection of which type of cancer?
A. Ovarian cancer B. Bone cancer
C. Lung cancer D. Oral cancer

Section-III : Elementary Mathematics (Numerical Ability)

Directions (Qs. No. 91 to 95) : *Answer the questions based on the information given in the following table. 1, 2, 3, 4, 5 denote companies and 2006, 2007, 2008, 2009 & 2010 denote years.*

Number of Units Manufactured (M) and Number of Units Sold (S) (in hundreds) by five different companies over the years.

	A		B		C		D		E	
	M	S	M	S	M	S	M	S	M	S
2006	2.8	1.3	3.3	2.2	2.6	1.7	3.0	2.2	1.9	1.4
2007	3.2	2.0	2.4	1.6	2.2	1.5	2.5	1.9	2.0	1.7
2008	1.9	0.9	2.9	1.6	2.1	1.0	2.3	1.5	1.6	1.1
2009	1.0	0.4	2.4	1.3	2.8	1.4	2.1	1.2	3.2	2.5
2010	2.5	1.5	2.3	1.2	2.6	2.1	1.8	1.1	3.1	2.6

91. What is the total number of units manufactured by Company C over all the years together?
A. 1420 B. 1030
C. 1230 D. 1320

92. What is the approximate per cent increase in the number of units sold by Company E in the year 2007 from the previous year?
A. 17 B. 36
C. 27 D. 21

93. The number of units sold by Company D in the year 2006 is what per cent of the number of units manufactured by it in that year? (*rounded off to two digits after decimal*)
A. 52.63 B. 61.57
C. 85.15 D. 73.33

94. What is the respective ratio of total number of units manufactured by Company A and B together in the year 2009 to those sold by them in the same year?
A. 2:01 B. 3:02
C. 5:02 D. None of the above

95. What is the average number of units sold by Company D over all the years together?
A. 166 B. 158
C. 136 D. 147

96. What is the value of (x) in the following equation?

$$x^{0.4} / 16 = 32 / x^{2.6}$$

A. 8 B. 9
C. 6 D. 7

97. The simplified value of $[(0.111)^3 + (0.222)^3 - (0.333)^3 + (0.333)^2 \times (0.222)]^3$ is:
A. 0.999 B. 0.111
C. 0 D. 0.888

98. When 2½ is added to a number and the sum is multiplied by 4½ and then 3 is added to the product and then the sum is divided by $1\frac{1}{5}$, the quotient becomes 25. What is that number?
A. 2½ B. 3½
C. 4½ D. 5½

99. If $x = (16^3 + 17^3 + 18^3 + 19^3)$, then x divided by 70 leaves a remainder of....
A. 0 B. 1
C. 69 D. 35

100. A man has 9 friends: 4 boys and 5 girls. In how many ways can he invite them, if there have to be exactly 3 girls in the invitees?
A. 320 B. 160
C. 80 D. 200

101. A group of 630 children is arranged in rows for a group photograph session. Each row contains three fewer children than the row in front of it. What number of rows is not possible?
A. 3 B. 4
C. 5 D. 6

102. A die is rolled twice. What is the probability that the sum of the numbers on the two faces is 5?
A. 3/13 B. 4/13
C. 6/13 D. 1/9

103. Two trains, one from Howrah to Patna and other from Patna to Howrah, start simultaneously. After they meet, the trains reach their destinations after 9 hours and 16 hours respectively. The ratio of their speed is.........
A. 2 : 03 B. 4 : 03
C. 6 : 07 D. 9 : 06

104. A watch which gains uniformly is 2 minutes slow at noon on Monday and is 4 minutes 48 seconds fast at 2 p.m. on the following Monday. When was it correct?
A. 2 p.m. on Tuesday
B. 2 p.m. on Wednesday
C. 3 p.m. on Thursday
D. 1 p.m. on Friday

105. A speaks truth in 75% cases and B in 80% of the cases. In what percentage of cases are they likely to contradict each other, narrating the same incident?
A. 5% B. 15%
C. 35% D. 45%

106. The sum of all the natural numbers from 200 to 600 (both inclusive) which are neither divisible by 8 nor by 12 is:
A. 1, 23, 968 B. 1, 33, 068
C. 1, 33, 268 D. 1, 87, 332

107. In a tournament, there are n teams $T_1, T_2, \dots T_n$, with $n > 5$. Each team consists of k players, $k > 3$. The following pairs of teams have one player in common T_1 and T_2, T_2 and T_3, ..., T_{n-1} and T_n, and T_n and T_1. No other pair of teams has any player in common. How many players are participating in the tournament, considering all the n teams together?

A. $k(n - 1)$
B. $n(k - 2)$
C. $k(n - 2)$
D. $n(k - 1)$

108. If $n^2 = 12345678987654321$, what is n?

A. 12344321
B. 1235789
C. 111111111
D. 11111111

109. Along a road lie an odd number of stones placed at intervals of 10 m. These stones have to be assembled around the middle stone. A person can carry only one stone at a time. A man carried out the job starting with the stone in the middle, carrying stones in succession, thereby covering a distance of 4.8 km. Then, the number of stones is:

A. 35
B. 15
C. 31
D. 29

110. What are the last two digits of 7^{2008}?

A. 01
B. 21
C. 61
D. 71

Section-IV : Legal Aptitude

Directions (Qs. No. 111 to 125) : *The question consist of two statements, one labelled as **PRINCIPLE** and other as **FACT**. You are to examine the principle and apply it to the given facts carefully and select the best option.*

111. PRINCIPLE : Whoever, intending to take dishonestly any movable property out of the possession of any person without that person's consent moves that property, such taking is said to commit theft.

FACTS : RAMU cuts down a tree on RINKU's ground, with the intention of dishonestly taking the tree out of RINKU's possession without RINKU's consent. A could not take the tree away.

A. RAMU can be prosecuted for theft
B. RAMU cannot be prosecuted for theft
C. RAMU can be prosecuted for attempt to theft
D. RAMU has neither committed theft nor attempt to commit theft

112. PRINCIPLE : injuria sine damnum *i.e.* injury without damage.

FACTS : SONU, who was a returning officer at a polling booth, wrongly refused to register a duly tendered vote of MONU, though he was a qualified voter. The candidate, whom MONU sought to vote, was declared elected.

A. MONU can sue SONU on the ground that he was denied to cast vote, which is a fundamental right.
B. MONU can sue SONU on the ground that he was denied to cast vote, which is a legal right.
C. MONU cannot sue SONU because there is no injury or damage cause to MONU.
D. MONU cannot sue SONU because to whom he sought to vote was declared elected.

113. PRINCIPLE : A person is said to be of sound mind for the purpose of making a contract if, at the time when he makes it. He capable of understanding it and of forming a rational judgment as to its effect upon his interests.

FACTS : Mr. X who is usually of sound mind, but occasionally of unsound mind enters into a contract with Mr. Y when he is of unsound mind. Y came to know about this fact afterwards and now wants to file a suit against Mr. X.

A. Mr. X cannot enter into contract because he is of unsound mind when he entered into contract.
B. Mr. X can enter into contract but the burden is on the other party to prove that he was of unsound mind at the time of contract.
C. Mr. X can enter into a contract but the burden is on Mr. X to prove that he was of unsound mind at the time of contract.
D. None of the above.

114. PRINCIPLE : When one person signifies to another his willingness to do or abstain from doing anything, with a view to obtaining the assent of that other to such act or abstinence, he is said to make a proposal.

FACTS : "Ramanuj telegrammed to the Shyamsunder, writing: "will you sell me your Rolls Royce CAR? Telegram the lowest cash price." Shyamsunder replied, too by telegram: 'Lowest price for CAR is ₹ 20 lacs.' Ramanuj immediately sends his consent through telegram stating: 'I agree to buy the CAR for ₹ 20 lacs asked by you.' Now Shyamsunder refused to sell the CAR.

A. He cannot refuse to sell the CAR because the contract has already been made.
B. He can refuse to sell the CAR because it was only invitation to offer and not the real offer.
C. It was not a valid offer because willingness to enter into a contract was absent.
D. None of the above.

115. PRINCIPLE : A master is liable for the acts committed by his servant in the course of employment.

FACTS : Sanjay is a driver working in Brookebond and Co. One day, the Manager asked him to drop a customer at the airport and get back at the earliest. On his way back from the airport, he happened to see his fiance Ruhina waiting for a bus to go home. He offered to drop her at home, which happened to be close to his office. She got into the car and soon thereafter; the car somersaulted due to the negligence of Sanjay. Ruhina was thrown out of the car and suffered multiple injuries. She seeks compensation from Brookebond and Co.

A. Brookebond and Co., shall be liable, because Sanjay was in the course of employment at the time of accident.
B. Brookebond and Co., shall not be liable, Sanjay was not in the course of employment when he took Ruhina inside the car.
C. Ruhina got into the car at her own risk, and therefore, she cannot sue anybody.
D. None of the above

116. PRINCIPLE : Nuisance as a tort (civil wrong) means an unlawful interference with a person's use or enjoyment of land, or some right over, or in connection with it.

FACTS : During the scarcity of onions, long queues were made outside the defendant's shop who having a license to sell fruits and vegetables used to sell only 1 Kg. of onion per ration card. The queues extended on to the highway and also caused some obstruction to the neighbouring shops. The neighbouring shopkeepers brought an action for nuisance against the defendant.

A. The defendant is liable for nuisance
B. The defendant was not liable for nuisance
C. The defendant was liable under the principle of strict liability
D. The plaintiff's suit should be decreed in his favour

117. PRINCIPLE : Nothing is an offence which is done by a person who, at the time of doing it, by reason of unsoundness of mind, is incapable of knowing the nature of the act, or that he is doing what is either wrong or contrary to law.

FACTS : A takes his son B who is three years old, for a bath to the well. He throws his son inside the well so that he could have a good bath. After 10 minutes he also jumped in the well to take a bath and take his son out of the well. Both were rescued by the villagers but his son was found dead.

A. A has committed culpable homicide not amounting to murder
B. A has committed murder
C. A has done no offence as he can plead the defence of unsoundness of mind
D. A's family should be responsible for this incident to let him take child to the well

118. PRINCIPLE : *Ignorantia juris non excusat and ingnorantia facit excusat.*

FACTS : George was a passenger from Zurich to Manila in a Swiss Plane. When the plane landed at the airport at Bombay on 28th Nov. 1962 it was found on search that George carried 34 kgs of gold bars in person and that he had not declared it in the 'Manifest for transit'. On 26th Nov. 1962 Government of India issued a notification and modified its earlier exemption and now it is necessary that, the gold must be declared in the "Manifest" of the aircraft.

A. George cannot be prosecuted because he had actually no knowledge about the new notification issued only two days ago.
B. George cannot be prosecuted because it is mistake of fact which is excusable.
C. George's will be prosecuted because mistake of law is not excusable.
D. George liability would depend on the discretion of the court.

119. PRINCIPLE : Everybody is under a legal obligation to take reasonable care to avoid an act or omission which he can foresee would injure his neighbour. The neighbour for this purpose, is any person whom he should have in his mind as likely to be affected by his act.

FACTS : Krishna, while driving a car at high speed in a crowded road, knocked down a cyclist. The cyclist died on the spot with a lot of blood spilling around, Lakshmi, a pregnant woman passing by, suffered from a nervous shock, leading to abortion. Lakshmi filed a suit against Krishna claiming damages.

A. Krishna will be liable, because he owed a duty of reasonable care to everybody on the road including Lakshmi
B. Krishna will not be liable, because he could not have foreseen Lakshmi suffering from nervous shock as a result of his act
C. Krishna will be liable to Lakshmi because he failed to drive carefully
D. None of the above

120. PRINCIPLE : Preparation is not an offence except the preparation of some special offences.

FACTS : Ramesh keeps poisoned halua in his house, wishing to kill Binoy whom he invited to a party and to whom he wishes to give it. Unknown to Ramesh, his only son takes the halua and dies. In this case.

A. Ramesh is liable for the murder.
B. He is not liable for murder since it is a preparation alone.
C. He is liable for culpable homicide.
D. None of the above

121. PRINCIPLE : Agreements, the meaning of which is not certain, or capable of being made certain, are void.

FACTS : A horse was bought for a certain price coupled with a promise to give ₹ 500 more if the horse proved lucky.

A. This is a valid agreement.
B. This agreement is void for uncertainty because it is very difficult to determine what luck, bad or good, the horse had brought to the buyer.
C. The agreement is partially valid and partially void.
D. None of the above.

122. PRINCIPLE : Mere silence as to facts likely to affect the willingness of a person to enter into a contract is not fraud, unless the circumstances of the case are such that, regard being had to them, it is the duty of the person keeping silence to speak, or unless his silence is, in itself, equivalent to speech.

FACTS : A sells, by auction, to B, a horse which A knows to be unsound. A says nothing to B about the horse's unsoundness.

A. A can be held liable for fraud
B. A can be held liable for misrepresentation
C. A cannot be held liable, because he did not say anything positive about the soundness of horse
D. A cannot be held liable because it is the buyer who must be aware of the things

123. PRINCIPLE : Any direct physical interference with the goods in somebody's possession without lawful justification is called trespass to goods.

FACTS : A purchased a car from a person who had no title to it and had sent it to a garage for repair. X, believing, wrongly, that the car was his, removed if from the garage.

A. X can be held responsible for trespass to goods
B. X cannot be held responsible for trespass to good as he was under a wrong belief
C. X has not committed any wrong
D. None of the above

124. PRINCIPLE : "Nobody shall unlawfully interfere with a person's use or enjoyment of land, or some right over, or in connection with it. The use or enjoyment, envisaged herein, should be normal and reasonable taking into account surrounding situation."

FACTS : Jeevan and Pavan were neighbours in a residential locality. Pavan started a typing class in a part of his house and his typing sound disturbed Jeevan who could not put up with any kind of continuous noise. He filed a suit against Pavan.

A. Pavan is liable, because he should not have started typing class in his house
B. Pavan is liable, because as a neighbour, he should have realised Jeevan's delicate nature
C. Pavan is not liable, because typing sound did not disturb anyone else other than Jeevan
D. None of the above

125. PRINCIPLE : Doctrine of Double Jeopardy: No person shall be prosecuted and punished for the same offence twice.

FACTS : Maqbool brought some gold into India without making any declaration to Custom department on the airport. The custom authorities confiscated the gold under the Sea Customs Act. Maqbool was later charged for having committed an offence under Foreign Exchange Regulation Act.

A. He cannot be prosecuted because it would amount to double jeopardy.
B. He can be prosecuted because confiscation of good by custom authorities does not amount to prosecution by Court.
C. Maqbool ought to have known that he can be stopped by the custom authorities.
D. None of the above.

Directions (Qs. No. 126 to 135) : *The question consist of two statements, one labelled as **Assertion (A)** and other as **Reason (R)**. You are to examine the two statements carefully and select the best option.*

126. Assertion: Custom per se is law, independent of prior recognition by the sovereign or the judge.

Reason: Custom is source of law but by itself is not law.

A. Both A and R are individually true and R is correct explanation to A
B. Both A and R are individually true but R is not correct explanation of A
C. A is true but R is false
D. A is false but R is true

127. Assertion: Idol is a person who can hold property.

Reason: Only human being can be called person not the lifeless things.

A. Both A and R are individually true and R is correct explanation to A
B. Both A and R are individually true but R is not correct explanation of A
C. A is true but R is false
D. A is false but R is true

128. Assertion: Laws are means of achieving an end namely social control.

Reason: The ultimate end of law is to secure greatest happiness to greatest number.

A. Both A and R are individually true and R is correct explanation to A
B. Both A and R are individually true but R is not correct explanation of A

C. A is true but R is false
D. A is false but R is true

129. Assertion: Every person should have the freedom of speech and expression.

Reason: If a person is stopped from speaking then mankind will lose the truth.
A. Both A and R are individually true and R is correct explanation to A
B. Both A and R are individually true but R is not correct explanation of A
C. A is true but R is false
D. A is false but R is true

130. Assertion: Attempt to commit an offence though does not result in any harm, should also be punished.

Reason: A person who tries to cause a prohibited harm and fails, is, in terms of moral culpability, not materially different from the person who tries and succeeds.
A. Both A and R are individually true and R is correct explanation to A
B. Both A and R are individually true but R is not correct explanation of A
C. A is true but R is false
D. A is false but R is true

131. Assertion: In India, every state has a High Court in its territory.

Reason: The Constitution of India provides for a High Court in each state.
A. Both A and R are individually true and R is correct explanation to A
B. Both A and R are individually true but R is not correct explanation of A
C. A is true but R is false
D. A is false but R is true

132. Assertion: The Council of Ministers at the centre is collectively responsible both to the Lok Sabha and Rajya Sabha.

Reason: The members of both Lok Sabha and Rajya Sabha are eligible to be ministers of the Union Government.
A. Both A and R are individually true and R is correct explanation to A
B. Both A and R are individually true but R is not correct explanation of A
C. A is true but R is false
D. A is false but R is true

133. Assertion: The reservation of thirty-three per cent of seats for women in Parliament and State Legislature does not require Constitutional Amendment.

Reason: Political parties contesting elections can allocate thirty-three per cent of seats they contest to women candidates without any Constitutional Amendment.
A. Both A and R are individually true and R is correct explanation to A
B. Both A and R are individually true but R is not correct explanation of A
C. A is true but R is false
D. A is false but R is true

134. Assertion: We, the people of India, having solemnly resolved to constitute India into a Democratic Republic.

Reason: A republic will ensure we have a head of state that is democratically elected and accountable to voters. As a result the head of state will be a more effective constitutional safeguard.
A. Both A and R are individually true and R is correct explanation to A
B. Both A and R are individually true but R is not correct explanation of A
C. A is true but R is false
D. A is false but R is true

135. Assertion: Republic Day is celebrated on 26th January every year in the country.

Reason: The Constitution of India came into force on 26th January 1950.
A. Both A and R are individually true and R is correct explanation to A
B. Both A and R are individually true but R is not correct explanation of A
C. A is true but R is false
D. A is false but R is true

Directions (Qs. No. 136 to 138) : *Read the definition and elements of the attempt, apply them on the given fact situations and answer the question:*

Definition of Attempt: Lord Blackburn has said that "*there is no doubt that there is difference between a preparation antecedent to an attempt and the actual attempt, but if the actual transaction has commenced which would have ended in the crime if not interrupted, there is clearly an attempt to commit the crime.*"

1. Fault element: Intention or knowledge requisite for committing an offence; and
2. Conduct Element: does any act towards its commission and has crossed the stage of preparation. This act is so closely connected with, and proximate to the commission that it fails in object because of facts not known to him or because of circumstances beyond his control.

136. 'RANI' ran to a well stating that she would jump into it, and she started running towards the well but she was caught before she could reach it.

A. She is not guilty of attempt to commit suicide because she might have changed her mind before jumping into the well
B. She is guilty of attempt to commit suicide
C. Right to life includes rights right to die hence a person should not be held responsible for attempt commit suicide
D. None of the above

137. 'SINY' with an intention to pick-pocket puts his hand into MINU's pocket. MINU had a loaded pistol in his pocket. The thief touches the pistol and trigger goes on, whereby MINU is shot dead.
A. SINY will be liable only for attempting to pick-pocket and not for killing because she cannot be treated differently from all other pick-pockets who steal under exactly similar circumstances and same intention, with no risk of causing death and with no greater care to avoid it.
B. SINY will be liable for attempting to murder
C. SINY will be liable for culpable homicide not amounting to murder as his intention was definitely not to kill
D. None of the above

138. 'JAM' denied food to his wife JANE for several days by keeping her confined in a room with an intention to accelerate her death. JANE ultimately managed to escape.
A. JAM is guilty for attempt to murder his wife.
B. JAM is not guilty for attempt to murder his wife and he was only doing preparation
C. JAM is not guilty for attempt to murder his wife as she always had option to escape
D. None of the above

Directions (Qs. No. 139 to 142) : *Fill in the blanks: Choose the pair of words which complete the sentence to make logical sense.*

139. The NDA led Government notified the .... and the National Judicial Appointments Commission Act, thus ending the over two-decade-old .... of appointing judges of Supreme Court and high courts. Under the new law, a six-member panel headed by .... will select judges of the apex court and state high courts.
A. 99th Constitutional (Amendment) Act 2015, collegium system, the Chief Justice of India
B. 121st Constitutional (Amendment) Act 2015, collegium system, the Union Law Minister
C. 121st Constitutional (Amendment) Act 2015, collegium system, the Prime Minister
D. 99th Constitutional (Amendment) Act 2015, cabinet system, the Prime Minister

140. The .... Legislative Assembly on 31st March 2015 passed a controversial Anti-Terrorism Law. Earlier, the passed bill was rejected two times by the then .... in 2004 and 2008.
A. Bihar, Presidents
B. Madhya Pradesh, Governors
C. Gujarat, Presidents
D. Maharashtra, Governors

141. The Union Government on the recommendation of the .... under the chairmanship of .... has decided to decriminalize Section .... of the Indian Penal Code.
A. 20th Law Commission, Justice A.P. Shah & 309
B. 20th Law Commission, Justice M.P. Shah & 307
C. Supreme Court, Justice H.L. Dattu & Section 309
D. Planning Commission, Law Minister, section 309

142. A bench headed by .... quashed allocation of 214 .... as ....
A. Justice H.L. Dattu, coal blocks, illegal and arbitrary
B. Justice R.M. Lodha, coal blocks, illegal and arbitrary
C. Justice T.S. Thakur, licenses, illegal and arbitrary
D. None of the above

143. Choose the best option for the following statement:

No one can be compelled to sing the National Anthem since:
1. It will be violative of the right to freedom of speech and expression.
2. It will be violative of the right to freedom of conscience and practice & propagation of religion.
3. There is no legal provision obliging anyone to sing the National Anthem.

A. 1 and 2 are correct B. 2 and 3 are correct
C. 1, 2 and 3 are correct D. None is correct

144. Five years' experience is a must to be able to practice as an advocate in the Supreme Court of India. This rule was prescribed by the ....
A. Bar Council of India
B. Supreme Court of India
C. High Court of Delhi
D. Ministry of Law and Justice, Government of India

145. Union Government recently approved 33 per cent Reservation for Women in:
A. Horizontally and each category (OBC, SC, ST, and others) in direct recruitment in all non-gazetted Police Posts in all Union Territories including Delhi.
B. Horizontally and each category (OBC, SC, ST, and others) in direct recruitment in all gazetted Police Posts in all Union Territories including Delhi.
C. Horizontally and each category (OBC, SC, ST, and others) in direct recruitment in all gazetted and non-gazetted Police Posts in all Union Territories including Delhi.
D. Horizontally and each category (OBC, SC, ST, and others) in direct recruitment in all gazetted and non-gazetted Posts in all Union Territories including Delhi.

146. As per Indian Protocol, who among the followings ranks highest in the order of precedence?
A. Deputy Prime Minister
B. Former President
C. Governor of a State within his State
D. Speaker of Lok Sabha

147. Consider the following statements and choose the best option:
1. The Chairman of the National Legal Services Authority (NALSA) is the Chief Justice of India.
2. Chief Justice Mr. Justice H.L. Dattu is the present Chairman of NALSA.
3. The Chairman of the National Legal Services Authority (NALSA) is the senior most judge (after CJI) of the Supreme Court of India.
4. Hon'ble Mr. Justice T.S. Thakur is the present Chairman of NALSA.

A. 1 and 2 are correct B. 2 and 3 are correct
C. 3 and 4 are correct D. None is correct

148. India and Britain recently signed an "extradition treaty". Extradition means:
A. Exports without double taxation
B. Order of Indian courts will apply to Indians living in the U.K.
C. India and the U.K. will deport criminals on reciprocal basis to each other
D. None of the above

149. What is a 'moot'?
A. A basic point of law
B. A basic fact of case
C. Mock court for practice by students in general
D. Another name for magistrate's court

150. The temporary release of a convicted prisoner from jail for a fixed period is called:
A. Bail B. Parole
C. Acquittal D. Discharge

151. The Railway authorities allowed a train to be over-crowded. In consequence, a legitimate passenger, Mr. X got his pocket picked. Choose appropriate answer:
A. Mr. X can sue the railway authorities for the loss suffered
B. Mr. X cannot sue because he had given his consent to travel in a over-crowded train
C. Mr. X cannot sue the railway authorities because there was no infringement of legal right and mere fact that the loss was caused does not give rise to a cause of action
D. None of the above

152. Choose the best option for the following statement:
The distinction between fraud and misrepresentation:
1. Fraud is more or less intentional wrong, whereas misrepresentation may be quite innocent.
2. In addition to rendering the contract voidable, is a cause of action in tort for damages. Simple misrepresentation is not a tort but a person who rightfully rescinds a contract is entitled to compensation for any damages which he has sustained through the non-fulfilment of the contract.
3. A person complaining of misrepresentation can be met with the defence that he had "the means of discovering the truth with ordinary diligence". But excepting fraud by silence in other cases of fraud it is no defence that "the plaintiff had the means of discovering the truth by ordinary diligence".
4. None of the above.

A. 1 is correct B. 1 and 2 are correct
C. 1, 2 and 3 are correct D. Only 4 is correct

153. In a recent case a Supreme Court bench comprising of Justice Dipak Misra and Justice Prafulla C Pant held that the amount of maintenance to be awarded under Section 125 of CrPC cannot be restricted for the iddat period (three months) only as the inherent and fundamental principle behind Section 125. Also, it said that an order under Section 125 CrPC can be passed if a person, despite having sufficient means, neglects or refuses to maintain the wife.
A. Shamima Farooqui *vs.* Shahid Khan
B. Mohd. Ahmad Khan *vs.* Shah Bano Begum
C. Hamida Bano *vs.* Abdul Rasheed
D. Abdul Kadir *vs.* Salima

154. Select the correct statements on Social Justice Bench constituted on social issue
1. Constituted by Supreme Court on 3 December 2014
2. Started operation on 12 December 2014
3. The brainchild of Chief Justice of India H.L. Dattu
4. Two-judge bench to be headed by Justice Madan B Lokur
5. The other member is Justice U U Lalit

A. 1, 2 and 5 are correct
B. 1, 2 and 3 are correct
C. 1, 3 and 4 are correct
D. All are correct

155. Select the correct statements about 14th Finance Commission which submitted its report to President
1. It covers the period between 1 April 2015 and 31 March 2020.
2. The Commission headed by former RBI Governor Y V Reddy.
3. Provides for devolution of tax receipts from the Centre to the States.
4. Article 280 of Constitution provides for appointment of Finance Commission
5. 1st and 13th Finance Commission was headed by K C Neogy and Dr Vijay Kelkar respectively.

A. 1, 3 and 5 are correct
B. 1, 2 and 3 are correct
C. 1, 3 and 4 are correct
D. All are correct

156. Who administers oath of office to the Governor of a State?
A. President of India
B. Chief Justice of High Court of the respective state
C. Chief Justice of India
D. Speaker of State Assembly

157. Governor of a State can make Laws during recess of State Legislative Assembly through ....
A. Act B. Bills
C. Notification D. Ordinance

158. Who called Indian Constitution as Quasi-Federal?
A. Austin B. K. C. Wheare
C. H. M. Servai D. Jennings

159. President of India exercises his powers..........
A. Either directly or through officers subordinate to him
B. Through ministers
C. Through Prime Minister
D. Through Cabinet

160. Vote on accounts is meant for ....
A. Vote on the report of CAG
B. To meet unforseen expenditure
C. Appropriating funds pending passing of budget
D. Budget

Section-V : Logical Reasoning

Directions (Qs. No. 161 to 168) : *W, X, Y, and Z are four friends, who do not mind exchanging items. X has two chessboards each costing ₹500, and a record player. Z originally had a cycle and a walkman. Each cricket bat costs ₹700. Both W and Z got a cricket bat from Y. X gave his record player costing ₹2000 to Y. Z get a camera costing ₹1500 from W. The cycle of Z costs ₹1000 and the walkman is for ₹700. Y had three cricket bats at the beginning and W had two cameras the total cost of which is ₹5000. X gave one of his chessboards to Z and took Z's cycle. Z gave his walkman to W.*

161. Total cost of materials Z had at the beginning was:
A. ₹ 1500 B. ₹ 1700
C. ₹ 1000 D. ₹ 2000

162. At the beginning who had the costliest items:
A. W. B. X
C. Y D. Z

163. Who did not have a cricket bat after the exchange of items was over?
A. W B. X
C. Y D. Z

164. Who became the gainer by highest amount through exchange?
A. W B. X
C. Y D. Z

165. The person incurring the highest amount of financial loss through exchange lost an amount of
A. ₹ 600 B. ₹ 1000
C. None D. ₹ 500

166. The amount of price of all the things remaining with the four persons lie between:
A. ₹ 800 – ₹ 900
B. ₹ 10000 – ₹ 12000
C. ₹ 9000 – ₹ 10000
D. ₹ 10000 – ₹ 11000

167. Even after exchanges, an item of highest value remained in possession of:
A. W B. X
C. Y D. Z

168. Among the things exchanged, which one faced the highest exchange value in percentage term.
A. Cricket Bat B. Record Player
C. Camera D. Cycle

Directions (Qs. No. 169 to 173) : *Read the following information and choose the best option.*

Recently, the answers of a test held nationwide were leaked to a group of unscrupulous people. The investigative agency has arrested the mastermind and nine other people A, B, C, D, E, F, G, H and I in this matter. Interrogating them, the following facts have been obtained regarding their operation. Initially, the mastermind obtains the correct answer-key. All the others create their answer-key from one or two people who already possess the same. These people are called his/her "sources". If the person has two sources, then he/she compares the answer-keys obtained for both sources. If the key to a question from both sources is identical, it is copied, otherwise it is left blank. If the person has only one source, he/she copies the source's answer into his/her copy. Finally, each person compulsorily replaces one of the answers (not a blank one) with a wrong answer in his/her answer key.

The paper contained 200 questions; so the investigative agency has ruled out the possibility of two or more of them introducing wrong answers to the same question. The investigative agency has a copy of the correct answer key and has tabulated the following data. This data represents question numbers.

Name	Wrong Answer(s)	Blank Answer(s)
A	46	...
B	96	46, 90, 25
C	27, 56	17, 46, 90
D	17	...
E	46, 90	...
F	14, 46	92, 90
G	25	...
H	46, 92	...
I	27	17, 26, 90

169. Which one of the following must have two sources?
A. A B. B
C. C D. D

170. How many people (excluding the mastermind) needed to make answer keys before C could make his answer key?
A. 2 B. 3
C. 4 D. 5

171. Both G and H were sources to...
A. F B. B
C. A D. None of the above

172. Which of the following statement is true?
A. introduced the wrong answer to question 27
B. E introduced the wrong answer to question 46
C. F introduced the wrong answer to question 14
D. H introduced the wrong answer to question 46

173. Which of the following two groups of people has identical sources?
(*i*) A, D and G
(*ii*) E and H
A. Only (*i*) B. Only (*ii*)
C. Neither (*i*) nor (*ii*) D. Both (*i*) and (*ii*)

Directions (Questions 174 to 178) : *In the following questions, a group of numerals is given followed by four groups of symbol/letter combinations lettered (A), (B), (C) and (D). Numerals are to be coded as per the codes and conditions. You have to find out which of the combinations (A), (B), (C) and (D) is correct and indicate your answer accordingly.*

Numerals:	3	5	7	4	2	6	8	1	0	9
Letter/symbol code:	*	B	E	A	@	F	K	%	R	M

Following conditions apply:
1. If the first digit as well as the last digit is odd, both are to be coded as 'X'.
2. If the first digit as well as the last digit is even, both are to be coded as '$'.
3. If the last digit is 'O', it is to be coded as #.

174. Find out the combination for : 487692
A. $KEFM@ B. AKEFM@
C. AKFEM@ D. $KEFM$

175. Find out the combination for : 713540
A. X%*BA# B. E%*BA#
C. E%*BAR D. None of the above

176. Find out the combination for : 765082
A. EFB#K@ B. XFBRK@
C. EFBRK@ D. None of the above

177. Find out the combination for : 364819
A. *FAK%X B. XFAK&M
C. *FAK%M D. None of the above

178. Find out the combination for : 546839
A. XAFK*X B. XAFK*M
C. BAFK*X D. None of the above

Directions (Questions 179 to 181) : *From the alternatives given below. Choose the best option that correctly classifies the four sentences as a:*

F: Fact: If it relates to a known matter of direct observation, or an existing reality or something known to be true.

J: Judgement: If it is an opinion or estimate or anticipation of common sense or intention.

I: Inference: If it is a logical conclusion or deduction about something based on the knowledge of facts.

179. 1. Everyday social life is impossible without interpersonal relationships.
2. The root of many misunderstandings has been cited in poor relations among individuals.
3. Assuming the above to be true, social life will be much better if people understand the importance of good interpersonal relations.
4. A study reveals that interpersonal relations and hence life in general can be improved with a little effort on the part of individuals.
A. FJIJ B. JFIF
C. FIFJ D. IFFJ

180. 1. The Cabinet minister definitely took the wrong step in giving the government contract.
2. Under the circumstances, he had many other alternatives.
3. The Prime Minister is embarrassed due to the minister's decision.
4. If he has put the government in jeopardy, the minister must resign.
A. JFFI B. IFJI
C. FFJI D. IFIJ

181. 1. If democracy is to survive, the people must develop a sense of consumerism.
2. Consumerism has helped improve the quality of goods in certain countries.
3. The protected environment in our country is helping the local manufacturers.

4. The quality of goods suffers if the manufacturers take undue advantage of this.

A. IJFJ B. JFJI
C. IJJF D. IFJJ

Directions (Questions 182 to 184) : *Questions consist of five statements followed by options consisting of three statements put together in a specific order. Choose the best option which indicates a valid argument, that is, where the third statement is a conclusion drawn from the preceding two statements.*

182. A. Traffic congestion increases carbon monoxide in the environment.

B. Increase in carbon monoxide is hazardous to wealth.

C. Traffic congestion is hazardous to health.

D. Some traffic congestion does not cause increase carbon monoxide.

E. Some traffic congestion is not hazardous to health.

A. CBA B. BDE
C. CDE D. BAC

183. A. MBAs are in great demand.

B. Samrat and Akshita are in great demand.

C. Samrat is in great demand.

D. Akshita is in great demand.

E. Samrat and Akshita are MBAs.

A. ABE B. ECD
C. AEB D. EBA

184. A. All software companies employ knowledge workers.

B. Infotech employees are knowledge workers.

C. Infotech is a software company.

D. Some software companies employ knowledge workers.

E. Infotech employs only knowledge workers.

A. ABC B. ACB
C. CDB D. ACE

Directions (Questions 185 and 186) : *Read the following information carefully to choose best option for the question:*

A. 'L % M' means that M is brother of L.

B. 'L × M' means that L is mother of M.

C. 'L ÷ M' means that L is the sister of M.

D. 'L = M' means that M is father of L.

185. Which of the following means "I is the nephew of Q?"

1. Q % J = I
2. Q ÷ M × B % I
3. C ÷ I = B % Q

A. Only 3 B. Only 1
C. Only 2 D. None of the above

186. If 'A $ B' means that A is the father of B, 'A * B' means that A is the mother of B, 'A @ B' means that A is the wife of B, then which of the following means that M is the grand-mother of N?

A. M * R $ T @ N B. M * R @ T @ N
C. M @ T $ N @ R D. M * T $ N @ R

Directions (Questions 187 to 189) : *The questions contain two statements numbered I and II.*

You have to decide whether the information provided in the statements are sufficient to answer the question. Read both the statements and give your answer as:

Answer (1) If the information in the statement I alone are sufficient to answer the questions.

Answer (2) If the information in the statement II alone are sufficient to answer the questions.

Answer (3) If the information either in the statement I alone or in statement II alone are sufficient to answer the questions.

Answer (4) If the information even in both statement I and II together are not sufficient to answer the questions.

187. Can a democratic system operate without an effective opposition?

I. The opposition is indispensable.

II. A good politician always learns more from his opponents than from his fervent supporters.

A. Answer (1) B. Answer (2)
C. Answer (3) D. Answer (4)

188. Do habits make men's life rigid?

I. It is out of habit that people envy others.

II. Men become slave of habits.

A. Answer (1) B. Answer (2)
C. Answer (3) D. Answer (4)

189. Does intelligence predict the child's ability to learn?

I. Intelligence is unaffected by bad teaching or dull home environment.

II. Children from poor home backgrounds do not do well in their school-work.

A. Answer (1) B. Answer (2)
C. Answer (3) D. Answer (4)

Directions (Questions 190 to 192) : *In the following questions some capital alphabets are written in a row, below them their coding has been given. In the questions, a particular word has been coded in a particular manner using codes as given below the capital letters.*

You have to understand the pattern of coding and have to answer the question asked subsequently.

A	B	C	D	E	F	G	H	I	J	K	L	M	N	O	P	Q	R	S	T	U	V	W	X	Y	Z
U	a	2	v	b	w	3	t	4	x	s	y	5	z	6	c	d	8	7	e	r	h	9	1	p	q

190. If DASH is 2a84, then SMASH is?

A. 7 5 U 7 t B. e y a 8 4
C. 8 z q e 3 D. 8 z q e 4

191. If FASHION is z64t7w, then POSITION is?

A. z 6 4 e 4 7 6 c B. z 6 4 e 4 7 c 6
C. c 6 7 4 e 4 6 z D. c 6 7 4 e 4 z 6

192. If LONDON is 5c62z5, then EURPOE is?

A. w h 7 c d w B. w h 7 z 6 v

C. b r 7 6 c b D. w h 7 6 c b

Directions (Questions 193 and 194) : *In questions contain two statements and two conclusions numbered I and II. You have to take the two given statements to be true even if they seem to be at variance from commonly known facts and decide which of the given conclusion(s) logically follow(s) from the two given statements.*

Answer (1) If only conclusion I follows.

Answer (2) If only conclusion II follows.

Answer (3) If neither I nor II follows.

Answer (4) If both I and II follow.

193. Statements:

I. Some players are singers.

II. All singers are tall.

Conclusions:

I. Some players are tall.

II. All players are tall.

A. Answer (1) B. Answer (2)

C. Answer (3) D. Answer (4)

194. Statements:

I. Some vegetables are fruits.

II. No fruit is black.

Conclusions:

I. Some fruits are vegetables.

II. No vegetable is black.

A. Answer (1) B. Answer (2)

C. Answer (3) D. Answer (4)

195. Amit first goes in South direction, then he turns towards left and travel for some distance. After that he turns right and moves certain distance. At last he turns left and travels again for some distance. Now, in which direction is he moving?

A. South B. West

C. East D. None of the above

196. There are six houses in a row. Mr. Aalekh has Mr. Mishra and Mr. Iliyas as neighbours. Mr. Mritynjay has Mr. Sandeep and Mr. Nayak as neighbours. Mr. Sandeep's house is not next to Mr. Mishra or Mr. Iliyas and Mr. Nayak does not live next to Mr. Iliyas. Who are Mr. Mishra's next door neighbours?

A. Mr. Aalekh and Mr. Mishra

B. Mr. Aalekh and Mr. Iliyas

C. Mr. Nayak and Mr. Aalekh

D. None of the above

197. From the word 'LAPAROSCOPY', how many independent meaningful English words can be made without changing the order of the letters and using each letter only once?

A. 1 B. 2

C. 3 D. 4

198. If Monday falls on 1st of October, which day will fall three days after the 20th in that month?

A. Monday B. Tuesday

C. Saturday D. Wednesday

199. In the word GRAPHOLOGIST, if 1st and 7th letters, 2nd and 9th letters, 3rd and 11th letters, 4th and 8th letters and 5th and 12th letters are mutually interchanged then which letter will be 6th letter from the left of 10th letter from the left side?

A. S B. T

C. G D. None of the above

200. The son of M is the father of N and grandfather (Mother's father) of R. S is the daughter of N and sister of B. On the basis of this information, how is M related to B?

A. Grandfather B. Grandmother

C. Grandmother's mother D. None of the above

ANSWERS

1	2	3	4	5	6	7	8	9	10
B	A	D	B	B	D	B	A	D	C
11	**12**	**13**	**14**	**15**	**16**	**17**	**18**	**19**	**20**
B	D	A	D	C	D	A	D	A	D
21	**22**	**23**	**24**	**25**	**26**	**27**	**28**	**29**	**30**
A	A	A	A	B	A	C	A	C	C
31	**32**	**33**	**34**	**35**	**36**	**37**	**38**	**39**	**40**
B	B	D	A	A	B	A	A	B	D
41	**42**	**43**	**44**	**45**	**46**	**47**	**48**	**49**	**50**
B	B	A	A	C	A	A	C	C	A
51	**52**	**53**	**54**	**55**	**56**	**57**	**58**	**59**	**60**
A	B	B	B	B	A	A	A	A	D

61	**62**	**63**	**64**	**65**	**66**	**67**	**68**	**69**	**70**
D	B	C	C	A	B	C	C	B	B
71	**72**	**73**	**74**	**75**	**76**	**77**	**78**	**79**	**80**
B	B	B	A	C	D	D	C	D	B
81	**82**	**83**	**84**	**85**	**86**	**87**	**88**	**89**	**90**
B	C	C	A	B	A	A	D	B	A
91	**92**	**93**	**94**	**95**	**96**	**97**	**98**	**99**	**100**
C	D	D	A	B	A	C	B	A	B
101	**102**	**103**	**104**	**105**	**106**	**107**	**108**	**109**	**110**
D	D	B	B	C	C	D	C	C	A
111	**112**	**113**	**114**	**115**	**116**	**117**	**118**	**119**	**120**
A	B	C	B	A	A	C	C	B	B
121	**122**	**123**	**124**	**125**	**126**	**127**	**128**	**129**	**130**
B	C	A	D	B	D	C	B	A	A
131	**132**	**133**	**134**	**135**	**136**	**137**	**138**	**139**	**140**
D	D	D	A	A	A	A	A	A	C
141	**142**	**143**	**144**	**145**	**146**	**147**	**148**	**149**	**150**
A	B	C	A	A	C	C	C	C	B
151	**152**	**153**	**154**	**155**	**156**	**157**	**158**	**159**	**160**
C	C	A	D	D	B	D	B	A	C
161	**162**	**163**	**164**	**165**	**166**	**167**	**168**	**169**	**170**
B	A	B	D	C	D	A	D	B	C
171	**172**	**173**	**174**	**175**	**176**	**177**	**178**	**179**	**180**
D	C	D	D	B	C	D	A	B	A
181	**182**	**183**	**184**	**185**	**186**	**187**	**188**	**189**	**190**
B	A	C	B	D	D	C	B	D	C
191	**192**	**193**	**194**	**195**	**196**	**197**	**198**	**199**	**200**
A	B	A	A	C	C	B	B	D	D

EXPLANATORY ANSWERS

91. Total number of units manufactured by company C over all the years together

$$= 2.6 + 2.2 + 2.1 + 2.8 + 2.6$$

$$= 12.3 \times 100$$

$$= \frac{123 \times 100}{10} = 1230$$

92. In 2006 the number of units sold by Company E

$$= 1.4 \times 100 = 140$$

In 2007 the number of units sold by Company E

$$= 1.7 \times 100 = 170$$

Increase in the number of units

$$= 170 - 140 = 30$$

$$\text{Required \%} = \frac{30}{140} \times 100$$

$$= \frac{150}{7} = 21\% \text{ (approx)}$$

93. The number of units sold by Company D in the year 2006

$$= 2.2 \times 100 = 220$$

The number of units manufactured by Company D in the year 2006

$$= 3.0 \times 100 = 300$$

According to the question,

$$220 = x\% \text{ of } 300$$

$$= \frac{x}{100} \times 300 = 3x$$

$$\Rightarrow \quad x = \frac{220}{3} = 73.33\%$$

94. Total number of units manufactured by Company A and B in 2009

$$= 1 \times 100 + 2.4 \times 100$$

$$= 100 + 240 = 340$$

Total number of units sold by Company A and B in 2009

$$= \frac{4}{10}\times 100 + \frac{13}{10}\times 100 = 40 + 130 = 170$$

Required ratio $= \dfrac{340}{170} = 2:01$

95. The average number of units sold by Company D over all the years together

$$= \left(\frac{2.2+1.9+1.5+1.2+1.1}{5}\right)\times 100$$

$$= \frac{79}{10\times 5}\times 100$$

$$= 79 \times 2 = 158$$

96. $\dfrac{x^{0.4}}{16} = \dfrac{32}{x^{2.6}}$

$\Rightarrow x^{0.4} \times x^{2.6} = 16 \times 32$

$\Rightarrow x^3 = 512 = (8)3$

$\Rightarrow x = 8$

97. $\because$ 0.111 + 0.222 – 0.333 = 0

$\therefore$ Required answer = 0

98. Let the number = x

$$\left[\left(x+\frac{5}{2}\right)\times\frac{9}{2}+3\right]\div\frac{6}{5} = 25$$

$$\Rightarrow \left[\left(\frac{2x+5}{2}\right)\times\frac{9}{2}+3\right]\div\frac{6}{5} = 25$$

$$\Rightarrow \left(\frac{18x+45}{4}+3\right)\times\frac{5}{6} = 25$$

$$\Rightarrow \left(\frac{18x+57}{4}\right)\times\frac{5}{6} = 25$$

$\Rightarrow 18x + 57 = 120$

$\Rightarrow 18x = 63$

$\Rightarrow x = \dfrac{63}{18} = \dfrac{7}{2} = 3\dfrac{1}{2}$

$\therefore$ Required number $= 3\dfrac{1}{2}$

99. $\because 1^3 + 2^3 + 3^3 + ... + n^3 = \left\{\dfrac{n(n+1)}{2}\right\}^2$

$16^3 + 17^3 + 18^3 + 19^3$

$= 1^3 + 2^3 + 3^3 + ... + 19^3 - (1^3 + 2^3 + ... + 15^3)$

$$= \left(\frac{19\times 20}{2}\right)^2 - \left(\frac{15\times 16}{2}\right)^2$$

$= (190)^2 - (120)^2$

$= (190 + 120)(190 - 120)$

$= 310 \times 70$

$\because \quad x = \dfrac{310\times 70}{70} = 310$

$\therefore$ Remainder = 0

102. $n(S) = 6 \times 6 = 36$

$n(E) = (1, 4), (3, 2), (2, 3), (4, 1)$

Required probability $= \dfrac{4}{36} = \dfrac{1}{9}$

103. $\because \quad \dfrac{S_1 t_1}{d_1} = \dfrac{S_2 t_2}{d_2}$

$\therefore \quad d_1 = d_2$

$\therefore \quad \dfrac{S_1}{S_2} = \dfrac{t_2}{t_1} = \dfrac{16}{9} = \dfrac{4}{3}$

$\therefore \quad S_1 : S_2 = 4 : 3$

104. It was correct 2 p.m. on Wednesday.

105. Required answer is 35%

108. $\because n^2 = 1\ 2\ 3\ 4\ 5\ 6\ 7\ 8\ 9\ 8\ 7\ 6\ 5\ 4\ 3\ 2\ 1$

$\therefore n = 111111111$

$\because \quad (1)^2 = 1$

$(11)^2 = 121$

$(111)^2 = 12321$

$(1111)^2 = 1234321$

$(11111)^2 = 123454321$

$(111111)^2 = 12345654321$

$(1111111)^2 = 1234567654321$

$(11111111)^2 = 123456787654321$

$\therefore (111111111)^2 = 12345678987654321$

$\because \quad n^2 = 12345678987654321$

$\Rightarrow \quad n^2 = (111111111)^2$

$\Rightarrow \quad n = 111111111$

109. Required no. of Stones = 31.

110. $(7)^2 = 49$

$(7)^3 = 343$

$(7)^4 = 2401$

$(7)^5 = 16807$

$(7)^6 = 117649$

$(7)^7 = 823543$

$(7)^8 = 5764801$

The last two digit of 7^{2008} = 01 because 2008 divisible by 4

$(7)^4, \ (7)^8, \ (7)^{12}, \ ..., \ (7)^{2008}$

the last two digit = 01.

161-168

Person	Item	Unit rate	Unit	Loss	Gain	Net exchange
W	Walkman (+ Z) Cricket bat (+ Y) Camera (– Z)	700 700 1500	1 1 2	 150	700 700	700 + 700 –1500 = – 100
X	Chess Board (– Z) Record Player (– Y) Cycle (+ Z)	500 2000 1000	2 1 1	500 2000	 1000	–2000 – 500 + 1000 = –1500
Y	Record player (+ X) Circket Bat (– W), (– Z)	2000 700	1 3	 700 700	2000	2000 –700 – 700 = 600
Z	Cycle (– X) Walkman (– W) Chess board (+ X) Circket bat (+ Y) Camera (+ W)	1000 700 500 700 1500	1 1 1 1 1	1000 700	 500 700 1500	 –1000 – 700 + 500 + 700 + 1500 = 1000

Note: Here (+ Z) means item is given by Z and (– Z) means item is given to Z.

161. In the beginning Z has 1000 + 700 = 1700.

162. The costliest item is Camera, possessed by W.

163. After the exchange, only X has not a cricket bat.

164. Net gain by Z = 500 + 700 + 1500

= 2700, which is highest amount of gain accomplished by one.

165. X Lost highest amount of financial loss through exchange an amount of ₹ 1500.

167. Even after exchange, an item of highest value *i.e.* Camera is possessed by W.

174. In '487692', first and last digit is even, so from given condition, code for 4 and 2 would be $.

So, '487692' will be coded as '$KEFM$'.

175. In '713540' last digit is '0', so from given condition, code for '0' is #. And '713540' will be coded 'E%*BA#'.

176. In '765082' first and last digit is odd and even respectively. So, code for '765082' will be 'EFBRK@'.

177. In '364819' first and last digit is odd, so code for 3 and 9 would be 'X'. Then code for '364819' will be 'XFAK%X'.

178. In '546839' first and last digit is odd, so code for '5' and '9' would be 'X' then, '546839' will be coded as 'XAFK*X'.

185. 1. Q % J means J is brother of Q.

2. Q ÷ M × B % I means.

Q is the sister of M, M is the mother of B and I is the brother of B.

i.e. I is the son of M (female), whose sister is Q.

3. C ÷ I = B % Q

C is the sister of I, B is the father of I and Q is the brother of B.

In this relation, I gender is not specified, so, I may be nephew or niece of Q.

186. Decoding of options:

A. M * R $ T @ N

M is the mother of R, R is the father of T and T is the wife of N.

Here, R is the father-in-law of N and M is the mother of R. So, M is the grand-mother-in-law of N.

B. M * R @ T @ N

M is the mother of R, R is the wife of T, and T is the wife of N.

This is not a valid relation.

C. M @ T $ N @ R

M is the wife of T, T is the father of N and N is the wife of R.

Hence, M is the mother of N.

D. M * T $ N @ R

M is the mother of T, T is the father of N and N is the wife of R.

Hence, M is the grand-mother of N.

187. In democratic system, the role of opposition has great importance. A democratic system operate effectively when opposition be strong and constructive. In democracy opposition is a indispensable part of the system. It is true that a good politician always learns more from his opponents then from his supporters.

190. From the given codes,

	D	A	S	H
	↓	↓	↓	↓
Code :	2	a	8	4
	↓	↓	↓	↓
Code of :	C	B	R	I

Similarly,

	S	M	A	S	H
	↓	↓	↓	↓	↓
Code :	8	z	q	e	3
	↓	↓	↓	↓	↓
Code of :	R	N	Z	T	G

191.

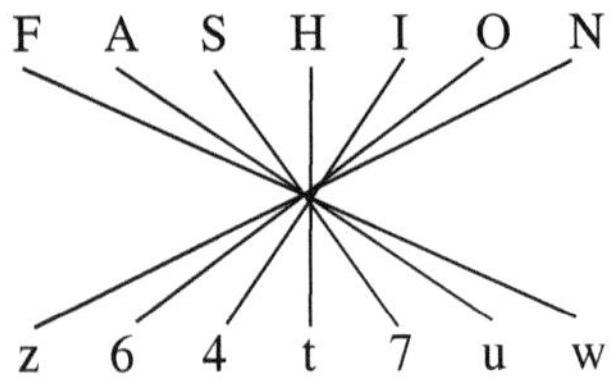

Similarly,

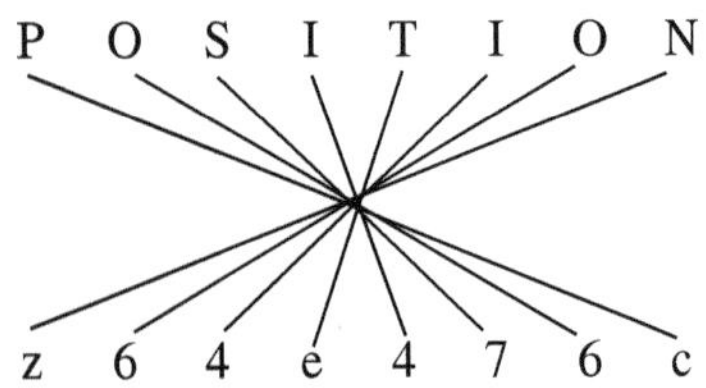

192.

	L	O	N	D	O	N
	↓	↓	↓	↓	↓	↓
Code:	5	c	6	2	z	5
	↓	↓	↓	↓	↓	↓
Code of:	M	P	O	C	N	M

Similarly,

	E	U	R	O	P	E
	↓	↓	↓	↓	↓	↓
Code:	w	h	7	z	6	v
	↓	↓	↓	↓	↓	↓
Code of:	F	V	S	N	O	D

193. As some singers are player and all singers are tall. So, some players are definitely tall.

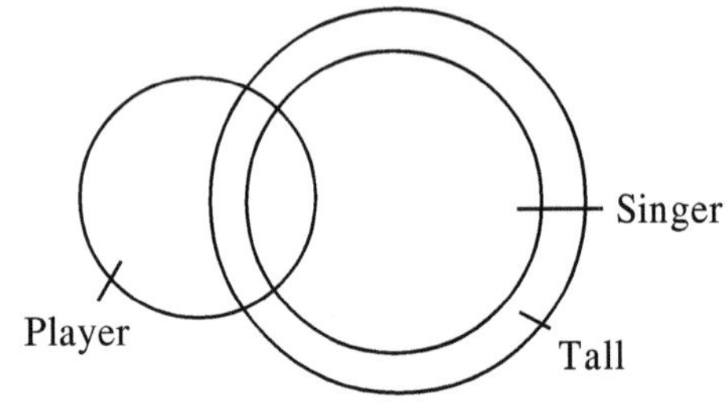

194. Some vegetables are fruits. So, some fruits are definitely vegetable.

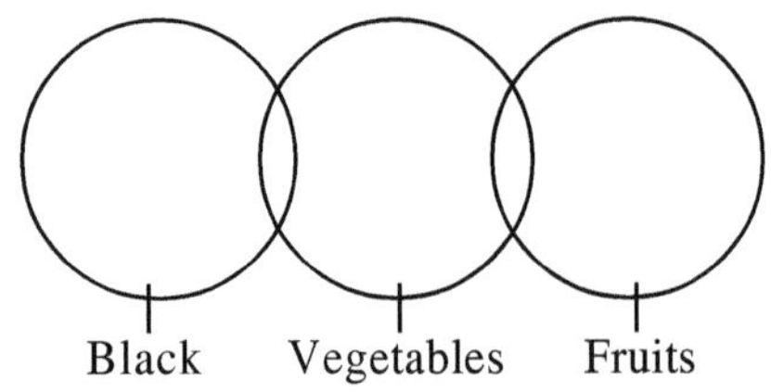

195.

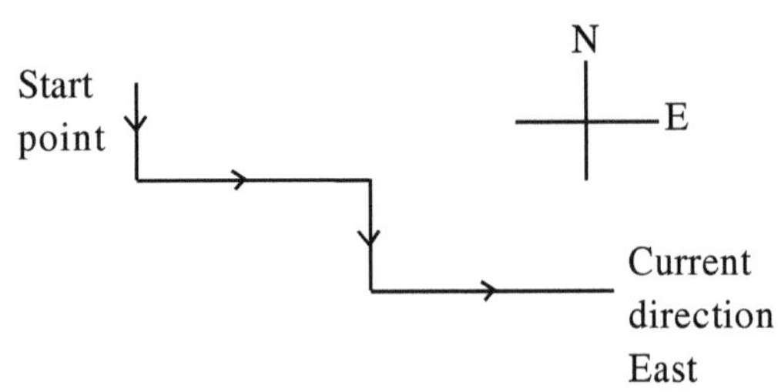

Previous Paper (Solved)

Common Law Admission Test (CLAT-UG)

Entrance Exam, 2014

Section-I : English Including Comprehension

Directions (Questions 1 to 5) : *Select the word that is spelt CORRECTLY.*

1. Which of the following spellings is correct?
A. Concensus B. Consencus
C. Consenssus D. Consensus

2. Which of the following spellings is correct?
A. Procede B. Proceed
C. Proceede D. Proced

3. Which of the following spellings is correct?
A. Accommodate B. Acommodate
C. Accomodate D. Acomodate

4. Which of the following spellings is correct 'for a page at the beginning of a book'?
A. Foreward B. Forword
C. Forworde D. Foreword

5. Which of the following spellings is correct?
A. Argueiment B. Argument
C. Arguiment D. Arguemint

Directions (Questions 6 to 10) : *Choose the explanation that best reflects the spirit of the idiom/proverb/phrase given in each question.*

6. To make clean breast of:
A. To tell the truth about something
B. To gain prominence
C. To destroy before it blooms
D. To praise oneself

7. A man of straw :
A. A creditable man
B. A very active man
C. A man of no or little substance
D. An unreasonable man

8. A wild-goose chase:
A. A wise search B. A fruitful search
C. A worthwhile hunt D. A futile pursuit

9. Put on the market:
A. To offer for sale B. Alongside the market
C. Already purchased D. None of the above

10. To meet someone halfway:
A. To show that you are prepared to strain your relationship with someone
B. To compromise with someone
C. Confrontation
D. Incongruity

Directions (Questions 11 to 20) : *The questions in this section are based on a single passage. The questions are to be answered on the basis of what is stated or implied in the passage. Kindly note that more than one of the choices may conceivably answer some of the questions. However, you are to choose the most appropriate answer; that is, the response that most accurately and completely answers the question.*

The spread of education in society is at the foundation of success in countries that are latecomers to development. In the quest for development, primary education is absolutely essential because it creates the base. But higher education is just as important, for it provides the ***cutting edge.*** And universities are the life-blood of higher education. Islands of excellence in professional education, such as Indian Institutes of Technology (IITs) and Indian Institutes of Management (IIMs), are valuable complements but cannot be substitutes for universities which provide educational opportunities for people at large.

There can be no doubt that higher education has made a significant contribution to economic development, social progress and political democracy in independent India. It is a source of dynamism for the economy. It has created social opportunities for people. It has fostered the vibrant democracy in our polity. It has provided a beginning for the creation of a knowledge society. But it would be a mistake to focus on its strengths alone. It has weaknesses that are a cause for serious concern.

There is, in fact, a quiet crisis in higher education in India that runs deep. It is not yet ***discernible*** simply because there are pockets of excellence, an enormous reservoir of talented young people and an intense competition in the admissions process. And, in some important spheres, we continue to reap the benefits of what was sown in higher education 50 years ago by the founding fathers of the Republic. The reality is that we have miles to go. The proportion of our population, in the age group 18-24, that enters the world of higher education is around 7 per cent, which is only one-half the average for Asia. The opportunities for higher education, in terms of the number of places in universities, are simply not enough in relation to our needs. What is more, the quality of higher education is most of our universities requires substantial improvement.

It is clear that the system of higher education in India faces serious challenges. It needs a systematic overhaul, so that we can educate much larger numbers without diluting academic standards. This is imperative because the transformation of economy and society in the 21st century would depend, in significant part, on the spread and the quality of education among our people, particularly in the sphere of higher education. It is only an inclusive society that can provide the foundations for a knowledge society.

The challenges that confront higher education in India are clear. It needs a massive expansion of opportunities for higher education, to 1500 universities nationwide, that would enable India to attain a gross enrolment ratio of at least 15 per cent by 2015. It is just as important to raise the average quality of higher education in every sphere. At the same time, it is essential to create institutions that are examplars of excellence at par with the best in the world. In the pursuit of these objectives, providing people with access to higher education in a socially inclusive manner is imperative. The realisation of these objectives, combined with access, would not only develop the skills and capabilities we need for the economy but would also help transform India into a knowledge economy and society.

11. The principal focus of the passage is:
A. Primary education
B. Intermediate education
C. Higher education
D. Entire education system

12. The style of the passage can be best described as:
A. Academic B. Critical and analytical
C. Comparative D. None of the above

13. What kind of society can provide the foundation for a knowledge society?
A. Elite society B. Contracted society
C. Exclusive society D. Inclusive society

14. According to the passage, which one of the following is INCORRECT?
A. There are no quality institutes providing excellent professional education in India.
B. Not many people go for higher education in India.
C. Education is the basis of success.
D. All the above options are correct.

15. According to the passage, the current state of affairs of higher education in India is:
A. Satisfactory.
B. Excellent, and there is no need of any expansion of opportunities for higher education.
C. Not good enough, and there is a need of expansion of opportunities for higher education, besides creating institutions and universities that are models of excellence.
D. Not explained in the passage.

16. According to the passage, which of the following is NOT a challenge that confronts higher education in India?
A. Expanding opportunities for higher education.
B. Creating institutions and universities that are exemplars of excellence.
C. Substantial improvement in the quality of higher education in most of our universities.
D. Getting into World University Rankings.

17. According to the passage, which of the following is CORRECT?
A. Primary education is very important.
B. Universities are the life-blood of higher education.
C. Transformation of economy and society in the 21st century would depend, in significant part, on the spread and the quality of education among our people, particularly in the sphere of higher education.
D. All the above propositions are correct.

18. Should the entire university system in India be modelled on premier institutes, such as, IITs and IIMs, providing professional education?
A. Yes
B. For sure
C. No
D. The passage is silent on this question

19. What is the antonym of the expression 'cutting edge'?
A. Conventional B. Avant-garde
C. Advanced D. Contemporary

20. What is the meaning of the world 'discernible'?
A. Unobtrusive B. Noticeable
C. Unremarkable D. Inconspicuous

Directions (Questions 21 to 30) : *Fill in the blank by choosing the most appropriate option.*

21. A vote of .... proposed at the end of the meeting.
A. thanks were B. thank was
C. thanks had been D. thanks was

22. During the recession many companies will .... lay off workers.
A. be forced to B. have the force to
C. forcefully D. be forced into

23. She has good .... over the famous foreign languages.
A. expertise B. command
C. control D. authority

24. The Chairman pointed out in favour of the manager that the profitability of the industrial plant had .... since he took over the administration.

A. arisen B. declined
C. added D. increased

25. When the examinations were over, ... went to Paris.
A. me and Rohan B. I and Rohan
C. Rohan and me D. Rohan and I

26. Let's go for a walk, ... ?
A. can we B. shall we
C. can't we D. shouldn't we

27. Had Anil been on time, he .... missed the train.
A. would not have been B. had not
C. will not have D. would not have

28. The most alarming fact is that infection is spreading .... the state and reaching villages and small towns.
A. over B. across
C. far D. from

29. In big cities people are cut .... from nature.
A. off B. down
C. away D. out

30. The dissidents .... a great problem in every political party.
A. give B. cause
C. pose D. hold

Directions (Questions 31 to 35) : *The sentences given in each question, when properly sequenced, form a coherent paragraph. Each sentence is labelled with a letter. Choose the most logical order of sentences from among the given choices to construct a coherent paragraph.*

31. (a) Payment for imports and exports is made through a system called foreign exchange. The value of the money of one country in relation to the money of other countries is agreed upon.
(b) The rates of exchange vary from time-to-time.
(c) For example, an American dollar or a British pound sterling is worth certain amounts in the money of other countries.
(d) Sometimes a US dollar is worth 60 rupees in India.
A. abcd B. bacd
C. acbd D. cabd

32. (a) When a dictionary is being edited, a lexicographer collects all the alphabetically arranged citation slips for a particular word.
(b) The moment a new word is coined, it usually enters the spoken language.
(c) The dictionary takes note of it and makes a note of it on a citation slip.
(d) The word then passes from the realm of hearing to the realm of writing.
A. abcd B. acbd
C. bacd D. bcad

33. (a) The impression that corruption is a universal phenomenon persists and the people do not co-operate in checking this evil.
(b) So there is hardly anything that the government can do about it now.
(c) It is regrettable that there is a widespread corruption in the country at all levels.
(d) Recently several offenders were brought to book, but they were not given deterrent punishment.
A. cdab B. adbc
C. adcb D. cbad

34. (a) In all social affairs convention prescribes more or less generally accepted rules of behaviour.
(b) Of course, there is nothing absolute about conventions.
(c) They vary from country-to-country, from age-to-age.
(d) Convention has a necessary part to play in the life of everyone.
A. abcd B. adbc
C. dacb D. dabc

35. (a) In fact, only recently there have been serious studies to find out how many of us actually have nightmares.
(b) Now that is changing.
(c) The study of nightmares has been curiously neglected.
(d) While results so far are inconclusive, it seems fair to say that at least half the population has occasional nightmares.
A. cadb B. abdc
C. adcb D. cbad

Directions (Questions 36 to 40) : *Given below are a few foreign language phrases which are commonly used. Choose the correct meaning for each of the phrases.*

36. *Ex officio*
A. By virtue of previously held position
B. Former official
C. By virtue of office
D. Outside the office

37. *Ultra Vires*
A. Within powers B. Full powers
C. Near powers D. Beyond powers

38. *Quid pro quo*
A. Something for nothing
B. Something for something
C. Everything for something
D. Something for everything

39. *Inter vivos*
A. between the living
B. among the living and the dead
C. between the dead
D. among the dead and the living

40. *Corpus juris*
A. body of judges B. group of jurists
C. body of law D. knowledge of law

Section-II : Elementary Mathematics (Numerical Ability)

41. There are 30 boys and 40 girls in a class. If the average age of boys is 10 yr and average age of girls is 8 yr, then the average age of the whole class is:

A. 8 yr B. 8.86 yr
C. 8.2 yr D. 9 yr

42. A person spends $\frac{1}{3}$ part of his income on food, $\frac{1}{4}$ part on house rent and remaining ₹ 630 on other items. The house rent is:

A. ₹ 504 B. ₹ 1512
C. ₹ 378 D. None of these

43. A person covers a certain distance by car at a speed of 30 km/h and comes back at a speed of 40 km/h. The average speed during the travel is:

A. 34.3 km/h B. 35 km/h
C. 37.5 km/h D. 32.8 km/h

44. An employer reduces the number of employees in the ratio 8 : 5 and increases their wages in the ratio 7 : 9. Therefore, the overall wages bill is:

A. Increased in the ratio 45 : 56
B. Decreased in the ratio 56 : 45
C. Increased in the ratio 13 : 17
D. Decreased in the ratio 72 : 35

45. Father is 3 yr. older than the mother and the mother's age is now twice the daughter's age. If the daughter is 20 yr. old now, then the father's age when the daughter was born is:

A. 20 yr. B. 40 yr.
C. 43 yr. D. 23 yr.

46. If 80% of A = 20% of B and B = $5x$% of A, then the value of x is:

A. 75 B. 80
C. 90 D. 85

47. A mixture of 40 L of alcohol and water contains 10% water. How much water should be added to this mixture, so that the new mixture contains 20% water?

A. 9L B. 5L
C. 7L D. 6L

48. 'A' can do a piece of work in 20 days and 'B' can do the same work in 15 days. How long will they take to finish the work, if both work together?

A. $13\frac{1}{2}$ days B. 10 days
C. $8\frac{4}{7}$ days D. $17\frac{1}{2}$ days

49. A man can row 5 km/h in still water. If the speed of the current is 1 km/h, it takes 3 h more in upstream than in the downstream for the same distance. The distance is:

A. 36 km B. 24 km
C. 20 km D. 32 km

50. A starts a business with ₹ 5000 and B joins the business 5 months later with an investment of ₹ 6000. After a year, they earn a profit of ₹ 34000. Find the shares of A and B in the profit amount depending on their individual investment.

A. ₹ 20000, ₹ 14000 B. ₹ 16000, ₹ 16000
C. ₹ 14000, ₹ 20000 D. None of these

51. A farmer has some hens and some goats. If the total number of animal heads is 80 and the total number of animal feet is 200, what is the total number of goats?

A. 40 B. 60
C. 20 D. Cannot be determined

52. A square field has its area equal to 324 m^2. The perimeter of the field is:

A. 36 m B. 72 m
C. 18 m D. 6561 m

53. A closed metal box measure 30 cm × 20 cm × 10 cm. Thickness of the metal is 1 cm. The volume of the metal required to make the box is:

A. 1041 cm^3 B. 6000 cm^3
C. 4536 cm^3 D. 1968 cm^3

54. The difference between the simple interest and the compound interest (compounded annually) on ₹ 2000 for 2 yr at 8% per annum will be:

A. ₹ 10 B. ₹ 20
C. ₹ 13 D. ₹ 25

55. A dealer marked his goods 20% above the cost price and allows a discount of 10%. Then the gain per cent is:

A. 2% B. 4%
C. 6% D. 8%

56. A man went to the Reserve Bank of India with ₹ 2000. He asked the cashier to give him ₹ 10 and ₹ 20 notes only in return. The man got 150 notes in all. How many notes of ₹ 10 did he receive?

A. 100 B. 150
C. 50 D. 70

57. The next number in the sequence is:

19, 29, 37, 43, ...

A. 45 B. 47
C. 50 D. 53

58. An unknown man is found murdered. The corpse has one gold plated tooth, right ear is pierced and a healed fracture of left hand thumb. A man with these characteristics is reported missing. What are the chances (probability) of the corpse being the missing man? (Given the occurrence of the gold-plated teeth in the area, 1 in 5000, left hand thumb fractures 1 in 20000 and of right ear pierces 1 in 100).

A. 1 in 1000 B. 1 in 1000,000
C. 1 in 1000,000,000 D. 1 in 10,000,000,000

59. Value of "A" in the expression,

$$5+12\times10\div\frac{120}{240}=A\times10,\ \text{is:}$$

A. 11 B. 24.5
C. 34 D. 6.5

60. The Least Common Multiple (L.C.M.) of 0.12, 9.60 and 0.60 is:

A. 9.60 B. 0.12
C. 0.6 D. None of these

Section-III : General Knowledge and Current Affairs

61. General Election is being held in India from 7 April to 12 May, 2014 to constitute:

A. 14th Lok Sabha B. 15th Lok Sabha
C. 16th Lok Sabha D. 17th Lok Sabha

62. Mention the name of the current Chief Justice of India:

A. Justice Altamas Kabir
B. Justice P Sathasivam
C. Justice R.M. Lodha
D. Justice H.L. Dattu

63. The 9th Ministerial Conference of the WTO, held during 3 December-6 December 2013, was concluded at:

A. Geneva, Switzerland
B. Kaula Lumpur, Malaysia
C. Warsaw, Poland
D. Bali, Indonesia

64. Nobel Prize in Literature for the year 2013 was awarded to:

A. Mo Yan B. James E Rothman
C. Lars Peter Hansen D. Alice Munro

65. Which one of the following satellites was successfully launched by the ISRO's Polar Satellite Launch Vehicle (PSLV-C24) on 4th April, 2014?

A. IRNSS-1B B. GSAT-14
C. INSAT-3D D. SARAL

66. Which of the following Judges of the Supreme Court of India is famously known as the 'Green Judge'?

A. Justice VR Krishna Iyyar
B. Justice PN Bhagwati
C. Justice Kuldip Singh
D. Justice BN Kirpal

67. Law Day is observed on:

A. 26th January B. 26th May
C. 15th August D. 26th November

68. In which year, Defence Research & Development Organisation (DRDO) was formed by the amalgamation of the Technical Development Establishment (TDE) of the Indian Army and the Directorate of Technical Development & Production (DTDP) with the Defence Science Organisation (DSO):

A. 1955 B. 1958
C. 1959 D. 1963

69. The Reserve Bank of India was established in the year:

A. 1858 B. 1935
C. 1947 D. 1950

70. Lord Buddha's image is sometimes shown with the hand gesture, called 'Bhumisparsha Mudra'. It signifies:

A. Buddha's calling of the Earth to watch over Mara and to prevent Mara from disturbing his meditation.
B. Buddha's calling of the Earth to witness his purity and chastity despite the temptations of Mara.
C. The gesture of debate or discussion/argument.
D. Both A and B are correct.

71. Which of the following statements is INCORRECT about Fundamental Duties under the Constitution of India? It shall be the duty of every citizen of India —

A. To uphold and protect the sovereignty, unity and integrity of India.
B. To strive towards excellence in all spheres of individual and collective activity so that the nation constantly rises to higher levels of endeavour and achievement.
C. Who is a parent or guardian to provide opportunities for education to his child, or, as the case may be, ward between the age of six and fourteen years.
D. To vote in public elections.

72. Which one of the following scripts of ancient India was mostly written from right to left?

A. Nandnagari B. Brahmi
C. Kharoshti D. Sharada

73. During the time of which Mughal Emperor did the East India Company establish its first factory in India?

A. Akbar B. Jahangir
C. Shahjahan D. Aurangzeb

74. Who among the following first translated the *Bhagwat Gita* into English?
A. Charles Wilkins
B. Alexander Cunningham
C. William Jones
D. James Prinsep

75. Match List-I with List-II and select the correct answer using the codes given below the lists:

List-I (Author)	List-II (Work)
(a) Devaki Nandan Khatri	(1) Chandrakanta
(b) Premchand	(2) Durgeshnandni
(c) Bankim Chandra Chattopadhyay	(3) Nil Darpan
	(4) Seva Sadan

Codes:
A. (a) – 4; (b) – 3; (c) – 1
B. (a) – 1; (b) – 4; (c) – 3
C. (a) – 2; (b) – 1; (c) – 3
D. (a) – 1; (b) – 4; (c) – 2

76. Match List-I with List-II and select the correct answer using the codes given below the lists:

List-I (Person)	List-II (Position)
(a) Nagendra Singh	(1) Chief Election Commissioner of India
(b) SH Kapadia	(2) President of the International Court of Justice
(c) NR Madhava Menon	(3) Former Chief Justice of India
(d) VS Sampath	(4) Legal educator and Founder-Director of National Law School of India University.

Codes:
A. (a) – 2; (b) – 3; (c) – 1; (d) – 4
B. (a) – 4; (b) – 3; (c) – 2; (d) – 1
C. (a) – 1; (b) – 2; (c) – 4; (d) – 3
D. (a) – 2; (b) – 3; (c) – 4; (d) – 1

77. Who was not a Chief Justice of India?
A. Justice M Patanjali Sastri
B. Justice KN Wanchoo
C. Justice HR Khanna
D. Justice MN Venkatachaliah

78. Who was the first Attorney-General for India?
A. CK Daphtary
B. MC Setalvad
C. Niren De
D. LN Sinha

79. Under the leadership of Mahatma Gandhi, the Civil Disobedience Movement, launched in 1930, started from?
A. Sabarmati
B. Dandi
C. Sevagram
D. Champaran

80. Match List-I with List-II and select the correct answer using the codes given below the lists:

List-I (Events)	List-II (Results)
(a) Dandi March	(1) Communal electorate
(b) Chauri Chaura	(2) Illegal manufacture of salt
(c) Simon Commission	(3) Country-wise agitation
(d) Morley Minto Reforms	(4) Withdrawal of a movement

Codes:
A. (a) – 1; (b) – 2; (c) – 3; (d) – 4
B. (a) – 4; (b) – 3; (c) – 2; (d) – 1
C. (a) – 2; (b) – 4; (c) – 3; (d) – 1
D. (a) – 1; (b) – 4; (c) – 3; (d) – 2

81. Which of the following planets has the maximum number of natural satellites?
A. Earth
B. Mars
C. Jupiter
D. Saturn

82. In India, the interest rate on savings accounts in all the nationalised commercial banks is fixed by?
A. Union Ministry of Finance
B. Union Finance Commission
C. Indian Banks' Association
D. None of the above

83. Solvents are the substances used to dissolve other substances. Consider the following substances: (1) Water (2) Ether (3) Toluene (4) Chloroform (5) Ethanol. Which of the above can be used as solvents?
A. (1) and (2)
B. (2) and (3)
C. (3), (4) and (5)
D. All of these

84. Viruses are parasitic, having DNA/RNA; but, they can be crystallised and lack respiration. Therefore, they are treated as:
A. Living beings
B. Non-living beings
C. Both living and non-living beings
D. None of the above

85. Who is the winner of the coveted Dadasaheb Phalke Award for the year 2013?
A. Javed Akhtar
B. Gulzar
C. AR Rahman
D. Indeevar

86. Who among the following has been recently appointed as brand ambassador for Central Reserve Police Force (CRPF):
A. Aamir Khan
B. M. S. Dhoni
C. MC Mary Kom
D. Sania Mirza

87. Till date (2014), how many people have been awarded the Bharat Ratna Award?
A. 40
B. 41
C. 42
D. 43

88. Which country Malala Yousafzai belongs to?
A. Pakistan
B. Afghanistan
C. The USA
D. England

89. Who recently became the first woman chief of the State Bank of India?

A. Arundhati Bhattacharya B. Shubhalakshmi Panse
C. Vijaylakshmi Iyer D. Chanda Kochhar

90. Who is the Chairman of the 14th Finance Commission?
A. Dr M Govinda Rao B. Dr Vijay Kelkar
C. Dr YV Reddy D. Dr. Raghuram Rajan

91. The Chairperson of the Seventh Pay Commission is:
A. Justice BN Srikrishna B. Justice DK Jain
C. Justice AP Shah D. Justice AK Mathur

92. Which one of the following is NOT correctly matched?

	United Nations Specialized Agency	Headquarters
A.	International Civil Aviation Organization	Montreal
B.	World Trade Organization	Geneva
C.	United Nations Industrial Development Organization	Brussels
D.	International Fund for Agricultural Development	Rome

93. The First Five Year Plan of India was based on:
A. John W Miller Model B. PC Mahalanobis Model
C. Gadgil Yojana D. Herrod-Domar Model

94. Which one of the following measures is NOT likely to aid in improving India's balance of payment position?
A. Promotion of import substitution policy
B. Devaluation of rupee
C. Imposition of higher tariff on imports
D. Levying the higher duty on exports

95. Find out the correct chronological sequence of the following persons' visit to India at one time or another:
(1) Fa-Hien (2) I-Tsing (Yijing)
(3) Megasthanese (4) Hiuen-Tsang
A. (1), (3), (2), (4) B. (1), (3), (4), (2)
C. (3), (1), (4), (2) D. (3), (1), (2), (4)

96. Which was the first newspaper to be published in India?
A. Bombay Samachar B. The Hindu
C. Bengal Chronicle D. Bengal Gazette

97. The change in the colour of stars is linked to:
A. Variation in their surface temperature
B. Variation in their distance from the earth
C. Fluctuations in their composition and size
D. Irregular absorption or scattering in earth's atmosphere

98. Which one of the following does NOT remain to be a planet now?
A. Neptune B. Uranus
C. Pluto D. Venus

99. Who was appointed as the 23rd Governor of the Reserve Bank of India?
A. KC Chakrabarty B. Urijit Patel
C. Raghuram Rajan D. D Subbarao

100. Which one of following offices is held during the pleasure of the President of India?
A. Vice-President
B. Governor of a State
C. Chief Justice of India
D. Comptroller and Auditor General of India

101. Who was the first winner of the prestigious Jnanpith Award?
A. Tarasankar Bandyopadhya
B. Kuppali Venkatappagowda Puttappa
C. G Sankara Kurup
D. Umashankar Joshi

102. Match List-I and List-II and choose the correct answer:

List-I	List-II
(a) Visakhadatta	1. Surgery
(b) Varahamihira	2. Drama
(c) Sushruta	3. Astronomy
(d) Brahmagupta	4. Mathematics

Codes :

	(a)	(b)	(c)	(d)
A.	1	3	4	2
B.	2	1	3	4
C.	2	3	1	4
D.	3	4	1	2

103. Who was among the following honoured with Arjun Award in Chess for the year 2013?
A. Kavita Chahal B. Parimarjan Negi
C. Ronjan Sodhi D. Abhijeet Gupta

104. Economic growth rate projected by the IMF for India in the fiscal year 2014-15 is:
A. 5.4 per cent B. 5.5 per cent
C. 5.6 per cent D. 5.7 per cent

105. Who was sworn in as the Prime Minister of Italy on 22nd February, 2014?
A. Oleksandr Turchynov B. Matteo Renzi
C. Enrico Letta D. Giorgio Napolitano

106. Which one of following is the highest peacetime gallantry award of India?
A. Param Vir Chakra B. Ashok Chakra
C. Maha Vir Chakra D. Kirti Chakra

107. Which one of the following gases is lighter than air?
A. Carbon dioxide B. Chlorine
C. Oxygen D. Hydrogen

108. Name the scientist who is known as the father of modern genetics:
A. Jean-Baptiste Lamarck B. Hugo de Vries
C. Gregor Johann Mendel D. Charles Darwin

109. Which year was designated by the United Nations as International Women's Year?
A. 1974 B. 1975
C. 1976 D. 1977

110. Mention the correct abbreviation for ATM:
A. Automated Teller Machine
B. Any Time Money
C. All Time Money
D. Auto-limited Teller Machine

Section-IV : Logical Reasoning

Directions (Questions 111 to 113) : *In each of the following questions, a related pair of words is followed by four pairs of words or phrases. Select the pair that best expresses a relationship similar to the one expressed in the question pair.*

111. India : Tricolour
A. China : Sickle and Hammer
B. UK : Red Cross
C. USA : Stars and Stripes
D. None of the above

112. Statute : Law
A. Proviso : Clause B. Chapter : Exercise
C. University : School D. Section : Illustration

113. Buddhists : Pagoda
A. Parsis : Temple B. Christians : Cross
C. Jains : Sun Temple D. Jews : Synagogue

Directions (Questions 114 and 115) : *Each question consists of five statements (a-e) followed by options consisting of three statements put together in a specific order. Choose the option which indicates a valid argument; that is, where the third statement is a conclusion drawn from the preceding two statements.*

114. a. Law graduates are in great demand.
b. Rajesh and Krishna are in great demand.
c. Rajesh is in great demand.
d. Krishna is in great demand.
e. Rajesh and Krishna are law graduates.
Choose the correct option:
A. abe B. ecd
C. aeb D. eba

115. a. All captains are great players.
b. Some captains are successful sports administrators.
c. Ritwik is a great player.
d. Ritwik is a captain and successful sports administrator.
e. Some successful sports administrators are great players.
Choose the correct option:
A. acd B. abe
C. dca D edc

Directions (Questions 116 to 118) : *Read the following information carefully and answer the questions given below:*

Five friends Satish, Rajesh, Rehman, Rakesh and Vineet – each presents one paper to their class on Physics, Zoology, Botany, English or Geology – one day a week, Monday through Friday.

(i) Vineet does not present English and does not give his presentation on Tuesday.
(ii) Rajesh makes the Geology presentation, and does not do it on Monday or Friday.
(iii) The Physics presentation is made on Thursday.
(iv) Rehman makes his presentation, which is not on English, on Wednesday.
(v) The Botany presentation is on Friday, and not by Rakesh.
(vi) Satish makes his presentation on Monday.

116. What day is the English presentation made?
A. Friday B. Monday
C. Tuesday D. Wednesday

117. What presentation does Vineet do?
A. English B. Geology
C. Physics D. Botany

118. What day does Rakesh make his presentation on?
A. Monday B. Tuesday
C. Wednesday D. Thursday

Directions (Questions 119 to 123) : *Each question contains a statement on relationship and a question regarding relationship based on the statement. Choose the correct option.*

119. Pointing to a photograph, a man said, "I have no brother or sister but that man's father is my father's son". Whose photograph was that?
A. His father's B. His own
C. His son's D. His nephew's

120. Ranjan introduces Abhay as the son of the only brother of his father's wife. How is Abhay related to Ranjan?
A. Son B. Brother
C. Cousin D. Uncle

121. Pointing to a lady on the stage, Bhumika said, "She is the sister of the son of the wife of my husband. How is the lady related to Bhumika?
A. Cousin B. Sister-in-law
C. Sister D. Daughter

122. Pinky, who is Victor's daughter, says to Lucy, "Your mother Rosy is the younger sister of my father, who is the third child of Joseph". How is Joseph related to Lucy?
A. Father-in-law B. Father
C. Maternal uncle D. Grandfather

123. Pramod told Vinod, "Yesterday I defeated the only brother of the daughter of my grand-mother". Whom did Pramod defeat?
A. Father B. Son
C. Father-in-law D. Cousin

Directions (Questions 124 to 128) : *Read the information given below to answer the questions.*

(i) In a family of six persons, there are people from three generations. Each person has separate profession and also each one likes different colours. There are two couples in the family.
(ii) Charan is a CA and his wife neither is a doctor nor likes green colour.
(iii) Engineer likes red colour and his wife is a teacher.
(iv) Vanita is mother-in-law of Namita and she likes orange colour.
(v) Mohan is grandfather of Raman and Raman, who is a principal, likes black colour.
(vi) Sarita is granddaughter of Vanita and she likes blue colour. Sarita's mother likes white colour.

124. Who is an Engineer?
A. Sarita B. Vanita
C. Namita D. Mohan

125. What is the profession of Namita?
A. Doctor B. Engineer
C. Teacher D. Cannot be determined

126. Which of the following is the correct pair of two couples?
A. Mohan — Vanita and Charan — Sarita
B. Vanita — Mohan and Charan — Namita
C. Charan — Namita and Raman — Sarita
D. Cannot be determined

127. How many ladies are there in the family?
A. Two B. Three
C. Four D. None of these

128. Which colour is liked by CA?
A. White B. Blue
C. Black D. None of these

Directions (Questions 129 to 133) : *Read the information given below carefully and answer the questions.*

129. Two buses start from the opposite points of a main road, 150 kms apart. The first bus runs for 25 kms and takes a right turn and then runs for 15 kms. It then turns left and runs for another 25 kms and takes the direction back to reach the main road. In the meantime, due to a minor breakdown, the other bus has run only 35 kms along the main road. What would be the distance between the two buses at this point?
A. 65 kms B. 75 kms
C. 80 kms D. 85 kms

130. 'G', 'H', 'I', 'J', 'K', 'L', 'M', 'N', are sitting around a round table in the same order for group discussion at equal distances. Their positions are clockwise. If 'M' sits in the north, then what will be the position of 'J' ?
A. East B. South-East
C. South D. South-West

131. Roshan, Vaibhav, Vinay and Sumit are playing cards. Roshan and Vaibhav are partners. Sumit faced towards North. If Roshan faces towards West, then who faces towards South ?
A. Vinay B. Vaibhav
C. Sumit D. Data is inadequate

132. Five boys are standing in a row facing East. Pavan is to the left of Tavan, Vipin, Chavan. Tavan, Vipin, Chavan are to the left of Nakul. Chavan is between Tavan and Vipin. If Vipin is fourth from the left, then how far is Tavan from the right?
A. First B. Second
C. Third D. Fourth

133. One morning after sunrise, Suraj was standing facing a pole. The shadow of the pole fell exactly to his right. Which direction was Suraj facing?
A. West B. South
C. East D. Data is inadequate

Directions (Questions 134 and 135) : *Read the information given below to answer the questions.*

Diana is three times older than Jackson; Edward is half the age of Stephen. Jackson is older than Edward.

134. Which one of the following can be inferred?
A. Jackson is older than Stephen
B. Diana is older than Stephen
C. Diana may be younger than Stephen
D. None of the above

135. Which one of the following information will be sufficient to estimate Diana's age?
A. Edward is 10 year old
B. Both Jackson and Stephen are older than Edward by the same number of years
C. Both A and B above
D. None of the above.

Directions (Questions 136 to 140) : *Study the sequence/pattern of letters or numbers carefully to work out the pattern on which it is based, and answer what the next item in the sequence must be. For example, the sequence 'A, C, E, G, ? has odd numbered letters of alphabet: therefore, the next item must be 'I'.*

136. 0, 3, 8, 15, ?
A. 24 B. 26
C. 35 D. None of these

137. 8, 16, 28, 44, ?
A. 60 B. 64
C. 62 D. 66

138. 0, 6, 24, 60, 120, 210, ?
A. 290 B. 240
C. 336 D. 504

139. POQ, SRT, VUW, ?
A. XYZ B. XZY
C. YZY D. YXZ

140. A1, C3, F6, J10, O15, ?
A. U21 B. V21
C. T20 D. U20

Directions (Questions 141 to 145) : *Two words, which have a certain relation, are paired. Select a correct option to substitute the question mark so as to make a similar relational pair with the word given after double colon (::).*

141. Bow : Arrow :: Piston : ?
A. Gun B. Shoot
C. Rifle D. Bullet

142. Eye : Wink :: Heart : ?
A. Throb B. Move
C. Pump D. Respirate

143. Ocean : Water :: Glacier : ?
A. Cooling B. Cave
C. Ice D. Mountain

144. *Prima facie* : One the first view :: *In pari delicto* : ?
A. Both parties equally at fault
B. While litigation is pending
C. A remedy for all disease
D. Beyond powers

145. Delusion : hallucination :: Chagrin : ?
A. Illusion B. Ordered
C. Cogent D. Annoyance

Directions (Questions 146 and 147) : *Each question comprises two statements (numbered as I and II). You have to take the statements as true even if they seem to be at variance with commonly known facts. Read all the conclusions and then decide which of the given conclusions logically follow from the given statements, disregarding commonly known facts.*

146. (I) All contracts are agreements
(II) All agreements are accepted offers.
Which of the following derivations is correct?
A. All accepted offers are contracts
B. All agreements are contracts
C. All contracts are accepted offers
D. None of the above

147. (I) Some beautiful women are actresses.
(II) All actresses are good dancers.
Which of the following derivations is correct?
A. Some beautiful women are good dancers
B. All good dancers are actresses
C. Both A and B
D. None of the above

Directions (Questions 148 to 150) : *Two statements are given below followed by two conclusions (I and II). You have to consider the two statements to be true even if they seem to be at variance with commonly known facts. You have to decide which of the conclusions, if any, follow from the given statements.*

148. Statements:
Some books are magazines.
Some magazines are novels.
Conclusions:
(I) Some books are novels.
(II) Some novels are magazines.
A. Only (I) follows
B. Only (II) follows
C. Both (I) and (II) follows
D. Neither (I) nor (II) follows

149. Statements:
All students like excursions.
Some students go for higher education.
Conclusions:
(I) Students who go for higher education also like excursions.
(II) Some students do not go for higher education, but like excursions.
A. Only (I) follows
B. Only (II) follows
C. Both (I) and (II) follows
D. Neither (I) nor (II) follows

150. Statements:
All good hockey players are in the Indian Hockey team.
'X' is not a good hockey player.
Conclusions:
(I) 'X' is not in the Indian Hockey team.
(II) 'X' wants to be in the Indian Hockey team.
A. Only (I) follows
B. Only (II) follows
C. Both (I) and (II) follows
D. Neither (I) nor (II) follows

Section-V : Legal Aptitude

Directions (Questions 151 to 200) : *This section consists of fifty (50) questions. Each question consists of legal propositions/principles (hereinafter referred to as 'principle') and facts. These principles have to be applied to the given facts to arrive at the most reasonable conclusion. Such principles may or may not be true in the real sense, yet you have to conclusively assume them to be true for the purposes of this section. In other words, in answering the following questions, you must not rely on any principles except the principles that are given herein below for every question. Further, you must not assume any facts other than those stated in the question. The objective of this section is to test your interest towards study of law, research aptitude and problem solving ability even if the 'most reasonable conclusion' arrived at may be unacceptable for any other reason. It is not the object of this section to test your knowledge of law.*

151. Principle: When two or more persons agree to do, or cause to be done, (1) an illegal act, or (2) an act which is not illegal by illegal means, through such an agreement such persons are said to have been engaged in a criminal conspiracy to commit an offence. It is said that no consummation of the crime need be achieved or even attempted.

Facts: 'X', 'Y' and 'Z' plan to kill 'D'. They agree that only one among them, that is 'Z', will execute the plan. In pursuance of it 'Z' buys a gun and loads it.

A. Only 'Z' can be charged with criminal conspiracy to kill 'D'.
B. All of them, *i.e.*, 'X', 'Y' and 'Z', can be charged with criminal conspiracy to kill 'D'.
C. 'X' and 'Y' cannot be charged with criminal conspiracy to kill 'D'.
D. None of them can be charged with criminal conspiracy to kill 'D'.

152. Principle: 'Wrongful gain' is gain by unlawful means of property to which the person gaining is not legally entitled. 'Wrongful loss' is the loss by unlawful means of property to which the person losing it is legally entitled.

Facts: 'X' takes away Y's watch out of Y's possession, without Y's consent and with the intention of keeping it.

A. 'X' causes 'wrongful gain' to 'Y'
B. 'Y' causes 'wrongful gain' to 'X'
C. 'X' causes 'wrongful loss' to 'Y'
D. 'Y' causes 'wrongful loss' to 'X'

153. Principle: Nothing is an offence by reason that it causes, or that it is intended to cause, or that it is known to be likely to cause, any harm, if that harm is so slight that no person of ordinary sense and temper would complain of such harm.

Facts: 'X' takes a plain sheet of paper from Y's drawer without Y's consent to write a letter to his friend.

A. 'X' has committed an offence in the above context
B. 'X' has committed no offence in the above context
C. 'Y' can sue 'X' for an offence in the above context
D. None of the above is correct in the above context.

154. Principle: When an act which would otherwise be a certain offence, is not that offence, by reason of the youth, the want of maturity of understanding, the unsoundness of mind or the intoxication of the person doing that act, or by reason of any misconception on the part of that person, every person has the same right of private defence against that act which he would have if the act were that offence.

Facts: 'X', under the influence of madness, attempts to kill 'Y'.

A. 'Y' has the right of private defence against 'X'
B. 'Y' does not have the right of private defence against 'X'
C. 'Y' has the right of private defence against 'X', only if 'X' is not under the influence of madness
D. 'X' has the right of private defence against 'Y'.

155. Principle: Where a person fraudulently or erroneously represents that he is authorized to transfer certain immovable property and professes to transfer such property for consideration, such transfer shall, at the option of the transferee, operate on any interest which the transferor may acquire in such property at any time during which the contract of transfer subsits.

Facts: 'A', a Hindu who has separated from his father 'B', sells to 'C' three fields, X, Y and Z, representing that 'A' is authorized to transfer the same. Of these fields Z does not belong to 'A', it having been retained by 'B' on the partition; but on B's dying 'A' as successor obtains Z, and at that time 'C' had not cancelled the contract of sale.

A. 'A' can sell Z to a third party
B. 'A' is not required to deliver Z to 'C'
C. 'A' is required to deliver Z to 'C'
D. None of the above statements is correct

156. Principle: Under the Transfer of Property Act, 1882 a property must be transferred by one living person to another living person. The Act deals only with transfer of property between living persons.

Facts: 'X' wants to transfer his property to the presiding deity in a temple situated within the estate of 'A'.

A. Transfer of property by 'X' will be valid
B. Transfer of property by 'X' will be invalid
C. Transfer of property by 'X' to the presiding deity will become a valid transfer to 'A'
D. None of the above is correct

157. Principle: Where there is transfer of ownership of one thing for the ownership of some other thing it is called exchange; while transfer of ownership for consideration of money is called sale, whereas, without consideration it becomes gift.

Facts: 'A' transfers his house worth ₹50 lakhs to 'B' for a shopping building worth the same amount, as consideration, from 'B'.

A. The transaction is a gift
B. The transaction is a sale
C. The transaction is an exchange
D. The transaction is a mortgage

158. Principle: One of the principles of natural justice is *Nemo judex in causa sua,* which means that no one should be a judge in his own cause. In other words, no person can judge a case in which he has an interest.

Facts: 'X', a member of the selection board for a government service, was also a candidate for selection for the same service. 'X' did not take part in the deliberations of the board when his name was considered and approved.

A. Selection of 'X' is against the principle of natural justice.
B. Selection of 'X' is not against the principle of natural justice.
C. Non-selection of 'X' will be against the principles of natural justice.
D. Non-participation of 'X' in the board deliberations will render his selection valid.

159. Principle: Strike is a collective stoppage of work by workmen undertaken in order to bring pressure upon those who depend on the sale or use of the products of work; whereas, lock-out is a weapon in the hands of the employer, similar to that of strike in the armoury of workmen, used for compelling persons employed by him to accept his terms or conditions of or affecting employment. While in closure there is permanent closing down of a place of employment or part thereof, in lay-off an employer, who is willing to employ, fails or refuses or is unable to provide employment for reasons beyond his control.

Facts: Workmen of a textile factory went on strike as per law, demanding the payment of bonus. Employer of the factory refused to pay any extra allowances, including bonus, and besides he closed down the factory till the strike was stopped.

A. Act of closing down the factory by the employer amounted to strike
B. Act of closing down the factory by the employer amounted to lay-off
C. Act of closing down the factory by the employer amounted to lock-out
D. Act of closing down the factory by the employer amounted to closure

160. Principle: Trade dispute means any dispute between employers and workmen or between workmen and workmen, or between employers and employers which is connected with the employment or non-employment, or the terms of employment or the conditions of labour, of any person. Disputes connected with the non-employment must be understood to include a dispute connected with a dismissal, discharge, removal or retrenchment of a workman.

Facts: 'X', an employee in a sugar factory, raised a dispute against 'Y', the employer, through trade union regarding certain matters connected with his suspension from the employment.

A. Matters connected with suspension can amount to a trade dispute
B. Matters connected with suspension cannot amount to a trade dispute
C. Only after dismissal, matters connected with suspension can amount to a trade dispute.
D. None of the above is correct.

161. Principle: When one person signifies to another his willingness to do or to abstain from doing anything, with a view to obtaining the assent of that other to such act or abstinence, he is said to make a proposal. The expression of willingness/desire results in a valid proposal only when it is made/addressed to some person(s).

Facts: 'X' makes the following statement in an uninhabited hall: 'I wish to sell my mobile phone for ₹ 1,000.'

Which of the following derivations is CORRECT ?

A. 'X' made a statement that resulted in a promise.
B. 'X' made a statement that resulted in a proposal.
C. 'X' made a statement that did not result in any proposal.
D. 'X' made a statement that resulted in an agreement.

162. Principle: A proposal (offer) should be made with an intention that after its valid acceptance, a legally binding promise or agreement will be created. The test for the determination of such intention is not subjective, rather it is objective. The intention of the parties is to be ascertained from the terms of the agreement and the surrounding circumstances under which such an agreement is entered into. As a general rule, in the case of arrangements regulating social relations, it follows as a matter of course that the parties do not intend legal consequences to follow. On the contrary, as a general rule, in the case of arrangements regulating business affairs, it follows as a matter of course that the parties intend legal consequences to follow. However, the above rules are just presumptive in nature, and hence, can be rebutted.

Facts: One morning while having breakfast, 'X', the father, says to 'Y' (X's son), in a casual manner, 'I shall buy a motorbike for you if you get through the CLAT.'

Which of the following derivations is CORRECT ?

A. 'X' made a statement that resulted in an enforceable promise
B. 'X' made a statement that resulted in a valid proposal
C. 'X' made a statement that resulted in an enforceable agreement
D. 'X' made a statement that did not result in any enforceable agreement

163. Principle: Acceptance (of offer) must be communicated by the offeree to the offeror so as to give rise to a binding obligation. The expression 'by the offeree to the offeror' includes communication between their authorised agents.

Facts: 'X' made an offer to buy Y's property for a stipulated price. 'Y' accepted it and communicated his acceptance to 'Z', a stranger.

Which of the following derivations is CORRECT ?
A. Y's acceptance resulted in an agreement
B. Y's acceptance did not result in any agreement
C. Y's acceptance resulted in a contract
D. Y's acceptance resulted in a promise

164. Principle : Acceptance should be made while the offer is still subsisting. The offeror is free to retract his offer at any time before his offer gets accepted by the offeree. Once the offer is withdrawn or is lapsed, it is not open to be accepted so as to give rise to a contract. Similarly, if a time is prescribed within which the offer is to be accepted, then, the offer must be accepted within the prescribed time. And, if no time is prescribed, then, the acceptance must be made within a reasonable time. 'What is a reasonable time', is a question of fact which is to be determined by taking into account all the relevant facts and surrounding circumstances.

Facts : 'X' makes an offer to 'Y' to sell his equipment for ₹ 1,000.00. No time is specified for the acceptance. 'Y' sends his reply two years after receiving the offer.

Which of the following derivations is CORRECT ?
A. There arises a contract between 'X' and 'Y' to sell/buy the equipment in question for ₹ 1,000.00.
B. There does not arise any contract between 'X' and 'Y' to sell/buy the equipment in question for ₹ 1,000.00.
C. 'X' is bound by his offer, and hence, cannot reject the acceptance made by 'Y'
D. There arises a promise by 'Y' to buy the equipment

165. Principle : Minor's agreement is void from the very beginning. It can never be validated. It cannot be enforced in the court of law.

Facts : 'A', a boy of 16 years of age, agrees to buy a camera from 'B', who is a girl of 21 years of age.

Which of the following derivations is CORRECT ?
A. There arises a contract between 'A' and 'B' to sell/buy the camera in question
B. There arise an enforceable agreement between 'A' and 'B' to sell/buy the camera in question
C. There does not arise any contract between 'A' and 'B' to sell/buy the camera in question
D. There arises a voidable contract between 'A' and 'B' to sell/buy the camera in question

166. Principle : A contract which is duly supported by real and lawful consideration is valid notwithstanding the fact that the consideration is inadequate. The quantum of consideration is for the parties to decide at the time of making a contract, and not for the courts (to decide) when the contract is sought to be enforced. An agreement to which the consent of the promisor is freely given is not void merely because the consideration is inadequate; but the inadequacy of the consideration may be taken into account by the Court in determining the question whether the consent of the promisor was freely given.

Facts : 'A' agrees to sell his mobile phone worth ₹ 20,000/- for ₹ 100/- only to 'B'. A's consent is freely given.

Which of the following derivations is CORRECT ?
A. There is a contract between 'A' and 'B'.
B. There is no contract between 'A' and 'B' because consideration is not adequate
C. There is no contract between 'A' and 'B' because a mobile phone worth ₹ 20,000 cannot be sold for just ₹ 100.
D. None of the above

167. Principle : The consideration or object of an agreement is unlawful if it is forbidden by law. Every agreement of which the object or consideration is unlawful is void.

Facts : 'X', promises to pay 'Y' ₹ 50,000, if he ('Y') commits a crime. 'X' further promises to indemnify him ('Y') against any liability arising thereof. 'Y' agrees to act as per X's promise.

Which of the following derivations is CORRECT ?
A. There is a contract between 'X' and 'Y'.
B. There is an agreement between 'X' and 'Y' which can be enforced by the court of law
C. There is an agreement between 'X' and 'Y' which cannot be enforced by the court of law
D. There is a voidable contract between 'X' and 'Y'

168. Principle : The consideration or object of an agreement is unlawful if the Court regards it as opposed to public policy. Every agreement of which the object or consideration is unlawful is void.

Facts : 'X' promises to obtain for 'Y' an employment in the public service, and 'Y' promises to pay ₹ 5,00,000/- to 'X'.

Which of the following derivations is CORRECT ?
A. There is a contract between 'X' and 'Y'.
B. There is a voidable contract between 'X' and 'Y'
C. There is an agreement between 'X' and 'Y' which can be enforced by the court of law
D. There is an agreement between 'X' and 'Y' which cannot be enforced by the court of law

169. Principle : Two or more persons are said to consent if they agree upon the same thing in the same sense. Consent is said to be free when it is not caused by coercion, or undue influence, or fraud, or misrepresentation, or mistake. When consent to an agreement is caused by coercion, undue influence, fraud or misrepresentation, the agreement is a contract voidable (rescindable or terminable) at the option of the party whose consent was so caused. However, when consent to an agreement is caused by mistake as to a matter of fact essential to the agreement, the agreement is void.

Facts: 'X' threatens to gun down 'Y', if he ('Y') does not sell his property worth ₹ 20,00,000 for ₹ 1,00,000 only. As a consequence, 'Y' agrees to sell it as demanded by 'X'.

Which of the following derivations is CORRECT?

A. There is a contract between 'X' and 'Y'.
B. There is an agreement between 'X' and 'Y' which can be enforced by the court of law
C. There is an agreement between 'X' and 'Y' which cannot be enforced by the court of law.
D. There is a contract between 'X' and 'Y' which voidable at the option of 'Y'.

170. Principle: Agreements in restraint of marriage are void.

Facts: 'X' enters into an agreement with 'Y' whereunder he agrees not to marry anybody else other than a person whose name starts with the letter 'A', and promises to pay ₹ 1,00,000/- to 'Y' if he ('X') breaks this agreement.

Which of the following derivations is CORRECT?

A. There is a contract between 'X' and 'Y'.
B. There is an agreement between 'X' and 'Y' which can be enforced by the court of law
C. There is an agreement between 'X' and 'Y' which cannot be enforced by the court of law
D. There is a voidable contract 'X' and 'Y'

171. Principle: Vicarious liability is the liability of the Master or Principal for the tort committed by his servant or agent, provided the tort is committed in the course of employment. The Master or Principal is not liable for private wrongs of the servant/agent.

Facts: 'X' hands over some cash money at his house to 'Y', who is his (X's) neighbour and is also cashier in a bank, to be deposited in A's account in the bank. Instead of depositing the money, 'Y' misappropriates it.

Which of the following statements depicts correct legal position in this given situation?

A. The bank would not be liable because 'Y' did not do any wrong in the course of his employment
B. The bank would be vicariously liable because 'Y' was the employee of the bank
C. The bank would not be liable because 'Y' did not do any wrong
D. The bank would be liable because 'Y' acted as bank's agent

172. Principle: A person has no legal remedy for an injury caused by an act to which he has consented.

Facts: 'R', a cricket enthusiast, purchases a ticket to watch a T20 match organised by the Indian Premier League (IPL). During the match, a ball struck for six hits 'R' on his body and injures him. He sues IPL for compensation for the medical expenses.

Which of the following derivations is CORRECT?

A. 'R' should be compensated as he purchased the ticket to get entertainment and not to get injured
B. 'R' would fail in his action, as he voluntarily exposed himself to the risk.
C. IPL would be liable as it did not ensure that the spectators were protected from the risk of such injuries.
D. None of the above.

173. Principle: Ignorance of law excuses no one.

Facts: 'X' fails to file his income tax returns for a considerable number of years. The Income Tax department serves upon him a 'show-cause notice' as to why proceedings should not be initiated against him for the recovery of the income tax due from him with interest and penalty.

Which of the following derivations is CORRECT?

A. 'X' may defend himself by taking the plea that his legal advisor had not advised him to file the return
B. 'X' would have to pay the due, as ignorance of law and failure to comply with law is no legal ground of defence
C. 'X' may defend himself successfully by taking the plea that he was unaware of any such law being in force
D. None of the above

174. Principle: Damage without the violation of a legal right is not actionable in a court of law. If the interference with the rights of another person is not unlawful or unauthorised, but a necessary consequence of the exercise of defendant's own lawful rights, no action should lie.

Facts: There was an established school ('ES') in a particular locality. Subsequently, a new school ('NS') was set up in the same locality, which charged lower fees, on account of which people started patronising the new school. Because of the competition, 'ES' had to reduce its fees. 'ES' filed a case against 'NS' saying that 'NS' had caused it ('ES') financial loss and, thus, claimed compensation.

Which of the following derivations is CORRECT?

A. Since no legal right of 'ES' had been violated, therefore, as such, no compensation could be granted
B. Since damage is caused to 'ES', therefore, it should be awarded compensation
C. 'ES' should be awarded compensation, as opening of school in competition is not good
D. No compensation could be granted, as reduction in fees is good for the public

175. Principle: Whenever there is an invasion of a legal right, the person in whom the right is vested, is entitled to bring an action though he has suffered no actual loss or harm, and may recover damages (compensation).

Facts: 'A' was a qualified voter for the Lok Sabha election. However, a returning officer wrongfully refused to take A's vote. In spite of such wrongful refusal, the candidate, for whom 'A' wanted to vote, won the election. But, 'A' brought an action for damages:

Which of the following derivations is CORRECT ?

A. Since no legal right of 'A' had been violated, therefore, as such, no compensation could be granted.
B. Since legal right of 'A' had been violated, therefore, compensation should be granted
C. No compensation could be granted, as 'A' had suffered no loss as his candidate won the election
D. Since no fundamental right of 'A' had been violated, therefore, as such, no compensation could be granted

176. Principle: In a civil action for defamation, truth of the defamatory matter is an absolute defence. However, the burden of proving truth is on the defendant; and he is liable if he does not successfully discharge this burden.

Facts: 'D', who was the editor of a local weekly, published a series of articles mentioning that 'P', who was a government servant, issued false certificates, accepted bribe, adopted corrupt and illegal means to mint money and was a 'mischief monger'. 'P' brought a civil action against 'D', who could not prove the facts published by him.

Under the circumstances, which of the following derivations is CORRECT ?

A. 'D' would be liable, since he could not prove the facts published by him
B. 'D' would not be liable, as such an action could curtail the right of expression and speech of press
C. 'D' would not be liable, as media could publish anything
D. None of the above

177. Principle: A gift comprising both existing and future property is void as to the latter.

Facts: 'X' has a house which is owned by him. He contracted to purchase a plot of land adjacent to the said house, but the sale (of the plot of land) in his favour is yet to be completed. He makes a gift of both the properties (house and land) to 'Y'.

Under the aforementioned circumstances, which of the following derivations is CORRECT ?

A. Gift of both the properties is valid
B. Gift of both the properties is void
C. Gift of house is void, but the gift of the plot of land is valid
D. Gift of house is valid, but the gift of the plot of land is void

178. Principle: *Caveat emptor, i.e.,* 'let the buyer beware' stands for the practical skill and judgement of the buyer in his choice of goods for purchase. It is the business of the buyer to judge for himself that what he buys has its use and worth for him. Once bought, and if the buy is not up to his expectations, then he alone is to blame and no one else.

Facts: For the purpose of making uniform for the employees, 'A' bought dark blue coloured cloth from 'B', but did not disclose to the seller ('B') the specific purpose of the said purchase. When uniforms were prepared and used by the employees, the cloth was found unfit. However, the cloth was fit for a variety of other purposes (such as, making caps, boots and carriage lining etc.)

Applying the afore-stated principle, which of the following derivations is CORRECT as regards remedy available to 'A' in the given situation?

A. 'A' (the buyer) would succeed in getting some remedy from 'B' (the seller)
B. 'A' (the buyer) would not succeed in getting any remedy from 'B' (the seller)
C. 'A' (the buyer) would succeed in getting refund from 'B' (the seller)
D. 'A' (the buyer) would succeed in getting a different variety of cloth from 'B' (the seller), but not the refund

179. Principle: The transferor of goods cannot pass a better title than what he himself possesses.

Facts: 'X' sells a stolen bike to 'Y'. 'Y' buys it in good faith.

As regards the title to bike, which of the following derivations is CORRECT ?

A. The real owner cannot get back the bike from 'Y'
B. 'Y' will get no title, as transferor's (X's) title was defective
C. 'Y' will get good title, as he is a *bonafide* buyer
D. 'Y' will get good title, as has not committed any wrong (stolen the bike)

180. Principle: Negligence is a breach of duty or a failure of one party to exercise the standard of care required by law, resulting in damage to the party to whom the duty was owed. A plaintiff can take civil action against the respondent, if the respondent's negligence causes the plaintiff injury or loss of property.

Facts: 'D' went to a café and ordered and paid for a tin/can of soft drink. The tin was opaque, and, therefore, the contents could not be seen from outside. She ('D') consumed some of the contents and then lifted the tin to pour the remainder of the content into a tumbler. The remains of a snail in decomposed state dropped out of the tin into the tumbler. 'D' later complained of a stomach pain and her doctor diagnosed her as having gastroenteritis and being in a state of severe shock. She sued the manufacturer of the drink for negligence.

Applying the afore-stated principle, which of the following derivations is CORRECT as regard liability of the manufacturer in the given situation?

A. The manufacturer is liable for negligence, as it owed a duty (to consumers) to take reasonable care to ensure that its products are safe for consumption
B. The manufacturer is not liable for negligence, as there is no direct contract between 'D' and the manufacturer. No duty is owed by the manufacturer towards a particular consumer ('D')
C. The manufacturer is not liable for negligence because it would otherwise become very difficult for the manufacturers to do business.
D. The manufacturer could be made liable under criminal law, but not for tort of negligence

181. Principle : Master is liable for the wrongful acts committed by his servant; provided the acts are committed during the course of employment. However, the master is not liable if the wrongful act committed by his servant has no connection, whatsover, with the servant's contract of employment.

Facts: 'D' is a driver employed by 'M', who is the owner of a company. During the lunch time, 'D' goes to a closeby tea shop to have a cup of tea. There he ('D') picks up fight with the tea shop owner ('T'), which resulted in some damage to his shop. 'T' wants to sue 'M' for claiming compensation for the damage caused by the fight.

Which of the following derivations is CORRECT ?

A. 'M' will be liable because 'D' is his servant
B. Both 'M' and 'D' will be liable
C. 'M' will not be liable because the wrongful act (picking up fight) was not committed in the course of D's employment
D. 'M' will be liable albeit the wrongful act (picking up fight) was not committed in the course of D's employment

182. Principle : The Constitution of India guarantees the 'right to life', which means 'right to live with human dignity'. The right to life under the Constitution, however, does not include the right to die.

Facts: 'M', who is 90, lives all alone as he has no family or children or grandchildren. He suffers from physical and mental distress, as there is no one to look after him. He has little means to foot his medical expenses. Under these circumstances, he approaches the court with a prayer that he should be granted the right to die with dignity because he does not want to be a burden on the society. Further, as it is his life, he has a right to put an end to it.

Which of the following derivations is CORRECT ?

A. The prayer can be granted, as suicide is not an offense in India
B. The prayer can be granted, as the right to life under the Constitution includes the right to die
C. The prayer can be granted, as a person cannot be forced to enjoy right to life to his detriment, disadvantage and disliking
D. The prayer cannot be granted, as the right to life under the Constitution does not include the right to die

183. Principle : Trespass to land means direct interference with the possession of land without lawful justification. Trespass could be committed either by a person himself entering the land of another person or doing the same through some tangible object(s).

Facts: 'A' throws some stones upon his neighbour's (B's) premises.

Which of the following derivations is CORRECT?

A. 'A' has committed trespass
B. 'A' has not committed trespass, as he has not entered B's premises
C. 'A' has committed nuisance
D. None of the above

184. Principle: Nuisance is an unlawful interference with a person's use or enjoyment of land or some right over or in connection with it. If the interference is 'direct', the wrong is trespass: whereas, if the interference is 'consequential', it amounts to nuisance.

Facts: 'A' plants a tree on his land. However, he allows its branches to project over the land of 'B'.

Which of the following derivations is CORRECT?

A. 'A' has committed trespass
B. 'A' has committed nuisance
C. 'A' has not committed nuisance
D. None of the above

185. Principle: Interference with another's goods in such a way as to deny the latter's title to the goods amounts to conversion, and thus it is a civil wrong. It is an act intentionally done inconsistent with the owner's right, though the doer may not know of, or intend to challenge, the property or possession of the true owner.

Facts: 'R' went to a cycle-stand to park his bicycle. Seeing the stand fully occupied, he removed a few bicycles in order to rearrange a portion of the stand and make some space for his bicycle. He parked his bicycle properly, and put back all the bicycles except the one belonging to 'S'. In fact, 'R' was in a hurry, and therefore, he could not put back S's bicycle. Somebody came on the way and took away S's bicycle. The watchman of the stand did not take care of it assuming that the bicycle was not parked inside the stand. 'S' filed a suit against 'R' for conversion.

Which of the following derivations is CORRECT?
A. 'R' could not be held liable for the negligence of the watchman
B. 'S' would succeed because R's act led to the stealing of his bicycle
C. 'S' would not succeed because 'R' did not take away the bicycle himself
D. 'S' would not succeed because R's intention was not bad

186. Principle: Nothing is an offence which is done by a person who is bound by law to do it.

Facts: 'A', a police officer, without warrant, apprehends 'Z', who has committed murder.
A. 'A' is guilty of the offence of wrongful confinement
B. 'A' is not guilty of the offence of wrongful confinement
C. 'A' may be guilty of the offence of wrongful restraint
D. 'A' cannot apprehend 'Z' without a warrant issued by a court of law

187. Principle: When a criminal act is done by several persons in furtherance of the common intention of all, each of such persons is liable for that act in the same manner as if it were done by him alone.

Facts: Roshan along with two of his friends, Tushar and Tarang proceeded to the house of Darshan in order to avenge an insult made by the brother of Darshan. They opened fire on the members of Darshan's family. It was found that the shots of Roshan did not hit anyone, but the shots of Tushar and Tarang succeeded in killing Darshan.
A. Roshan was not liable for the offence of murder of Darshan, as Roshan's shots did not hit Darshan
B. Only Tushar and Tarang were liable for the offence of murder of Darshan, as their shots hit Darshan
C. Roshan along with Tushar and Tarang was liable for the offence of murder of Darshan
D. Roshan was liable to a lesser extent comparing to his friends for the offence of murder of Darshan, as Roshan's shots did not hit Darshan

188. Principle: No communication made in good faith in an offence by reason of any harm to the person to whom it is made, if it is made for the benefit of that person.

Facts : 'A', a surgeon, in good faith, communicates to a patient his opinion that he cannot live. The patient dies in consequence of the shock.
A. 'A' has committed the offence of causing death of his patient
B. 'A' has not committed the offence of causing death of his patient
C. 'A' has only partially committed the offence of causing death of his patient
D. None of the above

189. Principle: Whoever, being legally bound to furnish information on any subject to any public servant, as such, furnishes, as true, information on the subject which he knows or has reason to believe to be false, has committed a punishable offence of furnishing false information.

Facts: Sawant, a landholder, knowing of the commission of a murder within the limits of his estate, willfully misinforms the Magistrate of the district that the death has occurred by accident in consequence of the bite of a snake.
A. Sawant is not guilty of the offence of furnishing false information to the Magistrate
B. Sawant is guilty of the offence of furnishing false information to the Magistrate
C. Sawant is not legally bound to furnish true information to the Magistrate
D. Sawant has the discretion to furnish true information to the Magistrate, as the murder was committed within the limits of his estate

190. Principle : Whoever unlawfully or negligently does any act which is, and which he knows or has reason to believe to be, likely to spread the infection of any disease dangerous to life, shall be guilty of a negligent act likely to spread infection of disease dangerous to life.

Facts: 'K', a person, knowing that he is suffering from Cholera, travels by a train without informing the railway officers of his condition.
A. 'K' has committed an unlawful and negligent act, which is likely to spread the infection of Cholera disease dangerous to the life of fellow-passengers
B. Railway officers are guilty of an unlawful and negligent act, as 'K' who is suffering from Cholera disease has travelled by the train
C. 'K' has not committed an unlawful and negligent act, which is likely to spread the infection of Cholera disease dangerous to the life of fellow-passengers
D. Both 'K' and Railway officers are guilty of an unlawful and negligent act, which is likely to spread the infection of Cholera disease dangerous to the life of fellow-passengers

191. Principle : Whoever drives any vehicle, or rides, on any public way in a manner so rash or negligent as to endanger human life, or to be likely to cause hurt or injury to any other person, has committed an offence, which shall be punished in accordance with the law.

Facts: 'X', a truck driver, driving his vehicle rashly and negligently at a high speed climbed the footpath and hit 'Y', a pedestrian, from behind causing his death.
A. 'X' is not guilty of rash and negligent driving
B. 'Y' should have taken sufficient care on the footpath

C. 'X' is guilty of rash and negligent driving
D. 'X' is only in part guilty of rash and negligent driving

192. Principle : Whoever causes death by doing an act with the intention of causing death, or with the intention of causing such bodily injury as is likely to cause death, or with the knowledge that he is likely by such act to cause death, commits the offence of culpable homicide.

Facts: 'A' knows 'Z' to be behind a bush. 'B' does not know it. 'A', intending to cause, or knowing it to be likely to cause Z's death, induces 'B' to fire at the bush. 'B' fires and kills 'Z'.

A. 'B' has committed the offence of culpable homicide
B. 'A' has committed the offence of culpable homicide
C. Both 'A' and 'B' have committed the offence of culpable homicide
D. None of them has committed the offence of culpable homicide

193. Principle : Whoever, intending to take dishonestly any movable property out of the possession of any person without that person's consent, moves that property in order to such taking, is said to commit theft.

Facts: 'Z', going on a journey, entrusts his plate to the possession of 'A', the keeper of a warehouse, till 'Z' shall return. Then, 'A' carries the plate to a goldsmith and sells it.

A. 'A' has committed theft
B. 'A' has not committed theft
C. 'A' lawfully sold the plate to the goldsmith
D. None of the above is true

194. Principle : Whoever makes any false document or part of a document with intent to cause damage or injury, to the public or to any person, or to support any claim or title, or to cause any person to part with property, or to enter into any express or implied contract, or with intent to commit fraud or that fraud may be committed, commits forgery.

Facts: 'A' without Z's authority, affixes Z's seal to a document purporting to be a conveyance of an estate from 'Z' to 'A', with the intention of selling the estate to 'B' and thereby of obtaining from 'B' the purchase-money.

A. 'B' has committed forgery
B. 'Z' has committed forgery
C. 'A' has committed forgery
D. 'A' and 'B' have committed forgery

195. Principle : Whoever intentionally uses force to any person, without that person's consent, in order to the committing of any offence, or intending by the use of such force to cause, or knowing it to be likely that by the use of such force he will cause injury, fear or annoyance to the person to whom the force is used, is said to use criminal force to that other.

Facts: 'Z' is riding in a palanquin. 'A', intending to rob 'Z', seizes the pole and stops the palanquin. Here 'A' has caused cessation of motion to 'Z', and 'A' has done this by his own bodily power.

A. 'A' has used criminal force to 'Z'
B. 'A' has no intention to use criminal force to 'Z'
C. 'A' has used force with the consent of 'Z'
D. None of the above is correct

196. Principle : One of the essential conditions for a marriage between any two persons to be solemnized under the Special Marriage Act, 1954 is that at the time of the marriage the male has completed the age of twenty-one years and the female the age of eighteen years. If the said condition is not fulfilled such a marriage is null and void.

Facts : 'A', a male aged twenty-two years, proposes to marry 'B', a female aged sixteen years, at Delhi in the month of June 2014 under the Special Marriage Act, 1954.

A. Marriage between 'A' and 'B' can be legally solemnized under the Special Marriage Act, 1954.
B. Marriage between 'A' and 'B' cannot be legally solemnized under the Special Marriage Act, 1954
C. Marriage between 'A' and 'B' can remain valid for A under the Special Marriage Act, 1954
D. None of the above is correct

197. Principle : Under the Hindu Marriage Act, 1955 either the husband or the wife can move a petition for a decree of divorce on the ground of desertion. The term 'desertion' means desertion of the petitioner by the other party to the marriage for a continuous period of not less than two years immediately preceding the presentation of the petition, without reasonable cause and without the consent or against the wish of such party and the includes the willful neglect of the petitioner by the other party to the marriage, and its grammatical variations and cognate expressions shall be construed accordingly. It is also said that desertion is withdrawal not from a place but from a state of things.

Facts: Rohan, a technocrat, went to US in January 2011 for pursuing his higher studies for a period of three years. In fact, Rohan went to US with the consent of his wife Basanti, who stayed at her parents' home, and with a promise of his return to India upon the completion of his studies. From US he has quite often been in touch with his wife. Subsequently, Rohan has got a job there in US and he wishes to take his wife. She refuses to go to US and, in the meanwhile, she files a petition for a decree of divorce on the ground of desertion by her husband.

A. Rohan's three year stay in US in the above context can amount to a ground of desertion for divorce.
B. Rohan's three year stay in US in the above context cannot amount to a ground of desertion for divorce.
C. Rohan's continued stay after three years can amount to a ground of desertion for divorce.
D. Basanti's refusal can amount to a ground of desertion for divorce.

198. Principle : Under the Hindu Adoptions and Maintenance Act, 1956, no person shall be capable of being taken in adoption unless he or she is a Hindu, he or she not already been adopted, he or she has not been married, unless there is a custom or usage applicable to the parties which permits persons who are married being taken in adoption, and he or she has not completed the age of fifteen years, unless there is a custom or usage applicable to the parties which permits persons who have completed the age of fifteen years being take in adoption.

Facts: Vijay being natural father had given Tarun, a boy aged 10 years, in adoption to Manoj in March 2010 in accordance with the Hindu Adoptions and Maintenance Act, 1956. In May 2012 Manoj gave Tarun in adoption to Sanjay. Subsequently in December 2013, Sanjay gave Tarun in adoption to Vijay.

A. Adoption of Tarun by Sanjay is valid
B. Adoption of Tarun by Vijay is valid
C. Adoption of Tarun by Manoj is valid
D. None of the above adoptions is valid

199. Principle : Under copyright law copyright subsists in original literary works also. A literary work need not be of literary quality. Even so prosaic a work as an index of railway stations or a railway guide or a list of stock exchange quotations qualifies as a literary work if sufficient work has been expended in compiling it to give it a new and original character.

Facts: Michael works hard enough, walking down the streets, taking down the names of people who live at houses and makes a street directory as a result of that labour.

A. Michael's exercise in making a street directory is sufficient to justify in making claim to copyright in that work which is ultimately produced
B. Michael's exercise in making a street directory is not enough to justify in making claim to copyright in that work
C. A street directory cannot be enough to be considered as a literary work
D. None of the above statements is correct

200. Principle: Every person shall be liable to punishment under the Indian Penal Code and not otherwise for every act or omission contrary to the provisions of the Code of which he shall be guilty within the territory of India. In other words, the exercise of criminal jurisdiction depends upon the locality of the offence committed, and not upon the nationality or locality of the offender.

Facts: 'X', a Pakistani citizen, while staying at Karachi, made false representations to 'Y', the complainant, at Bombay through letters, telephone calls and telegrams and induced the complainant to part with money amounting to over rupees five lakh to the agents of 'X' at Bombay, so that rice could be shipped from Karachi to India as per agreement. But the rice was never supplied to the complainant.

A. The offence of cheating under section 420 of the Code was committed by 'X' within India, even though he was not physically present at the time and place of the crime
B. The offence of cheating as per section 420 of the Code was not committed by 'X' within India, as he was not physically present at the time and place of the crime
C. Only the agents of 'X' had committed the offence of cheating under section 420 of the Code within India, as they were physically present at the time and place of the crime
D. 'Y' was also liable for the offence of cheating under section 420 of the Code within India, as he was physically present at the time and place of the crime

ANSWERS

1	2	3	4	5	6	7	8	9	10
D	B	A	D	B	A	C	D	A	B
11	12	13	14	15	16	17	18	19	20
C	B	D	A	C	D	D	C	A	B
21	22	23	24	25	26	27	28	29	30
D	A	B	D	D	B	D	B	A	B
31	32	33	34	35	36	37	38	39	40
C	D	A	D	D	C	D	B	A	C

41	42	43	44	45	46	47	48	49	50
B	C	A	B	D	B	B	C	A	A
51	52	53	54	55	56	57	58	59	60
C	B	D	C	D	A	D	D	B	A
61	62	63	64	65	66	67	68	69	70
C	C	D	D	A	C	D	B	B	D
71	72	73	74	75	76	77	78	79	80
D	C	B	A	D	D	C	B	A	C
81	82	83	84	85	86	87	88	89	90
D	D	D	C	B	C	D	A	A	C
91	92	93	94	95	96	97	98	99	100
D	C	D	D	C	D	A	C	C	B
101	102	103	104	105	106	107	108	109	110
C	C	D	A	B	B	D	C	B	A
111	112	113	114	115	116	117	118	119	120
C	A	D	C	B	B	D	D	C	C
121	122	123	124	125	126	127	128	129	130
D	D	A	D	D	B	B	D	A	D
131	132	133	134	135	136	137	138	139	140
A	D	B	B	C	A	B	C	D	A
141	142	143	144	145	146	147	148	149	150
D	A	C	A	D	C	A	B	C	D
151	152	153	154	155	156	157	158	159	160
B	C	B	A	C	B	C	A	C	A
161	162	163	164	165	166	167	168	169	170
C	D	B	B	C	A	C	D	D	C
171	172	173	174	175	176	177	178	179	180
A	B	B	A	B	A	D	B	B	A
181	182	183	184	185	186	187	188	189	190
C	D	A	B	B	B	C	B	B	A
191	192	193	194	195	196	197	198	199	200
C	B	B	C	A	B	B	C	A	A

EXPLANATORY ANSWERS

41. Total age of 30 boys = 30 × 10 = 300 years

Total age of 40 girls = 40 × 8 = 320 years

∴ Average age of the whole class $= \frac{620}{70}$ = 8.857 years = 8.86 years

42. Let the income = x

According to the question

$$x = \frac{1}{3}x + \frac{1}{4}x + 630$$

$$\Rightarrow x = \frac{4x + 3x + 630 \times 12}{12}$$

$$\Rightarrow 12x - 7x = 12 \times 630$$

$$\Rightarrow 5x = 12 \times 630$$

$$\Rightarrow x = \frac{12 \times 630}{5}$$

= 12 × 126 = ₹ 1512

Hence, the house rent = ₹ $\frac{1512}{4}$ = ₹378

43. Average speed $= \frac{2xy}{x+y} = \frac{2 \times 30 \times 40}{30 + 40}$

$$= \frac{2 \times 30 \times 40}{70} = \frac{240}{7}$$

= 34.3 km/hr

44. Let in initial number of workers $= 8x$
and at the present number of workers $= 5x$
Let wages of each worker $=$ ₹ $7y$
and at present wages of each worker $=$ ₹ $9y$
According to the question,
Ratio of wages of overall
$7y \times 8x : 9y \times 5x = 56xy : 45xy = 56 : 45$

45. $\because$ Present age of daughter $= 20$ years
$\therefore$ Mother's age $= 20 \times 2$
$= 40$ years
Father's age $= 40 + 3$
$= 43$ years
$\because$ Present age of father $= 43$ years
Hence, required age of father $= 43 - 20$
$= 23$ years.

46. $\because$ 80% of A = 20% of B
and B = $5x$% of A

$$\frac{80}{100} \times A = \frac{20}{100} \times B$$

$$\frac{4}{5}A = \frac{B}{5} = \frac{5x \times A}{100 \times 5}$$

$$\frac{4}{5} = \frac{5x}{100 \times 5}$$

$$\Rightarrow \frac{4}{5} = \frac{x}{100}$$

$$\Rightarrow 5x = 400$$

$$\Rightarrow x = \frac{400}{5} = 80$$

Hence, the value of $x =$ ₹ 80

47. Amount of water in 40 litres $= \frac{10}{100} \times 40 = 4$ litres.

Amount of alcohol in 40 litres $= 40 - 4 = 36$ litres.
Let x litre water added in the mixture

$$\therefore \frac{4+x}{40+x} = 20\%$$

$$\Rightarrow \frac{4+x}{40+x} = \frac{20}{100} = \frac{1}{5}$$

$$\Rightarrow 20 + 5x = 40 + x$$

$$\Rightarrow 5x - x = 40 - 20$$

$$\Rightarrow 4x = 20$$

$$\Rightarrow x = \frac{20}{4} = 5$$

Hence, 5 litre water should be added to this mixture so that the new mixture contains 20% water.

48. A's 1 day work $= \frac{1}{20}$

B's 1 day work $= \frac{1}{15}$

(A + B)'s 1 day work $= \frac{1}{20} + \frac{1}{15}$

$$= \frac{3+4}{60} = \frac{7}{60}$$

Hence, (A+B) can do this work in $\frac{60}{7}$ days

$$= 8\frac{4}{7} \text{ days.}$$

49. Let distance $= x$ km

$$\frac{x}{5-1} - \frac{x}{5+1} = 3$$

$$\Rightarrow \frac{x}{4} - \frac{x}{6} = 3$$

$$\Rightarrow \frac{3x - 2x}{12} = 3$$

$$\Rightarrow x = 36 \text{ km}$$

50. Amount of A in the business $= 5000 \times 12$
$=$ ₹ 60000
Amount of B in the business $= 6000 \times 7$
$=$ ₹ 42000
A : B = 60000 : 42000 = 10 : 7

Share of A $= \frac{10}{17} \times$ ₹ 34000 = ₹ 20000

Share of B $= \frac{7}{17} \times 34000$ = ₹ 14000

51. Let number of hens $= x$
$\therefore$ Number of goats $= 80 - x$
$\Rightarrow x(2) + (80 - x)(4) = 200$
$\Rightarrow 2x + 320 - 4x = 200$
$\Rightarrow -2x = -120$
$\Rightarrow x = 60$
$\therefore$ Number of hens $= 60$
Number of goats $= 80 - 60 = 20$

52. Area of square $= 324$ m^2
$\therefore$ Side of square $= \sqrt{324} = 18$ m
The perimeter of square $= 4 \times 18$
$= 72$ m.

53. Volume of the Box $= 30 \times 20 \times 10 - 28 \times 18 \times 8$
$= 6000 - 4032$
$= 1968$ cm^3

54. $$SI = \frac{2000 \times 8 \times 2}{100} = ₹\ 320$$

$$A = P\left(1+\frac{r}{100}\right)^t$$

$$= 2000\left(1+\frac{8}{100}\right)^2$$

$$= 2000 \times \frac{27}{25} \times \frac{27}{25}$$

$$= \frac{16\times 27\times 27}{5} = \frac{11664}{5}$$

$= 2332.8$

C.I. $= 2332.8 - 2000 = 332.8$

Difference $= 332.8 - 320 =$ ₹ 12.8

$\cong$ ₹ 13

55. Let CP = ₹ 100, then MP = ₹ 120

Discount $= \frac{10}{100} \times 120 =$ ₹ 12

SP $= 120 - 12 = 108$

Profit = SP – CP

$= 108 - 100 =$ ₹ 8

Profit % $= \frac{8}{100} \times 100 = 8\%$

56. Let no. of ₹ 10 $= x$

$\therefore$ Number of ₹ 20 $= (150 - x)$

$10(x) + (150-x)\,20 = 2000$

$\Rightarrow \quad 10x + 3000 - 20x = 2000$

$\Rightarrow \quad 10x = 1000$

$\Rightarrow \quad x = \frac{1000}{10} = 100$

Hence no. of ₹ 10 = 100

57. The next number in the sequence

19, 29, 37, 43, [47]

+ 10, + 8, + 6, + 4

19, 29, 37, 43, [53]

+ 10, + 8, + 6, + 10

58. 1 in 10,000,000,000

59. $5 + 12 \times 10 \div \frac{120}{240} = A \times 10$

$\Rightarrow \quad 5 + 12 \times 10 \div \frac{1}{2} = A \times 10$

$\Rightarrow \quad 5 + 12 \times 20 = A \times 10$

$\Rightarrow \quad A = \frac{245}{10} = 24.5$

60. LCM of $\frac{12}{100}, \frac{960}{100}$, and $\frac{60}{100}$

$$\text{LCM} = \frac{\text{LCM of Numerator}}{\text{HCF of denominator}} = \frac{960}{100} = 9.60$$

Previous Paper (Solved)

Common Law Admission Test (CLAT-UG) Entrance Exam, 2013

Section-I : English Including Comprehension

Directions (Questions 1 to 10) : *Read the given passage carefully and attempt the questions that follow and shade the appropriate answer in the space provided for it on the OMR answer sheet.*

It is an old saying that knowledge is power. Education is an instrument which imparts knowledge and therefore, indirectly controls power. Therefore, ever since the dawn of our civilisation, persons in power have always tried to supervise or control education. It has been handmaid of the ruling class. During the Christian era, the ecclesiastics controlled the institution of education and diffused among the people the gospel of the Bible and religious teachings. These gospels and teachings were no other than a philosophy for the maintenance of the existing society. It taught the poor man to be meek and to earn his bread with the sweat of his brow, while the priests and the landlords lived in luxury and fought duels for the slightest offence. During the Renaissance, education passed more from the clutches of the priest into the hands of the prince. In other words, it became more secular. Under the control of the monarch, education began to devise and preach the infallibility of its masters, the monarch or king. It also invented and supported fantastic theories like "The Divine Right Theory" and that the king can do no wrong, etc. With the advent of the industrial revolution, education took a different turn and had to please the new masters. It now no longer remained the privilege of the baron class, but was thrown open to the new rich merchant class of the society. The philosophy which was in vogue during this period was that of "Laissez Faire" restricting the function of the state to a mere keeping of laws and order while on the other hand, in practice the law of the jungle prevailed in the form of free competition and the survival of the fittest.

1. What does the theory "Divine Right of King" stipulate?
A. The kings are God
B. That the right of governing is conferred upon the kings by God
C. They have the right to be worshipped like Gods by their subjects
D. That the right of kings are divine and therefore sacred

2. Who controlled education during the Renaissance?
A. The common people
B. The prince
C. The church and the priests
D. None of these

3. What did the ruling class in the Christian Era think of the poor man?
A. That he is the beloved of God
B. That he deserves all sympathy of the rich
C. That he should be strong and lord over others
D. That he is meant for serving the rich

4. Who controlled the institution of education during the Christian Era?
A. The secular leaders of society
B. The church and the priests
C. The monarchs
D. The common people

5. What does the word "infallibility" mean?
A. That every man is open to error
B. Sensitivity
C. The virtue of not making mistake
D. That some divine power is responsible for determining the fate of the man

6. What do you mean by the "sweat of his brow"?
A. Very hard work
B. The tiny droplets of sweat on the forehead
C. The wrinkles visible on the forehead
D. The sign of innocence

7. What does the policy of "Laissez Faire" stand for?
A. Individual freedom in the economic field
B. State control over law and order in society
C. Joint control of the means of production by the state and private enterprise
D. Decontrol over law and order by the ruling class

8. Which of the following describes the writer?
A. Concerned
B. Unconcerned
C. Aggressive
D. Frustrated

9. Choose the correct synonym out of the four choices given:

Gospels

A. Chit chat
B. A teaching or doctrine of a religious teacher
C. Rumour
D. Guidance

10. Choose the correct synonym out of the four choices given:

Vogue

A. Uncertain
B. Out-dated
C. The prevailing fashion or style
D. Journey

Directions (Questions 11 to 15): *Select the word that is spelt correctly.*

11. A. paraphernalia B. paraphrenalia C. parapherenalia D. paraphrennalia

12. A. enterprenuer B. entrepreneur C. entrepenur D. enteruepeur

13. A. onomaetopoeia B. onomoatopoeia C. onomatopoeia D. onomatapoeia

14. A. hemorhage B. haemorhhage C. haemorrhage D. hemoorhage

15. A. dylexsia B. dyslexia C. dislexia D. dislecsia

Directions (Questions 16 to 25): *Select the best option from the four alternatives given below and shade the appropriate answer in the space provided for it in the OMR answer sheet.*

16. Unless he .... this office, I will not say anything.

A. Left B. Did not leave
C. Leaves D. Had left

17. ...., I would help all the poor people.

A. If I am rich B. If I was rich
C. If I were rich D. In case I am rich

18. I .... the news an hour ago.

A. Have heard B. Heard
C. Was hearing D. Have been hearing

19. He spoke .... about his prospects.

A. Confidentially B. Consciously
C. Confidently D. Conscientiously

20. The boy is not interested in playing, ...?

A. Doesn't he? B. Isn't he?
C. Didn't he? D. Is he?

21. He told us that we should never live beyond .... means.

A. His B. Their
C. Our D. Her

22. May I request .... you again to consider my case favourably.

A. To
B. Onto
C. Of
D. No proposition required

23. Known as devout and serious person, she also has .... sense of humour.

A. Better B. Quick
C. Good D. Beautiful

24. Galileo said, "The Earth .... around the sun".

A. Revolved B. Is revolving
C. Revolves D. Is revolved

25. We .... our work before the guests arrived at our house.

A. Shall finish B. Have finished
C. Had finished D. Shall have finished

Directions (Questions 26 to 30): *The sentences given in each question, when properly sequenced, form a coherent paragraph. Each sentence is labelled with a letter. Choose the most logical order of sentences form among the given choices to construct a coherent paragraph. Shade the appropriate answer in the space provided for it in the OMR sheet.*

26. a: People who start up their own business typically come from two extreme backgrounds: One is the business family background and the other is a steady professional family background.

b: Typically, people from different backgrounds face different kinds of basic problems.

c: The people from both the backgrounds find it very difficult to establish and manage an enterprise.

d: Starting up and managing a small business is no joke.

A. d b c a B. b a c d
C. d a c b D. c d a b

27. a: Venture capital is recommended as the ideal source of financing for a successfully small business.

b: Several companies including start ups have been funded by dedicated venture funds during this decade.

c: Despite this, an average Indian entrepreneur understands and appreciation of venture capital concept has been woefully inadequate.

d: In the Indian context, though venture capital has been a relatively late entrant, it has already made a reasonable impact.

A. a b c d B. a d b c
C. a c b d D. a d c b

28. a: Progress in diagnosis, in preventive medicine and in treatment, both medicinal and surgical, has been rapid and breathe taking.

b: Much in medicine which is not taken for granted was undreamt of even as recently as 20 years ago.

c: Presently small pox has been eradicated, poliomyelitis practically banished, tuberculosis has become curable and coronary artery disease surgically relievable.

d: The dramatic surge in the field of molecular biology and research by immunologists and geneticists has succeeded in controlling parasitic diseases like malaria and river blindness that affect millions of people round the world.

A. b d c a B. b a c d
C. b c a d D. b d a c

29. a: Instead, many deaths and injuries result from falling objects and the collapse of buildings, bridges and other structures.

b: Earthquakes almost never kill people directly.

c: Fire resulting from broken gas or power lines is another major danger during a quake.

d: Spills of hazardous chemicals are also a concern during an earthquake.

A. c a b d B. d a c b
C. d c a b D. b a c d

30. a: The Winchester or hard disk drives can store much more data than what can be stored on a floppy diskette.

b: Hard disks come sealed and they cannot be removed or changed like floppy diskettes.

c: Often floppy disk system is used in conjunction with the Winchester disk system.

d: This makes for an ideal system for secondary storage.

A. c a b d B. c b d a
C. b a c d D. a b c d

Directions (Questions 31 to 35) : *Given below are a few foreign language phrases which are commonly used. Choose the correct meaning for each of the phrases and shade the appropriate answer in the space provided for it in the OMR sheet.*

31. El Dorado
A. An imaginary place
B. High altitude
C. A literary man
D. A country full of gold and precious stones

32. Quantum ramifactus
A. The amount of damage suffered
B. The amount of damage caused
C. The amount of damage paid
D. The amount of damage received

33. Corpus delicti
A. Fake evidence of an offence
B. Hearsay evidence of an offence
C. Lack of evidence of an offence
D. An evidence which constitute an offence

34. Vis-a-vis
A. Direct B. Opposite
C. Face to face D. Agree

35. Carte blanche
A. Complete authority
B. Issue the warrant
C. No authority
D. Lack of authority

Directions (Questions 36 to 40) : *Choose the explanation that catches the spirit of the idiom given in each question.*

36. To blaze a trail
A. To set on fire
B. To blow the trumpet
C. To initiate work in a movement
D. To be hopeful

37. A snake in the grass
A. A secret or hidden enemy
B. An unreliable person
C. Unforeseen happening
D. A dangerous enemy

38. Have too many irons in the fire
A. Engaged in too many enterprises at the same time
B. Facing too many problems at the same time
C. Said or done too many things at the same time
D. To incite the feeling amongst the people

39. A fair weather friend
A. A friend who is fair to us at all the times
B. A friend who deserts us in difficulties
C. A friend whom we love the most
D. A friend who loves us the most

40. A Panacea
A. An injection that serves as a life line
B. A lecture full of precepts
C. A strong drug that induces sleep
D. A single cure for all diseases or troubles

Section-II : Elementary Mathematics (Numerical Ability)

41. 2/3 is a rational number whereas $\sqrt{2}/\sqrt{3}$ is:
A. Also a rational number
B. An irrational number
C. Not a number
D. A natural periodic number

42. Greatest number which divides 926 and 2313, leaving 2 and 3 remainders, respectively, is
A. 52 B. 54
C. 152 D. 154

43. A single discount equivalent to a discount series 15% and 5% is
A. 32% B. 20%
C. 10% D. 8.5%

44. By selling a cycle for ₹ 2,345, a student loses 19%. His cost price is nearly
A. ₹ 4,000 B. ₹ 5,000
C. ₹ 3,000 D. ₹ 3,500

45. Diagonals of a rhombus are 1 metre and 1.5 metre in lengths. The area of the rhombus is
A. 0.75 m^2 B. 1.5 m
C. 1.5 m^2 D. 0.375 m^2

46. An angle in a semi-circle is
A. π B. $\pi/4$
C. $\pi/2$ D. 2π

47. In a school for midday meal food is sufficient for 250 students for 33 days, if each student is given 125 gm meals. 80 more students joined the school. If same amount of meal is given to each student, then the food will last for
A. 20 days B. 40 days
C. 30 days D. 25 days

48. In a school of 500 students, 102 students can read Hindi and Tamil both, 200 students can read only Hindi. The students who can read only Tamil are
A. 98 B. 402
C. 302 D. 300

49. The value of k for which $kx + 3y - k + 3 = 0$ and $12x + ky = k$, have infinite solutions, is
A. 0 B. −6
C. 6 D. 1

50. Table shows the daily expenditure on food of 25 households in a locality

₹	100-150	150-200	200-250	250-300	300-350
Households	4	5	12	2	2

The mean daily expenditure on food is
A. ₹ 111 B. ₹ 161
C. ₹ 211 D. ₹ 261

51. A box contains 24 marbles, some are green and others are blue. If a marble is drawn at random from the jar, the probability that it is green is 2/3. The number of blue balls in the jar is
A. 13 B. 12
C. 16 D. 8

52. The population of a city is 250 thousand. It is increasing at the rate of 2% every year. The growth in the population after 2 years is
A. 2500 B. 10000
C. 252000 D. 10100

53. If a point (x, y) in a OXY plane is equidistant from (−1, 1) and (4, 3) then
A. $10x + 4y = 23$ B. $6x + 4y = 23$
C. $-x + y = 7$ D. $4x + 3y = 0$

54. Sum of first 15 multiples of 8 is
A. 960 B. 660
C. 1200 D. 1060

55. A rod of 2 cm diameter and 30 cm length is converted into a wire of 3 metre length of uniform thickness. The diameter of the wire is
A. 2/10 cm B. $2/\sqrt{10}$ cm
C. $1/\sqrt{10}$ cm D. 1/10 cm

56. Two straight poles of unequal length stand upright on a ground. The length of the shorter pole is 10 metres. A pole joins the top of the two vertical poles. The distance between the two tops is 5 metres. The distance between the poles along the ground is 4 metre. The area thus formed by the three poles with the ground is
A. 52 $metre^2$ B. 46 $metre^2$
C. 20 $metre^2$ D. 50 $metre^2$

57. Pipe A can fill a tank in 10 hours and Pipe B can fill the same tank in 12 hours. Both the pipes are opened to fill the tank and after 3 hours Pipe A is closed. Pipe B will fill the remaining part of the tank in
A. 5 hours B. 4 hours
C. 5 hours 24 minutes D. 3 hours

58. A ground 100 × 80 $metre^2$ has two cross roads in its middle. The road parallel to the length is 5 metre wide and the other road is 4 metre wide, both roads are perpendicular to each other. The cost of laying the bricks at the rate of ₹ 10 per m^2, on the roads, will be
A. ₹ 7,000 B. ₹ 8,000
C. ₹ 9,000 D. ₹ 1,000

59. If selling price of 10 articles is equal to cost price of 11 articles, then gain is
A. 8% B. 9%
C. 8.5% D. 10%

60. Angles of a quadrilateral are in the ratio 3 : 4 : 5 : 8. The smallest angle is
A. 20° B. 54°
C. 36° D. 18°

Section-III : General Knowledge and Current Affairs

61. The Headquarter of European Union is situated in
A. England B. Germany
C. France D. Belgium

62. India in 2008 successfully put CHANDRAYAAN-1 into its initial orbit by
A. PSLV – C12 B. PSLV – C11
C. PSLV – 14 D. GSLV – D3

63. Vishwanathan Anand retained the World Chess Championship in 2012 by defeating Boris Gelfand. Mr. Gelfand belongs to
A. Israel B. Russia
C. Poland D. USA

64. Kapilvastu Relics (fragments of Lord Buddha's bone), for the second time in 114 years, recently travelled from India to
A. China B. Sri Lanka
C. Myanmar D. Japan

65. Dr. Norman Borlaugh is famous as father of the Green Revolution in 1960s. His initial goal was to create varieties of wheat adapted to the climate of
A. Mexico B. India
C. USA D. China

66. A feature 'Bluetooth' now common in mobile phones, gets its name from a
A. Chinese 10th Century King
B. UK Software Company
C. Greek Goddess
D. Danish 10th Century King

67. Which pair of states does not touch each other?
A. Meghalaya, Manipur B. Chhattisgarh, U.P.
C. Rajasthan, Punjab D. J.K., H.P.

68. Baglihar dam, is constructed on river
A. Ravi B. Chenab
C. Indus D. Sutlej

69. Navjivan Trust was instituted with the objectives of propagating peaceful means of attaining third Swaraj, by
A. Mohan Das Karam Chand Gandhi
B. Lala Lajpat Rai
C. Bal Gangadhar Tilak
D. Dr. Ambedkar

70. World Cup Football 2014 and Olympics 2016 will be held in
A. USA B. Brazil
C. Russia D. South Africa

71. In 2012-13, India's target is to restrict the fiscal deficit to x% of the GDP, where x is
A. 10 B. 8.3
C. 15 D. 5.1

72. POSCO steel project to come up but being strongly protested by the people is located in
A. Chhattisgarh B. Jharkhand
C. Odisha D. Andhra Pradesh

73. Bharat Ratna and Padma Awards in our country were instituted in the year
A. 1952 B. 1954
C. 1962 D. 1964

74. Who was crowned the Miss World 2012 on August 18, 2012?
A. Ms. Jessica Kahawaty
B. Ms. Wenxia Yu
C. Ms. Vanya Mishra
D. Ms. Sophie Moulds

75. Vishwaroopam is a 2013 Tamil spy thriller film written, directed and co-produced by .... who also enacts the lead role.
A. Prakash Raj B. Rajni Kant
C. Kamal Haasan D. Chiranjeevi

76. Vijay Kumar, who clinched a silver medal in London Olympics in 2012 is associated with
A. Boxing B. Shooting
C. Weight Lifting D. Wrestling

77. Sushil Kumar who won a silver medal in London Olympics in 2012 is associated with
A. Shooting B. Boxing
C. Wrestling D. Weight Lifting

78. How many medals did India win in London Olympics 2012?
A. 3 B. 4
C. 5 D. 6

79. The present Pope chosen in March 2013 hails from which country?
A. Brazil B. Mexico
C. Argentina D. Panama

80. The first person to set foot on the moon on July 20, 1969 and who died on Aug. 25, 2012 was
A. Nevil Armstrong B. Neil Armstrong
C. Gagan Narang D. Michael Phelps

81. In which place, on Feb. 21, 2013, two powerful explosive devices planted on bicycles had exploded in Andhra Pradesh?
A. Dilrubnagar B. Dilsukhnagar
C. Dilkushnagar D. Dilshaknagar

82. On which date Maha Kumbh Mela started in Prayag this year?
A. 14-1-2013 B. 1-1-2013
C. 26-1-2013 D. 4-1-2013

83. On which date International Women's Day is celebrated?
A. 18th March B. 8th March
C. 28th March D. 18th Feb.

84. Duration of which Five Year Plan was 2007-2012?
A. X B. XII
C. IX D. XI

85. As per census 2011, which State has the lowest sex ratio (877 : 1000)?
A. Punjab B. Haryana
C. Uttar Pradesh D. Bihar

86. Hugo Chavez who died on March 5, 2013 after losing his battle with cancer, was the President of which country?
A. Argentina B. Cuba
C. Brazil D. Venezuela

87. Carlos Slim, who tops the list of world's wealthiest people, for the fourth year in a row, belongs to which country?
A. USA B. England
C. Mexico D. Germany

88. In the name P. Chidambaram, the present Union Finance Minister, what does 'P' stands for?
A. Palghat B. Pallakudi
C. Palaniappan D. Perumal

89. The earlier name of which city was New Amsterdam?
A. Chicago B. California
C. Washington D.C. D. New York City

90. The grant of Diwani of Bengal, Bihar and Orissa is associated with
A. Nawab Shuja-ud-Daula B. Nawab Asif-ud-Daula
C. Shah Alam I D. Shah Alam II

91. Where did Kuchipudi, an eminent dance form, originate?
A. Kerala B. Andhra Pradesh
C. Uttar Pradesh D. Tamil Nadu

92. Light Year is the unit of
A. Time B. Distance
C. Light D. None of these

93. The leaning tower of Pisa does not fall because
A. It is tapered at the top
B. It covers a large base area
C. Its C.G. is inside the tower
D. The vertical line passing through the C.G. of the tower falls within its base

94. "Paradise Regained" was written by
A. John Milton B. Michel Angelo
C. John Keats D. Lord Byron

95. Which is the richest temple in India?
A. Balaji Temple of Tirupathi
B. Padmanabha Swamy Temple of Thiruvananthapuram
C. Shirdi Sai Baba Temple
D. Jagannatha Temple of Puri

96. Who founded the Red Cross?
A. Henry Dunant B. Alexander
C. James Cook D. Bismark

97. World Literacy Day is celebrated on
A. 5th September B. 6th September
C. 8th September D. None of these

98. South African Paralympics icon Oscar Pistorius has been accused of killing
A. Julia Kamp B. Reeva Steenkamp
C. Pistorius Kamp D. Shakeera Kamp

99. In the month of March, 2013 the Supreme Court of India issued a notice that the ambassador of the following country shall not leave India without the permission of the Supreme Court.
A. Germany B. Maldives
C. Italy D. Nepal

100. The Constitution (One Hundred Seventeenth Amendment) Bill, 2012 makes provisions regarding
A. Reservation in matters of promotions for Scheduled Castes and Scheduled Tribes
B. Reservation in matters of appointments for Scheduled Castes and Scheduled Tribes
C. Reservation in matters of appointments and promotions for Scheduled Castes and Scheduled Tribes
D. None of the above

101. The number of High Courts in India is
A. 18 B. 24
C. 21 D. 28

102. The last British Emperor of India was
A. King George I B. King George III
C. King George V D. King George VI

103. Palaeolithic period is also known as
A. Mesolithic Age B. Late Stone Age
C. Old Stone Age D. Neolithic Age

104. Capital of India was transferred from Calcutta to Delhi in the year
A. 1901 B. 1911
C. 1921 D. 1922

105. The chairman of Fundamental Rights Sub-Committee of the Constituent Assembly was
A. Dr. Rajendra Prasad B. Dr. B.R. Ambedkar
C. Pt. Jawaharlal Nehru D. J.B. Kripalani

106. The Environment Protection Act was passed by the Parliament of India in the year
A. 1976 B. 1986
C. 1996 D. 2006

107. International Year of Biodiversity is/was/will be
A. 2010 B. 2011
C. 2012 D. 2014

108. The first Shaka king in India was
A. Rudradaman B. Menadar
C. Maues D. Damanrudra

109. Potential Energy is described by the expression
A. PE = mgh B. PE = ngh
C. PE = oph D. PE = pph

110. Where was 16th NAM Summit held?
A. Tehran B. Mehran
C. Turban D. Bagdad

Section-IV : Logical Reasoning

Directions (Questions 111 to 113): *Answer the following questions based on the statements given below:*

(*i*) There are 3 poles on each side of the road.
(*ii*) These six poles are labelled A, B, C, D, E and F.
(*iii*) The poles are of different colours namely Golden, Silver, Metallic, Black, Bronze and White.
(*iv*) The poles are of different heights.
(*v*) E, the tallest pole, is exactly opposite to the Golden coloured pole.
(*vi*) The shortest pole is exactly opposite to the Metallic coloured pole.
(*vii*) F, the Black coloured pole, is located between A and D.
(*viii*) C, the Bronze coloured pole, is exactly opposite to A.
(*ix*) B, the Metallic coloured pole, is exactly opposite to F.
(*x*) A, the White coloured pole, is taller than C but shorter than D and B.

111. What is the colour of the pole diagonally opposite to the Bronze coloured pole?
A. White B. Silver
C. Metallic D. Golden

112. Which is the second tallest pole?
A. A
B. D
C. B
D. Cannot be determined

113. Which is the colour of the tallest pole?
A. Golden B. Silver
C. Bronze D. None of these

Directions (Questions 114 and 115): *Answer the questions on the basis of the information given below:*

The head of a newly formed Government desires to appoint five of the six elected ministers P, Q, R, S, T and U to portfolios of Foreign, Industry and Commerce, Agriculture, Rural Development and Human Resources. U does not want any portfolio if S gets one of the five. R wants either Foreign or Human Resources or no portfolio. Q says that if S gets Industry and Commerce or Rural Development then she must get the other one. T insists on a portfolio if P gets one.

114. Which of the following is a valid assignment?
A. P – Foreign, Q – Industry and Commerce, R – Agriculture, S – Rural Development, T – Human Resources
B. R – Foreign, S – Industry and Commerce, P – Agriculture, Q – Rural Development, T – Human Resources
C. P – Foreign, Q – Industry and Commerce, T – Agriculture, S – Rural Development, U – Human Resources
D. Q – Foreign, U – Industry and Commerce, T – Agriculture, R – Rural Development, P – Human Resources

115. If P gets Foreign and R gets Human Resources, then which is not a valid assignment of Agriculture and Rural Development?
A. S – Agriculture, Q – Rural Development
B. U – Agriculture, Q – Rural Development
C. Q – Agriculture, T – Rural Development
D. Q – Agriculture, S – Rural Development

Directions (Questions 116 to 120): *In each of the following questions, a related pair of words is followed by four pairs of words or phrases. Select the pair that best expresses a relationship similar to the one expressed in the question pair.*

116. Action : Reaction
A. Introvert : Extrovert B. Assail : Defend
C. Diseased : Treatment D. Death : Rebirth

117. Sorrow : Misery
A. Love : Obsession B. Amity : Harmony
C. Happiness : Joy D. Enemy : Hatred

118. Drama : Audience
A. Brawl : Vagabonds B. Game : Spectators
C. Art : Critic D. Movie : Actors

119. Nuts : Bolts
A. Nitty : Gritty B. Bare : Feet
C. Naked : Clothes D. Hard : Soft

120. Book : Author
A. Rain : Flood B. Light : Switch
C. Symphony : Composer D. Song : Music

Directions (Questions 121 to 125): *Each question contains a statement on relationship and a question regarding relationship based on the statement. Select the correct option.*

121. Moni is daughter of Sheela. Sheela is wife of my wife's brother. How Moni is related to my wife?
A. Cousin B. Niece
C. Sister D. Sister-in-law

122. Annu is daughter of my mother's brother Abahi. Pari is granddaughter of my mother. Pari should call Annu as
A. Maternal Aunt B. Sister
C. Cousin D. Niece

123. Markandey is Rajiv's mother's father. Markandey has three brothers. One of them has grandson Abhi. Rajan is son of Abhi. Rajan is related to Rajiv as
A. Brother B. Nephew
C. Cousin D. Uncle

124. Deepak said to Nitin, "That boy playing with the football is the younger of the two brothers of the daughter of my father's wife". How is the boy playing football related to Deepak?
A. Son B. Brother
C. Cousin D. Brother-in-law

125. Pointing to a woman in the photograph, Rajesh said, "The only daughter of her grandfather is my wife". How is Rajesh related to that woman?
A. Uncle B. Father
C. Maternal Uncle D. Brother

Directions (Questions 126 to 130): *Read the information given below to answer the questions.*

(*i*) Kareena's dieting schedule consists of having only one fruit on a given day of the week.
(*ii*) Dietician has prescribed banana, papaya, pomegranate, apple and grape from Sunday to Friday, one day being a fasting day. Kareena cannot eat any fruit on Saturday.
(*iii*) Pomegranate day is neither on the first day nor on the last day but earlier than the papaya day.
(*iv*) Apple day is on the immediate next day of papaya day.
(*v*) Banana day is on the immediate previous day of the fasting day.
(*vi*) Apple day and grape day must have a gap of two days between them.
(*vii*) Grape day is the day immediately following the fasting day.

126. Which of the following is the fasting day?
A. Monday B. Tuesday
C. Wednesday D. Thursday

127. Banana day and apple day have a gap of how many days between them?
A. One B. Two
C. Three D. Four

128. Which day is grape day?
A. Monday B. Tuesday
C. Thursday D. Sunday

129. Which day is pomegranate day?
A. Sunday B. Monday
C. Tuesday D. Wednesday

130. Which of the following is the correct statement?
A. Apple day is after papaya day
B. Banana day is on Wednesday
C. Fasting day is on Tuesday
D. Papaya day is earlier than banana day

Directions (Questions 131 to 135): *Each question contains one statement and two courses of action I and II. Assuming the statements to be true, decide which of the two courses of action most logically follows.*

Codes:
A. If only I follows
B. If only II follows
C. If either I or II follows
D. If neither I nor II follows

131. Statement : Indian children are very talented but are instead weak in science and mathematics.
I : Teaching and textbooks are not available in mother language.
II : Education based on experiments in both the subjects is lacking.

132. Statement : Despite of child labour laws, children can be seen working in hotels, shops, houses very frequently.
I : The government should not make such laws which cannot be enforced.
II : A proper education system for the primary level particularly for lower caste community may eradicate this problem.

133. Statement : Kyoto protocol on environment is signed by almost every country of the world.
I : As a result air, water and soil pollution have come down.
II : Increasing production of automobiles, refrigerators and fertilisers do not affect our environment.

134. Statement : School dropout rate is very high in the rural areas as children support their parents in income earning activities.
I : Public awareness programme on primary education should be expanded immediately to educate parents.
II : Compensation is not a remedy.

135. Statement : Smoking is one of those human weaknesses which tend to test the will power of the smoker of the edge.

I : It is very difficult for the smoker to give up smoking even if they want to do so.

II : Human beings have other weaknesses as well.

Directions (Questions 136 to 140): *Complete the series by choosing the correct option.*

136. 0, 1, 1, 2, 3, 5, 8, 13, 21, ?

A. 34 B. 35
C. 33 D. 36

137. A – 10, E – 15, I – 20, M – 25, ...

A. Q – 5 B. Q – 30
C. P – 30 D. R – 30

138. 17, 36, 74, 150, ?, 606

A. 250 B. 303
C. 300 D. 302

139. 2, 1, 4, 3, 6, 5, 8, ?

A. 9 B. 10
C. 7 D. 8

140. 1, 4, 27, 256, ?

A. 625 B. 3125
C. 3025 D. 1225

Directions (Questions 141 to 145): *In each question below are given two statements numbered I and II. You have to take the two given statements as true even if they seem to be at variance with commonly known facts. Read all the conclusions and then decide which of the given conclusions logically follow from the given statements, disregarding commonly known facts.*

141. I : All vegetables have gravy.
II : All lunch has vegetable.

A. All lunch has gravy
B. All gravy has lunch
C. Both A and B
D. None of the above

142. I : Karan Johar is a good director.
II : Directors are intelligent.

A. All intelligent are directors
B. Karan Johar is intelligent
C. Both A and B
D. None of the above

143. I : Some blues are green.
II : Pink is green.

A. Some blue is pink
B. Some green is pink
C. Either A or B follows
D. Some pinks are blues

144. I : All boys are tall.
II : All Punjabi are tall.

A. All boys are Punjabi
B. Some boys are Punjabi
C. Both of the above
D. None of the above

145. I : All girls go to the college.
II : Rina does not go to the college.

A. Rina is not a girl
B. Going to college is not essential to be a girl
C. Rina is a girl
D. None of the above

Directions (Questions 146 to 150): *Read the information given below to answer the questions.*

A, B, C, D, E, F, G and H want to have a dinner on a round table and they have worked out the following seating arrangements.

(*i*) A will sit beside C
(*ii*) H will sit beside A
(*iii*) C will sit beside E
(*iv*) F will sit beside H
(*v*) E will sit beside G
(*vi*) D will sit beside F
(*vii*) G will sit beside B
(*viii*) B will sit beside D

146. Which of the following is wrong?

A. A will be to the immediate right of C
B. D will be to the immediate left of B
C. E will be to the immediate right of A
D. F will be to the immediate left of D

147. Which of the following is correct?

A. B will be to the immediate left of D
B. H will be to the immediate right of A
C. C will be to the immediate right of F
D. B will be to the immediate left of H

148. A and F will become neighbours if

A. B agrees to change her sitting position
B. C agrees to change her sitting position
C. G agrees to change her sitting position
D. H agrees to change her sitting position

149. During sitting

A. A will be directly facing C
B. B will be directly facing C
C. A will be directly facing B
D. B will be directly facing D

150. H will be sitting between

A. C and B
B. A and F
C. D and G
D. E and G

Section-V : Legal Aptitude

*Note: This section consists of **fifty (50)** questions. Each question consists of legal propositions/principles (hereinafter referred to as 'principle') and facts. These principles have to be applied to the given facts to arrive at the most reasonable conclusion. Such principles may or may not be true in the real sense, yet you have to conclusively assume them to be true for the purposes of this section. In other words, in answering the following questions, you must not rely on any principles except the principles that are given herein below for every question. Further you must not assume any facts other than those stated in the question. The objective of this section is to test your interest towards study of law, research aptitude and problem solving ability even if the "most reasonable conclusion" arrived at may be unacceptable for any other reason. It is not the objective of this section to test your knowledge of law.*

151. Principle : When an offer is accepted by a person to whom it is made, it becomes a promise. But this promise will become legally binding only when the acceptance of the offer is unconditional.

Facts : Ram makes an offer to sell his house to Shyam for ₹ 50 lacs. Shyam accepts this offer but wants to pay the price of the house in five quarterly instalments. Ram does not agree to it. Thereafter Shyam agrees to pay the price of the house in the way as originally desired by Ram. But Ram does not reply to it. Can Shyam compel Ram to sell his house to him?

A. Shyam can compel Ram to sell his house because Shyam ultimately agrees to pay the price as originally desired by Ram

B. Shyam can compel Ram to sell his house because Shyam in the first instance substantially complied with the desire of Ram

C. Shyam can compel Ram to sell his house because Ram's offer does not exclude the payment of price in instalments

D. Shyam cannot compel Ram to sell his house because Shyam imposes a new condition about payment of price of the house while accepting the offer which is not ultimately accepted by Ram

152. Principle : Generally an agreement without consideration is not valid. Therefore, in order to make a valid agreement, some consideration which may have some value in the eyes of law, is essentially required.

Facts : William has an old car of which he makes seldom use. He voluntarily enters into an agreement with Smith to sell this car for rupees ten thousand. Thereafter one Anson approaches William and offers to buy that car for rupees one lac as the car was one which Anson has been searching for long. Now William wants to cancel his agreement with Smith and refuses to deliver the car to him saying that consideration (price) for the car promised by Smith is negligible and, therefore, agreement with him cannot be said to be valid one.

A. William can cancel his agreement with Smith as the consideration involved in that is really inadequate

B. William cannot cancel his agreement with Smith as the sale of car for rupees ten thousand was voluntary and this price has some value in the eyes of law

C. William can cancel his agreement with Smith as he was ignorant about the value/price of the car for which it could be sold

D. William can cancel his agreement with Smith as he is entitled to get full market value/price of his car

153. Principle : In order to be eligible to appear in the semester examination, a student is required to attend, under all circumstances, at least 70% of the total classes held in that semester as per University rules.

Facts : Anand, an economically poor but a very brilliant student of LL.B. final semester, while going to his University by cycle received some leg injuries in road accident. Consequently Anand could not attend his classes for one week as he was advised rest by his doctor for that period. Due to this absence from the University, Anand failed to have 70% attendance essential to appear in the examination and, therefore, he was debarred from appearing in the examination by the University authorities. Anand challenges this decision in the court of law.

A. Anand will succeed in the court of law as the accident was beyond his control

B. Anand will definitely get favour of the court on humanitarian ground as he comes from a economically poor family and may not afford to take readmission

C. Anand will not succeed as he could very easily fulfil eligibility criteria for appearing in the examination by being reasonably regular in the class throughout the semester

D. Anand will succeed as requirement of 70% attendance may be declared arbitrary and, therefore, unreasonable by the court of law

154. Principle : A seller of goods cannot transfer better rights than he himself possesses in the goods sold to the buyer.

Facts : Komal leaves his watch by mistake on a seat in the park. Sonal finds that watch and immediately sells the same for good price to Monal who without inquiring whether Sonal is its owner or not. Komal later on claims that watch from Monal. Decide whether Komal can succeed.

A. Komal cannot succeed as Monal has paid good price of the watch
B. Komal cannot succeed as Monal is unaware of the fact that Sonal is not its owner
C. Komal cannot succeed as it was his carelessness and nothing else which enabled Sonal to sell the watch to Monal
D. Komal cannot succeed as Sonal is merely finder of the watch and, therefore, cannot transfer ownership rights thereon to Monal

155. Principle : All citizens shall have the Fundamental Right to carry on any occupation, trade or business. But reasonable restrictions on the exercise of such rights can be imposed by law in the interest of the general public.

Facts : A large number of persons had been carrying on the business of dyeing and printing in Rajkot area for the last 25 years providing employment to about 30000 families. From these business places untreated dirty water was being discharged on the roads thereby causing damage to the public health. A notice, therefore, was given to close this business till necessary measures to protect public health as provided under the environmental statutes were taken by those business men.

A. Notice cannot be justified as it will cause loss of employment to 30000 families
B. Notice cannot be justified as it amounts to violation of the Fundamental Right of the persons who have been carrying on the business for the last 25 years
C. The notice cannot be justified on the ground of damage to public health as the persons in that area have been voluntarily residing for long and have become used to that environment
D. The notice can be justified as the right to business is not absolute and reasonable restriction can be imposed law in the interest of the public

156. Principle : A contract cannot be enforced by or against a person who is not party to it. However, where some benefit is conferred on third party by the contract itself, there third party can be allowed to enforce that contract to get such benefit.

Facts : Dinesh is liable to pay ₹ 50,000 to Suresh. In order to discharge this liability Dinesh enters into a contract with Ramesh by which Dinesh sells his car to Ramesh for ₹ 1 lac. Ramesh takes the delivery of the car and promises/assures to pay its price at the earliest. Dinesh separately informs Suresh about this contract for his satisfaction. Ramesh fails to pay the car's price. Suresh wants to join Dinesh in filing suit against Ramesh for the recovery of price of the car. Whether Suresh is entitled to do so?

A. Suresh is entitled to do so because the contract was made for his benefit
B. Suresh is entitled to do so because Dinesh is liable to him and discharge of this liability depends upon the payment of the price of the car by Ramesh
C. Suresh is not entitled to do so because liability of Dinesh does not depend upon any assurance of Ramesh
D. Suresh is not entitled to do so because he is not a party to the contract between Dinesh and Ramesh

157. Principle : If a contract is made by post between two persons living in two different cities, then the contract is said to be complete as soon as the letter of acceptance is properly posted, and the place of completion of the contract is that city where acceptance is posted. It is worth mentioning here that in every contract there is always an offer from one party and the acceptance of the offer from the other party.

Facts : Sani, a resident of Patna, gives an offer by post to sell his house for ₹ 25 lacs to Hani, a resident of Allahabad. This offer letter is posted on 1st January 2013 from Patna and reaches Allahabad on 7th January 2013. Hani accepts this offer and posts the letter of acceptance on 8th January 2013 from Allahabad which reaches Patna on 16th January 2013. But Sani presuming that Hani is not interested in accepting his offer, sells his house to Gani at same price on 15th of January, 2013. Hani files a suit against Sani for the breach of contract in the competent court of Allahabad. Whether Hani will succeed?

A. Hani cannot succeed as Sani cannot be compelled by law to wait for the answer from Hani for an indefinite period of time
B. Hani cannot succeed as he could use some other effective and speedy mode for communicating his acceptance in minimum possible time
C. Hani can succeed as he properly posted the letter of acceptance and the delay was beyond his control
D. Hani can succeed as contract became complete in the eyes of law on the date of posting the letter of acceptance

158. Principle : He, who goes to the court of law to seek justice, must come with clean hands.

Facts : P enters into a contract with S under which S has to construct a house for P and has to complete the same within one year from the date of the contract. This contract includes two very important terms. According to first term, if there is price hike of the materials to be used in the construction, then the escalation charges at a particular rate shall be payable by P to S. According to second term, if the construction of the house is not completed within the period prescribed for it, then S will have to pay penalty at a particular rate to P. Before the completion of the construction work the workers of S go on strike and strike continues up to three months even after the expiry of one year. After that period workers return and the construction work again starts. During the last three months period of strike there was a considerable rise in the price of the building material. S claimed escalation cost from P. P did not agree to it. S filed a suit in the court of law either to order the payment of the price of the building material on the basis of escalated price or to allow him to stop the work without incurring any penal liability towards P.

A. S will succeed as strike by his workers was unexpected and beyond his control
B. S can succeed as there is an escalation clause in the contract
C. S cannot succeed as he has failed to complete the construction work in time and strike cannot be treated as a valid excuse for delay in work
D. S can succeed if he pays penalty to P for delay

159. Principle : If the object of an agreement is or becomes unlawful or immoral or opposed to public policy in the eyes of law, then the courts will not enforce such agreements. Law generally prohibits Child labour.

Facts : P enters into an agreement with T by which P has to let his house to T for two years and T has to pay ₹ 20,000.00 per month to P as rent. T starts a child care centre in that house. But after some time in order to earn some money for the maintenance of the centre, T starts sending the children of the centre on the rotation basis to work for four hour a day in some nearby chemical and hazardous factories. When P comes to know about this new development, he asks T either to stop the children from working in factories or to leave his house immediately. T neither agrees to leave the house nor to stop the children from working in the factories. P files a suit in the court of law for appropriate relief/action.

A. P cannot succeed as the agreement was for the two years and it cannot be terminated before the expiry of that period
B. P cannot succeed as the object at the time of making of the agreement was not clear
C. P will succeed as the object of the agreement has become unlawful
D. P will not succeed if T agrees to share the wages of the children with P

160. Principle : Whosoever by his act or omission causes environmental pollution shall be held liable for any loss caused by such pollution. It shall be no defence in such cases that all due diligence or reasonable care was taken while carrying out the act or omission in question.

Facts : Hari is carrying on a chemical and fertilizer industry near a bank of a river. In order to prevent and control any kind of harm to the environment, suitable waste treatment and disposal plants were installed in the factory. Due to some sudden mechanical/technical problem, these plants ceased to work properly and, therefore, caused environmental pollution, which ultimately caused substantial harm to the environment and to the people living around the factory. Victims of such pollution file a suit for suitable remedy.

A. Victims cannot succeed as necessary precautions to prevent any harm were taken by Hari
B. Victims cannot succeed as the mechanical/technical problem was sudden and, therefore, beyond the control of Hari
C. Victims can succeed as it is the duty of Hari to see that no harm is caused to the environment/people due to his activity under any circumstances
D. Victims could succeed if treatment/disposal plant were not installed in the factory

161. Principle : If a person transfers movable or immovable property with its full ownership and without any consideration to some other person, then it is called a gift.

Facts : S, who has no child of his own, makes a gift of his house worth ₹ 25 lacs to his nephew R. After completing all the legal formalities required for a valid gift, S says to R that in case of need R will provide that house to S for use without any questions. R does not react to it. After one year of this gift, S really needs that house and request R to make the house available to him, but R refuses to do so.

A. R cannot refuse as he got the house without paying any consideration for that
B. R cannot refuse as S is without children
C. R can refuse as he has become full owner of the house
D. R can refuse as he himself may be in need of that house

162. Principle : An agreement to do an act impossible in itself cannot be enforced by a court of law.

Facts : Ramesh agrees with his girl friend Shilpa to pluck stars from the sky through his extraordinary will power, and bring them down on earth for her within a week. After the expiry of one week, Shilpa filed a suit for damages against Ramesh for the breach of contract as Ramesh failed to perform his promise.

A. Shilpa can succeed in getting damages as Ramesh has deceived her
B. Ramesh cannot be held liable as he honestly believes that his love for Shilpa is true and, therefore, he will succeed in his endeavour

C. The court cannot entertain such suits as the act promised under the agreement is impossible in itself
D. Ramesh can be held liable for making an absurd promise

163. Principle : An agreement may be oral or written. However, if a law specifically requires that an agreement must be in writing then the agreement must be in writing. A law specifically requires that the agreements relating to transfer of the copyright in novel between an author of a novel and the producer of a motion picture must be in writing.

Facts : The author of a novel, *Love at Lost Sight*, had several rounds of discussion with a producer of motion picture regarding making of a motion picture based on *Love at Lost Sight*. During the last discussion, they decided to make a motion picture on *Love at Lost Sight*. The producer made a motion picture on *Love at Lost Sight* after making a payment of ₹ 10,00,000 (Ten Lac only) in cash to the author who happily accepted this amount as full and final payment. Later on, on the advice of his lawyer, the author brought a case in a court of law against the producer on the ground that there is no written agreement between the producer and him.

A. The author is likely to succeed in the case as the agreement is not in accordance with the law
B. The author cannot succeed in the case as he has given his consent to the agreement
C. The author is not likely to succeed in the case because he has already accepted the amount of ₹ 10,00,000 as full and final payment
D. The author can succeed in the case as the consideration is not adequate

164. Principle: A person is said to be of sound mind for the purpose of making a contract if, at the time when he makes it, he is capable of understanding it and of forming a rational judgement as to its effect upon his interest.

Facts: X who is usually of sound mind, but occasionally of unsound mind enters into a contract with Y when he (X) is of unsound mind. Y came to know about this fact afterwards and now wants to file a suit against X.

A. X cannot enter into contract because he is of unsound mind when he entered into contract
B. X can enter into contract but the burden is on the other party to prove that he was of unsound mind at the time of contract
C. X can enter into contract but the burden is on X to prove that he was of sound mind at the time of contract
D. None of these

165. Principle : Whosoever commits any act forbidden by the Indian Penal Code with a view to obtain the consent of any person to enter into an agreement, he cannot get the agreement enforced by law but the person whose consent has been so obtained may get the agreement enforced by law. The Indian Penal Code defines various offences and prescribes punishments therefore.

Facts : A obtains the consent of B to enter into an agreement by an act amounting to criminal intimidation under the Indian Penal Code. A brings a case against B for performance of agreement.

A. A will succeed in the case
B. A may succeed in the case
C. B will succeed in the case
D. B will not succeed in the case

166. Principle : A contract between the father and his son is a contract of utmost good faith. In such a type of contract law presumes that at the time of entering into the contract the father was in a position to dominate the will of his son. Where one of the parties was in position to dominate the will of the other party, the contract is enforceable only at the option of the party whose will was so dominated.

Facts : Ram had advanced a sum of ₹ 10,000 to his minor son Shyam. When Shyam became major, his father Ram misused his parental position and entered into an agreement with Shyam and obtained a bond from him for a sum of ₹ 30,000 in respect of the advance. Whether this agreement is enforceable?

A. The agreement is enforceable against Shyam only for ₹ 10,000, the actual amount of money advanced to him
B. The agreement is enforceable against Shyam for ₹ 30,000 because he has signed the bond
C. The agreement is enforceable against Shyam because he was major at the time of agreement
D. The agreement is not enforceable against Shyam because Ram has misused his position as father to obtain an unfair advantage

167. Principle : When at the desire of one person, any other person has done or abstained from doing something, such act or abstinence or promise is called a consideration for the promise. Only a promise coupled with consideration is enforceable by law.

Facts : X, the uncle of Y, made a promise to pay him an amount of ₹ 10,000 as reward if Y quits smoking and drinking within one year. X also deposited the above mentioned amount in a bank and informed Y that the said amount will be paid to him if he quits smoking and drinking within one year. Within a period of six months of making the promise X died. After the expiry of one year of making the promise by X, Y made a request to the legal heirs of X demanding the promised money. The legal heirs of X declined the request of Y.

A. The promise of X to Y is enforceable by law because Y has quitted smoking and drinking
B. The promise of X to Y is not enforceable by law because Y has benefitted by quitting smoking and drinking
C. The promise of X to Y is enforceable by law because the amount of ₹ 10,000 has been deposited in a bank
D. The promise of X to Y is enforceable by law because X has died within a period of six months of making the promise

168. Principle : 'Work' means literary work, artistic work, dramatic work, musical work, cinematographic film and sound recording but does not include acting in a cinematographic film. Only the works, as enumerated above, can be protected under copyright law.

Facts : A very famous actor acted in a cinematographic film. The actor was also the producer and director of cinematographic film.

A. The acting of the actor can be protected under copyright law
B. The acting of the actor can be protected under copyright law only as an artistic work
C. The acting of the actor cannot be protected under copyright law
D. The acting of the actor cannot be protected under copyright law as a cinematographic film

169. Principle : In case where the government is a party, the government shall be the first owner of the copyright in the work unless there is an agreement to the contrary.

Facts : The Government of the State of X entered into an agreement with a retired Professor of Botany. The Professor agreed to write a textbook on Botany. The Government agreed to pay a sum of ₹ Ten Lacs to the Professor for this work.

A. The Government of the State of X shall be first owner of copyright in the text book
B. The Professor shall be first owner of copyright in the text book
C. Both the Government of the State of X and the Professor shall be the joint owners of copyright in the text book
D. The Professor shall be first owner of copyright in the text book only if he refuses to accept the amount of ₹ Ten Lacs from the Government

170. Principle : Licence is an agreement whereby the owner of the copyright agrees to grant an interest in the copyright to the licencee. Assignment is an agreement whereby the owner of the copyright transfers all the property rights to the assignee. Property right is a bundle of rights consisting of right to possess, right to use, right to alienate and the right to exclude others.

Facts : A, an owner of copyright in a cinematographic film enters into an agreement with B, a film distributor. B agrees to distribute the film only in Mumbai. A also enters into many such agreement with other distributors for distribution of his film in other cities.

A. The agreement between A and B is more in the nature of assignment than in the nature of licence
B. The agreement between A and B is more in the nature of licence than in the nature of assignment
C. The agreement between A and B is both in the nature of assignment and licence
D. The agreement between A and B is neither in the nature of assignment nor in the nature of licence

171. Principle : *Qui facit per alium facit per se,* i.e. he who does things through others does it himself.

Facts : Nisha, the owner of a car, asked her friend Saurabh to take her car and drive the same to her office. As the car was near her office, it hit a pedestrian Srikant on account of Saurabh's negligent driving and injured him seriously. Now Srikant files a suit for damages against Nisha.

A. Nisha is not liable as it was the negligence of Saurabh
B. Saurabh is solely liable as Nisha was not driving the car
C. Nisha is liable as Saurabh was driving under her authority and for her purpose
D. Saurabh will be exempted from liability under the principle of inevitable accident

172. Principle : Words describing quality of things cannot be registered as trade mark. However, such words may be registered as trade mark if they acquire a secondary meaning. Words acquire secondary meaning when people start associating the descriptive words with a person specific.

Facts : A hatchery located in Raipur is owned by 'X'. X has been using the slogan "new laid eggs sold here" since 1970 to describe the quality of eggs sold in his hatchery. Over a period of time because of continuous use of this slogan, people started associating this slogan with X. X filed an application for registration of the words "new laid eggs" as trade mark in the year 1970.

A. The words will be registered as trade mark
B. The words will not be registered as trade mark
C. The words may be registered as trade mark
D. The words may not be registered as trade mark

173. Principle : Whoever takes away anything from the land of any person without that person's consent is said to commit theft. A thing so long as it is attached to the earth is not the subject of theft; but it becomes capable of being the subject of theft as soon as it is severed from the earth.

Facts : Y cuts down a tree standing on the land of X with the intention of dishonestly taking the tree out of X's possession without the consent of X. But Y is yet to take away the tree out of X's possession.

A. Y has committed theft as soon as he came to the land of X
B. Y has committed theft as soon as the tree has been completely cut down by him
C. Y has committed theft as soon as he has started cutting down the tree
D. Y has not committed theft because he is yet to take away the tree out of X's possession

174. Principle : *res ipsa loquitur* i.e. the thing speaks for itself.

Facts : Seema got herself operated for the removal of her uterus in the defendant's hospital, as there was diagnosed to be a cyst in one of her ovaries. Due the negligence of the surgeon, who performed the operation, abdominal pack was left in her abdomen. The same was removed by a second surgery.

A. Surgeon cannot be held responsible because it is merely a human error
B. Surgeon can be held responsible but Seema will have to prove in the court of law that the surgeon was grossly negligent
C. Surgeon will be responsible and Seema need not to prove surgeon's negligence because presence of abdominal pack in her abdomen is sufficient proof therefor
D. None of the above

175. Principle : Whoever takes away with him any minor person less than sixteen years of age if a male, or less than eighteen years of age if a female out of the keeping of parents of such minor person without the consent of such parent, is said to kidnap such minor person.

Facts : A female born on January 01, 1995 got admitted to an undergraduate program of a reputed University on July 01, 2012. She became friendly with one of the boys, born on June 01, 1994, of her class. The boy and the girl decided to marry. The parents of the boy agreed but the family of the girl did not agree. On December 15, 2012 the girl made a call from her Blackberry to the boy. The girl told the boy to come in his car at a particular place and time. The boy reached the stipulated place before the stipulated time. He waited there for about half an hour. The girl reached the stipulated place. She opened the door of the car and sat beside the boy who was on the driving seat. Without exchanging any pleasantries, the boy drove the car to an unknown place. The father of the girl lodged an FIR in the nearest police station on January 20, 2013.

A. The boy has committed the offence of kidnapping
B. The boy has not committed the offence of kidnapping
C. The boy has not committed the offence of kidnapping for there is a delay in filing the FIR
D. The boy has not committed the offence of kidnapping because the girl was his classmate

176. Principle : Whoever voluntarily has carnal intercourse against the order of nature with any man, woman or animal shall be punished.

Facts : Two adult men were found engaged in carnal intercourse by the police. The police arrested the men and produced them before the Court.

A. Court will punish the police officer who arrested the men
B. Court will not punish the men for they were adults
C. Court will punish the men
D. Court may be requested to declare the law unconstitutional

177. Principle : Wherever the causing of a certain effect, or an attempt to cause that effect, by an act or by an omission, is an offence, it is to be understood that the causing of that effect partly by an act and partly by an omission is the same offence.

Facts : A intentionally omitted to give food to his father. He also used to beat his father. Consequently A's father died.

A. A did not commit any offence
B. A committed only the offence of omitting to give food to his father
C. A committed only the offence of beating of his father
D. A committed the offence of killing of his father

178. Principle : Nothing is an offence which is done by a child under seven years of age.

Facts : A, a child born on January 01, 2005 killed another child 'B' on December 30, 2011.

A. A has committed no offence
B. A has committed the offence as it is heinous crime
C. Killing of one child by another child is not an offence
D. A has not committed the offence for on the date of killing of B, A was a minor

179. Principle : A pact, other than a pact to commit suicide, to suffer any harm is not an offence, provided the age of the person who has given his consent to suffer harm is above eighteen years.

Facts : A enters into a pact with B, a boy of less than 18 years of age, to fence with each other for amusement. They agreed to suffer any harm which, in the course of such fencing, may be caused without foul play.

A. A, while playing fairly, hurts B, A commits no offence
B. A, while playing only unfairly, hurts B, A commits an offence

C. A, while playing fairly, hurts B, A commits an offence
D. A, while playing unfairly, hurts B, A commits no offence

180. Principle : When an act, which would otherwise be an offence, is not that offence by reason of the youth, the want of maturity of understanding, the unsoundness of mind or the intoxication of the person doing that act, every person has the same right of private defence against that act which he would have if the act were that offence. Nothing is an offence which is done in the exercise of the right of private defence.

Facts : A, under the influence of madness, attempts to kill B. B in order to save his life causes grievous hurt to A.
A. A has committed an offence
B. A has not committed an offence
C. B has committed an offence
D. B has not committed any offence

181. Principle : Mere silence as to facts likely to affect the decision of a person to enter into a contract does not amount to fraud, unless his silence is in itself equivalent to speech.

Facts : A sells to B a horse which A knows to be of unsound mind. B says to A that if A does not say anything about the state of mind of horse, then B shall presume that the horse is of sound mind. A says nothing to B about the mental condition of horse.
A. A has committed fraud
B. A has committed misrepresentation
C. There cannot be a fraud because A says nothing about the mental condition of the horse
D. There cannot be a fraud because B did not ask A whether the horse is of sound mind

182. Principle : Whoever by words, either spoken or written brings or attempts to bring into hatred or contempt, or excites or attempts to excite disaffection towards the Government established by law in India shall be punished. However, comments expressing disapprobation of the administrative or other action of the Government without exciting or attempting to excite hatred, contempt or disaffection, do not constitute an offence.

Facts : A renowned Professor of Economics wrote a critical comment on the economic policies of the Government of India in a National Daily. This piece of writing generated academic debate not only in the print media but also on television and internet. A student of law asked the fellow Indians on a social networking website to assemble at a particular place for peaceful and silent demonstration against the said economic policies on a stipulated date and time. The crowd assembled at that venue and started shouting anti-government slogans. Police arrested the professor.
A. The professor has committed the offence
B. The professor has not committed any offence
C. The student of law has committed the offence
D. The crowd has committed an offence

183. Principle : Where two or more persons have made a complaint for the grant of compulsory licence to the Copyright Board, the licence shall be granted to that complainant only who, in the opinion of the Copyright Board, would best serve the interests of the general public.

Facts : Four persons made a complaint for the grant of compulsory licence to the Copyright Board.
A. Licence shall be granted to only one complainant
B. Licence may be granted to two complainants
C. Licence may be granted to three complainants
D. Licence must be granted to all the four complainants

184. Principle : Any police officer, not below the rank of a Sub-Inspector, may, if he is satisfied that an offence in respect of the infringement of copyright in any work has been, is being, or is likely to be, committed, seize without warrant, all copies of the work, and all plates used for the purpose of making infringing copies of the work, wherever found, and all copies and plates so seized shall, as soon as practicable, be produced before a Magistrate.

Facts : A Superintendent of Police (SP) conducted a raid on a shop and found pirated copies of books. The SP formed an opinion that infringement of copyright is taking place. He arrested the shop owner without warrant in the light of above mentioned propositions.
A. The arrest of the shop owner was within the power of the SP
B. The arrest of the shop owner was not within the power of the SP
C. The shop owner can never be arrested
D. SP was not competent to know whether infringement of copyright has taken place

185. Principle : Whoever attempts to commit an offence punishable by the Indian Penal Code and in such attempts does any act towards the commission of the offence, shall be punished. Stealing is an offence punishable by the Indian Penal Code.

Facts : A makes an attempt to steal some jewels by breaking open a box, and after so opening the box, finds that there is no jewel in it.
A. A has committed no offence
B. A has committed the offence of stealing
C. A has attempted to commit the offence of stealing
D. None of the above

186. Principle : Whoever by words either spoken or intended to be read, or by signs or by visible representations, makes or publishes any imputation concerning any person intending to harm, or knowing or having reason to believe that such imputation will harm, the reputation of such person, is said to defame that person.

Facts : In a community there is a custom of stealing shoes of bridegroom during the marriage ceremony. The shoes of the bridegroom were stolen by Y. 'A' announced that Z has stolen the shoes. Everyone present in the marriage party started staring at Z with great surprise. Z felt very ashamed.

A. A defamed Z
B. A did not defame Z
C. A defamed Z for Z felt very ashamed
D. A defamed the whole marriage party

187. Principle : An employer is liable for the negligence of his employee. But an employer is not liable for the negligence of his employee if the victim of such negligence is one of his other employees.

Facts : 'A' and 'B' were working in a factory as unskilled labourers. A was carrying a basket of stones on his head. B was sitting on the ground. When A crossed B, all of a sudden a stone fell down from the basket and hit B on his head. B died immediately.

A. The owner of the factory will be liable
B. A and the owner of the factory shall be jointly liable
C. The owner of the factory will not be liable
D. None of the above

188. Principle : Damages are the money recompense, as far as money can do, for the violation of a right.

Facts : A, an Indian citizen, having a right to vote, was not allowed to cast his vote on the polling booth, by the returning officer. Name of A was mentioned in the voter's list. A has also reported at the polling booth in time. However, the candidate in whose favour A would have cast his vote won the election. A filed a suit claiming damages.

A. A will be entitled to damages
B. A will not be entitled to damages
C. A will be entitled to only nominal damages
D. A will be entitled to exemplary damages

189. Principle : When a party to a contract has refused to perform, or disabled himself from performing, his promise in its entirety, the other party may put an end to the contract.

Facts : A engaged B on April 12 to enter his service on June 1, but on May 11, A wrote to B that his services would not be needed. On May 22, B joined C for employment.

A. B must wait till June 1
B. B must have joined C on May 11
C. B is not bound to wait till June 1
D. A must pay damages to B

190. Principle : When a person voluntarily agrees to suffer some harm, he is not allowed to complain for that.

Facts : 'A' was one of the spectators at a formula one car race, being held at Gurgaon, on a track owned by one 'M' company. During the race, there was a collision between two racing cars, one of which was thrown away amidst spectators, thereby causing an injury to 'A'. 'A' claims damages for the injuries caused to him.

A. M company will be liable for damages because the injury was caused during the race organized by it
B. M company will not be liable for damages because A had come to see the race on his own will
C. M company will not be liable for damages because the collision between the cars was beyond its control
D. M company will be liable because it has earned huge revenue by way of sale of tickets for the event

191. Principle : An interest which is created on a transfer of property and depends upon the fulfilment of a condition will fail if the fulfilment of the condition is impossible or is forbidden by law or is of such a nature that, if permitted, it would defeat the provisions of any law or is fraudulent or involves or implies injury to the person or property of another or the court regards it as immoral or opposed to public policy.

Facts : A gives ₹ Ten Lacs to B on condition that B shall marry A's daughter C. On the date on which A gave ₹ Ten Lacs to B, C was dead.

A. B's interest in ₹ Ten Lacs fails because of impossibility
B. B's interest in ₹ Ten Lacs fails because of immorality
C. B's interest in ₹ Ten Lacs fails because of prohibition by law
D. B's interest in ₹ Ten Lacs does not fail

192. Principle : A condition precedent must be complied with before the happening of the event to which such a condition is attached. Fulfilment of such a condition after the happening of the event is no fulfilment of condition.

Facts : A transfers ₹ 5,000 to B on condition that he shall marry with the consent of C, D and E. As C, D and E had to go abroad for some business purposes and as the date of marriage was already fixed, therefore, B marries without the consent of C, D and E, but obtains their consent after the marriage when C, D and E return to their country.

A. B has fulfilled the condition
B. B has not fulfilled the condition
C. B was free to marry any one without the consent of any body
D. B must divorce his wife as he married her without fulfilling the condition

193. Principle : In an agreement, a condition subsequent must be complied with, to claim the benefit of that agreement.

Facts : A agrees to transfer a farm to B, provided that, if B does not go to England within three years after the date of the agreement, his interest in the farm shall cease. B does not go to England within the term prescribed.

A. B's interest in the farm continues
B. B's interest in the farm does not continue
C. B has a fundamental right to go to England or not to go to England and hence the condition was illegal
D. The agreement between A and B was void

194. Principle : Existence of all the alleged facts is relevant whether they occurred at the same time and place or at different times and places.

Facts : A, a permanent resident in a foreign country who never visited India, is accused of waging war against the Government of India by taking part in an armed insurrection in which property is destroyed, troops are attacked and prisons are broken open.

A. The existence of all the above mentioned alleged facts is relevant
B. Only the alleged fact that A is accused of waging war against the Government of India is relevant
C. The fact that A was a permanent resident in a foreign country who never visited India is not relevant
D. Only the alleged fact of taking part by A in armed insurrection is relevant

195. Principle : Whoever desires any court to give judgement about any legal right or liability which depends on the existence of those facts which he asserts, must prove that those facts exist.

Facts : A asserts that B, C and D have committed an offence of criminal conspiracy and therefore A desires a Court to give judgement that B, C and D shall be punished for that crime which A says B, C and D have committed.

A. A must prove that B, C and D have committed the crime
B. B, C and D must prove that they have not committed the crime
C. A must prove that B, C and D were present at the place of crime
D. Police must prove that B, C and D have committed the crime

196. Principle : The fact that any person was born during the continuance of a valid marriage between his mother and any man, or within two hundred and eighty days after its dissolution, the mother remaining unmarried, shall be conclusive proof that he is the legitimate son of that man, unless it can be shown that the parties to the marriage had no access to each other at any time when he could have been begotten.

Facts : X and Y married on January 15, 1995. Y, the wife of X, never left her parental home and never went to her husband's home. A boy was born to Y on July 15, 1995. For the Court:

A. There shall be a conclusive proof that the boy is the legitimate son of X
B. There shall be no conclusive proof that the boy is the legitimate son of X
C. There shall be a conclusive proof that the boy is the illegitimate son of X
D. There shall be no evidence at all

197. Principle : An unlawful interference with a person's use or enjoyment of land, or some right over, or in connection with it, is a nuisance in law of tort.

Facts : During the scarcity of onions, long queues were made outside the defendant's shop who having a license to sell fruits and vegetables used to sell only 1 Kg. of onion per ration card. The queues extended on to the highway and also caused some obstruction to the neighbouring shops. The neighbouring shopkeepers filed a suit for nuisance against the defendant. Which one of the following decisions will be correct in this suit?

A. The defendant is liable for nuisance
B. The defendant is not liable for nuisance
C. The defendant is liable under the principle of strict liability
D. The plaintiff's suit should be decreed in favour of the neighbouring shopkeeper

198. Principle : Every agreement in restraint of the marriage of any person, other than a minor, is void.

Facts : Qadir Khan died in a road accident. Two co-widows, Sultana and Marjina enter into an agreement that if any of them will remarry, would forfeit her right to her share in the deceased husband's property.

A. The agreement is void because it was restraint of marriage
B. The agreement is not void because no restraint was imposed upon either of two widows for remarriage
C. The restraint was partial so agreement is valid
D. None of the above

199. Principle : Nothing is an offence merely by reason of its being done with the knowledge that it is likely to cause harm, if it be done without any criminal intention to cause harm, and in good faith for the purpose of preventing or avoiding other harm to a person or property.

Facts : Mr. Sharman, the Italian captain of a steam vessel, suddenly and without any fault or negligence on his part, finds himself near the Kochi coast in such a position that before he can stop his vessel, he must inevitably run down a boat B with twenty or thirty passengers on board, unless he changes the course of his vessel, and that by changing his course, he must incur risk of running down a boat C with only two passengers on board, which he may possibly clear. Whether Sharman has committed an offence?

A. Sharman has committed no offence because this was done out of necessity
B. Sharman can be held responsible for the act of criminal negligence
C. Sharman can be held responsible for culpable homicide
D. This is a clear case of accident so Sharman cannot be held responsible

200. Principle : Only the Parliament or the State Legislatures have the authority to enact laws on their own. No law made by State can take away a person's fundamental right.

Facts : Parliament enacted a law, which according to a group of lawyers is violating the fundamental rights of traders. The group of lawyers filed a writ petition against the Parliament for enacting such law and requests the court to quash the law and to direct the Parliament to make a new law.

A. No writ would lie against the Parliament, as the Court has no authority to direct the Parliament to enact or re-enact a law
B. The Court can quash the existing law if it violates fundamental right and can direct to make a new law
C. The Court can quash the existing law if it violates fundamental right but cannot direct the Parliament to make a new law
D. None of these

ANSWERS

1	**2**	**3**	**4**	**5**	**6**	**7**	**8**	**9**	**10**
B	B	D	B	C	A	D	A	B	C
11	**12**	**13**	**14**	**15**	**16**	**17**	**18**	**19**	**20**
A	B	C	C	B	C	C	A	C	D
21	**22**	**23**	**24**	**25**	**26**	**27**	**28**	**29**	**30**
C	D	C	C	C	C	B	D	D	D
31	**32**	**33**	**34**	**35**	**36**	**37**	**38**	**39**	**40**
A	A	D	C	A	D	A	C	B	D
41	**42**	**43**	**44**	**45**	**46**	**47**	**48**	**49**	**50**
B	D	B	C	A	C	D	A	C	C
51	**52**	**53**	**54**	**55**	**56**	**57**	**58**	**59**	**60**
D	D	A	A	B	B	C	D	D	B
61	**62**	**63**	**64**	**65**	**66**	**67**	**68**	**69**	**70**
D	B	A	B	A	D	A	B	A	B
71	**72**	**73**	**74**	**75**	**76**	**77**	**78**	**79**	**80**
D	C	B	B	C	B	C	D	C	B
81	**82**	**83**	**84**	**85**	**86**	**87**	**88**	**89**	**90**
B	A	B	B	B	D	C	C	D	D
91	**92**	**93**	**94**	**95**	**96**	**97**	**98**	**99**	**100**
B	B	D	A	B	A	C	B	C	A
101	**102**	**103**	**104**	**105**	**106**	**107**	**108**	**109**	**110**
B	D	C	B	D	B	A	C	A	A
111	**112**	**113**	**114**	**115**	**116**	**117**	**118**	**119**	**120**
D	D	B	B	D	B	C	B	C	C
121	**122**	**123**	**124**	**125**	**126**	**127**	**128**	**129**	**130**
B	A	B	B	B	A	D	B	D	A
131	**132**	**133**	**134**	**135**	**136**	**137**	**138**	**139**	**140**
D	B	A	A	D	A	B	D	C	B

141	142	143	144	145	146	147	148	149	150
A	B	B	D	A	C	B	D	C	B
151	152	153	154	155	156	157	158	159	160
D	A	C	B	D	B	A	C	C	C
161	162	163	164	165	166	167	168	169	170
A	C	A	C	B	D	D	D	A	B
171	172	173	174	175	176	177	178	179	180
C	C	B	C	C	C	D	D	C	D
181	182	183	184	185	186	187	188	189	190
C	B	A	B	C	B	C	D	C	A
191	192	193	194	195	196	197	198	199	200
A	C	B	A	A	A	B	A	A	C

EXPLANATORY ANSWERS

41. $\frac{2}{3}$ is a rational number whereas $\frac{\sqrt{2}}{\sqrt{3}}$ is an irrational number.

42. Required number = 154.

43. A single discount equivalent to a discount series

$$= \left(x + y - \frac{xy}{100}\right)\%$$

$$= \left(15 + 5 - \frac{15 \times 5}{100}\right)\%$$

$$= (20 - .75)\%$$

$$= 19.25\%$$

$$\cong 20\%.$$

44. Cost price $= \frac{100 \times 2345}{81}$

$$= ₹\,2895 \cong ₹\,3000.$$

45. Area of rhombus $= \frac{1}{2} \times d_1 \times d_2$

$$= \frac{1}{2} \times 1 \times 1.5$$

$$= \frac{1.5}{2} = .75\,\text{m}^2.$$

46. An angle in a semi circle is right angle $= \frac{\pi}{2}$.

47. Required days $= \frac{250 \times 33}{330} = 25\,\text{days}.$

48. $n(A \cup B) = n(A) + n(B) - n(A \cap B)$

$500 = 200 + x - 102$

$\Rightarrow \quad 300 = x - 102$

$\Rightarrow \quad x = 402.$

49. $kx + 3y = k - 3$

$12x + ky = k$

Since, the equations have infinite solutions

$$\therefore \quad \frac{a_1}{a_2} = \frac{b_1}{b_2} = \frac{c_1}{c_2}$$

$$\frac{k}{12} = \frac{3}{k} = \frac{k-3}{k}$$

(*i*) (*ii*) (*iii*)

from (*ii*) and (*iii*)

$3 = k - 3 \quad \Rightarrow \quad k = 6$

from (*i*) and (*ii*)

$k^2 = 36 \quad \Rightarrow \quad k = \pm 6$

from (*i*) and (*iii*)

$k^2 - 12k + 36 = 0$

$(k - 6)^2 = 0$

$k - 6 = 0 \quad \Rightarrow \quad k = 6$

Hence $k = 6$.

50.

C.I.	f	x	fx
100–150	4	125	500
150–200	5	175	875
200–250	12	225	2700
250–300	2	275	550
300–350	2	325	650
	25		5275

$$\bar{x} = \frac{5275}{25} = 211$$

The mean daily expenditure on food = ₹ 211.

51. Let blue ball in the jar = x

$\therefore$ no. of green ball = $24 - x$

According to the question,

$$\frac{2}{3} = \frac{24 - x}{24}$$

$\Rightarrow \quad 48 = 72 - 3x$

$\Rightarrow \quad 3x = 72 - 48$

$\Rightarrow \quad 3x = 24$

$\Rightarrow \quad x = 8$

number of blue balls = 8.

52. $A = P\left(1+\frac{r}{100}\right)^t$

$= 250000\left(1+\frac{2}{100}\right)^2$

$= 250000 \times \frac{51\times 51}{50\times 50}$

$= 260100$

The growth of population = 260100 – 250000
= 10100.

53.

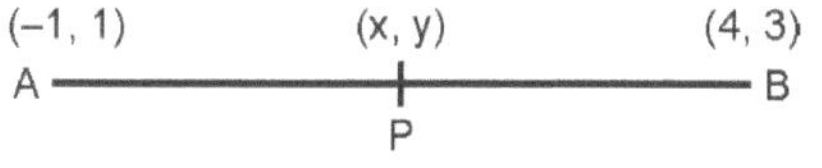

$AP = PB$

$\Rightarrow \quad AP^2 = PB^2$

$(x + 1)^2 + (y - 1)^2 = (4 - x)^2 + (3 - y)^2$

$\Rightarrow x^2 + 1 + 2x + y^2 + 1 - 2y =$
$16 + x^2 - 8x + 9 + y^2 - 6y$

$\Rightarrow \quad 10x + 4y = 23.$

54. 8 + 16 + 24 + 32 + ... + 120

= 8(1 + 2 + 3 + 4 + ... + 15)

$= 8\times\frac{15\times 16}{2} = 4\times 15\times 16 = 960$.

56.

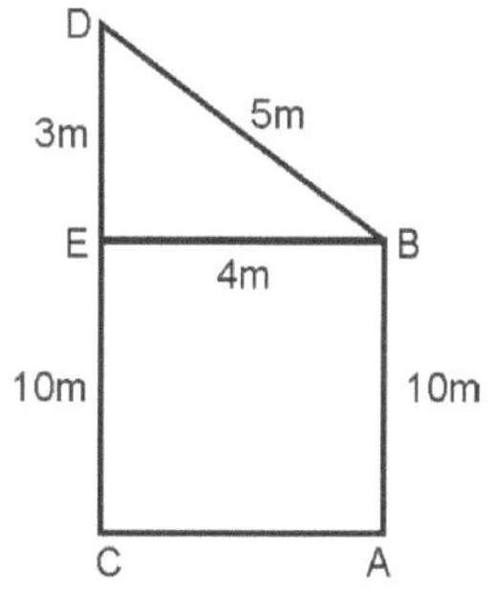

In Δ BED,

$ED^2 = (5)^2 - (4)^2 = 25 - 16 = 9$

$\therefore ED = \sqrt{9} = 3$ m

Area of ABCD $= \frac{1}{2}\times h\,(a+b)$

$= \frac{1}{2}\times 4\,(10+13)$

$= 2 \times 23 = 46$ m^2.

58.

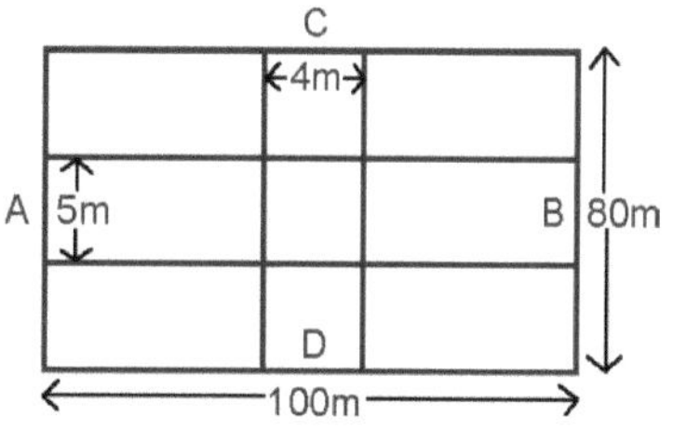

Area of AB road = 100 × 5 = 500 m^2

Area of CD road = 80 × 4 = 320 m^2

Area of (AB + CD) roads = 820 m^2

Common area = 5 × 4 = 20 m^2

Total area of roads = 820 – 20 = 800 m^2

Cost of 1 m^2 = ₹10

Cost of 800 m^2 = ₹10 × 800 = ₹ 8000.

59. 11 – 10 = 1

gain % $= \frac{1}{10}\times 100 = 10\%$.

60. $3x + 4x + 5x + 8x = 360°$

$20x = 360°$

$x = \frac{360}{20} = 18$

∴ Smallest angle = 18 × 3 = 54°.

Previous Paper (Solved)

Common Law Admission Test (CLAT-UG)

Entrance Exam, 2012

Section-I : English Including Comprehension

Instructions (1-5): *Choose the correct synonym out of the four choices given.*

1. Lethargy
A. serenity B. listlessness
C. impassivity D. laxity

2. Emaciated
A. tall B. languid
C. very thin D. wise

3. Latent
A. concealed B. apparent
C. lethargic D. prompt

4. Sporadic
A. epidemic B. whirling
C. occasional D. stagnant

5. Compendium
A. summary B. index
C. reference D. collection

Instructions (6-15): *Choose the correct option out of the four choices given.*

6. Given an example pertinent .... the case.
A. with B. on
C. for D. to

7. My voice reverberated .... the walls of the castle.
A. with B. from
C. in D. on

8. The reward was not commensurate .... the work done by us.
A. for B. on
C. with D. order

9. Our tragic experience in the recent past provides an index .... the state of lawlessness in this region.
A. of B. in
C. at D. by

10. Your conduct smacks .... recklessness.
A. of B. with
C. from D. in

11. A good judge never gropes .... the conclusion.
A. to B. at
C. on D. for

12. Nobody in our group is a genius .... winning friends and in convincing people.
A. for B. in
C. of D. at

13. If you are averse .... recommending my name, you should not hesitate to admit it.
A. about B. for
C. to D. against

14. Religious leaders should not delve .... politics.
A. in B. with
C. at D. into

15. What you say has hardly any bearing .... the lives of tribals.
A. about B. for
C. on D. with

Instructions (16-20): *Select the correct meaning of the italicized idioms and phrases out of the four choices given.*

16. He *burnt his fingers* by interfering in his neighbour's affair.
A. got himself into trouble B. burnt himself
C. got himself insulted D. got rebuked

17. Mr. Gupta, who is one of the trustees of a big charity, is suspected of *feathering his own nest.*
A. being lazy in doing his work
B. being too generous
C. neglecting his job
D. making money unfairly

18. Mrs. Hashmi has been *in the blues* for the last several weeks.
A. abroad B. unwell
C. depressed D. penniless

19. For the first week, the apprentice felt like *a fish out of water.*
A. frustrated B. homeless
C. disappointed D. uncomfortable

20. His friends failed to see why he should *ride the high horse* just because he had won an election.
A. become abnormal B. appear arrogant
C. indulge in dreams D. hate others

Instructions (21-25): *Given below are the jumbled sentences of a paragraph. The first and the last sentence of the jumbled paragraph are given in correct order. Arrange the middle sentences in the correct sequence.*

21. (*i*) On one hand we are proud of being Indians,
(*ii*) on the other hand we behave as if we were still at the dawn of our civilization
(*iii*) murders of our own brothers and sisters is not the way to please Ram or Rahim
(*iv*) the citizens of the land where Buddha and Gandhi taught
(*v*) the principles of love and non-violence,
(*vi*) nor does it fetch us any prosperity.
A. (*ii*), (*iii*), (*iv*), (*v*) B. (*iii*), (*iv*), (*v*), (*ii*)
C. (*iv*), (*v*), (*iii*), (*ii*) D. (*iv*), (*v*), (*ii*), (*iii*)

22. (*i*) On the basis of experiments with rats
(*ii*) health experts here say that
(*iii*) exercise more and consume vitamins,
(*iv*) they will live up to 100 years or more
(*v*) if humans eat less,
(*vi*) and be vigorous in their eighties and nineties.
A. (*ii*), (*iii*), (*v*), (*iv*) B. (*ii*), (*v*), (*iii*), (*iv*)
C. (*ii*), (*v*), (*iv*), (*iii*) D. (*v*), (*ii*), (*iii*), (*iv*)

23. (*i*) The release of atomic energy is the greatest achievement which science has yet attained
(*ii*) but the first invention to which their discoveries were applied was a bomb
(*iii*) the atom was split by physicists whose minds were set on the search for knowledge
(*iv*) it was more deadly than any other weapon invented so far
(*v*) it is with dread that scientists regard the first use to which their greatest discovery was put
(*vi*) however, they are gratified by the numerous applications of atomic energy for peaceful and constructive population.
A. (*ii*), (*iii*), (*iv*), (*v*) B. (*v*), (*iii*), (*ii*), (*iv*)
C. (*iii*), (*ii*), (*iv*), (*v*) D. (*iv*), (*v*), (*iii*), (*ii*)

24. (*i*) The problem of food is intimately connected with population
(*ii*) wages will seldom rise in proportion to the rising prices
(*iii*) the market is governed by demand and supply
(*iv*) without enough food, such people lack health, strength of efficiency
(*v*) if too many people demand goods to go round, prices will rise and poor classes will starve
(*vi*) they fall an easy prey to all sorts of diseases.
A. (*iii*), (*v*), (*ii*), (*iv*) B. (*ii*), (*iii*), (*iv*), (*v*)
C. (*iv*), (*ii*), (*v*), (*iii*) D. (*v*), (*iii*), (*iv*), (*ii*)

25. (*i*) India's message has always been one of love and peace.
(*ii*) our Buddha was the light of Asia
(*iii*) it has been a source of light and wisdom to the rest of the world
(*iv*) Ashoka, moved by the horrors of Kalinga War, adopted the message of non-violence
(*v*) the greatest apostle of non-violence in recent years was Mahatma Gandhi
(*vi*) he shook the foundation of the British rule in India through non-violence.
A. (*ii*), (*v*), (*iii*), (*iv*) B. (*iv*), (*ii*), (*iii*), (*v*)
C. (*v*), (*iv*), (*iii*), (*ii*) D. (*iii*), (*ii*), (*iv*), (*v*)

Instructions (26-30): *Given below are a few commonly used foreign language phrases, select the correct answer from the four options given below.*

26. Mala fide
A. generous B. bad intention
C. trustworthy D. genuine

27. Tabula rasa
A. clean slate B. agitated
C. deprived D. creative

28. Carte blanche
A. slavery B. complete discretion
C. anarchy D. dependent

29. De jure
A. illegal B. heir
C. concerning law D. forbidden

30. Raison d'etre
A. logical conclusion B. reason for existence
C. free choice D. dubious argument

Instructions (31-40): *Read the given passage carefully and attempt the questions that follow.*

The work which Gandhiji had taken up was only regarding the achievement of political freedom but also the establishment of a new social order based on truth and non-violence, unity and peace, equality and universal brotherhood and maximum freedom for all. This unfinished part of his experiment was perhaps even more difficult to achieve than the achievement of political freedom. In the political struggle, the fight was against a foreign power and all one could do was either join it or wish it success and given it his/her moral support. In establishing a social order on this pattern, there was a strong possibility of a conflict arising between diverse groups and classes of our own people. Experience shows that man values his possessions even more than his life because in the former he sees the means for perpetuation and survival of his descendants even after his body is reduced to ashes. A new order cannot be established without radically changing the mind and attitude of men towards property and, at some stage or the other, the 'haves' have to yield place to the 'have-nots'. We have seen, in our time, attempts to achieve a kind of egalitarian society and the picture of it after it was achieved. But this was done, by and large, through the use of physical force.

In the ultimate analysis it is difficult, if not impossible, to say that the instinct to possess has been rooted out or that it will not reappear in an even worse form under a different guise. It may even be that, like a gas kept confined within containers under great pressure, or water held back by a big dam, once the barrier breaks, the reaction will one day sweep back with a violence equal in extent and intensity to what was used to establish and maintain the outward egalitarian form. This enforced egalitarianism contains, in its bosom, the seed of its own destruction.

The root cause of class conflict is possessiveness or the acquisitive instinct. So long as the ideal that is to be achieved is one of securing the maximum material satisfaction, possessiveness is neither suppressed nor eliminated but grows on what it feeds. Nor does it cease to be possessiveness, whether it is confined to only a few or is shared by many.

If egalitarianism is to endure, it has to be based not on the possession of the maximum material goods by a few or by all but on voluntary, enlightened renunciation of those goods which cannot be shared by others or can be enjoyed only at the expense of others. This calls for substitution of material values by purely spiritual ones. The paradise of material satisfaction, which is sometimes equated with progress these days, neither spells peace nor progress. Mahatma Gandhi has shown us how the acquisitive instinct inherent in man can be transmuted by the adoption of the ideal of trusteeship by those who 'have' for the benefit of all those who 'have not' so that, instead of leading to exploitation and conflict, it would become a means and incentive for the amelioration and progress of society respectively.

31. According to the passage, egalitarianism will not survive if
- A. It is based on voluntary renunciation.
- B. It is achieved by resorting to physical force.
- C. Underprivileged people are not involved in its establishment.
- D. People's outlook towards it is not radically changed.

32. According to the passage, why does man value his possessions more than his life?
- A. He has inherent desire to share his possession with others.
- B. He is endowed with the possessive instinct.
- C. Only his possession helps him earn love and respect from his descendants.
- D. Through his possessions he can preserve his name even after his death.

33. According to the passage, which was the unfinished part of Gandhi's experiment?
- A. Educating people to avoid class conflict.
- B. Achieving total political freedom for the country.
- C. Establishment of an egalitarian society.
- D. Radically changing the mind and attitude of men towards truth and non-violence.

34. Which of the following statements is 'not true' in the context of the passage?
- A. True egalitarianism can be achieved by giving up one's possessions under compulsion.
- B. Man values his life more than his possessions.
- C. Possessive instinct is a natural desire of human beings.
- D. In the political struggle, the fight was against alien rule.

35. According to the passage, true egalitarianism will last only if
- A. It is thrust upon people.
- B. It is based on truth and non-violence.
- C. People inculcate spiritual values instead of material values.
- D. 'Haves' and 'have-notes' live together peacefully.

36. According to the passage, people ultimately overturn a social order...........
- A. which is based on coercion and oppression.
- B. which does not satisfy their basic needs.
- C. which is based upon conciliation and rapprochement.
- D. which is not congenital to the spiritual values of the people.

37. According to the passage, the root cause of class conflict is
- A. The paradise of material satisfaction.
- B. Dominant inherent acquisitive instinct in man.
- C. Exploitation of the 'have-nots' by the 'haves'.
- D. A Social order where the unprivileged are not a part of the establishment.

38. Which of the following statements is 'not true' in the context of the passage?
- A. A new order can be established by radically changing the outlook of people towards it.
- B. Adoption of the ideal of trusteeship can minimize possessive instinct.
- C. Enforced egalitarianism can be the cause of its own destruction.
- D. Ideal of new order is to secure maximum material satisfaction.

39. Which of the following conclusions can be deduced from the passage?
- A. A social order based on truth and non-violence alone can help the achievement of political freedom.

B. After establishing the social order of Gandhiji's pattern, the possibility of a conflict between different classes of society will hardly exist.
C. It is difficult to change the mind and attitude of men towards property.
D. In an egalitarian society, material satisfaction can be enjoyed only at the expense of others.

40. According to the passage, what does "adopting of the ideal of trusteeship" mean?
A. Equating peace and progress with material satisfaction.
B. Adoption of the ideal by the 'haves' for the benefit of 'have-nots'.
C. Voluntary enlightened remuneration of the possessive instinct by the privileged class.
D. Substitution of spiritual values by material ones by those who live in the paradise of material satisfaction.

Section-II : General Knowledge/Current Affairs

41. The longest highway in India runs from
A. Kolkata to Jammu
B. Shillong to Amritsar
C. Ambala to Nagercoil
D. Varanasi to Kanyakumari

42. The longest irrigation canal in India is called
A. Upper Bari Doab Canal
B. Indira Gandhi Canal
C. Sirhind Canal
D. Yamuna Canal

43. Leukemia is a disease related to
A. Kidney B. Throat
C. Blood D. Eyes

44. In which city was Osama Bin Laden killed in May 2011?
A. Islamabad B. Abbottabad
C. Faisalabad D. Peshawar

45. The XI Five Year Plan envisaged the highest growth in the sector of
A. Industry B. Agriculture
C. Services D. Manufacturing

46. Light year is a unit of
A. Distance B. Time
C. Sound D. Light intensity

47. The IV summit of BRICS was held in New Delhi on
A. 11th January, 2012 B. 1st April, 2012
C. 29th March, 2012 D. 28th February, 2012

48. An indigenous nuclear submarine still under construction has been named as
A. Chakra B. Sudarshan
C. Arihant D. Ghaatak

49. Government of India has launched a publicity campaign for census 2011 in association with which of the following UN organization?
A. United Nations Development Programme (UNDP)
B. World Health Organization (WHO)
C. United Nations Children's Emergency Fund (UNICEF)
D. United Nations Population Fund (UNPF)

50. Mahatma Gandhi National Rural Employment Guarantee Act (MGNREGA) completed how many years of operation in 2011?
A. 3 years B. 4 years
C. 5 years D. 6 years

51. The first ever formula one race in India was held in
A. Greater Noida B. New Delhi
C. Faridabad D. Pune

52. Name the actor who has been honoured with the Dadasaheb Phalke Award in 2012.
A. Naseerudin Shah B. Kamal Hasan
C. Soumitra Chatterjee D. Amol Paleker

53. In which city was the Arab Summit held in the last week of March 2012?
A. Baghadad B. Cairo
C. Beirut D. Riyadh

54. The two Supreme Court Judges who delivered the famous 2-G judgment in February 2012 were
A. Justice G.S. Singhvi and Justice Gyan Sudha Mishra
B. Justice G.S. Singhvi and Justice A.K. Ganguly
C. Justice S.H. Kapadia and Justice A.K. Ganguly
D. Justice Chandramauli Kumar Prasad and Justice H.L. Gokhale

55. Who presides over the joint sitting of both houses of Parliament?
A. Speaker of Lok Sabha
B. President
C. Chairman of Rajya Sabha
D. Prime Minister

56. Christian Lagarde heads the
A. World Bank
B. UNICEF
C. International Monetary Fund
D. WHO

57. The seat of International Criminal Court is at
A. The Hague B. Geneva
C. Washington D. Tokyo

58. First Indian to ski to North Pole is
A. Arun Nayyar B. Ajeet Bajaj
C. Sq. Ldr. Sanjay Thapar D. Neal Paramjeet

59. First woman Director General of Police in India was
A. Kanchan Choudhary B. Kavitha Choudhary
C. Kiran Bedi D. Aswathy Tonge

60. Which countries co-hosted the One-day cricket World Cup in 2011?
A. India, Bangladesh and Sri Lanka
B. India, Bangladesh and Pakistan
C. India, Sri Lanka and Pakistan
D. India, Sri Lanka, Bangladesh and Pakistan

61. Priyanka Chopra has been named National Ambassador of
A. WHO
B. UNICEF
C. UNESCO
D. International Red Cross Society

62. Who is leading in the Republican primaries to contest the American Presidential election scheduled in November 2012?
A. Sara Palin B. Newt Gingrich
C. Rick Santorum D. Mitt Romney

63. Supreme Court recently declared 'Salva Judum' unconstitutional. What is 'Salva Judum'?
A. A terrorist outfit
B. An armed civilian group formed to combat Maoists
C. A money-chain business
D. Custom of killing a girl for inter-caste marriage in the name of honour

64. As per the Indian Union Budget of 2012-13, the income-tax exemption limit for persons below 65 years of age is
A. ₹ 175000 B. ₹ 200000
C. ₹ 250000 D. ₹ 190000

65. The U.N. Climate Change Conference 2011 was held in
A. New Delhi B. Doha
C. Durban D. Geneva

66. Who said that, 'Man is a social animal'?
A. Socrates B. Aristotle
C. Kahn D. Plato

67. World Computer Literacy day is celebrated on
A. November 14 B. November 3
C. December 2 D. July 5

68. Whose teaching inspired the French Revolution?
A. Rousseau B. Locke
C. Hegel D. Wagner

69. The II Africa-India Summit was held in May 2011 in
A. New Delhi B. Lagos
C. Nairobi D. Addis Ababa

70. The famous Akshardham temple is situated in the city of
A. Jamnagar B. Gandhinagar
C. Jammu D. Madurai

71. Who out of the following was the recipient of Dhyan Chand Award in 2011?
A. Satish Pillai B. Hukam Singh
C. Shabbir Ali D. Mukh Bain Singh

72. Name the annual fair of Rajasthan that is famous for its camel trading event
A. Maru Mela B. Pushkar Mela
C. Suraj Kund Mela D. Sonepur Mela

73. The 38th G-8 summit will be held in 2012 in
A. USA B. UK
C. Germany D. Canada

74. Who was awarded the Nobel Prize for literature in 2011?
A. Paul Lauterbur B. Bill Clinton
C. Tomas Transtromer D. Shirin Ebadi

75. Who was awarded the UNESCO King Sejong Literacy Prize in 2011?
A. Nelson Mandela
B. National Literacy Service, Burundi
C. Medha Patkar
D. National Literacy Mission, India

76. December 10 is observed as
A. World Health Day B. U. N. Day
C. Red Cross Day D. Human Rights Day

77. Which is the largest gland in human body?
A. Pancreas B. Liver
C. Thyroid D. Pituitary

78. The book titled 'The Google Story' has been authored by
A. David A. Vice B. Shobha Dey
C. Fredrick Forsyth D. Vikram Seth

79. Which strait separates Europe from Africa
A. Mallaica B. Gibralter
C. Berring D. Palk

80. Taiwan was earlier known as
A. Fuchow B. Marshall Island
C. Formosa D. Macau

81. Identify the Indian Tennis player who has turned Hollywood filmmaker?
A. Vijay Amritraj B. Mahesh Bhupathi
C. Leander Paes D. Ashok Amritraj

82. Where will the next Olympic Games be held in 2012?
A. Tokyo B. Berlin
C. London D. Toronto

83. Which of the following teams has won the Santosh Trophy Football Championship in 2011?
A. Punjab B. West Bengal
C. Goa D. Railways

84. Excess of money supply as compared to supply of goods results in
A. Depression B. Deflation
C. Trade deficit D. Inflation

85. The largest living flightless bird is
A. Emu B. Kiwi
C. Ostrich D. Penguin

86. Which of the following oceans has the shape of the English letter 'S'?
A. Atlantic B. Pacific
C. Indian D. Arctic

87. Which is the longest shipping canal in the world?
A. Panama Canal
B. Suez Canal
C. White Sea-Baltic Canal
D. Kiel Canal

88. Le Corbusier, the architect of Chandigarh was a national of
A. Britain B. Portugal
C. France D. Netherlands

89. India became a member of UNO in
A. 1945 B. 1947
C. 1950 D. 1952

90. To which country does India export the largest quantity of iron ore?
A. USA B. Japan
C. Egypt D. Germany

Section-III : Elementary Mathematics (Numerical Ability)

91. In the number series 4, 10, 23, 50, 104, 216, 439 the wrong number is:
A. 10 B. 23
C. 104 D. 50

92. The price of 2 trousers and 4 shirts is ₹ 1,600. With the same amount one can buy 1 trouser and 6 shirts. If one wants to buy 12 shirts, he has to pay
A. ₹ 2400 B. ₹ 4800
C. ₹ 1200 D. ₹ 3700

93. If $x=\left(\frac{3}{2}\right)^2\left(\frac{2}{3}\right)^{-4}$, the value of x^{-2} is

A. $\left(\frac{2}{3}\right)^{12}$ B. $\left(\frac{3}{2}\right)^{12}$

C. $\left(\frac{6}{5}\right)^{-12}$ D. $\left(\frac{5}{6}\right)^{-12}$

94. A dealer buys an article for ₹ 380.00. What price should he mark so that after allowing a discount of 5% he still makes a profit of 25% on the article?
A. ₹ 500 B. ₹ 475
C. ₹ 95 D. ₹ 465

95. In a factory, the production of scooters rose to 48400 from 40000 in 2 years. The rate of growth per annum is
A. 20% B. 10%
C. 30% D. 8%

96. If $x+\frac{1}{x}=3$, then $x^2+\frac{1}{x^2}$ will be
A. 9 B. 10
C. 27 D. 7

97. When $16x^4 + 12x^3 - 10x^2 + 8x + 20$ is divided by $4x - 3$, the quotient and the remainder are, respectively

A. $4x^3 + 6x^2 + 2x$ and $\frac{61}{2}$

B. $4x^3 + 6x^2 + \frac{7}{2}$ and $\frac{51}{2}$

C. $6x^2+2x+\frac{2}{7}$ and $\frac{61}{2}$

D. $4x^3+6x^2+2x+\frac{7}{2}$ and $\frac{61}{2}$

98. The sum of two numbers is 2490. If 6.5% of one number is equal to 8.5% of the other, the numbers are
A. 1411 and 1079 B. 1412 and 1080
C. 1141 and 1709 D. 1214 and 1800

99. 120 men had food provision for 200 days. After 5 days, 30 men died of an epidemic. The food will last for further
A. 280 days B. 260 days
C. 290 days D. 252 days

100. Out of the total income, X spends 20% on house rent and 70% of the remaining amount on household expenditure. If X saves ₹ 1800, the total income is
A. ₹ 8000 B. ₹ 9500
C. ₹ 7500 D. ₹ 8500

101. P sells a table to Q at a profit of 10% and Q sells it to R at a profit of 12%. If R pays ₹ 246.40 for it, then how much had P paid for it?
A. ₹ 200.00 B. ₹ 300.00
C. ₹ 248.00 D. ₹ 346.00

102. The least value of x, for which the expression $x^2 + x + 17$ will not give a prime number, is
A. 7 B. 11
C. 13 D. 17

103. A train 300 meters long is running at a speed of 25 metres per second, it will cross a bridge 200 metres long in
A. 5 seconds B. 10 seconds
C. 20 seconds D. 25 seconds

104. If 0.06% of a number is 84, then 30% of that number is
A. 25.2 B. 420
C. 42000 D. 2520

105. A sum was divided among P, Q & R. R got double than P who got double than Q. If the difference between the shares of Q and R is ₹ 3675.00, then the sum in rupees is
A. 4900 B. 8575
C. 11025 D. 7350

106. If the ratio of the areas of two squares is 25 : 36, then the ratio of their perimeters is
A. 5 : 6 B. 25 : 36
C. 6 : 5 D. 36 : 25

107. The denominator of a fraction is greater than its numerator by 11. If 8 is added to both its numerator and denominator, then it becomes ¾. The fraction is
A. 25/26 B. 35/26
C. 26/35 D. 25/36

108. The value of $\frac{1}{x^2}+\frac{1}{y^2}$, where $x=2+\sqrt{3}$ and $y=2-\sqrt{3}$, is
A. 12 B. 16
C. 14 D. 10

109. If the volume of a sphere is divided by its surface area, we obtain 27 cm. The radius of the sphere is:
A. 9 cm B. 81 cm
C. 27 cm D. 24 cm

110. One-third of one-fourth of a number is 12. Then the number is
A. 96 B. 144
C. 108 D. 36

Section-IV : Logical Reasoning

Instructions (111-113): *Read the following information carefully and then answer the questions.*

Four friends W, X, Y and Z are students of Class 10th. W and X are good in Hindi but poor in English. W and Y are good in Science but poor in Mathematics. Y and Z are good in English but poor in Social Studies. Z and X are good in Mathematics as well as in Science.

111. Who amongst the following friends is not good in Mathematics but good in Hindi?
A. W B. Y
C. X D. Z

112. Which of the following pairs of friends are good, both in English and Science?
A. W and Y B. W and Z
C. Y and Z D. Z and X

113. Which of the following statements is definitely true?
A. Y and Z are good in English as well as in Hindi
B. All four friends are good in Science
C. W is good in Social Studies, Hindi and Science
D. Y is not good in Mathematics, Hindi and Social Studies

Instructions (114-116): *Select the statement which logically follows the two given statements.*

114. Statements:
I. No athletes are vegetarians.
II. All players are athletes.
III. Therefore ....
A. no players are vegetarians
B. all players are vegetarian
C. some players are vegetarian
D. all vegetarians are players

115. Statements:
I. All persons who have done any creative work can be responsible critics
II. Z has not done any creative work
III. Therefore ....
A. Z can be a responsible critic
B. Z cannot be a responsible critic
C. Z can become a responsible critic
D. Z cannot become a responsible critic

116. Statement:

I. One who has squared a circle is not a mathematician

II. Therefore ....

A. No one who has squared a circle is a mathematician

B. All non-mathematicians have squared a circle

C. Some mathematicians have squared a circle

D. All mathematicians square a circle

117. Statement: The Supreme Court of India is encouraging Public Interest Litigation

Reasons:

I. To increase the reach of justice to the disadvantaged sections of society

II. To quicken the pace of Justice

Identify the correct reason for the aforementioned statement.

A. Both I and II are correct reasons of the statement

B. I is the correct reason of the statement

C. Both I and II are not correct reasons of the statement

D. II is the correct reason of the statement

118. Yoga has become a very popular exercise, but it may not be for everyone. If you are interested in high energy and fast workouts, yoga may not be the best choice. Therefore, evaluate your fitness requirement before joining yoga classes.

This paragraph best supports the statement that:

A. Yoga is more popular than high energy exercise

B. Yoga is changing the concept of fitness in various ways

C. Before opting for Yoga, assess your fitness requirements

D. Yoga is a holistic fitness regime

119. Statistics allows us to understand the reality. It indicates developmental directions. Statistics is good for exposing reality, but it can also be manipulated to perpetuate untruth and misunderstanding. Data has power to mislead people.

This paragraph best supports the statement that:

A. Words are more truthful than numbers

B. Study of statistics is more important than any other discipline

C. Numbers never lie

D. Numbers can be used to mislead people.

120. Technology has developed out of stone tools which were used in ancient times. At first, development of new technology was slow, but after neo-liberal economic policy was adopted there has been a tremendous growth in technology sector.

This paragraph best supports the statement that:

A. Stone tools were not really technology

B. Stone tools were in use in Ancient India

C. Today new technologies are developing at a fast pace

D. New technology has nothing in common with the stone tools

Instructions (121-125): *Given below is a pair of events I and II. You have to decide their nature of relationship. Assume that the given information is correct and final.*

121. I. Prices of toys in the market have gone down.

II. Government has reduced import duty on toys.

A. I is the main cause and II is the main effect

B. I is effect but II is not the main cause

C. II is the main cause and I is the main effect

D. II is an effect but I is not the main cause.

122. I. Inflation rate in India has come down.

II. Reserve Bank of India has increased interest rate.

A. I is the main cause and II is the main effect

B. I is effect but II is not the main cause

C. II is the main cause and I is the main effect

D. II is an effect but I is not the main cause.

123. I. More and more students are opting for legal education.

II. Bar Council of India has introduced Bar Examination.

A. I is the main cause and II is the main effect

B. I is effect but II is not the main cause

C. II is the main cause and I is the main effect

D. II is an effect but I is not the main cause.

124. I. Sea level is steadily rising.

II. Global Warming is a serious problem which the world is facing.

A. I is the main cause and II is the main effect

B. I is effect but II is not the main cause

C. II is the main cause and I is the main effect

D. II is an effect but I is not the main cause.

125. I. Financial Institutions are largely unregulated.

II. Today, world is passing through a serious phase of economic crisis.

A. I is the main cause and II is the main effect

B. I is effect but II is not the main cause

C. II is the main cause and I is the main effect

D. II is an effect but I is not the main cause.

126. An argument is given below, on the basis of that argument; find out the parallel argument from the given list of subsequent arguments

Argument: Himalayan Sparrows are disappearing. This bird is an Indian bird; therefore, Indian birds are disappearing.

Subsequent Arguments:

A. Industrialists pay most of the taxes. 'Z' is a wealthy man therefore 'Z' must pay most taxes

B. A pineapple is a fruit, a mango is a fruit therefore pineapple is a mango

C. Snow tigers are an endangered species; all endangered species must be protected; therefore snow-tiger must be protected

D. John is his father's favourite son, and John knows this must be true because his father told him this; and no father would lie to his favourite son

Instructions (127-130): *Each question below is followed by arguments. Choose the most appropriate choice from the options given.*

127. Question : Should Judicial Activism be discouraged?

Argument I : No, it would lead to executive dictatorship.

Argument II : Yes, Judiciary should stay in the constitutional limits.

A. Argument I is strong
B. Argument II is strong
C. Both the arguments are strong
D. Both the arguments are weak

128. Question : Should the Judiciary be independent of Executive and Legislature?

Argument I : Yes, this is necessary to ensure impartiality in the administration of Justice.

Argument II : No, it will develop inertia in Executive and Legislature.

A. Argument I is strong
B. Argument II is strong
C. Both the arguments are strong
D. Both the arguments are weak

129. Question : Should E-Governance be introduced at every level of public administration?

Argument I : Yes, it will reduce corruption.

Argument II : No, it will lead to unemployment.

A. Argument I is strong
B. Argument II is strong
C. Both the arguments are strong
D. Both the arguments are weak

130. Question : Should there be a world Government?

Argument I : Yes, it will eliminate inter-state conflicts.

Argument II : No, Rich and Powerful countries will dominate it.

A. Argument I is strong
B. Argument II is strong
C. Both the arguments are strong
D. Both the arguments are weak

131. "Some philosophers believe that a concept which cannot be verified can still be valid because of its inner logic which ennobles it."

Statement : "Every person has certain inherent and inalienable rights which must be protected by Rule of Law."

A. True
B. False
C. Difficult to determine
D. Both True and False

Instructions (132-137): *Given below are some statements followed by two arguments. Read carefully and decide which of the arguments strongly support the statement.*

132. Statement: Should the pay scale and conditions of service of government employees be made applicable to private sector employees?

Arguments:

(*i*) No, this will develop inertia, inefficiency and would adversely affect spirit of competition.

(*ii*) Yes, this will enhance dedication to work and institutional loyalty.

A. Argument (*i*) is strong
B. Argument (*ii*) is strong
C. Both (*i*) and (*ii*) are strong
D. Neither (*i*) nor (*ii*) is strong

133. Statement: Should a strong institution of ombudsman be created in India?

Arguments:

(*i*) Yes, this will bring transparency and accountability in the administration.

(*ii*) No, this will develop lack of initiative and flexibility in the administration.

A. Argument (*i*) is strong
B. Argument (*ii*) is strong
C. Both (*i*) and (*ii*) are strong
D. Neither (*i*) nor (*ii*) is strong

134. Statement: Should internal assessment in colleges and universities be abolished?

Arguments:

(*i*) Yes, this will eliminate the possibility of favouritism.

(*ii*) No, teaching faculty will lose control over the students and this would adversely affect their academic growth.

A. Argument (*i*) is strong
B. Argument (*ii*) is strong
C. Both (*i*) and (*ii*) are strong
D. Neither (*i*) nor (*ii*) is strong

135. Statement: Should military training be made compulsory for all college and university students?

Arguments:

(*i*) Yes, this will develop in them a sense of punctuality and discipline

(*ii*) No, military training should be given only to those students who are physically fit.

A. Argument (*i*) is strong
B. Argument (*ii*) is strong
C. Both (*i*) and (*ii*) are strong
D. Neither (*i*) nor (*ii*) is strong

136. Statement: Should students' union in colleges and universities be abolished?

Arguments:

(*i*) Yes, it detracts students from academic and career development.
(*ii*) No, all great leaders have been students' union leaders.

A. Argument (*i*) is strong
B. Argument (*ii*) is strong
C. Both (*i*) and (*ii*) are strong
D. Neither (*i*) nor (*ii*) is strong

137. Statement: Should the age of marriage be raised to 25 years for boys and 21 for girls?

Arguments:

(*i*) No, it is difficult to change a social practice in Indian conditions.
(*ii*) Yes, by that age people develop a sense of responsibility and also complete their education.

A. Argument (*i*) is strong
B. Argument (*ii*) is strong
C. Both (*i*) and (*ii*) are strong
D. Neither (*i*) nor (*ii*) is strong

Instructions (138-141): *Each question contains six statements followed by four sets of combination of three. Choose the set in which the statements are logically related.*

138. Statements:

(*i*) X and Y are siblings.
(*ii*) X and Y do not quarrel.
(*iii*) Siblings are known to quarrel often.
(*iv*) X and Y quarrel often.
(*v*) All those who quarrel are siblings.
(*vi*) X and Y cannot be siblings.

A. (*ii*), (*iv*), (*v*) B. (*i*), (*iv*), (*vi*)
C. (*i*), (*iii*), (*iv*) D. (*i*), (*ii*), (*v*)

139. Statements:

(*i*) All mangoes are fruits.
(*ii*) All mangoes are green.
(*iii*) All mangoes are oval shaped.
(*iv*) All fruits are sweet.
(*v*) All mangoes are sweet.
(*vi*) All fruits are expensive.

A. (*i*), (*ii*), (*iii*) B. (*i*), (*iv*), (*v*)
C. (*ii*), (*iii*), (*iv*) D. (*iv*), (*v*), (*vi*)

140. Statements:

(*i*) All frogs are amphibians.
(*ii*) All amphibians are not frogs.
(*iii*) All amphibians are cold blooded.
(*iv*) All frogs lay eggs.
(*v*) All amphibians lay eggs.
(*vi*) Frogs are cold blooded.

A. (*i*), (*iii*), (*vi*) B. (*i*), (*iv*), (*v*)
C. (*i*), (*ii*), (*v*) D. (*ii*), (*v*), (*iv*)

141. Statements:

(*i*) Some men are of short-height.
(*ii*) Short-heighted men are intelligent.
(*iii*) Sudhir is a man.
(*iv*) Sudhir is of short-height.
(*v*) Sudhir is intelligent.
(*vi*) All men are intelligent.

A. (*i*), (*ii*), (*vi*) B. (*iii*), (*iv*), (*ii*)
C. (*ii*), (*iv*), (*v*) D. (*ii*), (*iv*), (*vi*)

Instructions (142-144): *Of the four alternatives given in each of the following questions, find the one which is different from the rest.*

142. A. Fast-Slow B. Bright-Dark
C. Day-Night D. Valley-Depth

143. A. Body-Hand B. Foot-Ankle
C. Eye-Ear D. Wrist-Finger

144. A. Snake-Frog B. Goat-Hen
C. Dog Cat D. Tiger-Deer

Instructions (145-147): *Each question below has two statements followed by four conclusions I, II, III and IV. You have to accept the given statements to be true, even if they appear to be at variance from commonly known facts. Read all the conclusions and then decide which of the given conclusions logically follows from the two statements:*

145. Statement One: All girls are students.
Statement Two: All doctors are students.

Conclusions:

I. All girls are students.
II. Some students are girls.
III. Some students are doctors.
IV. All doctors are girls.

A. Only I follows
B. Only I and II follows
C. Only II and IV follows
D. Only I and II and III follows

146. Statement One: All researchers are sociologists
Statement Two: Some researchers are professors.

Conclusions:

I. All researchers are professors.
II. Some researchers are professors.
III. Some professors are sociologists.
IV. Some sociologists are researchers.

A. Only III and II follow
B. Only II, III and IV follow
C. Only III follows
D. None follows

147. Statement One: Some democracies are dictatorship.
Statement Two: No dictatorship is a monarchy.
Conclusions:
I. No democracy is a monarchy.
II. No dictatorship is a democracy.
III. Some democracies are monarchy.
IV. Some dictatorships are democracies.
A. None follows
B. Only IV follows
C. II and III follow
D. I, II and IV follow

Instructions (148-150): *The following questions comprise of one or more statements. Answer the questions on the basis of the given statement(s). Accept the factual assumptions required by the question, even if you believe that the statement is false.*

148. Statements:
I. Cheese is bad for people with high-cholesterol.
II. Sumeet does not eat cheese.

Assuming that I and II are true, which of the following statement follows?
A. Sumeet has high-cholesterol
B. Cheese is bad for Sumeet
C. People with high-cholesterol do not eat cheese
D. None of the above

149. Statement:
I. Democrats are secularists.

Which of the following statements, if true, would show that the above statement is false?
A. My father is a secularist but he is not a democrat
B. My father is a democrat but he is secularist
C. My father is a democrat and he is secularist
D. My father is neither a democrat nor a secularist

150. Statement:

"Where there is a cloud, there is a rain." Which of the following statements, if true, would show that the above statement is false?
A. Sometimes there is cloud, but there is no rain
B. Sometimes there is rain, but there is no cloud
C. There is no rain where there is no cloud
D. None of the above

Section- V : Legal Aptitude

Instructions (151-165): *Each of the next fifteen questions consists of two statements, one labelled as 'Assertion' (A) and other as 'Reason' (R). You are to examine these two statements carefully and select the correct answers.*

151. Assertion (A): A void contract is not necessarily illegal.

Reason (R): Every illegal contract is void.
A. Both A and R are individually true and R is the correct explanation of A
B. Both A and R are individually true but R is not the correct explanation of A
C. A is true but R is false
D. A is false but R is true

152. Assertion (A): The Indian Constitution was adopted on 26th November, 1949.

Reason (R): Law Day is celebrated in India on 26th November every year.
A. Both A and R are individually true and R is the correct explanation of A
B. Both A and R are individually true but R is not the correct explanation of A
C. A is true but R is false
D. A is false but R is true

153. Assertion (A): The state shall not make any law, which takes away or abridges the rights conferred by Part III (Fundamental Rights) and any law made in contravention of this clause shall, to the extent of the contravention, be void.

Reason (R): The fundamental rights are the rights reserved by the people and for this reason they are eternal and sacrosanct.
A. Both A and R are individually true and R is the correct explanation of A
B. Both A and R are individually true but R is not the correct explanation of A
C. A is true but R is false
D. A is false but R is true

154. Assertion (A): Directive Principles of State Policy contained in Part IV shall not be enforceable by any court, but the principles therein laid down are nevertheless fundamental in the governance of the country and it shall be the duty of the State to apply these principles in making laws.

Reason (R): Directive Principles of State Policy and Fundamental Rights are both complementary to each other but in case of any controversy fundamental rights will prevail.
A. Both A and R are individually true and R is the correct explanation of A
B. Both A and R are individually true but R is not the correct explanation of A
C. A is true but R is false
D. A is false but R is true

155. Assertion (A): All minorities, whether based on religion or language, shall have the right to establish and administer educational institutions of their choice.

Reason (R): Institutions established by the minorities are not entitled to governmental aid and government is not under an obligation to give aid.

A. Both A and R are individually true and R is the correct explanation of A
B. Both A and R are individually true but R is the correct explanation of A
C. A is true but R is false
D. A is false but R is true

156. Assertion (A): The right to move the Supreme Court under Article 32 of the Constitution by appropriate proceedings for the enforcement of the fundamental rights is guaranteed as a fundamental right.

Reason (R): Supreme Court of India has been appointed as the guardian of the Constitution.

A. Both A and R are individually true and R is the correct explanation of A
B. Both A and R are individually true but R is not the correct explanation of A
C. A is true but R is false
D. A is false but R is true

157. Assertion (A): If the budget presented to the Rajya Sabha is not passed in the stipulated period, the budget proposals are not affected.

Reason (R): The Lok Sabha is more powerful, in financial matters, than the Rajya Sabha.

A. Both A and R are individually true and R is the correct explanation of A
B. Both A and R are individually true but R is not the correct explanation of A
C. A is true but R is false
D. A is false but R is true

158. Assertion (A): In the Event of violation of any legal right (tort) the aggrieved party is entitled to recover unliquidated damages.

Reason (R): The object of awarding damages to the aggrieved party is to put him in the same position in which he would have been if the wrong would not have been committed. Damages are therefore, assessed on that basis.

A. Both A and R are individually true and R is the correct explanation of A
B. Both A and R are individually true but R is not the correct explanation of A
C. A is true but R is false
D. A is false but R is true

159. Assertion (A): During inflation, there is increase in money supply and rise in price level.

Reason (R): The rise in prices is due to shortage in supply of essential consumer goods.

A. Both A and R are individually true and R is the correct explanation of A
B. Both A and R are individually true but R is not the correct explanation of A
C. A is true but R is false
D. A is false but R is true

160. Assertion (A): X, because of unsound state of mind and not knowing the nature of the act, attacks Y, who in self defense and in order to ward off the attack, hits thereby injuring him. Y has not committed an offence.

Reason (R): Y had a right of private defense against X under Section 98 of the Indian Penal Code.

A. Both A and R are individually true and R is the correct explanation of A
B. Both A and R are individually true but R is not the correct explanation of A
C. A is true but R is false
D. A is false but R is true

161. Assertion (A): X and Y independently entertained the idea to kill Z. Accordingly; each of them separately inflicted wounds on Z who died as a consequence. X and Y are liable for murder under Section 341 IPC.

Reason (R): When a criminal act is done by several persons in furtherance of common intention of all, each of such persons is liable as if the whole act was done by him alone.

A. Both A and R are individually true and R is the correct explanation of A
B. Both A and R are individually true but R is not the correct explanation of A
C. A is true but R is false
D. A is false but R is true

162. Assertion (A): A person claims compensation for his non-gratuitous act.

Reason (R): A person who enjoys benefit from lawful, non-gratuitous act of another must compensate him even though there is no contract.

A. Both A and R are individually true and R is the correct explanation of A
B. Both A and R are individually true but R is not the correct explanation of A
C. A is true but R is false
D. A is false but R is true

163. Assertion (A): Freedom of Speech is the most important civil liberty of people in a democratic polity.

Reason (R): State can regulate free speech in the interest of public order.

A. Both A and R are individually true and R is the correct explanation of A
B. Both A and R are individually true but R is not the correct explanation of A
C. A is true but R is false
D. A is false but R is true

164. **Assertion (A):** Austin's concept of law is known as imperative theory.

Reason (R): Austin emphasized on the commanding character of law.

A. Both A and R are individually true and R is the correct explanation of A
B. Both A and R are individually true but R is not the correct explanation of A
C. A is true but R is false
D. A is false but R is true

165. **Assertion (A):** The essence of joint liability under Section 149 of the IPC is that the criminal act must have been done with a view to fulfil the common object of an unlawful assembly.

Reason (R): Any sudden and provocative act done by a member of an unlawful assembly would render the other members of that assembly liable.

A. Both A and R are individually true and R is the correct explanation of A
B. Both A and R are individually true but R is not the correct explanation of A
C. A is true but R is false
D. A is false but R is true

166. The following are enshrined in the Preamble of the Constitution of India

I. Equality of status and of opportunity
II. Liberty of thought, expression, belief, faith and worship
III. Justice-social, economic and political
IV. Fraternity assuring the dignity of the individual
V. Unity and Integrity of the nation

Which of the following is the correct order in which they appear in the preamble?

A. V-I-II-IV-III B. III-II-I-IV-V
C. III-I-II-V-IV D. I-I-IV-III-V

167. Which one of the following statements is correct? Right to free and compulsory education for all children of the age of 6 to 14 years is:

A. a fundamental right enforceable in law
B. a fundamental duty
C. a directive principle of state policy
D. a fundamental right which, however, can be enforced only if the state makes an enabling legislation

168. Affirmative action connotes:

I. Measures taken by the state to help the socially disadvantaged groups.
II. Positive discrimination.
III. Strict quotas for the socially and educationally backward class in school/college admissions and jobs.

Which of the above mentioned is true?

A. I and II only B. II only
C. I, II and III D. II and III only

169. Identify the correct statement:

A. Federalism implies a system of government which embodies a division of powers between a central and a number of regional authorities
B. Federalism implies a system of government which embodies a division of powers between Legislature, Executive and Judiciary
C. Federalism implies a system of government which embodies Parliamentary supremacy
D. None of these

170. Consider the following statements:

I. In a recent Supreme Court verdict pronounced by Justice Markandeya Katju and Justice Gyan Sudha Mishra, the court upheld the constitutionality of the Haj subsidy.
II. Muslims are not the only beneficiaries of the secular state's generosity. Hindus have also received substantial financial support from the Government.

With reference to the statements mentioned above, which of the following is correct?

A. I only B. II only
C. Both I and II D. Neither I nor II

171. X, a married woman, agreed to live in adultery with B and also agreed to serve him as his housekeeper. In return, B agreed to pay X ₹ 500 per month for living in adultery and ₹ 500 per month for housekeeping. The agreement is

A. Valid
B. Void
C. Void as to the first object but valid with respect to the second object
D. Unlawful as being opposed to public policy

172. Ramu applied for the post of Director in an organization. The governing body of the organization passed a resolution appointing him to the post. After the meeting, one of the members of the governing body informed him privately of the resolution. Subsequently, the resolution was rescinded. Ramu claims damages. Which one of the following is the correct legal proposition in the case?

A. Ramu cannot claim damages as he had not resigned from his existing post in anticipation of getting the appointment letter
B. Ramu cannot claim damages as there was no formal communication
C. Ramu can claim damages as governing body cannot rescind the resolution once passed
D. Ramu can claim damages as there was private communication

173. The Railway authorities allowed a train to be over crowded. In consequence, a legitimate passenger Mr. X got his pocket picked. Choose the appropriate answer:

A. Mr. X can sue the Railway authorities for the loss suffered
B. Mr. X cannot sue because he had given his consent to travel in a over-crowded train
C. Mr. X cannot sue railway authorities because there was no infringement of his legal right and mere fact that the loss was caused does not give rise to a cause of action
D. None of these

174. Z is carried off by a tiger. X fires at the tiger, knowing that the shot might kill Z, but with no intention to kill Z, and in good faith trying to save Z. X's shot, however, gives Z a mortal wound. Choose the correct option:

A. X has committed an offence of a grievous nature
B. X has no moral duty to save Z therefore he can be held liable
C. X has not committed any offence, as the act was in good faith and for the benefit of Z
D. None of the above

175. Ms. Usha wants to file a suit against Bhagyalaxmi Theatre praying for a permanent injuction (stay order) restraining the theatre from running the film named "Jai Santoshi Maa". Her contention is that the film hurt her religious feelings and sentiments as Goddess Saraswati, Laxmi and Parvati were depicted as jealous and were ridiculed.

A. She cannot file a suit because injury to religious feelings is not a legally recognized right
B. She cannot file a suit because the Theatre has a fundamental right to speech and expression
C. She can file a suit as injury to religious feelings has been legally recognized as a right (*injuria sine damnum*)
D. It is a case of complete judicial discretion

176. Match schedule I and II and choose the appropriate answer:

	Schedule I		Schedule II
(*i*)	Concurrent list	1.	Constitution of Japan
(*ii*)	Rule of Law	2.	Constitution of Ireland
(*iii*)	Directive Principle of State Policy	3.	British Constitution
(*iv*)	Procedure established by law	4.	Constitution of Australia

	(*i*)	(*ii*)	(*iii*)	(*iv*)
A.	1	2	3	4
B.	2	4	3	1
C.	1	3	4	2
D.	4	3	2	1

177. P, Q and R made a joint promise to give S a sum of ₹ 3000. S recovered the whole amount from P. Q was declared insolvent and cannot give anything. Which statement out of the following is correct?

A. P cannot get anything from R
B. P can recover ₹ 1000 from R
C. P can recover ₹ 1500 from R
D. P can recover ₹ 2000 from R

178. X went to Y's house and forgot his bag which contained 1 kg sweets. Y's children consumed the sweets. Decide the liability of Y.

A. Y is bound to pay the price of sweets to X
B. Y is not bound to pay anything
C. Y is bound to pay half the price of sweets
D. Y would not have to pay anything because X loves Y's children

179. Which one of the following is not correct?

A. Freedom of speech and expression includes freedom of press.
B. Right to life and personal liberty includes right to carry on any trade and profession
C. Right to equality includes the principles of natural justice
D. Freedom of conscience includes the wearing and carrying of kirpans by the Sikhs

180. Y makes an attempt to steal some jewels by breaking open a box and finds, after opening the box, that there is no jewel in it. Choose the appropriate answer.

A. Y is not guilty of attempt to theft because the box was empty
B. Y is guilty of attempt to commit theft
C. Y is guilty of trespass
D. Y is not guilty of any offence

181. A lady wanted to get a railway ticket but finding a crowd near the ticket window at the station, asked Raju, who was near the window, to get a ticket for her and handed him money for the same. Raju took the money and instead of getting the ticket, ran away with it. What offence has been committed by Raju?

A. No offence
B. Criminal breach of trust
C. Criminal misappropriation
D. Theft

182. The Right to Equality is guaranteed by:

A. Article 14 to 18
B. Article 14
C. Article 14 and 15
D. Article 14, 15 and 16

183. Mr. Samay was severely hurt while working in his factory and fell unconscious. He was rushed to a hospital by his fellow workers. In the hospital (at emergency/casualty ward) the doctors opined that he should be operated immediately. While conducting preliminary examinations, he was found to be HIV positive. The doctors are in a dilemma regarding what should they do first:

A. Doctors should operate first
B. Doctors should inform his family members
C. Doctors should inform his employers
D. Doctors should not inform anyone because it would violate patient's right of privacy.

184. Match schedule I and II and choose the appropriate answer:

	Schedule I	Schedule II
(*i*)	Republic	1. Head of the state is elected by the people
(*ii*)	Secular	2. State does not recognize any religion as religion of the state
(*iii*)	Democracy	3. The government which gets authority from the will of the people

	(*i*)	(*ii*)	(*iii*)
A.	1	2	3
B.	1	3	2
C.	2	3	1
D.	3	2	1

185. In which of the following cases can a Constitutional amendment be passed just by a simple majority in Parliament?

A. Election matters
B. Change in the name and boundaries of states
C. Powers of the President
D. None of the above

186. **Principle:** Only Parliament or State Legislatures have the authority to enact laws on their own. No law made by the State can take away a person's fundamental right.

Facts: Parliament enacted a law, which according to a group of lawyers is violating the fundamental rights of traders. A group of lawyers files a writ petition challenging the Constitutional validity of the statue seeking relief to quash the statue and further direct Parliament to enact a new law.

A. No writ would lie against Parliament, as the court has no authority to direct Parliament to enact or re-enact a law
B. The court can quash existing law if it violates fundamental rights and can direct Parliament to make a new law
C. The court can quash the existing law if it violates fundamental rights but cannot direct Parliament to make a new law
D. None of the above

187. **Principle:** When one person signifies to another his willingness to do or abstain from doing anything, with a view to obtaining the assent of that person to such an act or abstinence, he is said to have made a proposal.

Facts: "Ramanuj telegraphed to Shyam Sunder, writing: "*Will you sell me your Rolls Royce CAR? Telegram the lowest cash price.*" Shyam Sunder also replied by telegram: "*Lowest price for CAR is ₹ 20 lakh.*" Ramanuj immediately sent his consent through telegram stating: "*I agree to buy the CAR for ₹ 20 lakh asked by you.*" Shyam Sunder refused to sell the car.

A. He cannot refuse to sell the CAR because the contract has already been made.
B. He can refuse to sell the CAR because it was only invitation to offer and not the real offer
C. It was not a valid offer because willingness to enter into a contract was absent
D. None of these

188. **Principle:** Every person, who is of the age of majority, is competent to contract according to the law to which he is subject.

Facts: A minor mortgaged his house in favour of Thakur Das, a money lender, to secure a loan of ₹ 20000. A part of this, *i.e.*, ₹ 10500 was actually advanced to him. While considering the proposed advance, the attorney who was acting for the moneylender, received information that the plaintiff was still a minor. Subsequently the minor commenced an action stating that he was underage when he executed the mortgage and the same should, therefore, be cancelled. He prayed for setting aside the mortgage. The mortgagee moneylender prayed for the refund of ₹ 10500 from the minor.

A. As a minor's contract is void, any money advanced to a minor can be recovered
B. A minor's contract is void ab initio, any money advanced to a minor cannot be recovered
C. A minor's contract is voidable; any money advanced to a minor can be recovered
D. Advanced money can be recovered because minor has given wrong information about his age

189. **Principle:** A person is said to be of sound mind for the purpose of making a contract if, at the time when he makes it, he is capable of understanding it and of forming a rational judgment as to its effect upon his interests.

Facts: Mr. X who is usually of sound state of mind, but occasionally of unsound state of mind, enters into a contract with Mr. Y when he was of unsound state of mind. Mr. Y having come to know about this fact afterwards, wants to file a suit against Mr. X

A. Mr. X cannot enter into contract because he is of unsound state of mind when he entered into contract.

B. Mr. X can enter into contract but the burden is on the other party to prove that he was of unsound state of mind at the time of contract.
C. Mr. X can enter into contract but the burden is on Mr. X to prove that he was of sound state of mind at the time of contract.
D. None of these

190. Principle:

(1) The state shall not deny to any person equality before the law and equal protection of the laws within the territory of India.
(2) The state shall not discriminate against any citizen on grounds only of religion, race, caste, sex and place of birth or any of them.

Facts: The Government of Rajasthan, passed an order providing for reservations for the Scheduled Castes/ Scheduled Tribes and Socially and Educationally Backward Classes (including Muslims), and Women, in all institutions of higher education, including private educational institutions, both aided as well as unaided, in the following manner: Scheduled Caste-15%; Scheduled Tribe-7.5%, Socially and Educationally Backward Classes (including Muslims)-27%

I. The reservation policy of the government is violative of the principle of equality envisaged in the Constitution.
II. The reservation policy is unconstitutional because it is based on 'caste' which is a prohibited marker.
III. Reservation does not violate equality clause as it entails "like should be treated like and unlike should be treated differently."
IV. Reservation does not violate equality clause as the Constitution itself enables the State to make special provision for the advancement of socially and educationally backward classes of citizens or for the Scheduled Castes and Scheduled Tribes.

A. I is correct
B. I and II are both correct answers
C. III is correct answer
D. III and IV both are correct answers

191. Principle: Nothing is an offence merely by reason of its being done with the knowledge that it is likely to cause harm, if it be done without any criminal intention to cause harm, and in good faith for the purpose of preventing or avoiding other harm to a person or property.

Facts: Mr. Sharman, the Captain of a steam vessel, suddenly and without any fault or negligence on his part, finds himself in such a position that, before he can stop his vessel, he must inevitably run down a boat B, with twenty or thirty passengers on board, unless he changes the course of his vessel, and that, by changing his course, he must incur the risk of running down a boat C with only two passengers on board and which he may possibly clear.

A. Sharman has committed no offence because this was done out of necessity
B. Sharman can be held responsible for the act of criminal negligence
C. Sharman can held responsible for culpable homicide
D. This is a clear case of accident so Sharman cannot be held responsible

192. Principle: Willful rash driving is an offense.

Facts: Mr. Tiwari was driving his car after drinking alcohol. Police books him for willful negligent driving. Is the act of the police lawful?

A. No, because Mr. Tiwari was not driving rashly; he was drunk while driving.
B. No, this is not a negligent act.
C. Yes, because Mr. Tiwari was driving rashly.
D. Yes, because the police has the power to arrest a person driving rashly.

193. Principle: Whoever, intending to take dishonestly any movable property out of the possession of any person without that person's consent, moves that property with an intention to take it, is said to commit theft.

Facts: Y cuts down a tree on Z's ground, with the intention of dishonestly taking it out of Z's possession without Z's consent. Y could not take away the tree.

A. Y can be prosecuted for theft
B. Y cannot be prosecuted for theft
C. Y can be prosecuted for attempt to theft
D. Y has neither committed theft nor attempted to commit theft

194. Principle: *Injuria Sine Dammum i.e.* Injury (violation of legal right) without damage.

Facts: X, who was the returning officer at a polling both in Amethi, wrongly refused to register a duly tendered vote of Y in the recent UP elections, even though Y was an eligible voter. The candidate in whose favour Y wanted to vote, was declared elected. Give the appropriate answer:

A. Y can sue X on the ground that he was denied the right to cast vote, which is a fundamental right
B. Y can sue X on the ground that he was denied the right to cast vote, which is a legal right
C. Y cannot sue X because there is no injury or damage caused to Y
D. Y cannot sue X because the candidate in whose favour he wanted to vote was declared elected

195. Principle: Nothing is an offence which is done by a person who, at the time of doing it, by reason of unsound state of mind, is incapable of knowing the nature of the act, or something that he is doing is either wrong or contrary to law.

Facts: X takes his son Y who is three years old, for bathing to the well. He throws his son inside the well so that the son can have a good bath. After 10 minutes he also jumps into the well to take bath and get his son out of the well. Both were rescued by the villagers but his son was found dead.

A. X has committed culpable homicide amounting to murder
B. X has committed murder
C. X has done no offence as he can plead the defense of unsound state of mind
D. X's family should be held responsible for allowing him to take the child to the well

196. Principle: Ignorance of Fact is excused but ignorance of law is no excuse.

Facts: X was a passenger from Zurich to Manila in a Swiss Plane. When the plane landed at the Airport of Bombay on 28 Nov. 1962 it was found on searching that X carried 34 kg of Gold Bars on his person and that he had not declared it in the 'Manifest for Transit'. On 26th Nov. 1962 the Government of India had issued a notification modifying its earlier exemption, making it mandatory now that the gold must be declared in the "Manifest" of the aircraft.

A. X cannot be prosecuted because he had actually no knowledge about the new notification issued two days ago
B. X cannot be prosecuted because ignorance of fact is excusable
C. X can be prosecuted because ignorance of law is not excusable
D. X's liability would depend on the discretion of the court

197. Principle: Proposal (communication) + Acceptance (communication) + Consideration = Contract. The communication of a proposal is complete when it comes to the knowledge of the person to whom it is made.

Facts: X's nephew absconded from home. He sent his servant in search of the boy. After the servant had left, X by handbills offered to pay ₹ 501 to anybody finding his nephew. The servant came to know of this offer only after he had already traced the missing child. He, therefore, brought an action to recover the reward.

A. His action would fail because he was not aware of the offer
B. His action would not fail because it was a general offer
C. The fact that he was aware of the offer does not make any difference and hence it was a valid contract. It is a mere formality
D. None of the above

198. Principle: Agreements, the meaning of which is not certain, or not capable of being made certain, are void.

Facts: A horse was bought for a certain price coupled with a promise to give ₹ 500 more if the horse is proved lucky.

A. This is a valid agreement.
B. This agreement is void for uncertainty because it is very difficult to determine what luck, bad or good, the horse has brought to the buyer
C. The agreement is partially valid and partially void
D. None of the above

199. Principle: Mere silence as to the facts likely to affect the willingness of a person to enter into a contract is not a fraud, unless the circumstances of the case are such that, on close examination it is found to be the duty of the person keeping silent to speak, or unless his silence is, in itself, equivalent to speech.

Facts: X sells by auction to Y, a horse which X knows to be of unsound state of mind. X says nothing to Y about the horse's unsound state of mind. Give the correct answer:

A. X can be held liable for fraud
B. X can be held liable for misrepresentation
C. X cannot be held liable, because he did not say anything positive about the mental state of the horse
D. X cannot be held because it is the buyer who must be aware of the things

200. Principle: Any direct physical interference with goods in somebody's possession without lawful justification is called trespass of goods.

Facts: Z purchased a car from a person who had no title to it and sent it to a garage for repair. X believing wrongly that the car was his, removed it from the garage.

A. X can be held responsible for trespass of goods
B. X cannot be held responsible for trespass of goods as he was under a wrong belief
C. X has not committed any wrong
D. None of the above

ANSWERS

1	**2**	**3**	**4**	**5**	**6**	**7**	**8**	**9**	**10**
B	B	A	C	D	D	B	C	A	A
11	**12**	**13**	**14**	**15**	**16**	**17**	**18**	**19**	**20**
D	B	C	D	C	A	D	C	B	B
21	**22**	**23**	**24**	**25**	**26**	**27**	**28**	**29**	**30**
D	B	C	A	B	B	A	B	C	B
31	**32**	**33**	**34**	**35**	**36**	**37**	**38**	**39**	**40**
D	D	C	B	C	A	B	D	B	B
41	**42**	**43**	**44**	**45**	**46**	**47**	**48**	**49**	**50**
D	B	C	B	C	A	C	C	C	D
51	**52**	**53**	**54**	**55**	**56**	**57**	**58**	**59**	**60**
A	C	A	B	A	C	A	B	A	A
61	**62**	**63**	**64**	**65**	**66**	**67**	**68**	**69**	**70**
C	D	B	B	C	B	C	A	D	B
71	**72**	**73**	**74**	**75**	**76**	**77**	**78**	**79**	**80**
C	B	A	C	B	D	B	A	B	C
81	**82**	**83**	**84**	**85**	**86**	**87**	**88**	**89**	**90**
D	C	B	D	C	A	B	C	A	B
91	**92**	**93**	**94**	**95**	**96**	**97**	**98**	**99**	**100**
C	A	A	A	B	D	D	A	B	C
101	**102**	**103**	**104**	**105**	**106**	**107**	**108**	**109**	**110**
A	D	C	C	B	A	D	C	B	B
111	**112**	**113**	**114**	**115**	**116**	**117**	**118**	**119**	**120**
A	C	B	A	A	A	B	C	D	C
121	**122**	**123**	**124**	**125**	**126**	**127**	**128**	**129**	**130**
C	C	B	C	D	C	C	A	C	C
131	**132**	**133**	**134**	**135**	**136**	**137**	**138**	**139**	**140**
A	B	A	A	D	D	B	C	A	D
141	**142**	**143**	**144**	**145**	**146**	**147**	**148**	**149**	**150**
C	D	A	B	D	B	D	C	B	A
151	**152**	**153**	**154**	**155**	**156**	**157**	**158**	**159**	**160**
A	A	A	B	C	A	D	D	A	A
161	**162**	**163**	**164**	**165**	**166**	**167**	**168**	**169**	**170**
D	A	A	A	C	B	D	C	A	D
171	**172**	**173**	**174**	**175**	**176**	**177**	**178**	**179**	**180**
C	A	C	C	C	D	C	B	B	B
181	**182**	**183**	**184**	**185**	**186**	**187**	**188**	**189**	**190**
B	A	D	A	B	C	C	B	A	D
191	**192**	**193**	**194**	**195**	**196**	**197**	**198**	**199**	**200**
D	A	A	B	C	A	C	B	C	B

EXPLANATORY ANSWERS

91. $4 \times 2 + 2 = 10$

$10 \times 2 + 3 = 23$

$23 \times 2 + 4 = 50$

$50 \times 2 + 5 = \boxed{105}$ *given 104, wrong no.*

$105 \times 2 + 6 = 216$

$216 \times 2 + 7 = 439$

92. $2x + 4y = 1600$ ...(*i*)

$1x + 6y = 1600$ ...(*ii*)] × 2

$2x + 12y = 3200$ ...(*iii*)

from (*i*) and (*iii*)

$2x + 4y = 1600$

$2x + 12y = 3200$

$- \quad - \qquad -$

$-8y = -1600$

$y = 200$

$\because$ Cost of 1 shirt = ₹ 200

$\therefore$ Cost of 12 shirts = ₹ 200 × 12 = ₹ 2400.

93. $x = \left(\frac{3}{2}\right)^2\left(\frac{2}{3}\right)^{-4} = \left(\frac{3}{2}\right)^2\left(\frac{3}{2}\right)^4$

$x = \left(\frac{3}{2}\right)^6$

$x^2 = \left[\left(\frac{3}{2}\right)^6\right]^2 = \left(\frac{3}{2}\right)^{12}$

$x^4 = \left(\frac{3}{2}\right)^{24}$

$\frac{x^2}{x^4} = \left(\frac{3}{2}\right)^{-12}$

$\Rightarrow x^{-2} = \left(\frac{2}{3}\right)^{12}$.

94. Let MP = ₹ 500

then discount = $500 \times \frac{5}{100}$ = ₹ 25

SP = ₹ 500 – ₹ 25 = ₹ 475

CP = ₹ 380

Profit = SP – CP = 475 – 380 = ₹ 95

$\text{Profit \%} = \frac{\text{Profit}}{\text{CP}} \times 100$

$= \frac{95}{380} \times 100 = 25\%$

$\therefore$ MP = ₹ 500 (correct answer).

95. $A = P\left(1+\frac{r}{100}\right)^2$

$48400 = 40000\left(1+\frac{r}{100}\right)^2$

$\frac{48400}{40000} = \left(1+\frac{r}{100}\right)^2$

$\left(\frac{22}{20}\right)^2 = \left(1+\frac{r}{100}\right)^2$

$1+\frac{r}{100} = \frac{22}{20}$

$\Rightarrow \frac{r}{100} = \frac{22}{20}-1$

$= \frac{2}{20}$

$\therefore r = 10\%$.

96. $\because x+\frac{1}{x} = 3$

$\left(x+\frac{1}{x}\right)^2 = (3)^2$

$x^2+\frac{1}{x^2}+2 = 9$

$x^2+\frac{1}{x^2} = 7$

97. $4x-3\overline{)16x^4+12x^3-10x^2+8x+20}\left(4x^3+6x^2+2x+\frac{7}{2}\right.$

$16x^4-12x^3$
$-\quad+$

$24x^3-10x^2+8x+20$

$24x^3-18x^2$
$-\quad+$

$8x^2+8x+20$

$8x^2-6x$
$-\quad+$

$14x+20$

$14x-\frac{21}{2}$
$-\quad+$

$20+\frac{21}{2} = \frac{61}{2}$

$\therefore Q = 4x^3+6x^2+2x+\frac{7}{2}$

$r = \frac{61}{2}$.

98. Let first number = x

$\therefore$ other number = $2490 - x$

According to the question,

$(6.5\%)x = (8.5\%)(2490-x)$

$\frac{65x}{1000} = \frac{85}{1000}(2490-x)$

$65x = 85 \times 2490 - 85x$

$150x = 85 \times 2490$

$x = \frac{85 \times 2490}{150} = 1411$

first number = 1411

other number = 2490 – 1411

= 1079

$\therefore$ numbers are 1411 and 1079.

99. 120 – 30 = 90 men

200 – 5 = 195 days

$\because$ for 120 men had food provision 195 days.

$\therefore$ for 1 man had food provision = 195 × 120 days

$\therefore$ 90 men had food provision = $\frac{195 \times 120}{90}$

= 260 days

100. Let total income = ₹ x

$$20\% \text{ of } x = \frac{20x}{100} = \frac{x}{5}$$

$$\text{remaining} = x - \frac{x}{5} = \frac{5x - x}{5} = \frac{4x}{5}$$

$$70\% \text{ of } \frac{4x}{5} = \frac{70}{100} \times \frac{4x}{5} = \frac{14x}{25}$$

$$\text{Saving} = \frac{4x}{5} - \frac{14x}{25} = \frac{6x}{25}$$

According to the question,

$$\frac{6x}{25} = 1800$$

$$x = \frac{25 \times 1800}{6} = 7500$$

∴ Total income = ₹ 7500.

101. Let CP of P = ₹ x

$$10\% \text{ of } x = \frac{10x}{100} = \frac{x}{10}$$

$$x + \frac{x}{10} = \frac{11x}{10}$$

$$12\% \text{ of } \frac{11x}{10} = \frac{12}{100} \times \frac{11x}{10} = \frac{132x}{1000}$$

$$\frac{11x}{10} + \frac{132x}{1000} = \frac{1100x + 132x}{1000} = \frac{1232x}{1000}$$

According to the question,

$$\frac{1232x}{1000} = \frac{24640}{100}$$

$$\Rightarrow \quad 1232x = 246400$$

$$x = \frac{246400}{1232} = 200$$

∴ C.P. of P = ₹ 200.

102. $x^2 + x + 17$

Put $x = 17$

$(17)^2 + 17 + 17 = 289 + 34 = 323$

323 is not a prime number because 323 is divisible by 19

∴ Least value of $x = 17$.

103. Distance = 300 + 200 = 500 m

Speed = 25 m/sec

$$\because \quad \text{Speed} = \frac{\text{dis.}}{\text{time}}$$

$$\text{Time} = \frac{\text{dis.}}{\text{speed}} = \frac{500}{25} = 20 \text{ seconds}.$$

104. 0.06% of $x = 84$

$$\frac{6x}{100 \times 100} = 84$$

$$x = \frac{840000}{6} = 140000$$

$$30\% \text{ of } x = \frac{30}{100} \times 140000$$

$$= 42000.$$

105. Let Q's share = ₹ x

P's share = ₹ $2x$

R's share = ₹ $4x$

According to the question,

$$4x - x = 3675$$

$$3x = 3675$$

$$x = 1225$$

Total share = 1225 + 2450 + 4900 = ₹ 8575.

106. ∵ Ratio of areas of squares = 25 : 36

Ratio side of squares = $\sqrt{25} : \sqrt{36} = 5:6$

∴ Ratio of their perimeter = 5 : 6.

107. Let numerator = x

∴ denominator = $x + 11$

$$\therefore \text{ fraction} = \frac{x}{x+11}$$

According to the question,

$$\frac{x+8}{x+11+8} = \frac{3}{4}$$

$$\Rightarrow \quad \frac{x+8}{x+19} = \frac{3}{4}$$

$$4x + 32 = 3x + 57$$

$$x = 25$$

$$\therefore \text{ fraction} = \frac{x}{x+11} = \frac{25}{25+11} = \frac{25}{36}.$$

108. $\because \; x = 2 + \sqrt{3}$

$$\Rightarrow \quad \frac{1}{x} = \frac{1}{2+\sqrt{3}} \times \frac{2-\sqrt{3}}{2-\sqrt{3}} = \frac{2-\sqrt{3}}{4-3} = 2 - \sqrt{3}$$

$$y = 2 - \sqrt{3}$$

$$\Rightarrow \quad \frac{1}{y} = \frac{1}{2-\sqrt{3}} \times \frac{2+\sqrt{3}}{2+\sqrt{3}} = \frac{2+\sqrt{3}}{4-3} = 2 + \sqrt{3}$$

$$\frac{1}{x^2}+\frac{1}{y^2} = \left(\frac{1}{x}\right)^2+\left(\frac{1}{y}\right)^2$$

$$= \left(\frac{1}{x}+\frac{1}{y}\right)^2 - 2\left(\frac{1}{x}\right)\left(\frac{1}{y}\right)$$

$$= \left(2-\sqrt{3}+2+\sqrt{3}\right)^2 - 2\left(2-\sqrt{3}\right)\left(2+\sqrt{3}\right)$$

$$= (4)^2 - 2\,(4-3)$$

$$= 16 - 2$$

$\therefore$ The value of $\frac{1}{x^2}+\frac{1}{y^2} = 14.$

109. Volume of sphere = $\frac{4}{3}\pi r^3$

Surface area of sphere = $4\pi r^2$

According to the question,

$$\frac{4\pi r^3}{3\times 4\pi r^2} = 27$$

$$r = 27 \times 3 = 81 \text{ cm.}$$

110. Let the number be x

According to the question,

$$\frac{1}{3}\times\frac{1}{4} \text{ of } x = 12$$

$$\frac{x}{12} = 12$$

$$x = 144$$

$\therefore$ number = 144.

For 111 to 113

	Hindi	English	Science	Maths	Social Studies
W	√	×	√	×	
X	√	×	√	√	
Y		√	√	×	×
Z		√	√	√	×

114. 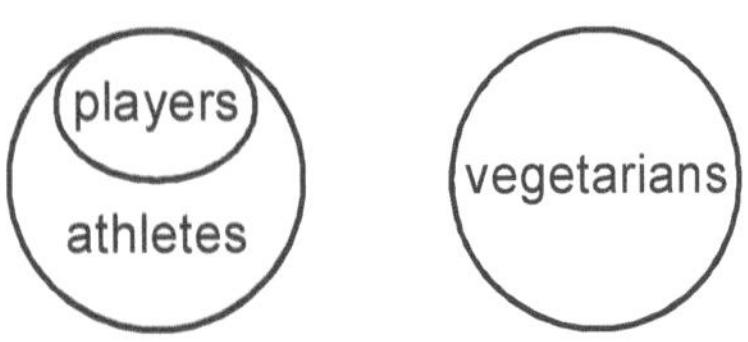

115. 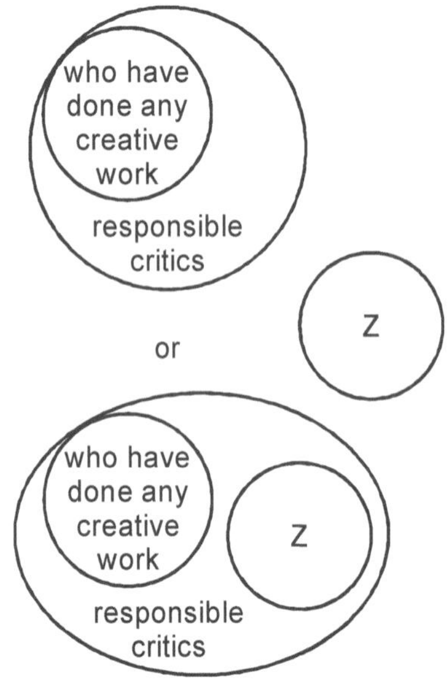

142. Except option D, in all options the words are opposite to each-other.

143. Except option A, in all options all words are the name of body parts.

144. Except, option B, in all options the second is game of the first.

145. 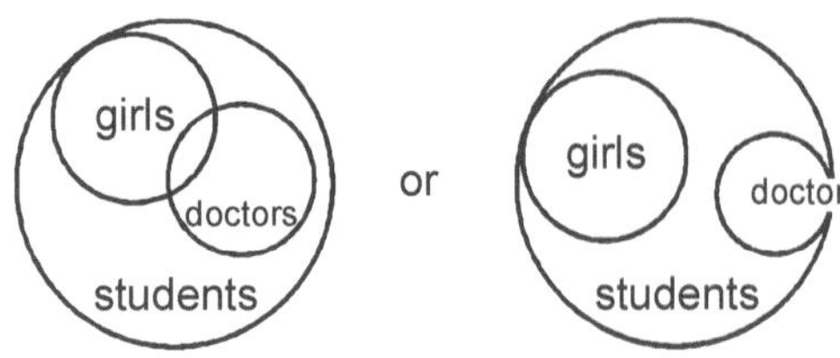

146. 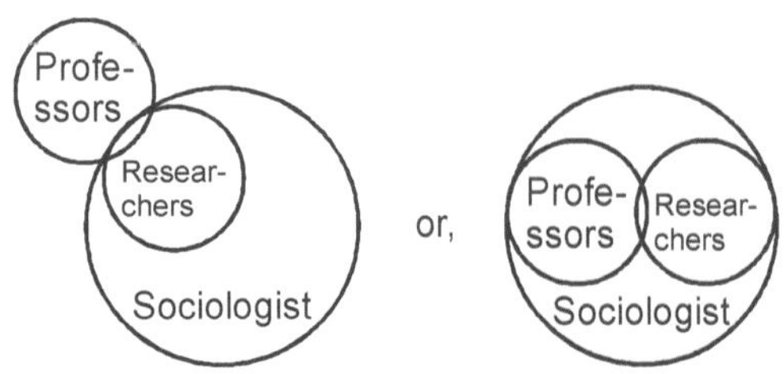

147. 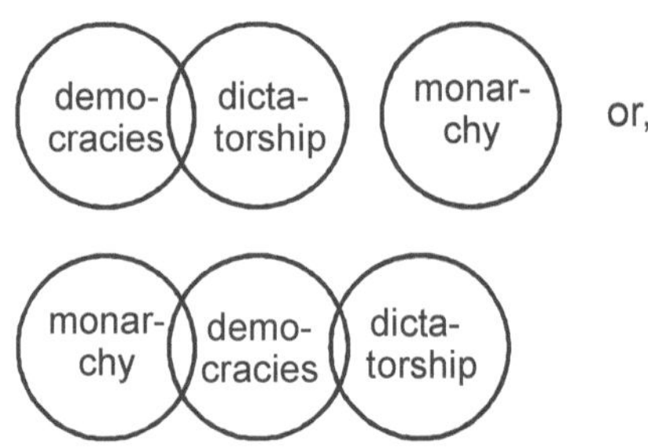

Previous Paper (Solved)

Common Law Admission Test (CLAT-UG) Entrance Exam, 2011

Section-I : English Comprehension

The questions in this section are based on a single passage. The questions are to be answered on the basis of what is stated or implied in the passage.

Please note that for some of the questions, more than one of the choices could conceivably answer the question. However, you are to choose the best answer; that is, the response that most accurately and completely answers the question.

Passage for Questions 1 to 10

If religion and community are associated with global violence in the minds of many people, then so are global poverty and inequality. There has, in fact, been an increasing tendency in recent years to justify policies of poverty removal on the ground that this is the surest way to prevent political strife and turmoil. Basing public policy—international as well as domestic—on such an understanding has some evident attractions. Given the public anxiety about wars and disorders in the rich countries in the world, the indirect justification of poverty removal—not for its own sake but for the sake of peace and quiet in the world—provides an argument that appeals to self-interest for helping the needy. It presents an argument for allocating more resources on poverty removal because of its presumed political, rather than moral, relevance.

While the temptation to go in that direction is easy to understand, it is a perilous route to take even for a worthy cause. Part of the difficulty lies in the possibility that if wrong, economic reductionism would not only impair our understanding of the world, but would also tend to undermine the declared rationale of the public commitment to remove poverty. This is a particularly serious concern, since poverty and massive inequality are terrible enough in themselves, and deserve priority even if there were no connection whatsoever with violence. Just as virtue is its own reward, poverty is at least its own penalty. This is not to deny that poverty and inequality can—and do—have far reaching consequences with conflict and strife, but these connections have to be examined and investigated with appropriate care and empirical scrutiny, rather than being casually invoked with unreasoned rapidity in support of a ''good cause''.

Destitution can, of course, produce provocation for defying established laws and rules. But it need not give people the initiative, courage, and actual ability to do anything very violent. Destitution can be accompanied not only by economic debility, but also by political helplessness. A starving wretch can be too frail and too dejected to fight and battle, and even to protest and holler. It is thus not surprising that often enough intense and widespread suffering and misery have been accompanied by unusual peace and silence.

Indeed, many famines have occurred without there being much political rebellion or civil strife or intergroup warfare. For example, the famine years in the 1840s in Ireland were among the most peaceful, and there was little attempt by the hungry masses to intervene even as ship after ship sailed down the river Shannon with rich food. Looking elsewhere, my own childhood memories in Calcutta during the Bengal famine of 1943 include the sight of starving people dying in front of sweetshops with various layers of luscious food displayed behind the glass windows, without a single glass being broken, or law or order being disrupted.

1. Select the statement that can be most plausibly inferred from the aforesaid passage:
   - A. A society plagued by recurrent famines can never witness political revolution.
   - B. Religious discrimination inevitably leads to violence and strife.
   - C. Destitution of the masses leads to peace and social stability.
   - D. Famines and starvation do not necessarily result in political rebellion.

2. The author believes that it may not be advisable to emphasise on the connection between poverty and violence as:
   - A. Emphasis on such connection appeals only to self-interest of persons.
   - B. Linking poverty and violence undermines the moral character of anti-poverty measures.
   - C. The absence of any essential connection between poverty and violence may then weaken the very rationale of anti-poverty policies.
   - D. There is no necessary link between poverty and inequality.

3. Which of the following best captures the central argument of this passage:
   A. Religion is inextricably linked with violence.
   B. Famines may not necessarily result in civil unrest.
   C. Global poverty and inequality are one of the fundamental causes of global violence and strife.
   D. Basing anti-poverty programmes on the need for avoidance of violence and strife is dotted with many pitfalls.

4. In the given passage, the word 'perilous' means:
   A. Scared B. Costly
   C. Futile D. Dangerous

5. The author refers to his own experience as a child during the Bengal famine of 1943 in order to:
   A. Illustrate how religiosity may instill passive acceptance of even the worst forms of starvation among people.
   B. Repudiate the argument that religious discrimination usually tends to inspire violent protests.
   C. Substantiate his assertion that it is not unusual to have the most intense suffering and misery coexist with complete peace.
   D. Demonstrate that people confronted with acute starvation are rendered too helpless to protest ever at all.

6. The word 'destitution' in this passage can be best substituted by:
   A. Dejection B. Indigence
   C. Default D. Dereliction

7. Which of the following statement is least likely to be inferred from the passage:
   A. History is replete with instance of famines that have occurred without there being much violent protest.
   B. Many writers and critics are increasingly advocating for stronger policies on poverty removal on the ground that this would help prevent political turmoil.
   C. The author believes that the links between poverty and violence must never be emphasized at all.
   D. Economic debility in turn inhibits political freedom.

8. The author asserts that basing anti-poverty measures on the avowed connections between poverty and violence has certain apparent benefits because:
   A. Poverty is similar to religious exploitation in terms of the potential violent consequences.
   B. It leads to allocation of more resources on anti-poverty policies.
   C. The widespread concern about war and violence provides a rationale for poverty-removal that appeals to the 'self-interest' of persons.
   D. Otherwise, there would not have been the tendency to justify anti-poverty policies on the ground that they prevent political turmoil.

9. 'Economic reductionism' in this passage means:
   A. Neglecting the economic connection between poverty and violence.
   B. Excessive accent on poverty and inequality.
   C. Emphasizing on the linkage between violence, poverty and economic equality.
   D. The view that every conflict is caused by underlying economic tensions.

10. "A sense of encroachment, degradation and humiliation can be even easier mobilize for rebellion and revolt." Select the most appropriate word out of the four options for filling the blank space in the aforesaid sentence:
    A. for B. as
    C. into D. to

Passage for Questions 11 to 20

In 1954, a Bombay economist named A.D. Shroff began a Forum of Free Enterprise, whose ideas on economic development were somewhat at odds with those then influentially articulated by the Planning Commission of the Government of India. Shroff complained against the 'indifference, if not discouragement' with which the state treated entrepreneurs.

At the same time as Shroff, but independently of him, a journalist named Philip Spratt was writing a series of essays in favour of free enterprise. Spratt was a Cambridge communist who was sent by the party in 1920s to foment revolution in the subcontinent. Detected in the act, he spent many years in an Indian jail. The books he read in the prison, and his marriage to an Indian woman afterwards, inspired a steady move rightwards. By the 1950s, he was editing a pro-American weekly from Bangalore, called *MysIndia*. There he inveighed against the economic policies of the government of India. These, he said, treated the entrepreneur 'as a criminal who has dared to use his brains independently of the state to create wealth and give employment'. The state's chief planner, P.C. Mahalanobis, had surrounded himself with Western leftists and Soviet academicians, who reinforced his belief in 'rigid control by the government over all activities'. The result, said Spratt, would be 'the smothering of free enterprise, a famine of consumer goods, and the tying down of millions of workers to soul-deadening techniques'.

The voices of men like Spratt and Shroff were drowned in the chorus of popular support for a model of heavy industrialization funded and directed by the governments. The 1950s were certainly not propitious times for free marketers in India. But from time-to-time their ideas were revived. After the rupee was devalued in 1966, there were some moves towards freeing the trade regime, and hopes that the licensing system would also be liberalized. However, after Indira Gandhi split the Congress Party in 1969, her government took its 'left turn', nationalizing a fresh range of industries and returning to economic autarky.

11. Which of the following statements can most reasonably be inferred from the information available in the passage:
   A. P.C. Mahalanobis believed in empowering private entrepreneurs and promoting free market.
   B. Phillip Spratt preferred plans that would create economic conditions favourable for a forward march by the private enterprise.
   C. Restrictions on free markets enriched large Indian companies.
   D. Philip Spratt opposed the devaluation of rupee in 1966.

12. Which of the following statements is least likely to be inferred from the passage:
   A. Acceptance of A.D. Shroff's plans in the official circles smothered free enterprise in India.
   B. The views of the Forum of Free Enterprise ran against the conception of development then prevalent among the policy makers.
   C. A.D. Shroff believed that state should actively support the private sector.
   D. Philip Spratt had been educated in Cambridge.

13. Select the statement that best captures the central purpose of this passage:
   A. Highlight that even though there were advocates for free-market and private enterprise in the early years of independent India, they were crowded out by others who supported a dominant role for state over private enterprise.
   B. Explain the politics behind Indira Gandhi's decision to nationalise the banks.
   C. Demonstrate with the help of statistics how the preference of policy makers for Soviet-style economic policies prevented India's economic growth.
   D. Establish that devaluation of rupee in 1966 was vindicated by subsequent experience.

14. Philip Spratt came to India because he:
   A. Fell in love with an Indian women
   B. Wanted to protest against the economic policies of the Indian government.
   C. Was offered the editorship of *MysIndia.*
   D. Had been instructed to work towards the goal of inciting a revolution in India.

15. The author avers that A.D. Shroff's ideas were somewhat at odds with the views of Planning Commission because:
   A. A.D. Shroff was in favour of rigid governmental control over all economic activities.
   B. Shroff had opposed government's decision to devalue Indian rupee.
   C. The hostility of the government to private entrepreneurs was complained against by A.D. Shroff.
   D. Shroff had been critical of the influence of Soviet academicians over India's economic policy.

16. The ideological shift of Philip Spratt to the right was caused by:
   A. The demise of the Soviet Union.
   B. The start of the weekly called *MysIndia.*
   C. The books that he encountered in the prison.
   D. The dissolution of his first marriage to his college friend.

17. Select the statement that could be most plausibly inferred from this passage:
   A. Philip Spratt and A.D. Shroff were members of the Forum for Free Enterprise.
   B. The first two Five Year Plans emphasised on the importance of private enterprise as the spearhead of economic growth.
   C. P.C. Mahalanobis had mooted the expulsion of foreign firms like Coca Cola and IBM from India.
   D. The hopes that the licensing regime would be liberalized after the devaluation of Indian rupee were belied in the aftermath of the split in the Congress Party.

18. The author alludes to nationalization of industries in 1969 in order to:
   A. Show the contradictions between AD Shroff's economic views and the official economic policies of the Government of India.
   B. Exemplify the shift of the Indira Gandhi led government to the 'left'.
   C. Demonstrate the ideological changes in the worldview of Philip Spratt.
   D. Highlight the negative political repercussions of the decision to devalue the Indian currency.

19. "Neither Philip Spratt nor A.D. Shroff .... able to convince Mahalanobis." Select the most appropriate phrase out of the four options for filling the blank space in the aforesaid sentence.
   A. were   B. are
   C. was   D. is

20. The word 'inveighed' in this passage means:
   A. Praised   B. Recited
   C. Proclaimed   D. Remonstrated

Passage for Questions 21 to 30

In Manu Joseph's debut novel *Serious Men,* the protagonist, Ayyan Mani, is a sly, scheming Dalit-Buddhist who almost gets away with passing off his partially deaf son, Adi, as a prodigy, a genius who can recite the first 1,000 prime numbers. The garb of satire—where almost every character cuts a sorry figure—gives the author the licence to offer one of the most bleak and pessimistic portrayals of urban Dalits. Despite his savage portrayal of Dalit (and female) characters—or perhaps because of it?—*Serious Men* has won critical appreciation from a cross-section of readers and critics.

At a time when a formidable body of Dalit literature—writing by Dalits about Dalit lives—has created a distinct space for itself, how and why is it that a novel such as *Serious Men,* with its gleefully skewed portrayal of an angry Dalit man, manages to win such accolades? In American literature—and particularly in the case of African-American authors and characters—these issues of representation have been debated for decades. But in India, the sustained refusal to address issues related to caste in everyday life—and the continued and unquestioned predominance of a Brahminical stranglehold over cultural production—have led us to place where non-Dalit portrayal of Dalits in literature, cinema and art remains the norm.

The journey of modern Dalit literature has been a difficult one. But even though it has not necessarily enjoyed the support of numbers, we must engage with what Dalits are writing—not simply for reasons of authenticity, or as a concession to identity politics, but simply because of the aesthetic value of this body of writing, and for the insights it offers into the human condition. In a society that is still largely unwilling to recognise Dalits as equal, rights-bearing human beings, in a society that is inherently indifferent to the everyday violence against Dalits, in a society unwilling to share social and cultural resources equitably with Dalits unless mandated by law (as seen in the **anti-reservation discourse**), Dalit literature has the potential to humanise non-Dalits and sensitise them to a world into which they have no insight. But before we can understand what Dalit literature is seeking to accomplish, we need first to come to terms with the stranglehold of non-Dalit representations of Dalits.

Rohinton Mistry's *A Fine Balance,* published 15 years ago, chronicles the travails of two Dalit characters—uncle Ishvar and nephew Omprakash—who migrate to Bombay and yet cannot escape brutality. While the present of the novel is set at the time of the Emergency, Ishvar's father Dukhi belongs to the era of the anti-colonial nationalist movement. During one of Dukhi's visits to the town, he chances upon a meeting of the Indian National Congress, where speakers spread the ''Mahatma's message regarding the freedom struggle, the struggle for justice,'' and wiping out ''the disease of untouchability, ravaging us for centuries, denying dignity to our fellow human beings.''

Neither in the 1940s, where the novel's past is set, nor in the Emergency period of the 1970s—when the minds and bodies Ishvar and Omprakash, are savaged by the state—do we find any mention of a figure like B.R. Ambedkar or of Dalit movements. In his 'nationalist' understanding of modern Indian history, Mistry seems to have not veered too far from the road charted by predecessors like Mulk Raj Anand and Premchand. Sixty years after Premchand, Mistry's literary imagination seems stuck in the empathy-realism mode, trapping Dalits in abjection. Mistry happily continues the broad stereotype of the Dalit as a passive sufferer, without consciousness of caste politics.

21. Which of the following is the closest description of the central argument of this passage:

A. Manu Joseph's novel presents a scathing portrayal of Dalits.

B. Contemporary American literature is very cautious on politically correct representation of minorities.

C. The last two decades have witnessed the rise of a very vibrant Dalit literature.

D. Portrayal of Dalits by non-Dalits merely as passive victims has been the dominant norm in Indian literature, cinema and art.

22. According to this passage, Premchand and Mulk Raj Anand:

A. Presented a stereotyped version of Dalit characters in their writings.

B. Excelled in writing satires on social inequality.

C. Were politically opposed to the views of B.R. Ambedkar.

D. Were closely involved with the leadership of the nationalist movement.

23. The writer refers to the 'anti-reservation discourse' in order to argue that:

A. Dalit literature has had a very difficult journey since its origins.

B. Manu Joseph is viscerally opposed to Dalits.

C. Persons belonging to the upper castes are inherently indifferent to routine violence against Dalits.

D. Indian society is not yet ready to equitably share, on its own, social, cultural and political space with Dalits.

24. Which of the following statements is least likely to be inferred from this passage:

A. The author of *Serious Men* has used the literary device of satire to present an unflattering picture of women characters.

B. Issues of representation of minorities have been debated extensively in American literature.

C. The writer of this passage believes that engagement with Dalits is necessary only because such engagement affirms the importance identity politics.
D. The writer believes that Rohinton Mistry presented a stereotypical representation of Dalits character in his book.

25. According to the information available in the passage, the writer attributes the prevalence of representation of Dalits by non-Dalits in literature, art and media to:
A. The nationalist understanding of Indian history.
B. Marginalisation of B.R. Ambedkar from nationalist movement.
C. The anti-reservation discourse.
D. Brahminical control over cultural production.

26. Which of the following is not among the reasons suggested by the writer for engaging with Dalit writing:
A. Dalit literature has the potential to sensitize non-Dalits about the experiences of the former.
B. Dalit writing is more authentic than representation of Dalits by non-Dalits.
C. Dalit literature does not have the support of numbers.
D. The aesthetic value of Dalit writing.

27. Which of the following statement cannot be inferred from the passage:
A. Upper-castes have dominated the instruments of cultural production in Indian society.
B. Indian society is unwilling to recognise Dalits as equal, rights-bearing human beings.
C. Dalit writers have carved out a space for writings on Dalit experience and world view.
D. The judiciary in India, in its opposition to reservation, has betrayed its unwillingness to acknowledge Dalits as equal bearer of rights.

28. The writer of this passage is critical of Rohinton Mistry's *A Fine Balance* for the reason that:
A. It is an example of a book on Dalit characters by a non-Dalit.
B. The book suggests that Dalits are nothing more than passive sufferers without any agency.
C. The book ignores the everyday violence that Dalits have to confront with.
D. It bares the passive literary style of the author, Rohinton Mistry.

29. Which of the following words would be the best substitute for the word 'sly' in this passage:
A. bright B. wise
C. devious D. dim

30. ''It is not as if Dalit movements .... not active during the periods that form *A Fine Balance*'s backdrop.'' Select the most appropriate choice to fill in the blank in the above sentence:
A. is B. was
C. were D. are

Passage for Questions 31 to 40

In recent weeks, the writers William Dalrymple and Patrick French, among others, have come before a **fusillade** of criticism in India, much of it questioning not their facts, not their interpretations, but their foreignness.

"Who gets to write about India?" The Wall Street Journal asked on Wednesday in its own report on this Indian literary feuding. It is a complicated question, not least because to decide who gets to write about India, you would need to decide who gets to decide who gets to write about India. Rather than conjecturing some Committee for the Deciding of the Deciding of Who Gets to Write About India, it might be easier to let writers write what they please and readers read what they wish.

The accusations pouring forth from a section of the Indian commentariat are varied. Some criticism is of a genuine literary nature, fair game, customary, expected. But lately a good amount of the reproaching has been about identity.

In the case of Mr. Dalrymple, a Briton who lives in New Delhi, it is—in the critics' view—that his writing is an act of re-colonization. In the case of Mr. French, it is that he belongs to a group of foreign writers who use business-class lounges and see some merit in capitalism and therefore do not know the real India, which only the commentariat member in question does.

What is most interesting about these appraisals is that their essential nature makes reading the book superfluous, as one of my Indian reviewers openly admitted. (His review was not about the book but his refusal to read the book.) The book is not necessary in these cases, for the argument is about who can write about India, not what has been written.

For critics of this persuasion, India surely seems a lonely land. A country with a millennial history of Hindus, Christians, Jews, Muslims and Buddhists living peaceably together; a country of hundreds of dialects in which so many Indians are linguistic foreigners to each other, and happily, tolerantly so; a country that welcomes foreign seekers (of yoga poses, of spiritual wisdom, of ancestral roots) with open arms; a country where, outside the elite world of South Delhi and South Bombay, I have not heard an Indian ask whether outsiders have a right to write, think or exist on their soil.

But it is not just this deep-in-the bones pluralism that challenges the **who-gets-to-write-about-India contingent.** It is also that at the very heart of India's multifarious changes today is this glimmering idea: that Indians must be rewarded for what they do, not who they are.

Identities you never chose—caste, gender, birth order—are becoming less important determinants of fate. Your deeds—how hard you work, what risks you take—are becoming more important.

It is this idea, which I have found pulsating throughout the Indian layers, that leaves a certain portion of the intelligentsia out of sync with the surrounding country. As Mr. French has observed, there is a tendency in some of these writers to value social mobility only for themselves. When the new economy lifts up the huddled masses, then it becomes tawdry capitalism and rapacious imperialism and soulless globalization.

Fortunately for those without Indian passports, the nativists' vision of India is under demographic siege. The young and the relentless are India's future. They could not think more differently from these literatis.

They savour the freedom they are gaining to seek their own level in the society and to find their voice; and they tend to be delighted at the thought that some foreigners do the same in India and love their country as much as they do.

31. Which of the following statements is least likely to be inferred from the passage:
   A. Younger generations of Indians are more tolerant of foreign scribes who write about their country.
   B. The writer believes that a section of Indian intelligentsia is very hostile to upward economic mobility.
   C. Mr. William Dalrymple has been accused of recolonising India through his writings.
   D. Most of the criticism that has been recently directed at Patrick French has emphasized mainly on the writer's underwhelming literary style.

32. Which of the following would be the best substitute for the word, 'fusillade' in the passage?
   A. Barrage B. Breach
   C. Temper D. Row

33. The writer uses the phrase, 'who-gets-to-write-about-India contingent' in this passage to refer to:
   A. Foreign writers who have written books on India.
   B. Critics who have attacked foreign writers writing on India for their mere foreignness.
   C. Elite residents of South Delhi and South Bombay.
   D. Cultural pluralists.

34. The writer believes that the most peculiar aspect of the criticisms that Patrick French and William Dalrymple have received is that:
   A. Most such condemnation has emerged from elite Indians.
   B. Such critics are hostile to upward immobility.
   C. These censures are not centered on the books of such writers or their literary styles but are targeted at their identity instead.
   D. These critics ignore the plural ethos of India.

35. Which of the following statements can be inferred from the passage:
   A. Ascriptive identities like caste, tribe, etc. are becoming more and more important with the passage of time.
   B. Patrick French believes that the new market friendly economic policies followed for the last decades have resulted in the rise of tawdry capitalism and rapacious imperialism.
   C. The writer is of the opinion that a section of the intelligentsia is divorced from the views of their compatriots.
   D. While India has historically been very hospitable to a variety of religions, it has not been equally open to linguistic foreigners.

36. According to the information available in the passage, the writer is of the opinion that:
   A. Writers like Patrick French do not know the real India.
   B. Most of the condemnation heaped on Dalrymple, French and himself has been on expected lines.
   C. India's reputation of pluralism is cosmetic at best, one that hides deep rooted hatred towards foreigners.
   D. The new generation of Indians have internalized the idea that people should be rewarded for what they do and not who they are.

37. The writer refers to the history of Hindus, Christians, Jews, Muslims and Buddhists living peaceably together in India for millions of years in order to:
   A. Show India's openness to foreigners who have visited Indian in the quest for yoga.
   B. Argue that India is a country of hundreds of dialects.
   C. Demonstrate the religiosity pervading in an average Indian.
   D. India's deep-in the bones pluralism.

38. The writer argues that the nature of criticism he, Dalrymple and French have received for their books renders reading their books superfluous because:
   A. Such criticism has been limited to a very small minority of Indians.
   B. These writers are popular among Indian youth, even among those who have not read their books.
   C. The literary styles of these writers are not the sole focus of such criticism.
   D. Such criticism is less about what has been written in their books than about who can write on India.

39. According to the passage, the question 'who gets to write about India' is complicated because:
   A. India has been historically open to and tolerant of foreign writers and artists.

B. This issue can be satisfactorily resolved only if we can decide who gets to decide who gets to write about India.
C. Ascriptive identities are becoming more and more important in a globalised world.
D. This would result in a shift of attention from what has been written to who has written.

40. ''But with many outsiders' India-related books recently hitting bookstores there, the sensitivity .... flared into about of vigorous literary nativism, with equally vigorous counterpunches.'' Select the most appropriate choice to fill in the blank in the above sentence:
A. has B. have
C. was D. did

Section-II : General Knowledge/Current Affairs

41. Which prominent Barrister-politician, who was closely linked with the emergency proclamation of 1975, breathed his last in Kolkata on 6th November 2010?
A. Jyoti Basu
B. Siddhartha Shankar Ray
C. Hiren Mukherjee
D. Indrajit Gupta

42. Who is the author of the book 'Great Soul: Mahatma Gandhi and his Struggle with India', criticised for its content?
A. Nirad C. Chaudhury B. Joseph Lelyveld
C. Khushwant Singh D. Hermann Kallenbach

43. Which *Gharana* of Classical singing did Late Pandit Bhimsen Joshi belong to?
A. Dhrupad B. Maihar
C. Kirana D. Etawah

44. 14th March 2011 was the 80th Anniversary of the first Indian sound Film (talkie). Which Movie was it?
A. Jahan Ara B. Alam Ara
C. Noorjehan D. None of the above

45. Which internationally renowned musician collaborated with Rahul Sharma to release a music album titled *'Namaste India'*?
A. Richard Clayderman B. Kenny G
C. Yanni D. Ricky Martin

46. ''War on Terrorism or American Strategy for Global Dominance'' is authored by which of the following authors?
A. Noam Chomsky B. Demetrios Caraley
C. Lea Brilmayer D. Manzoor Alam

47. Mohammad Asif, Mohammad Amir and Salman Butt (Cricket players of Pakistan) have been banned for being found guilty of spot fixing. To which of the following institutions have they applead?
A. Pakistan Cricket Board
B. Anti-Corruption Tribunal of the Asian Cricket Council
C. Court of Arbitration for Sport
D. Anti-Corruption Tribunal of the International Cricket Council

48. Indian driver Karun Chandok was recently in the news for which of the following?
A. Being selected as a reserve driver by Team Force India for the 2011 Formula One season.
B. Being selected as a reserve driver by Team Lotus for the 2011 Formula One season.
C. Being selected as a reserve driver by Team Ferrari for the 2011 Formula One season.
D. None of the above.

49. The United Nations Framework Convention on Climate Change meeting of 2010 December was held in which of the following placcs?
A. Colorado B. Canberra
C. Cancun D. None of the above

50. Which of the following pairings is incorrect?
A. Muammar Gaddafi – Syria
B. Fidel Castro – Cuba
C. Pol Pot – Cambodia
D. Hosni Mubarak – Egypt

51. The Right of Children to Full and Compulsory Education Act 2009 requires private schools to ensure that .... per cent of their students come from weaker sections and disadvantaged groups?
A. 2 B. 15
C. 25 D. 40

52. Srikrishna Committee, which recently submitted its report, was constituted for which of the following issues?
A. Mumbai bomb blast case
B. Malegaon blast case
C. Telengana issue
D. 2G Spectrum corruption issue

53. Why was Arundhati Roy investigated for sedition?
A. For committing contempt of court
B. For saying that Kashmir is not an integral part of India
C. For sympathising with the Maoists
D. For condemning nuclear tests conducted by India

54. Damon Galgut's 'In a Strange Room' was recently in news for:
A. Man Booker Prize shortlist
B. Winning the Pulitzer Prize
C. Winning the Orange Prize for fiction
D. None of the above

55. Who was recently in the news when the Supreme Court of India rejected her plea for Euthanasia, but paved the way for legalization of passive euthanasia?
A. Aruna Shanbaug B. Aruna Roy
C. Mary Roy D. Medha Patkar

56. Nagoya Protocol, signed by India on 30th October, 2010 is:
A. an international treaty of bilateral investment between India and Japan
B. an international treaty to ensure that local produce are exploited only under license and for the common good of the mankind
C. an international treaty to ensure that the benefits of natural resources and their commercial derivatives are shared with local communities
D. None of the above

57. Julian Assange, the founder of WikiLeaks, was arrested in which of the following nations?
A. U.K. B. Sweden
C. U.S.A. D. Denmark

58. Which of the following are the five countries that have decided to bid for 2017 World Athletics Championships?
A. Qatar, USA, China, Sri Lanka and Brazil
B. Germany, Britain, Hungary, Qatar and Spain
C. Germany, Qatar, India, Spain and China
D. Germany, Britain, China, Qatar and Spain

59. The recent Tunisian revolution is known as:
A. Orange Revolution B. Jasmine Revolution
C. Purple Revolution D. Crescent Revolution

60. 'The Naive and the Sentimental Novelist' is a 2010 publication of Harvard University Press of which of the following authors?
A. Orhan Pamuk B. J.M. Coetzie
C. Partha Chatterjee D. Ben Okri

61. Who replaced Lalit Modi as the IPL Chairman and Commissioner from this year's edition of the IPL?
A. Chirayu Amin B. Rajiv Shukla
C. Ratnakar Shetty D. Shashank Manohar

62. Which one of the following films was officially selected to compete in the *Un Certain Regard* (A Certain Glance) category at the 2010 Cannes Film Festival?
A. Udaan B. My Name is Khan
C. Wednesday D. Dhobi Ghat

63. Rani Kumudini Devi, whose birth centenary is being celebrated in 2011, was the:
A. First woman barrister of India
B. First woman Mayor of Hyderabad
C. First woman photographer in India
D. First woman doctor of India

64. The Supreme Court in 2010 upheld an order of the Bombay High Court to lift a four-year-old ban imposed by the Maharashtra government on publication and circulation of a controversial book, authored by American scholar James Laine. Identify the book from the following:
A. Chatrpati Shivaji
B. Shivaji – The Warrior King
C. Shivaji – The Hindu King in Muslim India
D. None of the above

65. In which case did the Nagpur Bench of the Bombay High Court on July 14, 2010 commute the death sentence of six accused to rigorous life imprisonment?
A. Khairlanji Case B. Bhopal Gas Leak Case
C. Bhagalpur Case D. Nithari Case

66. The Shunglu panel was constituted for which of the following issues?
A. Investigate the 2G Spectrum Scam
B. Suggest Civil Service Reforms
C. Probe the Commonwealth Games Scam
D. Suggest reforms on centre-state relationship

67. Who was appointed as the Chairman of the National Innovation Council in August 2010?
A. Shashi Tharoor
B. Chetan Bhagat
C. Arindam Chaudhury
D. Sam Pitroda

68. Name the Kenya-born political lobbyist who runs a firm called Vaishnavi Corporate Communications, and has recently been in news?
A. Barkha Dutt B. Vir Sanghhvi
C. Vina Ramani D. Niira Radia

69. Irom Sharmila has been fasting for the last 10 years to protest against which of the following issues?
A. Rape case against Indian Army in Manipur
B. Emergency in Manipur
C. Prevention of Terrorism Act 2005
D. Application of the Armed Forces (Special Powers) Act 1958 in Manipur

70. Thein Sein is the newly-appointed President of which of the following nations?
A. Indonesia B. Malaysia
C. Myanmar D. Thailand

71. Baglihar dam has been a matter of dispute between which nations?
A. Bangladesh and Myanmar
B. Myanmar and China
C. India and China
D. India and Pakistan

72. Who is the author of the book ''TINDERBOX —The Past and Future of Pakistan''?
A. Husain Haqqani
B. Yasmeen Niaz Mohiuddin
C. Ishrat Husain
D. M.J. Akbar

73. On 25th January 2011, BJP leaders Sushma Swaraj and Arun Jaitley were prevented from entering Srinagar and unfurl the national flag. What was that *Rath Yatra* called?
A. Swabhimaan Yatra B. Ekta Yatra
C. Mukti Yatra D. Swaraj Yatra

74. Who is chairing the Joint Parliamentary Committee (JPC) on the 2G Spectrum allocation issue?
A. Murli Manohar Joshi B. A Raja
C. M. Thambi Durai D. P.C. Chacko

75. Saina Nehwal recently defeated Ji Hyun Sung of South Korea to win which of the following titles?
A. Swiss Open Grand Prix Gold Badminton
B. Commonwealth Games
C. Singapore Open
D. Hong Kong Open

76. *'Moner Manush'*, the film to win the 'Golden Peacock' at the 41st International Film Festival of India was based on the life of which legendary 19th century folk singer and spiritual leader?
A. Kabir B. Surjya Sen
C. Kabir Suman D. Lalan Fakir

77. Justice P.C. Phukan Commission of Inquiry was constituted to enquire into which of the following incidents?
A. Clashes between Nagas and Lepchas in Nagaland on 14th August 2008
B. Clashes between Bodos and Muslims in Northern Assam's Udalguri district on August 14th 2008
C. Clashes between Assamese and Bengalis in Guwahati on August 14th 2008
D. None of the above

78. The first woman Secretary General of SAARC is from which country?
A. Maldives B. Bhutan
C. Sri Lanka D. India

79. Under whose premiership was the Women's Reservations Bill (to secure quotas for women in Parliament and state legislative assemblies) first introduced in Parliament?
A. Rajiv Gandhi B. HD Deve Gowda
C. Atal Bihari Vajpayee D. Manmohan Singh

80. Which Irish player scored the fastest Century in the history of World Cup Cricket?
A. Niall O' Brien B. Kevin O' Brien
C. A. Cusack D. Ed Joyce

81. Which of the following report brought out the 2G spectrum scam?
A. CBI report B. WikiLeaks
C. CAG report D. None of the above

82. In February 2011, Gopa Sabharwal was appointed as the first Vice Chancellor of which University of international stature?
A. Jawaharlal Nehru University
B. Azim Premji University
C. Visva-Bharati University
D. Nalanda International University

83. With which Hindutva association are Sadhvi Pragya Singh Thakur and Swami Aseemanand allegedly associated?
A. Vishwa Hindu Parishad
B. Shri Ram Sena
C. Abhinav Bharat
D. Arya Samaj

84. With which of the following do your associate the name P.J. Thomas?
A. Central Vigilance Commission
B. Lokpal
C. Anti-corruption Ombudsman
D. Banking Ombudsman

85. The 17th Commonwealth Law Conference was held in which city?
A. Delhi B. Bangalore
C. Kolkata D. Hyderabad

86. Gustavo Santaolall who composed the music to the song ''Stranger Lives'' in the movie ''Dhobi Ghat'', is from which of the following nations?
A. Chile B. Peru
C. Argentina D. Mexico

87. Which one of the following was not awarded a portion of the contested land by the judgment of the Allahabad High Court in 2010 pertaining to the Ayodhya dispute?
A. Nirmohi Akhada
B. Sunni Central Board of Waqfs
C. Rashtriya Swayamsevak Sangh
D. Bhagwan Sri Ram Lala Virajman

88. Sania Mirza claimed silver in the tennis mixed doubles category in the Asian Games in Guanzhou in November 2010. Who was her Partner?
A. Mahesh Bhupathi B. Somdev Devvarman
C. Leander Paes D. Vishnu Vardhan

89. China objected to the Dalai Lama's recent visit to Tawang in Arunachal Pradesh. What was he visiting in Tawang?
A. A Buddhist monastery
B. A memorial to Tibetans massacred by the Chinese army
C. The residence of Panchen Lama
D. None of the above

90. Which one of the following tribes lives in the Niyamgiri Hills, which is at the heart of the controversy surrounding Vedanta Resources' mining operations?
A. Manna Dhora
B. Dongria Kondh
C. Pardhan
D. Mal Pahariya

Section-III : Mathematics

91. Ranjeetha walks around the circular park in 15 minutes. If she walks at the rate of 5 km/hr, how much distance would she have to travel, at the minimum, to reach the centre of the park from any point on its perimeter?
A. 100 metre B. 200 metre
C. 250 metre D. 300 metre

92. If $(9/7)^3 \times (49/81)^{2x-6} = (7/9)^9$, then the value of x is:
A. 12 B. 9
C. 8 D. 6

93. Francis has 18 eggs out of which 12 eggs were sold at 10% loss than the cost price. At what mark up should he sell the remaining eggs to cover his losses?
A. 5% B. 10%
C. 15% D. 20%

94. If the length and height of a brick increases by 10% each respectively, and the breadth reduces by 20%, what is the percentage change in the volume of the brick?
A. 28 B. 30
C. 32 D. 36

95. A flag pole 18 m high casts a shadow 9.6 m long. What is the distance of the top of the pole from the far end of the shadow?
A. 20 metres B. 20.04 metres
C. 20.4 metres D. 24 metres

96. The 10th term of the series: 5, 8, 11, 14, ... is:
A. 32 B. 35
C. 38 D. 185

97. A bag contains 19 red balls, 37 blue balls and 27 green balls. If a ball is picked up from this bag at random, what is the probability of picking a blue ball?
A. 19/83 B. 37/87
C. 34/81 D. None of the above

98. A cylindrical tennis ball container can contain maximum three balls stacked on one another. The top and bottom balls also touch the lid and the base of the container respectively. If the volume of a tennis ball is 240 cm^3, then what is the volume of the container?
A. 1080 cm^3 B. 840 cm^3
C. 1440 cm^3 D. 720 cm^3

99. Akbar will turn 50 when his son Jehangir turns 18. What will be Akbar's age when it will be exactly 5 times that of Jehangir?
A. 36 years B. 40 years
C. 44 years D. 48 years

100. Arun can climb a Coconut tree by 1.5 feet by each lift; however he slips 0.5 feet every time he makes the next life. How many individual lifts he will have to reach the top of the Coconut tree of 18.5 feet?
A. 20 B. 19
C. 18 D. 17

101. Jogen's taxable income for 2010-11 is ₹ 5,00,000. The tax rates are (*i*) nil for first 1,50,000, (*ii*) 10% or 150,001 – 3,00,000 and (*iii*) 20% for the remaining. His Tax liability is:
A. ₹ 45,000 B. ₹ 50,000
C. ₹ 55,000 D. ₹ 60,000

102. The ratio of two numbers is 4 : 5. But, if each number is increased by 20, the ratio becomes 6 : 7. The sum of such numbers is:
A. 90 B. 95
C. 100 D. 60

103. During the academic session 2009-10, in Banaras Hindu University, Varanasi, the number of students studying Arts, Law and Commerce was in the ratio of 5 : 6 : 7. If during the academic session 2010-11 the number of students studying Arts, Law and Commerce increased by 20%, 30% and 40% respectively, what will be new ratio?
A. 26 : 42 : 63 B. 36 : 44 : 73
C. 26 : 39 : 49 D. 30 : 39 : 49

104. A customised jewellery was sold at ₹ 1000 with 90% discount on the 'making charges'. If the payment made for making charges was ₹ 100, what is the *approximate* rate of discount on the product?
A. 35 B. 45
C. 47 D. 90

105. A man walks from his house to the Railway station to catch a train, which is running as per schedule. If he walks at 6 km/hr, he misses the train by 9 minutes. However, if he walks at 7 km/hr, he reaches the station 6 minutes before the departure of train. The distance of his home to the Railway Station is:
A. 2 km B. 1.5 km
C. 1.05 km D. 1.25 km

106. Difference between two numbers is 9 and difference between their squares is 981. Lowest of the two numbers is:
A. 40 B. 50
C. 55 D. 59

107. Ms. Jhulan Goswami scores 102 runs in the 18th innings of her career and thus increases her average by 5. After the 18th inning, her average is:
A. 17 B. 21
C. 26 D. 28

108. In a staff room of 29 teachers, 13 drink black coffee, 7 milk coffee, 9 drink both tea and either type of coffee, and everyone drinks either of the beverages. How many teachers drink only tea?
A. insufficient information
B. 5
C. 6
D. 9

109. A box contains 90 discs which are numbered from 1 to 90. If one disc is drawn at random from the box, the probability that it bears a perfect square number is:
A. 1/10 B. 1/11
C. 1/90 D. 1/9

110. Two coins are tossed simultaneously. The probability of getting at the most one head is:
A. 1/4 B. 1/2
C. 3/4 D. 1

Section-IV : Logical Reasoning

For the following eight questions, study the sequence of letters, numbers or words carefully to work out the pattern on which it is based, and therefore what the next item in the sequence must be. For example, the sequence 'A, C, E, G, ...', has odd-numbered letters of the alphabet; therefore, the next item must be 'I'. The meanings of the words are irrelevant.

111. A, B, D, G, K, P, ...
What is the last alphabet in this sequence?
A. Z B. Y
C. V D. X

112. B, C, E, G, K, M, Q, S, ...
What is the next alphabet in this sequence?
A. T B. U
C. V D. W

113. Z, X, T, N, ...
What is the next alphabet in this sequence?
A. E B. F
C. G D. H

114. 'Apple, Application, ..., Approval, Apricot, April'.
Which of the following best fits in the blank?
A. Arrogant B. April
C. Appropriate D. Apiary

115. 'Sunday, Monday, Wednesday, Saturday, Wednesday, Monday, Sunday, ...'.
Which of the following best fits in the blank?
A. Sunday B. Tuesday
C. Saturday D. Thursday

116. '387924, ..., 3724, 423, 32, 2'. Which number is missing?
A. 42978 B. 42783
C. 42983 D. 42783

117. 'Gym, hymn, lynx, pygmy, rhythm'
Which of the following words does not belong to the above set?
A. Myrrh B. Mythic
C. Flyby D. Syzygy

118. Aadvark, Eerie, Iiwi, Oolong, ...
Which of the following words follows the pattern of this series?
A. Uvula B. Uulium
C. Uranium D. Uranus

In the following three questions, assume that a 'fact' expresses something that can be proved by clear and objective data. An opinion expresses a judgment, view, attitude, or conclusion that is not backed by data.

119. Which one of the following statements is best described as an assertion of opinion rather than an assertion of fact?
A. Brazil, China and India are now among the largest emitters of greenhouse gases.
B. Scientists agree that human activity is an important cause of climate change.
C. The Indian government's policy on climate change is misguided.
D. The Indian government's policy on climate change has changed significantly in the last five years.

120. '(a) The number of people migrating into Bengaluru has increased significantly in recent years. (b) This is because Bengaluru provides more economice opportunities than the towns and villages from which these migrants come. (c) This sudden influx of migrants has made the city less pleasant to live in. (d) The success of the government's rural employment guarantee act might have the effect of stemming some rural-urban migration.'

Which one of the above statements is best described as an assertion of opinion rather than an assertion of fact?

A. (a) B. (b)
C. (c) D. (d)

121. Which one of the following statements, if true, is best described as an assertion of opinion rather than an assertion of fact?

A. Mumbai is larger than Pune
B. Mumbai is smaller than Pune
C. Mumbai is more cultured than Pune
D. Mumbai is more crowded than Pune

For the following three questions, there are two or more statements along with four conclusions deduced from the statements. You are required to answer on the basis of the statements and the conclusions. Make the factual assumptions required by the question even if you believe the statement is actually false.

122. Statement 1 : Some aeroplanes are balloons.
Statement 2 : Some balloons are rockets.

Conclusions:

(a) Some aeroplanes are rockets.
(b) Some rockets are tables.
(c) All the rockets are balloons.
(d) All the balloons are aeroplanes.

Assuming that statements 1 and 2 are true, which conclusions follow:

A. Only (b) and (d) B. Only (a) and (c)
C. Only (d) D. None of the above

123. Statement 1 : All whales are fish.
Statement 2 : Some fish are not amphibians.
Statement 3 : All whales are amphibians.
Statement 4 : Some amphibians are not fish.

Conclusions:

(a) Some fish are amphibians.
(b) Some amphibians are fish.
(c) Only whales are both fish and amphibians.
(d) All amphibians are fish.

Assuming only that statements 1, 2, 3 and 4 are true, which of the above conclusions may be deduced?

A. Only (a) and (b) B. Only (c)
C. Only (d) D. None of the above

124. Statement 1 : All libraries are laboratories.
Statement 2 : No laboratories are hostels.

Conclusions:

(a) All laboratories are libraries.
(b) Some hostels are libraries.
(c) Some libraries are hostels.
(d) No library is a hostel.

Assuming that statements 1 and 2 are true, which conclusions follow:

A. Only (a) and (b) B. Only (b) and (c)
C. Only (c) and (d) D. Only (d)

For the following sixteen questions, read the given passage carefully and answer the questions that follow.

Passage for Questions 125 to 127

'Instead of being concerned with what actually happens in practice... [economics] is increasingly preoccupied with developing pseudo-mathematical formulas. These provide models of behaviour which never quite fit what actually happens, in a way which resembles the physical sciences gone wrong: instead of equations describing reality, economics produces equations describing ideal conditions and theoretical clarity of a type which never occurs in practice'.

125. Which of the following best summarises the argument of this paragraph?

A. Economics ought to be more like the physical sciences.
B. Theoretical clarity is undesirable in economics.
C. The physical sciences are wrong to emphasise mathematic formulae.
D. The mathematical equations used by economists do not accurately describe the real world.

126. Which of the following claims is *not* implied in the paragraph above?

A. Economists should stop using mathematical models.
B. Equations describing ideal conditions should not be mistaken for equations describing reality.
C. Theoretical clarity should not come at the expense of accuracy.
D. Models of human behaviour should be true to the complexity of human nature.

127. Which of the following, *if true,* would most *weaken* the argument of the passage above?

A. The physical sciences are themselves reducing their reliance on mathematical formulae.
B. The real world in fact closely approximates ideal theoretical conditions.
C. We do not at present have the mathematical expertise to model the full complexity of the world economy.
D. Academic economists need to be more sensitive to human nature.

Passage for Questions 128 and 129

'Religions, like camel caravans, seem to avoid mountain passes. Buddhism spread quickly south from Buddha's birth-place in southern Nepal across the flat Gangetic plain to Sri Lanka. But it took a millennium to reach China ... The religious belt stretched eventually to Mongolia and Japan, but in Afghanistan Buddhism filled only a narrow belt that left pagans among the valleys to the east and west in Kailash and Ghor'.

128. Which of the following best summarises the subject of this paragraph?
- A. The Afghan people were hostile to Buddhism.
- B. Geography has considerable impact on the spread of religions.
- C. Buddhism does not flourish in mountainous regions.
- D. Religion has a considerable impact on geography.

129. Which of the following, if true, would most *weaken* the conclusion to the above argument?
- A. Christianity took several centuries to cross the Atlantic Ocean to America.
- B. The Hindukush mountains made no difference to the speed with which Islam spread.
- C. Buddhism is strongest in mountainous regions.
- D. Jainism is less popular in cold climates.

Passage for Questions 130 and 131

'Friendship was indeed a value for the villagers, more for men than for women. Two good friends were said to be 'like brothers' (literally, 'like elder brother-younger brothers', *annatammandirahage*). I heard this expression several times and I could not help recalling the statement of an elderly English colleague who had told me that he and his brother were very close and had written to each other every week. He had added, 'We are very good friends.' That is, friendship connoted intimacy in England while in Rampura (as in rural India everywhere), brotherhood conveyed intimacy'.

130. Which of the following best summarises the conclusion of the argument of this paragraph?
- A. Friendship has greater value for men than for women.
- B. People in England have different attitudes to brotherhood and friendship than people in rural India.
- C. Brotherhood has greater value in rural India than in England.
- D. Friendship has greater value in England than in India.

131. Which of the following, if true, would directly *contradict* the conclusion of the above argument?
- A. People are less likely to have large families in England.
- B. People in England are no longer close to their family members.
- C. People in England do not think that friendship connotes intimacy.
- D. People in rural India think that sisters cannot be intimate.

Passage for Questions 132 and 133

'A language is most easily learnt when it is in tune with the social context. To teach an Indian child in English at the primary stage ... strengthens distinctions of class and status and warps the mind. Failure to resort to regional languages in literacy campaigns also hampers their success'.

132. Which of the following best summarises the argument of the passage above?
- A. Learning English warps the mind.
- B. Language policy should be devised with an eye to social context.
- C. Literacy campaigns in India have failed.
- D. English should be taught at the secondary school level.

133. Which of the following claims, if true, would *weaken* the argument in the passage above?
- A. Literacy campaigns are more successful when conducted in English.
- B. Learning English at an early age has been found to weaken class distinctions.
- C. Children who learn English at the primary-school stage have been found to show greater intellectual ability than those who learn English only at the secondary level.
- D. All of the above.

Passage for Questions 134 to 136

'The tribes should develop their own culture and make their contribution to the cultural richness of the country. It is unnecessary to cause them to change their customs, habits or diversions so far as to make themselves indistinguishable from other classes. To do so would be to rob rural and pastoral life of its colour and stimulating diversity.'

134. Which of the following conclusions is *not* implied by the passage above?
- A. It is good for India's tribal people to develop their culture.
- B. Tribal customs should not be allowed to change in any respect.
- C. Forcing tribal people to change their customs reduces the diversity of rural life.
- D. Tribal culture is part of the cultural richness of India.

135. Which of the following claims runs directly counter to the spirit of the passage above?
- A. Tribal people should be able to decide what elements of the modern world to adopt.

B. The government should make modern science and medicine available to tribal people.
C. Tribal people should not be subjected to any coercion to conform to non-tribal cultural norms as long as they do not violate the law.
D. The tribals should assimilate as far as possible into non-tribal culture as a condition of full citizenship.

136. Which of the following is *not* an assumption required by the above argument?
A. Colour and diversity are desirable things.
B. Tribal people are capable of contributing to India's cultural diversity.
C. Changing tribal customs is a necessary condition of making modern medicine available to tribal people.
D. Rural life is presently full of colour and diversity.

Passage for Questions 137 and 138

'India is the only country in the world where, in the States which are governed by the Communist party, human rights are fully respected—and that is only because the Bill or Rights is firmly entrenched in our national constitution. We can proudly say that our Constitution gave us a flying start and equipped us adequately to meet the challenges of the future.'

137. Which of the following conclusions is *not* implied by the passage above?
A. Communist states often do not respect human rights.
B. Communist states never respect human rights.
C. The entrenchment of the Bill of Rights is what ensures that even Communist-governed states respect human rights.
D. The Indian constitution prepared India for the challenges of independence.

138. Which of the following if true, would *weaken* the above argument?
A. Communist governments are motivated to respect human rights out of Communist principles, not Constitutional ones.
B. The Constitution of India is itself sympathetic to Communist principles.
C. Human rights need to be enforceable to have any meaning.
D. Countries without a strong culture of human rights are prone to oppressing minorities.

Passage for Questions 139 and 140

'Poverty is ... more restrictive and limiting than anything else. If poverty and low standards continue then democracy, for all its fine institutions and ideals, ceases to be a liberating force. It must therefore aim continuously at the eradication of poverty and its companion unemployment. In other words, political democracy is not enough. It must develop into economic democracy also'.

139. Which of the following is *not* implied by the above passage?
A. Democracy has ceased to be a liberating force.
B. Democracies should aim to eliminate poverty.
C. Poverty and unemployment go hand in hand.
D. Political democracy should develop into economic democracy.

140. Which of the following views, if true, would *weaken* the argument of the above passage?
A. Political democracy is inseparable from economic democracy.
B. Poverty does not in fact restrict freedom.
C. Democracy flourishes most in poor societies.
D. Economic democracy is a necessary condition for the elimination of unemployment.

The following six questions comprise of one or more statements. Please answer the questions on the basis of the given statement(s). Please make the factual assumptions required by the question even if you believe the statement is false.

141. 'Where there is smoke, there is fire'.

Which of the following statements, *if true,* would show that the above statement is false?
A. There is sometimes smoke where there is no fire.
B. There is sometimes fire where there is no smoke.
C. There is no fire where there is no smoke.
D. None of the above.

142. 'Where there is poverty, there are always thieves.'

Which of the following statements, *if true*, would show that the above statement is false?
A. America is a rich country and there are thieves in America.
B. Bhutan is a poor country and there are no thieves in Bhutan.
C. Bangladesh is a poor country and there are many thieves in Bangladesh.
D. Nepal is a rich country and there are no thieves in Nepal.

143. **Statement 1 :** Sugar is bad for people with diabetes.

Statement 2 : Leela does not eat sugar.

Assuming that Statements 1 and 2 are true, which of the following statements follows?
A. Leela has diabetes.
B. Sugar is bad for Leela.
C. People with diabetes do not eat sugar.
D. None of the above.

144. **Statement 1 :** People who read fashion magazines do not like to read fiction.

Statement 2 : Tenzin does not read fashion magazines.

Assuming that Statements 1 and 2 are true, which of the following conclusions might be said to follow?

A. Tenzin likes to read fiction.
B. Tenzin may or may not like to read fiction.
C. Tenzin does not like to read fiction.
D. Tenzin does not like fashion magazines.

145. **Suleiman :** All Communists are atheists.

Sheeba : That is not true.

Which of the following, *if true*, would make Sheeba's reply the most convincing?

A. My uncle is an atheist but he is not a Communist.
B. My uncle is a Communist but he is not an atheist.
C. My uncle is a Communist and an atheist.
D. My uncle is neither a Communist nor an atheist.

146. **Statement 1 :** All pingos are byronic.

Statement 2 : Shalisto is byronic.

Statement 3 : Therefore ....

Fill in the blank.

A. Shalisto is a pingo
B. Shalisto is not a pingo
C. Shalisto is not byronic
D. None of the above

For the following nine questions, read the given argument or statement carefully, making any factual assumptions necessary. Then choose the best answer out of the four choices to the question asked. Note that not all the facts given will be relevant for determining the answer.

147. 'China has a higher literacy rate than India. This is due to the greater efficiency of the Communist system. Efficiency is sorely lacking in India's democratic system. Therefore, democracy is the biggest obstacle to India's achieving 100% literacy.'

Which of the following, *if true,* would directly undermine the above argument?

A. Inefficiency is equally a problem in democracies and Communist countries.
B. Communist systems do not respect human rights.
C. Freedom is more important than literacy.
D. China is slowly making the transition to democracy.

148. 'In 399 BC, a jury in Athens condemned Socrates to death for impiety and corrupting the morals of the youth. Socrates' friends offered to help him escape, but Socrates refused. Socrates argued that the fact that he had lived in Athens for so many years meant that he had committed himself to obeying its laws. It would therefore be wrong for him to break those very laws he was implicitly committed to obeying'.

Which one of the following claims constitutes the most plausible challenge to Socrates' argument?

A. Long residence only commits someone to obeying just laws and Socrates was convicted under an unjust law.
B. Long residence by itself does not imply a commitment to obeying laws since one never made any explicit commitment.
C. Obedience to the law is not always required.
D. There is no point in escaping from prison since one will anyway be captured again.

149. 'Soft drinks have been shown by scientists to be bad for the teeth. Therefore, the government would be justified in banning all soft drinks from the Indian market.'

Assuming that the factual claim in the above argument is true, what else needs to be assumed for the conclusion to follow?

A. The government is justified in banning anything that is bad for dental health.
B. Soft drinks are also bad for gastric health.
C. Dental hygiene is a matter of great concern.
D. No further assumptions are necessary.

150. 'In order to be eligible for election to the Lok Sabha, a person must be at least 25 years of age. Moreover, one must not be bankrupt. Therefore, Jatinder Singh, over 50 years of age and without any criminal convictions, cannot be the Speaker of the Lok Sabha since he has just filed for bankruptcy.'

Which of the following must be assumed for the conclusion to follow logically?

A. Anyone over 50 years of ago is eligible to be Speaker of the Lok Sabha as long as he or she has no criminal convictions.
B. People without criminal convictions cannot be elected to the Lok Sabha even if they are not bankrupt.
C. Only those eligible for election to the Lok Sabha are eligible to be the Speaker of the Lok Sabha.
D. There is no minimum age requirement for the Speaker of the Lok Sabha.

151. 'As a century draws to a close, people start behaving much like people coming to the end of a long life. People approaching death often start reflecting on the events of their lives. Similarly, people alive in 1999 ....'

Which of the following most logically completes the paragraph above?

A. ... started reflecting on the events of the twentieth century.
B. ... started to reflect on the events of their lives.
C. ... started to fear death.
D. ... started to wonder what the year 2000 would bring.

152. 'The Roman poet and philosopher Lucretius proposed the following thought experiment. If the universe has a boundary, we can throw a spear at this boundary. If the spear flies through, then it is not a boundary. If the spear bounces back, there must something beyond this boundary that is itself in space, which means it is not a boundary at all. Either way, it turns out that the universe has no boundary.'

How best can the form of Lucretius' argument for the infinity of space be described?

A. Lucretius shows that positing finite space leads to a contradiction.
B. Lucretius shows that finite space is inconsistent with physics.
C. Lucretius shows that finite space is inconsistent with mathematics.
D. Lucretius shows that finite space is inconceivable.

153. 'Utilitarians believe that the right action is that which produces the most happiness.'

Which of the following claims is *incompatible* with the utilitarian view?

A. The right thing to do is to make the consequences of our actions as good as possible.
B. The right thing to do is to do our duty, whatever the consequences.
C. The right thing to do is to act on a rule which, if followed widely, produces the most happiness.
D. The right thing to do is to act from motivations which produce the most happiness.

154. 'Senthil goes to Ambala for the first time in his life. On the way from the railway station to his hotel, he sees twelve people, all of them male. He concludes that there are no women in Ambala. As a matter of fact, there are many thousands of women in Ambala.'

Which of the following best describes Senthil's error?

A. Senthil was misled by irrelevant details.
B. Senthil generalised on the basis of insufficient evidence.
C. Senthil was biased against women.
D. Senthil was bad at counting.

155. 'It took many centuries before the countries of Europe could resolve their internal problems of violence and corruption to become the stable nation-states they are. Therefore, it will take many centuries for India to achieve internal stability.'

Assuming that the factual claims in the argument above are true, what must be assumed in order for the conclusion to follow?

A. Countries everywhere must follow the same paths towards stability.
B. India is gradually progressing towards internal stability.
C. Indian can learn how to achieve stability by studying Europe's example.
D. India has no hope achieving stability in the near future.

Section- V : Legal Aptitude

Instructions to Candidates:

*This section consists of **ten** problems (with **45 questions**) in total. Each problem consists of a set of rules and facts. Apply the **specified rules** to the set of **facts** and answer the questions.*

*In answering the following questions, you should **not** rely on any rule(s) except the rule(s) that are supplied for every problem. Further, you should not assume any fact other than those stated in the problem. The aim is to test your ability to properly apply a rule to a given set of facts, even when the result is absurd or unacceptable for any other reason. It is **not** the aim to test any knowledge of law you may already possess.*

Problem 1 (For Questions 156 to 160)

Rules:

(a) Whoever intending to take any moveable property out of the possession of any person without that person's consent, moves that property out of his or her possession, is said to commit theft.

(b) A person who, without lawful excuse, damages any property belonging to another intending to damage any such property shall be guilty of causing criminal damage.

(c) Damage means any impairment of the value of a property.

Facts:

Veena, an old lady of 78 years, used to live with her granddaughter Indira. Veena was ill and therefore bed-ridden for several months. In those months, she could not tolerate any noise and it became quite difficult to clean her room. After she died, Indira hired a cleaner, Lucky, to clean the room and throw away any rubbish that may be there.

There was a pile of old newspapers which Veena had stacked in a corner of her room. Lucky asked Indira if he should clear away the pile of old newspapers, to which she said yes. Lucky took the pile to a municipality rubbish dump. While Lucky was sorting and throwing away the newspapers, he was very surprised to find a beautiful painting in between two sheets of paper. He thought that

Indira probably wouldn't want this old painting back, especially because it was torn in several places and the colour was fading. He took the painting home, mounted it on a wooden frame and hung it on the wall of his bedroom. Unknown to him, the painting was an old masterpiece, and worth twenty thousand rupees. Before mounting the painting, Lucky pasted it on a plain sheet of paper so that it does not tear any more. By doing so, he made its professional restoration very difficult and thereby reduced its value by half.

Lucky's neighbour Kamala discovered that the painting belonged to Indira. With the motive of returning the painting to Indira, Kamala climbed through an open window into Lucky's room when he was away one afternoon and removed the painting from his house.

156. Has Lucky committed theft?
  A. Yes, Lucky has committed theft of the newspapers and the painting.
  B. No, Lucky has not committed theft because he had Veena's consent.
  C. Yes, Lucky has committed theft of the painting, but not of the newspapers.
  D. No, Lucky has not committed theft because he has not moved the painting out of Veena's possession.

157. Is Lucky guilty of criminal damage?
  A. No, Lucky is not guilty of criminal damage as he did not intentionally impair the value of the painting.
  B. Yes, Lucky is guilty of criminal damage as he intentionally stuck the paper on to the painting.
  C. No, Lucky is not guilty of criminal damage as he does not have the painting in his possession anymore.
  D. No, Lucky is not guilty of criminal damage as he has not destroyed the painting.

158. If Lucky had discovered the painting before leaving Indira's house rather than at the rubbish dump, would he have been guilty of theft in this case?
  A. Yes, he would be guilty of theft of the newspapers and the paintings.
  B. No, he would not be guilty of theft.
  C. Yes, he would be guilty of theft of the painting.
  D. None of the above.

159. Is Kamala guilty of theft?
  A. No, Kamala is not guilty of theft since the person she took the painting from (Lucky) was not its lawful owner.
  B. No, Kamala is not guilty of theft since she took the painting only with the motive of returning it to Indira.
  C. Yes, Kamala is guilty of theft as she took the painting out of Lucky's possession without his consent.
  D. None of the above.

160. Which of the following propositions could be inferred from the facts and the rules specified,
  A. Kamala is guilty of criminal damage as the person she took the painting from (Lucky) was not its lawful owner.
  B. Kamala is guilty of criminal damage as she took the painting without Lucky's consent.
  C. Kamala is not guilty of criminal damage as the painting has not been completely destroyed.
  D. None of the above.

Problem 2 (For Questions 161 to 164)

Rules:

  A. When land is sold, all 'fixtures' on the land are also deemed to have been sold.
  B. If a moveable thing is attached to the land or any building on the land, then it becomes a 'fixture'.

Facts:

Khaleeda wants to sell a plot of land she owns in Baghmara, Meghalaya and the sale value decided for the plot includes the fully-furnished palatial six-bedroom house that she has built on it five years ago. She sells it to Gurpreet for sixty lakh rupees. After completing the sale, she removes the expensive Iranian carpet which used to cover the entire wooden floor of one of the bedrooms. The room had very little light and Khaleeda used this light-coloured radiant carpet to negate some of the darkness in the room. Gurpreet, after moving in, realises this and files a case to recover the carpet from Khaleeda.

161. As a judge you would decide in favour of:
  A. Gurpreet because when the price was agreed upon, Khaleeda did not inform her about removing the carpet.
  B. Gurpreet because the carpet was integral to the floor of the bedroom and therefore attached to the building that was sold.
  C. Khaleeda because a fully-furnished house does not entail the buyer to everything in the house.
  D. Khaleeda because by virtue of being a carpet it was never permanently fixed to the floor of the building.

Assume that in the above fact scenario, Khaleeda no longer wants the carpet. She removes the elaborately carved door to the house after the sale has been concluded and claims that Gurpreet has no claim to the door. The door in question was part of Khaleeda's ancestral home in Nagercoil, Tamil Nadu for more than 150 years before she had it fitted as the entrance to her Baghmara house.

162. As a judge you would decide in favour of:

A. Khaleeda because while the rest of the building belongs to Khaleeda exclusively, the door is ancestral property and therefore the decision to sell it cannot be Khaleeda's alone.

B. Gurpreet because the door is an integral part of the building as it is attached to it.

C. Khaleeda because the door can be removed from the building and is therefore not attached to it.

D. Gurpreet because the contract is explicitly for the whole house and since the door is part of house, it cannot be removed subsequent to the sale.

163. Amongst the following options, the most relevant consideration while deciding a case on the basis of the above two principles would be:

A. Whether the moveable thing was included in the sale agreement.

B. Whether the moveable thing was merely placed on the land or building.

C. Whether the moveable thing had become an inseparable part of the land or building.

D. Whether the moveable thing could be removed.

164. Rule C: If a moveable thing is placed on land with the intention that it should become an integral part of the land or any structure on the land it becomes a fixture.

Applying Rules A and C, to the fact situations in Questions 161 and 162, as a judge you would decide in favour of:

A. Khaleeda in both situations

B. Gurpreet only in 161

C. Khaleeda only in 161

D. Gurpeet in both situations

Problems 3 (For Questions 165 to 169)

Rule A : An owner of land has the right to use the land in any manner he or she desires. The owner of land also owns the space above and the depths below it.

Rule B: Rights above the land extend only to the point they are essential to any use or enjoyment of land.

Rule C: An owner cannot claim infringement of her property right if the space above his or he land is put to reasonable use by someone else at a height at which the owner would have no reasonable use of it and it does not affect the reasonable enjoyment of his or her land.

Ramesh's case: Ramesh owns an acre of land on the outskirts of Sullurpeta, Andhra Pradesh. The Government of India launches its satellites into space frequently from Sriharikota, near Sullurpeta. The Government of India does not deny that once the satellite launch has travelled the distance of almost 7000 kilometres it passes over Ramesh's property. Ramesh files a case claiming that the Government of India has violated his property rights by routing its satellite over his property, albeit 7000 kilometres directly above it.

165. Applying **only** Rule A to Ramesh's case, as a judge you would decide:

A. In favour of the Government of India because the transgression was at a height at which Ramesh could not possibly have any use for.

B. That ownership of land does not mean that the owner's right extends infinitely into space above the land.

C. In favour of Ramesh because he has the right to infinite space above the land he owns.

D. In favour of the Government of India because it would lead to the absurd result that Ramesh and most other property owners would have a claim against airline companies and other countries of the world whose satellites orbit the earth.

Shazia's case: Shazia owns a single storeyed house in Ahmedabad which has been in her family for more than 75 years. The foundation of the house cannot support another floor and Shazia has no intention of demolishing her family home to construct a bigger building. Javed and Sandeep are business partners and own three storey houses on either side of Shazia's house. Javed and Sandeep are also Ahmedabad's main distributors for a major soft drinks company. They have erected a huge hoarding advertising their products, with the ends supported on their roofs but the hoarding also passes over Shazia's house at 70 feet and casts a permanent shadow on her terrace. Shazia decides to hoist a huge Indian flag, going up to 75 feet, on her roof. She files a case, asking the court to order Javed and Sandeep to remove the hoarding for all these reasons.

166. Applying **only** Rule B to Shazia's case, you would decide in favour of:

A. Javed and Sandeep because Shazia can easily hoist a flag below 70 feet.

B. Shazia because she has the right to put her land to any use and the court cannot go into her intentions for hoisting a flag at 75 feet.

C. Shazia because she has the absolute right to the space above her land.

D. Javed and Sandeep because hoisting a flag 75 feet above one's roof is not essential to the use and enjoyment of the land.

167. Applying **only** Rules A **and** B to Shazia's case, you would decide:

A. In favour of Shazia only under Rule A.

B. In favour of Shazia under Rule A as well as B.

C. Against Shazia under Rule B.

D. Against Shazia under Rule A as well as B.

168. Applying **only** Rule B **and** C to Ramesh's case, you would decide:

A. In favour of Ramesh only under Rule B.

B. In favour of Ramesh under Rule B as well as C.

C. Against Ramesh under Rule C.

D. Against Ramesh under Rule B as well as C.

169. Applying Rule C to Shazia's case, you would decide:

A. In her favour because hoisting a 75 feet high flag is reasonable.

B. Against her because hoisting a 75 feet high flag is not reasonable.

C. Against her because the hoarding is a reasonable use of the space above her land.

D. In her favour because the permanent shadow cast by the hoarding affects the reasonable enjoyment of her land.

Problem 4 (For Questions 170 to 174)

Rules

A. The fundamental right to freedom of association includes the right to form an association as well as not join an association.

B. The fundamental right to freedom of association also includes the freedom to decide with whom to associate.

C. The fundamental right to freedom of association does not extend to the right to realise the objectives of forming the association.

D. Fundamental rights are applicable only to laws made by or administrative actions of the State and do not apply to actions of private persons.

E. Any law in contravention of fundamental rights is unconstitutional and therefore cannot bind any person.

Facts

Gajodhar Pharmaceuticals, a private company, offered an employment contract of two years to Syed Monirul Alam. One of the clauses in the employment contract provided that Syed Monirul Alam must join Gajodhar Mazdoor Sangh (GMS), one of the trade unions active in Gajodhar Pharmaceuticals.

Questions

170. Decide which of the following propositions can be most reasonable inferred through the application of the stated legal principles to the facts of this case:

A. The employment contract offered to Monirul Alam to join GMS is legal as it does not restrict his freedom not to join any association.

B. The condition requiring Monirul Alam to join GMS cannot bind him as it impinges on his freedom not to join any association.

C. Syed Monirul Alam cannot claim a fundamental right to freedom of association against Gajodhar Pharmaceuticals and therefore, the contract would bind him even though his freedom of association is restricted.

D. The employment contract infringes Syed Monirul Alam's freedom to decide with whom to associate and therefore is legally not enforceable.

171. If Parliament enacts a law which requires every employee to join the largest trade union in their workplace mandating Syed Monirul Alam to join GMS, then:

A. Such a law would merely govern private action to which fundamental rights do not apply.

B. Such a law would not curtail any individual's right to freedom of association.

C. Neither the employment contract, nor the law of the parliament would be enforceable as they would curtail the freedom of association.

D. The law of parliament would violate an individual's freedom not to join any association and therefore be unconstitutional.

172. If Parliament enacts a law that requires a trade union to open its membership to all the employees, then:

A. Such a law would not infringe any fundamental right to freedom of association.

B. The law of the parliament would curtail an individual's right not to join any association.

C. Such a law would curtail the union members' right to decide with whom they would like to associate.

D. Such a law would render the employment contract offered by Gajodhar Pharmaceuticals to Syed Monirul Alam unenforceable.

173. If Gajodhar Pharmaceuticals enter into an agreement with GMS wherein the former agrees to hire only the existing members of GMS as employees, then:

A. The agreement would be illegal as it would curtail the union members' right to decide with whom they would like to associate.

B. Such an agreement would infringe the union's right to decide with whom to associate and therefore is legally not enforceable.

C. The agreement would not be enforceable as it would infringe upon the employer's right not to join an association.

D. The constitutionality of this agreement cannot be contested on grounds of contravention of fundamental rights as such rights are not applicable to private persons.

174. If Parliament enacts a legislation prohibiting strikes by trade unions of employees engaged in pharmaceutical industry, then:

A. The legislation would not violate the right to freedom of association.

B. The legislation would curtail the right of trade unions to strike, and therefore violate freedom of association.

C. Since strike is only one of the objectives with which a trade union is formed, right to strike is not protected by the right to freedom of association.

D. None of the above.

Problem 5 (For Questions 175 to 177)

Rule

Whoever finds an unattended object can keep it unless the true owner claims that object. This does not affect the property owner's right to the ownership of the property on which the object is found. The right to ownership of a property does not include the right to ownership of unattended objects on that property.

Facts

Elizabeth is the CEO of a global management services company in Chennai and is on her way to Ranchi to deliver the convocation address at India's leading business school on the outskirts of Ranchi. Flying business class on Dolphin Airlines, she is entitled to use the lounge owned by the airline in Chennai Airport while waiting for her flight. She finds a diamond ear-ring on the floor of the lounge and gives it to the staff of Dolphin Airlines expressly stating that in the event of nobody claiming the ear-ring within six months, she would claim it back. The airline sells the ear-ring after eight months and Elizabeth files a case to recover the value of the ear-ring from the airline when she is informed about its sale.

175. As a judge you would order that:

A. Elizabeth is not entitled to compensation because the ear-ring was found on the property of the airline and therefore, the airline is entitled to sell it.

B. The airline must compensate Elizabeth because owning the lounge does not give the airline the right over all things that might be found on it.

C. The airline must compensate Elizabeth because while accepting the ear-ring from Elizabeth they had agreed to return it if nobody claimed it within six months.

D. Elizabeth is not entitled to compensation because she did not claim the ear-ring after the expiry of six months and the airline waited for a couple more months before selling it.

176. Assume now that Elizabeth was only an economy class passenger and was not entitled to use the airline's lounge. However, she manages to gain entry and finds the ear-ring in the lounge. The rest of the above facts remain the same. Will her illegal entry into the Lounge affect Elizabeth's right to keep the ear-ring (or be compensated for its value)?

A. Yes, the airline claims that Elizabeth's entry into the lounge was illegal and therefore has no right over anything she found there.

B. No, because Elizabeth's class of travel has no bearing on the outcome in this case.

C. Cannot be determined as we need to know how Elizabeth was able to access the airline's lounge.

D. None of the above.

177. To the original fact scenario, the following fact is added: In the lounge there are numerous signboards which proclaim 'Any unattended item will be confiscated by Dolphin Airlines'. In this case, you would:

A. Order the airline to pay compensation to Elizabeth because the board in the lounge cannot grant property rights over unattended objects to the airline.

B. Deny Elizabeth compensation because the signboard makes it evident that the airline, as owner of the lounge, is exercising all rights over all unattended items in the lounge and the ear-ring is one such item.

C. Deny Elizabeth compensation because she knew any unattended item belonged to the airline.

D. Order the airline to pay compensation to Elizabeth because the property rights of the airline are relevant only if the item is unattended. The moment Elizabeth found the ear-ring, it belonged to her.

Problem 6 (For Questions 178 to 182)

Rule A :

The State shall not discriminate, either directly or indirectly, on the grounds of sex, race, religion, caste, creed, sexual orientation, marital status, disability, pregnancy, place of birth, gender orientation or any other status.

Rule B :

Direct discrimination occurs when for a reason related to one or more prohibited grounds a person or group of persons is treated less favourably than another person or another group of persons in a comparable situation.

Rule C :

Indirect discrimination occurs when a provision, criterion or practice which is neutral on the face of it would have the effect of putting persons having a status or a characteristic associated with one or more prohibited grounds at a particular disadvantage compared with other persons.

Rule D :

Discrimination shall be justified when such discrimination is absolutely necessary in order to promote the well-being of disadvantaged groups, such as women, dalits, religious minorities, sexual minorities or disabled persons.

Facts :

On 2nd October 2010, the Governor of the state of Bihar ordered the release of all women prisoners who were serving sentence of less than one year imprisonment to mark the occasion of Mahatma Gandhi's birthday.

178. Which of the following is correct with respect to the Governor's order?

A. It discriminates directly on the ground of sex.

B. It discriminates indirectly on the ground of sex.

C. It does not discriminate on the ground of sex.
D. It discriminates directly as well as indirectly on the ground of sex.

179. Is the governor's order justified under Rule D?
A. Yes, because it is for the well-being of women prisoners.
B. No, because it is not absolutely necessary for the well-being of women prisoners.
C. No, because it does not promote the well-being of women prisoners or the society.
D. None of the above.

180. Assume that the Governor also made a second order requiring the release of all persons under the age of 25 and over the age of 65 who were serving a sentence of less than one year's imprisonment. Under the Rules, this order is:
A. Directly discriminatory
B. Indirectly discriminatory
C. Not discriminatory
D. Discriminatory, but justifiable

181. Assume further that the government made a third order, releasing all graduate prisoners who are serving a sentence of less than one year's imprisonment. Which of the following statistics would have to be true for this order to be indirectly discriminatory?
A. Only 13% of the prison population in Bihar have a graduation degree.
B. Of the graduate prisoners, 89% belong to upper castes.
C. Only 25% women in Bihar get a graduation degree.
D. All of the above.

Rule E :

'A discriminatory act shall be justified if its effect is to promote the well-being of disadvantaged groups, such as women, dalits, religious minorities, sexual minorities or disabled persons'.

182. Would the first order of release of all women prisoners be justified under Rule E?
A. Yes, because it promotes the well-being of women.
B. No, because it does not promote the well-being of women prisoners.
C. No, because it does not promote the well-being of all disadvantaged groups equally.
D. None of the above.

Problem 7 (For Questions 183 to 187)

Rules :

A. A minor is a person who is below the age of eighteen. However, where a guardian administers the minor's property the age of majority is twenty-one.
B. A minor is not permitted by law to enter into a contract. Hence, where a minor enters into a contract with a major person, the contract is not enforceable. This effectively means that neither the minor nor the other party can make any claim on the basis of the contract.
C. In a contract with a minor, if the other party hands over any money or confers any other benefit on the minor, the same shall not be recoverable from the minor unless the other party was deceived by the minor to hand over money or any other benefit. The other party will have to show that the minor misrepresented her age, he was ignorant about the age of the minor and that he handed over the benefit on the basis of such representation.

Facts :

Ajay convinces Bandita, a girl aged 18 that she should sell her land to him. Bandita's mother Chaaru is her guardian. Nonetheless Bandita, without the permission of Chaaru, sells the land to Ajay for a total sum of rupees fifty lakh, paid in full and final settlement of the price. Chaaru challenges this transaction claiming that Bandita is a minor and hence the possession of the land shall not be given to Ajay. Thus Ajay is in a difficult situation and has no idea how to recover his money from Bandita.

183. Chaaru is justified in challenging the sale transaction because:
A. Bandita is of unsound mind and is not in a position to make rational decisions.
B. Though Bandita is eighteen year old, she will be treated as a minor, as Chaaru is her guardian.
C. Though Bandita is eighteen year old, she cannot sell the land without the permission of her mother.
D. Though Bandita is eighteen year old she should not be treated like a person who has attained the age of majority.

184. Ajay can be allowed to recover the money only if he can show that:
A. He was deceived by Bandita who misrepresented her age.
B. He honestly believed that Bandita was empowered under the law to sell the land.
C. He was an honest person who had paid the full price of the land to Bandita.
D. Both A and B.

185. In order to defend the sale, Bandita will need to show that:
A. Bandita has attained the age of majority.
B. Bandita is mature enough to make rational decisions regarding her own affairs.
C. The sale transaction was beneficial to her interest and will enhance her financial status.
D. None of the above.

186. Which of the following is correct?
- A. Ajay should be allowed to recover the money because even though is no contract, Bandita and Chaaru should not be allowed to unjustly benefit from Ajay's money.
- B. Ajay should be allowed the possession of the land because Chaaru can always decide to approve the transaction between Ajay and Bandita.
- C. Ajay should not be allowed to recover because the induced Bandita, a minor, to sell the land.
- D. None of the above.

187. Which of the following is correct?
- A. If Ajay is allowed to recover the money, that will defeat the law framed for protecting the minors against fraudulent persons.
- B. If Ajay is not allowed to recover that will cause him injustice as he has not paid off the entire sale price.
- C. If Ajay is allowed to recover, Chaaru will benefit from both the money and the land.
- D. None of the above.

Problem 8 (For Questions 188 to 191)

Rules :

- **A.** The act of using threats to force another person to enter into a contract is called coercion.
- **B.** The act of using influence on another and taking undue advantage of that person is called undue influence.
- **C.** In order to prove coercion, the existence of the use of threat, in any form and manner, is necessary. If coercion is proved, the person who has been so threatened can refuse to abide by such contract.
- **D.** In order to prove undue-influence, there has to be a pre-existing relationship between the parties to a contract. The relationship has to be of such a nature that one is in a position to influence the other. If it is proven that there has been undue influence, the party who has been so influenced need not enforce the contract or perform his obligations under the contract.

Facts :

Aadil and Baalu are best friends. Aadil is the son of multi millionaire business person, Chulbul who owns Maakhan Pharmaceuticals. Baalu is the son of a bank employee, Dhanraj. One day, Aadil is abducted from his office by Baalu. Chulbul receives a phone call from Dhanraj telling him that if he does not make Baalu the CEO of Maakhan Pharmaceuticals, Aadil will be killed. Chulbul reluctantly agrees to do the same. Subsequently Chulbul and Baalu sign an employment contract. However, as soon as Aadil is released and safely returns home, Chulbul tells Baalu that he shall not enforce the employment contract. Baalu and Dhanraj are not sure as to what is to be done next.

188. As per the rules and the given facts, who coerces whom:
- A. Aadil coerces Baalu
- B. Baalu coerces Chulbul
- C. Dhanraj coerces Chulbul
- D. None of the above

189. In the above fact situation:
- A. There is undue influence exercised by Dhanraj on Baalu.
- B. There is undue influence exercised by Aadil on Chulbul.
- C. There is no undue influence.
- D. None of the above.

190. Chulbul is:
- A. Justified in refusing to enforce the employment contract as Chulbul was coerced by Dhanraj.
- B. Justified in refusing to enforce the employment contract as Baalu was complicit in the coercive act.
- C. Not justified in refusing to enforce the employment contract as Baalu was an innocent person and has not coerced Chulbul.
- D. Both A and B.

191. Baalu will succeed in getting the employment contract enforced if he can show that:
- A. He is the best friend of Aadil.
- B. It was his father, and not he, who used coercion against Chulbul.
- C. Chulbul has promised his father to employ him.
- D. None of the above.

Problem 9 (For Questions 192 to 195)

Rule A :

When a State undertakes any measure, the effects of the measure have to be the same for all those who are affected by it.

Facts :

100 mountaineers embarked on an extremely risky climbing expedition in Leh. Weather conditions worsened five days into the expedition and the mountaineers are trapped under heavy snow. The government received information of this tragedy only two weeks after the unfortunate incident and has only 24 hours in which to send rescue helicopters. Weather stations across the world confirm that this particular region of Leh will experience blizzards of unprecedented intensity for almost two weeks after this 24 hours window rendering any helicopter activity in the region impossible and certain death for anyone left behind. The government has only five rescue helicopters with a maximum capacity of 50 people (excluding pilots and requisite soldiers) and these helicopters can fly only once in 24 hours to such altitudes.

As the Air Force gets ready to send the helicopters, an emergency hearing is convened in the Supreme Court to challenge this measure as this would leave 50 people to die.

192. If you were the judge required to apply Rule A, you would decide that:

A. As many lives must be saved as possible.

B. If everyone cannot be rescued, then everyone must be left behind.

C. A law cannot be upheld at the cost of 50 lives.

D. It must be left to those who are trapped to decide if they want half amongst them to be saved and leave the rest to die.

Rule B :

When a State undertakes any measure, everyone affected must have an equal chance to benefit from it.

193. As the government prepares to send in rescue helicopters, which option would be acceptable only under Rule B and not Rule A:

A. A lottery to choose the 50 survivors excluding those diagnosed with terminal illnesses from participating in the lottery.

B. A lottery to decide the 50 survivors with single parents of children below five years of age automatically qualifying to be rescued.

C. The 50 youngest people should be rescued.

D. None of the above.

194. Choosing 50 survivors exclusively by a lottery would be:

A. Permissible under Rules A and B.

B. Impermissible under Rule A and B.

C. Permissible only under Rule B.

D. Permissible only under Rule A.

195. If the government decides that it will either save everyone or save none, it would be:

A. Permissible under Rules A and B.

B. Impermissible under Rule A and B.

C. Permissible only under Rule A.

D. Permissible only under Rule B.

Problem 10 (For Questions 196 to 199)

Rules :

A. A person is an employee of another if the mode and the manner in which he or she carries out his work is subject to control and supervision of the latter.

B. An employer is required to provide compensation to his or her employees for any injury caused by an accident arising in the course of employment. The words 'in the course of the employment' mean in the course of the work which the employee is contracted to do and which is incidental to it.

Facts :

Messrs. Zafar Abidi and Co. (Company) manufactures bidis with the help of persons known as 'pattadars'. The pattadars are supplied tobacco and leaves by the Company and are required to roll them into bidis and bring the bidis back to the Company. The pattadars are free to roll the bidis either in the factory or anywhere else they prefer. They are not bound to attend the factory for any fixed hours of work or for any fixed number of days. Neither are they required to roll up any fixed number of bidis. The Company verifies whether the bidis adhere to the specified instructions or not and pays the pattadars on the basis of the number of bidis that are found to be of right quality. Aashish Mathew is one of the pattadars of the Company. He was hit by a car just outside the precinct of the factory while he was heading to have lunch in a nearby food-stall. Aashish Mathew has applied for compensation from the Company.

196. Which of the following statements can most plausibly be inferred from the application of the rules to the given facts:

A. Aashish Mathew is an employee of the Company because the latter exercises control over the manner in which Aashish Mathew carries out his work.

B. Aashish Mathew is not an employee but an independent contractor as he does not have a fixed salary.

C. Aashish Mathew is an employee because the Company exercises control over the final quality of the bidis.

D. Verification of the quality of bidis amounts to control over the product and not control over the mode and method of work and therefore, Aashish Mathew is not an employee of the Company.

197. In case the pattadars were compulsorily required to work in the factory for a minimum number of hours every day, then it would be correct to state that:

A. The injury was not caused by an accident in the course of employment.

B. Aashish Mathew would not be an employee as the Company would have still not exercised control over the manner of work.

C. The injury suffered by Aashish Mathew could not be held to be caused by an accident.

D. Stipulations on place and hours of work relate to manner and mode of work and therefore, Aashish Mathew would be held to be an employee of the Company.

198. According to the facts and the rules specified, which of the following propositions is correct:

A. The Company is not liable to pay compensation as the injury to Aashish Mathew was not caused by an accident arising in the course of employment.

B. The Company is liable to pay the compensation.

C. Since the injury did not arise in the course of employment, the Company would not be liable to pay the compensation even though Aashish Mathew is an employee of the Company.

D. The Company is liable to pay the compensation as Aashish Mathew is a contracted pattadar with the company.

199. Select the statement that could be said to be most direct inference from specified facts:

A. The injury to Aashish Mathew did not arise in the course of employment as he was not rolling bidis at the time when he was hit by the car.

B. Since the Aashish Mathew is a contracted pattadar with the Company, it shall be presumed that the injury was caused by an accident in the course of employment.

C. Since there was no relationship of employment between Aashish Mathew and the Company, the injury suffered by Aashish Mathew could not be held to be one arising in 'the course of employment' notwithstanding the fact that the concerned injury was caused while he was involved in an activity incidental to his duties.

D. None of the above

Instructions : (Question 200): *A principle/principles and a fact situation are given in the following question. Decide only on the basis of the principle(s).*

200. Principles

(*i*) Neighbour principle—A person is liable if he harms his neighbour. A neighbour is one whose action affects another

(*ii*) One is liable only for contractual relations

Facts:

X manufactures a food item and sells his food item to Y, a whole seller. Y appoints Z, a retailer to retail these items. Z sells the food item to a consumer who after eating them falls ill. X is liable to the consumer because

A. of contractual relations

B. of the Food Adulteration Act

C. the consumer is the neighborur of X

D. of the consumer protection law

ANSWERS

1	**2**	**3**	**4**	**5**	**6**	**7**	**8**	**9**	**10**
D	C	C	D	C	D	D	A	C	D
11	**12**	**13**	**14**	**15**	**16**	**17**	**18**	**19**	**20**
B	C	A	D	C	C	D	B	A	C
21	**22**	**23**	**24**	**25**	**26**	**27**	**28**	**29**	**30**
C	B	D	D	D	C	D	B	C	C
31	**32**	**33**	**34**	**35**	**36**	**37**	**38**	**39**	**40**
D	A	A	C	D	D	A	D	A	A
41	**42**	**43**	**44**	**45**	**46**	**47**	**48**	**49**	**50**
B	B	C	B	B	D	C	B	C	C
51	**52**	**53**	**54**	**55**	**56**	**57**	**58**	**59**	**60**
C	C	B	A	A	C	A	B	B	A
61	**62**	**63**	**64**	**65**	**66**	**67**	**68**	**69**	**70**
A	A	B	C	A	C	D	D	D	C
71	**72**	**73**	**74**	**75**	**76**	**77**	**78**	**79**	**80**
D	D	B	D	A	D	D	A	B	B
81	**82**	**83**	**84**	**85**	**86**	**87**	**88**	**89**	**90**
C	D	C	A	D	C	D	C	A	B
91	**92**	**93**	**94**	**95**	**96**	**97**	**98**	**99**	**100**
B	D	D	C	C	A	D	A	B	B
101	**102**	**103**	**104**	**105**	**106**	**107**	**108**	**109**	**110**
C	A	D	B	C	B	A	A	A	B
111	**112**	**113**	**114**	**115**	**116**	**117**	**118**	**119**	**120**
C	D	B	B	A	B	D	B	C	D
121	**122**	**123**	**124**	**125**	**126**	**127**	**128**	**129**	**130**
C	D	B	D	D	B	B	D	B	B
131	**132**	**133**	**134**	**135**	**136**	**137**	**138**	**139**	**140**
C	B	C	C	C	A	B	A	A	A
141	**142**	**143**	**144**	**145**	**146**	**147**	**148**	**149**	**150**
A	B	D	B	B	D	C	B	B	C
151	**152**	**153**	**154**	**155**	**156**	**157**	**158**	**159**	**160**
B	D	D	B	B	B	A	C	C	D
161	**162**	**163**	**164**	**165**	**166**	**167**	**168**	**169**	**170**
D	D	D	D	C	B	B	D	D	C

171	172	173	174	175	176	177	178	179	180
D	A	D	A	B	B	A	A	B	C
181	**182**	**183**	**184**	**185**	**186**	**187**	**188**	**189**	**190**
B	A	B	B	A	A	B	C	C	A
191	**192**	**193**	**194**	**195**	**196**	**197**	**198**	**199**	**200**
D	A	B	C	C	D	D	A	C	A

EXPLANATORY ANSWERS

92. $\left(\frac{9}{7}\right)^3 \times \left(\frac{49}{81}\right)^{2x-6} = \left(\frac{7}{9}\right)^9$

$\Rightarrow \left(\frac{9}{7}\right)^3 \times \left(\frac{7}{9}\right)^{2(2x-6)} = \left(\frac{7}{9}\right)^9$

$\Rightarrow \left(\frac{7}{9}\right)^{4x-12} = \left(\frac{7}{9}\right)^{12}$

$\Rightarrow 4x - 12 = 12$

$\Rightarrow x = 6.$

98. Let radius of ball = r

A/Q, height of the cylinder = $2r + 2r + 2r = 6r$

Now volume of three balls = $3 \times 240 = 720$ cm^3

Again volume of cylinder = $\pi r^2 \cdot 6r$

$= \frac{3}{4} \times \frac{4}{3}\pi r^3 \times 6 = \frac{6}{4} \times 3 \times \frac{4}{3}\pi r^3$

$= \frac{6}{4} \times 720 = 1080$ cm^3.

100. Total distance climb in one step

= 1.5 – 0.5 = 1 feet

∴ Total number of steps = 18 + 1 = 19.

103. Let number of students in Arts = $5x$

Law = $6x$

And Commerce = $7x$

A/Q, number of students in Arts = $5x\left(1+\frac{20}{100}\right)$

$= 5x \times \frac{6}{5} = 6x$

Number of students in Law increases

$= 6x\left(1+\frac{30}{100}\right) = 6x \times \frac{13}{10} = \frac{39x}{5}$

Number of students in Commerce = $7x\left(1+\frac{40}{100}\right)$

$= \frac{49x}{5} = 6x : \frac{39x}{5} : \frac{49x}{5}$

$= 30 : 39 : 49.$

107. Let the average of runs after 17th innings = x

∴ Total runs = $17 \times x = 17x$

In 18th innings, she scores 102

∴ After 18th innings her total score = $17x + 102$

Now her average increases to $(x + 5)$

∴ Total runs after 18th innings = $18(x + 5)$

$\Rightarrow 18(x + 5) = 17x + 102$

$\Rightarrow 18x + 90 = 17x + 102$

$\Rightarrow x = 12$

Average runs after 18th innings = 12 + 5 = 17.

109. Perfect square numbers between 1 to 90 are 1, 4, 9, 16, 25, 36, 49, 64, 81

∴ $n(s) = 90$

$n(E)$ = Perfect square numbers = 9

∴ $P(E) = \frac{n(E)}{n(s)} = \frac{9}{90} = \frac{1}{10}.$

110. $S = \{(HT), (TH), (H, H), (T, T)\}$

∴ $n(s) = 4$

$n(E) = (H, T)(T, H) = 2$ ∴ $P(E) = \frac{2}{4} = \frac{1}{2}.$

111. $A \xrightarrow{+1} B \xrightarrow{+2} D \xrightarrow{+3} G \xrightarrow{+4} K \xrightarrow{+5} P \xrightarrow{+6} \boxed{V}$

112. $B \xrightarrow{+1} C \xrightarrow{+2} E \xrightarrow{+2} G \xrightarrow{+4}$

$K \xrightarrow{+2} M \xrightarrow{+4} Q \xrightarrow{+2} S \xrightarrow{+4} \boxed{W}$

115. Sunday +1 = Monday, Monday + 2 = Wednesday

Wednesday + 3 = Saturday, Saturday + 4 = Wednesday

Wednesday + 5 = Monday, Monday + 6 = Sunday

Sunday + 7 = $\boxed{\text{Sunday}}$.

117.

+1 +4 +4 +2 +1

Gym hymn lynx pygmy rhythm $\boxed{\text{syzygy}}$

Thus, all the words start with the next letter.

118. Aadvark Eerie Iiwi Oolong $\boxed{\text{Uulium}}$

122. 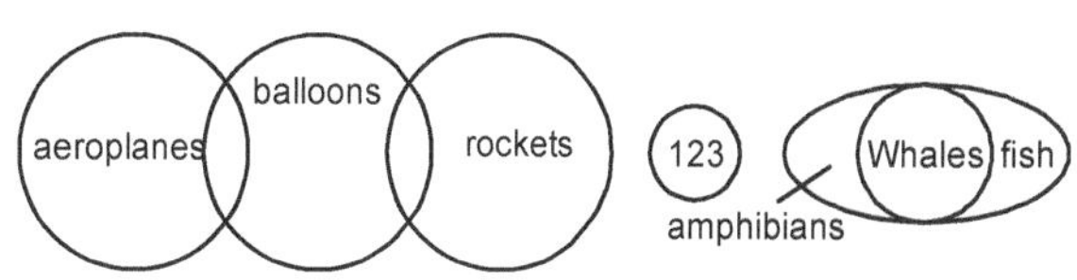

124. 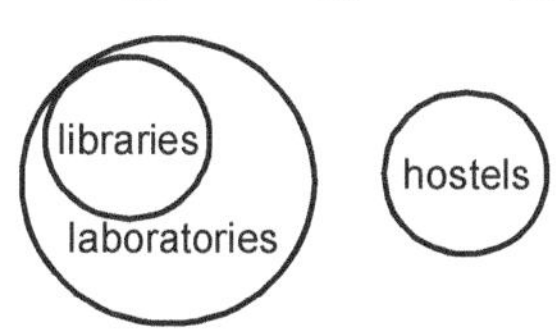

Previous Paper (Solved)

Common Law Admission Test (CLAT-UG) Entrance Exam, 2010

Section-I : English Including Comprehension

Instructions (Questions 1-3): *Substitute the underlined phrases with any of the given choices to express the opposite meaning in the sentences.*

1. She always praises everything I say
A. picks holes in B. dislikes
C. rebukes D. picks holes to

2. He often says how wonderful his school is?
A. says how unworthy B. appreciates
C. runs up D. runs down

3. She said I was the best boss they'd ever had. It was obvious she was praising me sincerely.
A. not appreciating me B. befooling me
C. buttering me up D. disliking me

Instructions (Questions 4-6): *Identify the part of speech of the underlined words in the given sentences.*

4. I must perfect the operation to make the perfect robot.
A. verb B. adverb
C. adjective D. noun

5. A kindly person is one who behaves kindly.
A. noun B. preposition
C. adverb D. verb

6. He is not normally a very fast runner, but he runs fast in major events.
A. adverb B. adjective
C. verb D. noun

Instructions (Questions 7-16): *Read the following passage carefully and answer the question below.*

Antigone was one of the daughter of Oedipus, that tragic figure of male power who had been cursed by Gods for mistakenly killing his father and subsequently marrying his mother and assuming the throne of Thebes. After the death of Oedipus civil war broke out and a battle was waged in front of the seventh gate of Thebes—his two sons led opposing factions and at the height of the battle fought and killed each other. Oedipus' brother, Creon, uncle of Antigone, was now undisputed master of the city. Creon resolved to make an example of the brother who had fought against him, Polynices, by refusing the right of honourable burial. The penalty of death was promulgated against any who should defy this order.

Antigone was distraught. Polynices had been left unburied, unwept, a feast of flesh for keen eyed carrion birds. Antigone asks her sister Ismene, for it was a challenge to her royal blood. "Now it is time to show weather or not you are worthy of your royal blood. Is he not my brother and yours? Whether you like it or not? I shall never desert him-never!" But Ismene responds, "How could you dare—when Creon has expressly forbidden it? Antigone, we are women, it is not for us to fight against men." With a touch of bitterness, Antigone releases her sister from the obligation to help her, but argues she cannot shrug off the burden. "If I die for it what happiness! Live, if you will live, and defy the holiest of laws of heaven."

7. What is the main theme of the story of Antigone?
A. One must be truthful and honest
B. There is a conflict between the laws of men and heavenly laws
C. One must be true to one's kins
D. War is an evil

8. Why did Antigone decide to defy the orders of Creon?
A. She loved her brother
B. She was to give an honorable burial to her brother
C. She felt she was bound by her heavenly obligation
D. To teach Creon a lesson

9. What, in your opinion, would have been the logical end of the story?
A. Antigone might have agreed with her sister and refrained from giving a burial to Polynices
B. Antigone might have been allowed by Creon to give a decent burial to her brother
C. Antigone might have defied the order of Creon but forgiven by him
D. Antigone might have been executed for defying the order of the king

10. What was the status of women in the contemporary society? They
A. were liberated
B. could have taken their own decisions
C. considered themselves inferior and subordinate to men
D. claimed equality with men

11. Why did a civil war break out in Thebes? The war broke out because
A. of the curse of the Gods
B. the brothers of Antigone were greedy
C. there was a fight among sons of Oedipus for the inheritance of the kingdom
D. there was a conflict between a son of Oedipus and Creon

12. A carrion bird is a bird
A. of prey
B. which eats human flesh
C. which eats dead bodies
D. which eats only grain

13. Why did Creon deny decent burial to Polynices? He did so because
A. he did not love Polynices
B. Polynices fought against Creon
C. Polynices was disobedient to Creon
D. Polynices did not show bravery

14. Why did Ismene not support Antigone? Ismene
A. was weak and did not have the courage to defy orders of the powerful king
B. did not consider it right to defy the king
C. did not think it fit to defy her uncle especially after the death of her father
D. did not believe that Polynices deserved better treatment

15. Why did the Gods curse Oedipus? Because Oedipus
A. killed his father and married his mother
B. killed his father
C. married his mother
D. committed an unknown sin

16. Does the story approve the principle of vicarious liability? If so how?
A. No, it does not
B. Yes, it does, because of the acts of Oedipus his children suffered
C. Yes, it does, because his father was killed by Oedipus
D. Yes, it does, because he married his mother

Instructions (Questions 17-22): *Select the meaning of the underlined idioms and phrases in sentences.*

17. I have <u>hit upon</u> a good plan to get rid of him.
A. found B. chanced upon
C. decided to beat him D. borrowed

18. He is <u>sticking out for</u> better terms.
A. threatens to take action
B. insists on using the force
C. decides to give concessions
D. persists in demanding

19. He <u>broke off</u> in the middle of the story.
A. failed B. began crying
C. stopped suddenly D. felt uneasy

20. He refused to be <u>led by the nose.</u>
A. to follow like an animal
B. to be treated as a fool
C. to follow submissively
D. to be treated violently

21. The new cotton mill is mortgaged <u>up to the eye.</u>
A. apparently B. completely
C. deceptively D. actually

22. When they embraced a new religion, it is safe to say they did it for <u>loaves and fishes.</u>
A. selflessly B. honest reasons
C. material benefits D. because of fear

Instructions (Questions 23-27): *Choose the correct spelling out of four choices in questions.*

23. A. Misogynists B. Mysogynists
C. Mysoginists D. Mysagynists

24. A. Aracnophobia B. Aranchophobia
C. Arochnophobia D. Arachnophobia

25. A. Cinamon B. Cinnamon
C. Cinnaman D. Cinaman

26. A. Alcohol B. Alchohol
C. Alchohal D. Alchohel

27. A. Bioclymatalogy B. Bioclimatalogy
C. Bioclimatology D. Bioclimatelogy

Instructions (Questions 28-32): *Select the correct meanings of the given words in given questions.*

28. Lexicon
A. number B. legal document
C. dictionary D. captain's dog

29. Hex
A. crude person B. herb
C. parrot D. evil spell

30. Seminary
A. chapel B. college
C. convocation hall D. hostel

31. Liturgy
A. prayer B. priest
C. ritual D. church

32. Laity
A. church members not baptized
B. church members baptized
C. priest
D. church members who are not ordained priests

Instructions (Questions 33-37): *Fill in the blanks in given questions.*

33. Slavery was not done away .... until the last century.
A. with B. for
C. to D. off

34. Does he not take .... his father?
A. before B. for
C. after D. like

35. We will have to take .... more staff if we're to take on more work
A. up B. onto
C. into D. on

36. Mother takes everything in her ....
A. steps B. face
C. stride D. work

37. Sale have really taken .... now.
A. up B. on
C. of D. off

Instructions (Questions 38-40): *The constituent phrases of a sentence are jumbled up in given question. Select the most appropriate sequence meaningful.*

38. (*i*) built on the site of a church destroyed
(*ii*) in the hilly area of the city is the famous Shandon Steeple
(*iii*) the bell tower of St. Anne's Church
(*iv*) when the city was besieged by the Duke of Marlborough
A. (*ii*), (*iii*), (*i*), (*iv*) B. (*ii*), (*i*), (*iii*), (*iv*)
C. (*iv*), (*iii*), (*i*), (*ii*) D. (*iii*), (*ii*), (*i*), (*iv*)

39. (*i*) no law giving effect to the policy of the state towards securing all or any of the principles laid in part IV
(*ii*) notwithstanding anything contained in Article 13
(*iii*) and no law containing a declaration that it is for giving effect to such policy shall be called in question in any court on the ground that it does not give effect to such policy
(*iv*) shall be deemed to be void on the ground that it is inconsistent with or takes away or abridges any of the rights conferred by Article 14 or 19
A. (*ii*), (*i*), (*iii*), (*iv*) B. (*iv*), (*i*), (*ii*), (*iii*)
C. (*ii*), (*i*), (*iv*), (*iii*) D. (*i*), (*ii*), (*iii*), (*iv*)

40. (*i*) neither House shall proceed further with the Bill
(*ii*) if he does so, the houses shall meet accordingly
(*iii*) but the President may at any time after the date of his notification summon the Houses to meet in a joint sitting for the purpose specified in the notification and
(*iv*) where the President has under clause (1) notified his intention of summoning the Houses to meet in a joint sitting
A. (*iv*), (*i*), (*iii*), (*ii*) B. (*iv*), (*i*), (*ii*), (*iii*)
C. (*iv*), (*ii*), (*iii*), (*i*) D. (*i*), (*ii*), (*iii*), (*iv*)

Section-II : General Knowledge/Current Affairs

41. Lumbini is the place where the Buddha
A. attained nirvana
B. attained enlightenment
C. was born
D. was married

42. Galvanometer is an instrument to measure
A. relative density of liquids
B. electric currents
C. pressure of gases
D. distances

43. Who wrote 'Mudra Rakshasa'?
A. Vishakhadatta
B. Bana Bhatta
C. Kalidasa
D. Jaya Dev

44. The venue of Asian Games in 1970 was
A. Beijing B. Jakarta
C. Bangkok D. New Delhi

45. 1929 is known for
A. visit of Simon Commission to India
B. Congress resolution for complete independence of India
C. coming of Indian National Congress under the leadership of Mahatma Gandhi
D. Burma was made a part of India

46. I.N.S. Airavat is India's
A. amphibious ship B. submarine
C. destroyer D. frigate

47. Astra-Missile is
A. surface to surface missile
B. surface to air missile
C. air to surface missile
D. air to air missile

48. Nehru Institute of Mountaineering is situated at
A. Nainital B. Darjeeling
C. Shimla D. Uttarkashi

49. The chief guest on the 60th Republic day of India was the President of
A. Uzbekistan B. Tajikistan
C. Kazakastan D. South-Africa

50. Which of the following was not the base of L.T.T.E. before being captured by Srilankan Forces?
A. Elephant Pass B. Kilinochchi
C. Mullaithivu D. Murid ke

51. Who was given Col. C. K. Nayudu Life Time Achievement Award for 2007-2008 for exemplary contribution to cricket
A. Kapil Dev B. Gundappa Vishwanath
C. Sunil Gavaskar D. Vijay Hazare

52. Who is the foreign minister of European Union?
A. Baroness Ashlon B. Massimo D'Alema
C. David Miliband D. Carl Bildt

53. Who is the author of 'Godan'?
A. Bhisma Sahani
B. Premchand
C. Manohar Shyam Joshi
D. Shrad Chandra Chattopadhyay

54. Which political party does Raj Babbar belong to?
A. Samajwadi B. Bhratiya Janta Party
C. Congress D. Bahujan Samaj Party

55. In which year Bastille fell on 14th of July?
A. 1879 B. 1789
C. 1787 D. none of them

56. Alberto Fujimori is the former president of
A. Japan B. Peru
C. South Korea D. Vietnam

57. Which of the following is the national river of India?
A. Brahmaputra B. Narmada
C. Ganga D. Kaveri

58. The highest number of telephone users are in
A. China B. U.S.A.
C. Canada D. India

59. The president of Maldives is
A. Maumoom Abdul Gayoom
B. Mohammad Ashraf
C. Mahmood Alam
D. Mohammed Nasheed

60. Arabinda Rajkhowa is a member of
A. BJP B. Assam Gana Parishad
C. Maoist Centre D. Ulfa

61. The breakthrough in the ideas of Darwin on the evolution of species came after his visit to a cluster of islands and where he saw that each island supported its own form of finch. Name the islands?
A. Ice land B. Greenland
C. Galapagos D. Christian Islands

62. Mahatma Gandhi never became a Nobel Laureate, but he was nominated five times. In which of the following years he was not nominated?
A. 1937 B. 1939
C. 1948 D. 1940

63. Which of the following countries has not, till the end of 2009, decoded the entire genome of a human being?
A. India B. Russia
C. China D. Canada

64. When was the University of Bombay established?
A. 1861 B. 1857
C. 1909 D. 1890

65. Harare is the capital of
A. Zambia B. Zaire Republic
C. Zimbabwe D. Yemen

66. Before the Indian team left for Conference on Climate Change at Copenhagen, Jairam Ramesh announced that India would work for voluntary reduction of
A. 40 to 45 percent B. 20 to 25 percent
C. 30 to 35 percent D. 10 to 15 percent

In energy intensity in 2020 compared to 2005

67. Which is the largest island in the world (if Australia is not considered an island)?
A. Iceland B. Borneo
C. Sumatra D. Greenland

68. Indo-Pak summit between Parvez Mushrraf and Atal Bihari Bajpayee was held in 2001 at
A. Delhi B. Shimla
C. Agra D. Mumbai

69. In 2009, Sultan Azlan Shah Cup was won by
A. India B. Pakistan
C. Canada D. New Zealand

70. Which of the following is not a union territory?
A. Tripura B. Daman and Diu
C. Lakshadweep D. Puducherry

71. Who was the founder editor of "Kesari"?
A. Lala Lajpat Rai
B. Bal Gangadhar Tilak
C. Gopal Krishna Gokhle
D. Dadabhai Naoroji

72. With whose permission did the English set up their first factory at Surat?
A. Akbar B. Shahjahan
C. Jahangir D. Aurangzeb

73. The group of nations known as G-8 started as G-7. Which among the following was not one of them?
A. Canada B. Italy
C. Russia D. Japan

74. Emperor Akbar the Great, died in the year
A. 1505 B. 1605
C. 1606 D. 1590

75. What was the name of Emperor Shahjahan before he became Emperor?
A. Kusrau B. Khurram
C. Parvez D. Shaheryar

76. Which of the following trees has medicinal value?
A. pine B. teak
C. oak D. neem

77. Identify the main principle on which the Parliamentary system operates?
A. Responsibility of executive to legislature
B. Supremacy of democracy
C. Rule of law
D. Supremacy of the constitution

78. Great tennis player Bjorn Borg belongs to which country?
A. Italy B. Latvia
C. U.S.A. D. Sweden

79. Which of the following is the national song of India?
A. Vande Mataram...
B. Jana gana mana adhinayak...
C. Ye mera chaman, ye mera chaman...
D. Sare jahan se achcha...

80. Which country was known as sick man of Europe?
A. Greece B. Latvia
C. Turkey D. Austria

81. In Malaysia, the word 'bhumiputra' refers to
A. Malays B. Chinese
C. Indians D. Buddhists

82. What was the real name of Munshi Premchand?
A. Nabab Rai
B. Dhanpat Rai
C. Ram Chandra Srivastava
D. Hari Shankar

83. Who is the author of 'Old Man and the Sea'?
A. John Ruskin B. Raja Rao
C. Gunter Grass D. Ernest Hemingway

84. Prophet Mohammed was born in
A. 570 A.D. B. 720 A.D.
C. 620 A.D. D. 510 A.D.

85. When was the First World War declared?
A. 1914 B. 1915
C. 1918 D. 1913

86. Deodhar trophy is given for the game of
A. Cricket B. Football
C. Hockey D. Golf

87. Pariyar Wild-Life sanctuary is situated in the state of
A. Tamilnadu B. Karnataka
C. Kerala D. Andhra-Pradesh

88. Nepanagar in Madhya Pradesh is known for
A. steel mill B. sugar mills
C. potteries D. news print factory

89. Who destroyed the Somnath temple in Gujarat?
A. Mohammed Ghori B. Mahmud Ghaznavi
C. Changhez Khan D. Taimur Lang

90. In Cape Trafalgar, the famous battle of Trafalgar was fought in 1805. Where is Cape Trafalgar situated?
A. Italy B. Greece
C. Spain D. Portugal

Section-III : Legal Aptitude

91. The manager of waqf is known as
A. Sajjadanashin B. Khadim
C. Mutawalli D. Mujawar

92. "Ipso facto" means—
A. in place of B. by reason of that fact
C. by the same source D. by the way

93. 'Requisition' means
A. permanent transfer of the title of the property
B. supervision of property
C. taking control of property temporarily
D. taking possession permanently

94. 'Corroborative evidence' means
A. main evidence in a case
B. evidence which supports other evidence
C. evidence that proves the guilt of an accused person
D. evidence of a person who supports the accused

95. Ex parte decision means a decision given
A. after hearing both the parties
B. without proper procedure
C. after observing proper procedure
D. without hearing the opponent

96. Which of the following constitutions is a unitary constitution
A. U.S. B. British
C. Indian D. Australian

97. Which of the following is not a fundamental rights in India?
A. right to form association
B. freedom of religion
C. right to property
D. right to move throughout the territory of India

98. Which of the following marriages is approved by Islamic law? Between a Muslim
A. male and a Christian female
B. female and a Hindu male
C. female and a Christian male
D. female and a Jew male

99. Which of the following constitutions when framed did not provide for judicial review?
A. Indian B. Pakistani
C. U.S. D. Australian

100. Ratio decidendi means
A. a judicial decision
B. part of the judgment which possesses authority
C. any observation made by the court which goes beyond the requirement of the case
D. an observation made by a judge

101. 'Dyarchy' under the government of India Act 1919 meant
A. division of powers between the central and provincial government
B. separation of judiciary from executive
C. division of executive departments under elected ministers and the members of the governor's executive council
D. separation between legislature and executive

102. Fringe benefit tax is a tax
A. paid by an employer in respect of the fringe benefits provided or deemed to have been provided by an employer to his employee
B. paid by an employer for the benefits which he enjoys
C. paid by a person for the benefits which he gets from his employer
D. paid by a member of scheduled castes and scheduled tribes for benefits they receive from the government

103. Which of the following is not true about a criminal proceeding?
A. the court may ask to pay a fine
B. the court may order the transfer of the ownership of the property
C. there is prosecution
D. the court may discharge an accused

104. In Ram v/s Shyam, Ram cannot be a
A. plaintiff B. appellants
C. defendant D. prosecutor

105. Cr. P.C. Stands for
A. Criminal proceedings code
B. Criminal proceedings court
C. Crime prevention code
D. Criminal procedure code

106. Medical Science used for investigating crimes is known as
A. Criminal Medicine
B. Epistemological Science
C. Forensic science
D. Ontological Science

107. A puisne judge of a High Court is
A. a judge other than a Chief Justice
B. the Chief Justice
C. a temporary judge
D. a retired judge

108. Intra vires means
A. within the powers
B. outside the powers
C. within the scope of fundamental rights
D. regular

109. X, the servant of Y, takes a hundred rupee note from Y's pocket and hides it under the carpet in the house of Y. X tells Z another servant of Y, about the currency note and both agree to share the money when the currency note is taken by X from the hiding place. Before X could recover the note, it was found by Y. Decide if an offence was committed and if so who committed the offence?
A. No offence was committed
B. Only X committed the offence
C. Both X and Z committed the offence
D. Only Z committed the offence

110. Moots, in law schools, are
A. exercises of law teaching
B. legal problems in the form of imaginary cases, argued by two opposing students before a bench pretending to be a real court
C. imaginary class room where a student acts as a teacher
D. a debate on a legal problem

111. Scheduled Tribe status is
A. restricted to Hindus
B. religiously neutral
C. restricted to Hindus and Christians
D. restricted to Hindus and Muslims

112. Which of the following has not been a woman judge of the Supreme Court of India, till 2009?
A. Justice Gyan Sudha Mishra
B. Justice Sujata Manohar
C. Justice Ruma Pal
D. Justice Fathima Beevi

113. What is the meaning of chattel?
A. any property B. immovable property
C. movable property D. cattle

114. In a civil suit, the person who files suit and the person against whom the suit is filed are called
A. accused, prosecutor B. accuser, defendant
C. appellant, respondent D. plaintiff, defendant

115. In a criminal case, an accused person, who in consideration of his non-prosecution offers to give evidence against other accused, is called
A. accomplice B. hostile witness
C. approver D. hostile accomplice

116. The President of India is elected by an electoral college consisting of
A. all the members of both the Houses of Parliament and all the members of all the Legislative Assemblies
B. all the elective members of both the Houses of Parliament and all the members of all the Legislative Assemblies
C. all the members of both the Houses of Parliament and all the elected members of all the Legislative assemblies
D. all the elected members of both the Houses of Parliament and all the elected members of all the Legislative assemblies

117. Which of the following is not a fundamental right?
A. freedom of speech B. right to life
C. right to equality D. right to work

118. International Labour Organization has its headquarters at
A. The Hague B. Geneva
C. New York D. London

119. The Child Marriage Restraint Act 2006 is applicable to
A. only Hindus
B. all Indians except Muslims as the minimum age of marriage among Muslim girls is puberty (beginning of menstruation) in Muslim personal law
C. all irrespective of religion
D. all except Muslim, Christians and Jews

120. X, a shopkeeper, leaves a sealed 5 kilogram bag of a branded wheat flour at the door of Y with a note "you will like this quality wheat flour and pay Rupees 100 for this bag" without being asked to do so. Y on coming back, collects the bag from his door, opens the seal of the bag, and uses a quarter of kilogram for making chapattis (unleavened bread). But next day returns the bag. Is he bound to pay for the bag? He is
A. not bound to pay as he did not ask the shopkeeper to deliver the bag
B. bound to pay as he has opened the bag
C. bound to pay only for the quantity used
D. neither bound to pay nor return the bag

121. Within the jurisdiction of which High Court does Lakshdweep fall
A. Bombay High Court B. Kerala High Court
C. Madras High Court D. Delhi High Court

122. Which of the following is not the function of the International Court of Justice? It
A. gives advisory opinion at the request of general Assembly
B. gives advisory opinion at the request of Security Council
C. interprets treaties when considering legal disputes bought before it by nations
D. decides international crimes

123. Bank nationalization case relates to the nationalization of
A. some banks by the government of India after economic liberalisation in 1991.
B. some banks under a law during the Prime Ministership of Mrs. Indira Gandhi.
C. all the private Indian Banks during the Prime Ministership of Narasimha Rao.
D. all the private Indian Banks during the Prime Ministership of Mrs. Indira Gandhi.

124. Which of the following is not included within the meaning of intellectual property?
A. Patents
B. Copyrights
C. Trade mark
D. Property of an intellectual

125. The main aim of the competition Act 2002 is to protect the interests of
A. the multinational corporation
B. the Indian companies
C. the consumers
D. the market

126. Which of the following judges had never been the chairman of the Law Commission of India?
A. Justice R.C. Lahoti
B. Justice A.R. Lakshamanan
C. Justice Jeevan Reddy
D. Justice Jagannadha Rao

127. Who among the following was the first chief Information Commissioner of India?
A. Wajahat Habibullah B. Irfan Habib
C. Tahir Mahmood D. Najma Heptullah

128. R.T.I. stands for
A. Revenue Transactions in India
B. Research and Technology Institute
C. Rural and Transparency Infrastructure
D. Right to Information

129. Fiduciary relationship is relationship based on
A. contract B. trust
C. blood relationship D. money

130. Human rights day is observed on
A. 14th February
B. 26th November
C. 2nd October
D. 10th December

131. 'No-fault liability' means
A. liability for damage caused through negligence
B. liability for damage caused through fault
C. absolute liability even without any negligence or fault
D. freedom from liability

132. An 'encumbrance' in legal parlance is a
A. liability on property B. grant of property
C. gift of property D. restriction on property

133. A husband and wife have a right to each other's company. This right is called
A. matrimonial right B. consortium right
C. marital right D. conjugal right

134. Release of prisoner before completion of his sentence is called
A. release B. parole
C. acquittal D. lease

135. Result of successful prosecution is
A. acquittal B. discharge
C. conviction D. charge sheeting

Section-IV : Logical Reasoning

136. Six students A, B, C, D, E and F are sitting. A and B are from Mumbai, rest are from Delhi. D and F are tall but others are short. A, C and D are girls, others are boys. Which is the tall girl from Delhi?
A. F B. D
C. E D. C

137. P is the brother of Q. R is the sister of Q. S is the Sister of R. How is Q related to S?
A. brother B. sister
C. brother or sister D. son

Instructions (Questions 138-140): *In the following questions two sets of words have certain relation. Select a word to replace the question mark so as to make a similar relational pair with the other word in the third set.*

138. Cat-Kitten; Goat-kid; Sheep-?
A. colt B. filly
C. lamb D. wool

139. Cataract-eye; jaundice-liver; pyorrhea-?
A. breath B. tongue
C. ears D. teeth

140. Blue-moon; blue-black; black-?
A. sheep B. goat
C. sky D. star

Instructions (Questions 141-145): *A principle/principles and a fact situation are given in the following question. Decide only on the basis of the principle(s).*

141. Principles
(*i*) Neighbour principle-A person is liable if he harms his neighbour. A neighbour is one whose action affects another
(*ii*) One is liable only for contractual relations

Facts
X manufactures a food item and sells his food item to Y, a whole seller. Y appoints Z, a retailer to retail these items. Z sells the food item to a consumer who after eating them falls ill. X is liable to the consumer because
A. of contractual relations
B. of the Food Adulteration Act
C. the consumer is the neighbor of X
D. of the consumer protection law

142. Principles
(*i*) Freedom consists in making choices out of two or more alternatives
(*ii*) Everyone has freedom to speak

Facts
X says his freedom to speech includes freedom not to speak. X's assertion is
A. wrong
B. right
C. wrong because the freedom to speak cannot mean freedom not to speak
D. right because X may opt to speak or not to speak

143. Principles
(*i*) A master is liable for the wrongful acts of his servant
(*ii*) A person can be called a servant only if there is a relation of employment and he acts under the order and on behalf of his master

Facts
X bank launched a saving scheme for poor sections of the society and the customer can deposit ₹ 10 per day. Y an unemployed youth collected money from several customers, and on behalf of them deposited the money at the Bank every day. The bank gave to Y a small

commission. After sometime, Y disappeared without depositing the money given by the customers. The customers bring a suit alleging that the Bank is liable. Decide

A. the Bank is liable because it paid commission to Y
B. the Bank is liable because Y was their servant
C. the Bank is not liable because Y was not their servant
D. No one is liable

144. Principle

X propounds the principle that everyone in this world always speaks lies

Facts

X wants to know weather this principle is logically true or false

A. logically the principle may be true
B. everyone in the whole of this world does not always speak lies
C. logically X is also speaking lies
D. everyone is basically an honest person

145. Principle

Whosoever enters into or upon the property in the possession of another, with intent to commit an offence or to intimidate or annoy any person in possession of the property, and remains there with intent thereby to intimidate or annoy another person or with intent to commit an offence is guilty of criminal trespass

Facts

The accused entered at night into a house to carry on intimate relations with an unmarried major girl on her invitation and information that her family members are absent. However, he was caught by her uncle before he could get away. Is the accused guilty of criminal trespass? He is

A. guilty of criminal trespass as he annoyed the uncle
B. guilty because he entered the house to commit a crime against the girl
C. guilty because no one should enter into the house of another at night
D. not guilty of criminal trespass

146. In a code every letter of the alphabet is replaced by some other letter. The code for the name Ram Kumar is

A. Ten Ronet B. Len Finol
C. Pen Sinet D. Elephant

Instructions (Questions 147 and 148): *Four of the given five are alike in a certain way and form a group. Which is the one that does not belong to that group in the following questions.*

147. (I) 217 (II) 143 (III) 214
(IV) 157 (V) 131

A. I B. V
C. I D. III

148. (1) gourd (2) radish (3) spinach
(4) cucumber (5) beetroot

A. radish B. beetroot
C. potatoes D. Spinach

Instructions (Questions 149-151): *Point out the entry which does not form a class with the other entries in the following questions.*

149. A. house B. mortgage
C. hypothecation D. immovable property

150. A. Law B. Court
C. Morality D. Judge

151. A. Freedom of speech B. Right to equality
C. Freedom of religion D. Right to make contract

Instructions (Questions 152-156): *In the following questions a question and two arguments are given. Arguments in relation to the question are either weak or strong. Use this key to give your responses*

A. Argument I is strong
B. Argument II is strong
C. Both I and II are strong
D. Both I and II are weak

152. Question: Should there be complete ban on manufacture of fire crackers in India?
Argument I: No, This will render thousands of workers jobless.
Argument II: Yes, the fire cracker manufacturers use child labour.

153. Question: Should private operators be allowed to operate passenger train service in India?
Argument I: No private operators do not agree to operate on non profitable sectors.
Argument II: Yes, it will improve the quality of Indian Railway Service.

154. Question: Should the system of reservation of posts for scheduled castes be introduced in private sector?
Argument I: Yes, this would give more opportunity of development to these groups
Argument II: No, this would affect merit

155. Question: Would the problem of old parents be solved if children are made legally responsible to take care of their parents in old age?
Argument I: Yes, such problems can be solved only through law.
Argument II: Yes, this will bring relief to old parents.

156. Question: Should right to primary education be made a fundamental right?
Argument I: We should first complete other developmental project, education of children may wait.

Argument II: Yes, without primary education for all there cannot be inclusive development.

157. Pramesh is heavier than Jairam but lighter than Gulab. Anand is heavier than Gulab. Mohan is lighter than Jairam. Who among them is the heaviest?
A. Jairam B. Anand
C. Gulab D. Pramesh

158. Ravi is the brother of Amit's son. How is Amit related to Ravi?
A. Cousin B. Father
C. Son D. Grandfather

159. If CABLE is coded ZCDAY, then STABLE will be coded as
A. TPADAY B. TPCDCY
C. TPCDAY D. TPCYAY

160. If CHARTER is coded UMOEPYE then PARTNER will be coded as
A. AONPCYE B. AEEPCYE
C. AOEACYE D. AOEPCYE

Instructions (Questions 161-170): *In the given questions two words are paired which have a certain relation. Select a correct option to substitute question mark so as to make a similar relational pair with the word given after double colon (::)*

161. Constituent Assembly : Constitution :: Parliament : ?
A. Statute B. Legislative bills
C. Speaker D. Prime Minister

162. Right : Duty :: Power : ?
A. Wrong B. Weak
C. Powerless D. Liability

163. Elephant : Calf :: Tiger : ?
A. Pup B. Tigress
C. Cub D. Baby Tiger

164. Patient : Doctor :: Litigant : ?
A. Advisor B. Help
C. Legal aid D. Lawyer

165. Prosecutor : Accused :: plaintiff : ?
A. Appellant B. Defendant
C. Plaint D. Suit

166. Lok Sabha : Meera Kumar :: Rajya Sabha : ?
A. Hameed Ansari B. Najma Heptullah
C. Sushma Swaraj D. Arun Jaitely

167. President of India : 35 :: Member of Parliament (Rajya Sabha) : ?
A. 18 B. 21
C. 25 D. 30

168. India : Parliamentary System :: U.S.A. : ?
A. Democratic System B. Presidential System
C. Federal System D. Republican system

169. Executive : President :: Judiciary : ?
A. Supreme Court
B. Chief Justice
C. Constitution
D. Government of India

170. World War II : United Nations :: World War I : ?
A. Treaty of Versailles
B. International Commission of Jurists
C. League of Nations
D. International court of Justice

Instructions (Questions 171-175): *In the given questions two statements are given. There may or may not be cause and effect relationship between the two statements. Mark your answer using this code.*
A. Statement I is the cause and statement II is the effect
B. Statement II is the cause and statement I is the effect
C. Both the statements are independent causes
D. Both the statements are independent effects

171. Statement I: School education has been made free for children of poor families.
Statement II: Literacy rate among the poor is steadily growing.

172. Statement I: Hallmarking of gold jewellary has been made compulsory.
Statement II: Many persons do not prefer to buy Hallmarked jewellary.

173. Statement I: Many vegetarians are suffering from stomach ailments.
Statement II: Many dead fish were found near the lake shore.

174. Statement I: Ahmed is a healthy boy.
Statement II: His mother is very particular about the food he eats.

175. Statement I: Rate of crime is very low in this city.
Statement II: The police is efficient in this city

Instructions (Questions 176-180): *In the given questions a statement is followed by two assumptions. These assumptions may or may not be implicit in the statement. Select your response in accordance with the following code*
A. Only assumption I is implicit
B. Only assumption II is implicit
C. Both assumptions I and II are Implicit
D. Neither of the assumptions I and II is implicit

176. Statement: If Ram has finished reading the instructions, let him begin activities accordingly.
Assumption I: Ram has understood the instructions.
Assumption II: Ram would be able to act accordingly.

177. Statement: Children below the age of seven should not be prosecuted for crimes.

Assumption I: Generally children below seven cannot distinguish between right and wrong.
Assumption II: Children below the age of seven are generally mentally unsound.

178. Statement: The employer has a right to reject the application of any candidate for employment without assigning any reason while short-listing candidates for interview.
Assumption I: The employer is impartial and believes in transparency in employment practices.
Assumption II: The employer wants to call only those candidates for interview, who in his opinion are eligible.

179. Statement: The government has decided to reduce custom duty on computers.
Assumption I: The government wants to make computer accessible to larger number of people.
Assumption II: Prices in domestic market may go up in near future.

180. Statement: You can win over new friends by your warm smile.
Assumption I: It is necessary to win over new friends.
Assumption II: It is always better to smile warmly to new persons.

Section-V : Elementary Mathematics (Numerical Ability)

181. Average age of ten persons learning yoga is 32 years. When the age of their instructor is added, the average age becomes 34 years. The age of their instructor is?
A. 54 B. 52
C. 46 D. 56

182. Find 12% of 5000
A. 620 B. 600
C. 680 D. 720

183. Square root of 400 is
A. 40 B. 25
C. 20 D. 100

184. What is the place (location) value of 5 in 3254710?
A. 10000 B. 5
C. 54710 D. 50000

185. 6 × 3 (3 – 1) is equal to
A. 53 B. 36
C. 20 D. 19

186. Y travels 15 kilometers due South, then 5 kilometers due west, then 18 kilometers due north, then 3 kilometers due south, then 5 kilometers due East. How far is he from the starting point?
A. 6 kilometers B. 3 kilometers
C. 0 kilometers D. 9 kilometers

Instructions (Questions 187 and 188): *Select appropriate number to fill in the blanks in the series given in the following questions.*

187. 3,9, ..., 6561
A. 18 B. 27
C. 81 D. 61

188. 100, 50, 33.33, ..., 20
A. 25 B. 30
C. 22 D. 21

189. Which of the following fractions has the highest value 3/5, 4/3, 2/5, 1/2
A. 3/5 B. 4/3
C. 2/5 D. 1/2

190. Four gardeners with four grass mowers mows 400 square meters of ground in four hours. How long would it take for eight gardeners with eight grass mowers to mow 800 square meters of ground?
A. 8 hours B. 6 hours
C. 12 hours D. 4 hours

Instructions (Questions 191-193): *Select one of the given numbers to replace question mark in the series in the given question.*

191. 2, 3, 4, 6, 7, 8, 9, 11, 12, 13, 14, 15, 17, 18, 19, 20, 21, ?
A. 22 B. 23
C. 24 D. 25

192. 117, 104, 91, 78, ?
A. 39 B. 60
C. 65 D. 36

193. 88, 96, 104, ?
A. 100 B. 110
C. 120 D. 112

194. Ram borrows Rupees 520 from Govind at a simple interest of 13% per annum. What amount of money should Ram pay to Govind after six months to be absolved of the debt? Rupees
A. 552.80 B. 553.80
C. 453.80 D. 353.80

195. Which of the following is a prime number?
A. 19 B. 20
C. 21 D. 22

196. The square root of 289 is
A. 13 B. 17
C. 27 D. 23

197. Find the factors of 330
A. $2 \times 4 \times 5 \times 11$ B. $2 \times 3 \times 7 \times 13$
C. $2 \times 3 \times 5 \times 13$ D. $2 \times 3 \times 5 \times 11$

198. Find the factors of 1122
A. $3 \times 9 \times 17 \times 2$ B. $3 \times 11 \times 17 \times 2$
C. $9 \times 9 \times 17 \times 2$ D. $3 \times 11 \times 17 \times 3$

199. Which of the following is not a prime number?
A. 23 B. 29
C. 43 D. 21

200. If the numbers from 1 to 24, which are divisible by 2 are arranged in descending order, which number will be at the 8th place from the bottom?
A. 10 B. 12
C. 16 D. 18

ANSWERS

1	2	3	4	5	6	7	8	9	10
A	A	B	A	B	D	B	B	D	C
11	**12**	**13**	**14**	**15**	**16**	**17**	**18**	**19**	**20**
C	C	B	A	A	B	A	D	C	C
21	**22**	**23**	**24**	**25**	**26**	**27**	**28**	**29**	**30**
B	A	A	D	B	A	C	C	D	B
31	**32**	**33**	**34**	**35**	**36**	**37**	**38**	**39**	**40**
C	D	A	C	A	C	A	A	A	A
41	**42**	**43**	**44**	**45**	**46**	**47**	**48**	**49**	**50**
C	B	A	C	B	A	D	D	C	D
51	**52**	**53**	**54**	**55**	**56**	**57**	**58**	**59**	**60**
B	A	B	C	B	B	C	A	D	D
61	**62**	**63**	**64**	**65**	**66**	**67**	**68**	**69**	**70**
C	D	A	B	C	B	D	C	A	A
71	**72**	**73**	**74**	**75**	**76**	**77**	**78**	**79**	**80**
B	C	C	B	B	D	B	D	A	C
81	**82**	**83**	**84**	**85**	**86**	**87**	**88**	**89**	**90**
A	B	D	A	A	A	C	D	B	C
91	**92**	**93**	**94**	**95**	**96**	**97**	**98**	**99**	**100**
C	C	C	B	D	B	C	A	C	B
101	**102**	**103**	**104**	**105**	**106**	**107**	**108**	**109**	**110**
C	A	B	C	D	C	A	A	A	B
111	**112**	**113**	**114**	**115**	**116**	**117**	**118**	**119**	**120**
B	A	C	D	C	C	D	B	B	B
121	**122**	**123**	**124**	**125**	**126**	**127**	**128**	**129**	**130**
B	D	B	C	D	A	A	D	B	D
131	**132**	**133**	**134**	**135**	**136**	**137**	**138**	**139**	**140**
C	D	B	B	C	B	C	C	D	A
141	**142**	**143**	**144**	**145**	**146**	**147**	**148**	**149**	**150**
D	C	A	A	D	A	D	D	C	C
151	**152**	**153**	**154**	**155**	**156**	**157**	**158**	**159**	**160**
D	A	B	C	B	B	B	B	C	D
161	**162**	**163**	**164**	**165**	**166**	**167**	**168**	**169**	**170**
B	D	C	D	A	A	D	B	B	C
171	**172**	**173**	**174**	**175**	**176**	**177**	**178**	**179**	**180**
B	D	D	B	B	C	A	C	A	B
181	**182**	**183**	**184**	**185**	**186**	**187**	**188**	**189**	**190**
A	B	C	A	B	C	C	A	B	D
191	**192**	**193**	**194**	**195**	**196**	**197**	**198**	**199**	**200**
A	C	D	B	A	B	D	B	D	A

EXPLANATORY ANSWERS

146. In name Ram Kumar, R is replaced by T, m is replaced by n, a is replaced by e. In the given option except option (A) no one follows the rule.

147. Only 214 is even number.

148. Only spinach is leaves.

149. House → a building that is made for people to live in.
Mortgage → money borrowed to buy a house.
Hypothecation → the situation that have not yet happened.
Immovable property → property that can't be moved.

150. Rest three are the part of judiciary.

151. Rest three are fundamental rights.

157. P > J, P < G, A > G, M < J

$\therefore$ A > G > P > J > M.

$\therefore$ Anand is heaviest.

158. $\boxed{\text{Ravi}} \xrightarrow{\text{brother}} \boxed{\text{X}} \xrightarrow{\text{son}} \boxed{\text{Amit}}$

$\therefore$ Amit is father of Ravi.

159. Through the given option (C).

160. Through the given option (D)

181. Total age of ten persons = 10 × 32 = 320 years

Total age of eleven persons (instructor is included) = 11 × 34 = 374 years.

Age of Instructor = 374 – 320 = 54 years.

182. 12 % of 5000 = $\frac{5000 \times 12}{100} = 600$

183. $\sqrt{400} = \sqrt{20 \times 20} = 20$

185. 6 × 3 (3 – 1) = 6 × 3 × 2 = 36

186.

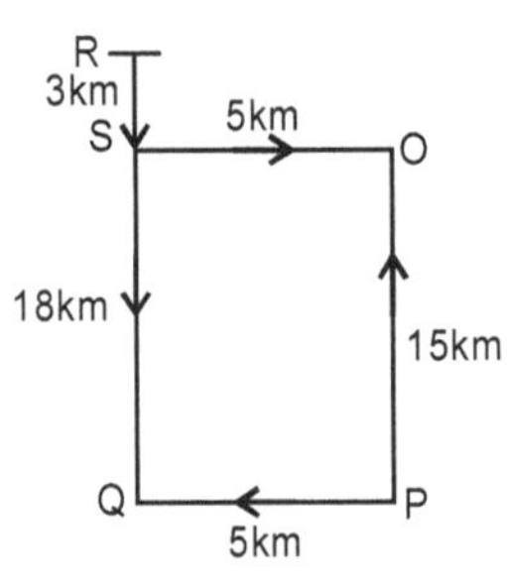

= 0 kilometers.

187. 3, 9 (3^2), 9^2 (81), 81^2 (6561)

$\therefore$ 81

188. 100, $\frac{100}{2}$ (50), $\frac{100}{3}$ (33.33), $\frac{100}{4}$ (25), $\frac{100}{5}$ (20)

189. Clearly $\frac{4}{3}$ is highest fraction because Numerator is greater than Denominator.

191. 2, 3, 4 6, 7, 8, 9 11, 12, 13, 14, 15 17, 18, 19 20, 21 22

192. Difference between their consecutive terms is 13 from right to left.
Hence, 65 is correct answer.

193. Difference is 8

$\therefore$ 112 is correct answer.

194. S.I. = $\frac{P \times R \times T}{100} = \frac{520 \times 13 \times 6}{12 \times 100}$

S.I. = 33.80

$\therefore$ After 6 months Govind pays = ₹ 553.80.

196. 289 = 17 × 17

$\therefore$ Square root = 17.

197.

2	330
3	165
5	55
	11

= 2 × 3 × 5 × 11

198.

2	1122
11	561
3	51
	17

= 2 × 3 × 11 × 17

200. 24, 22, 20, 18, 16, 14, 12, $\boxed{10}$, 8, 6, 4, 2

Previous Paper (Solved)

Common Law Admission Test (CLAT-UG)

Entrance Exam, 2009

Section-I : English Including Comprehension

Instructions (Qs. No. 1-10): *Read the given passage carefully and answer the questions that follow. Shade the appropriate answer.*

There is a fairly universal sentiment that the use of nuclear weapons is clearly contrary to morality and that its production probably so, does not go far enough. These activities are not only opposed to morality but also to law if the legal objection can be added to the moral, the argument against the use and the manufacture of these weapons will considerably be reinforced. Now the time is ripe to evaluate the responsibility of scientists who knowingly use their expertise for the construction of such weapons, which has **deleterious** effect on mankind.

To this must be added the fact that more than 50 per-cent of the skilled scientific manpower in the world is now engaged in the armaments industry. How appropriate it is that all this valuable skill should be **devoted** to the manufacture of weapons of death in a world of poverty is a question that must touch the scientific conscience.

A meeting of biologists on the Long-Term Worldwide Biological consequences of nuclear war added frightening dimension to those forecasts. Its report suggested that the long biological effects resulting from climatic changes may at least be as serious as the immediate ones. Sub-freezing temperatures, low light levels, and high doses of ionizing and ultraviolet radiation extending for many months after a large-scale nuclear war could destroy the biological support system of civilization, at least in the Northern Hemisphere. Productivity in natural and agricultural ecosystems could be severely restricted for a year or more. Post war survivors would face starvation as well as freezing conditions in the dark and be exposed to near lethal doses of radiation. If, as now seems possible, the Southern Hemisphere were affected also, global disruption of the biosphere could ensue. In any event, there would be severe consequences, even in the areas not affected directly, because of the inter-dependence of the world economy. In either case the extinction of a large fraction of the earth's animals, plants and micro-organism seems possible. The population size of Homo sapiens conceivably could be reduced to prehistoric levels or below, and extinction of the human species itself cannot be excluded.

1. Choose the word, which is most opposite in meaning of the word, printed in bold as used in the passage Deleterious.
   A. Beneficial B. Harmful
   C. Irreparable D. Non-cognizable

2. The author's most important objective of writing the above passage seems to ....
   A. Highlight the use of nuclear weapons as an effective population control measures
   B. Illustrate the devastating effects of use of nuclear weapons on mankind
   C. Duly highlight the supremacy of the nations which possess nuclear weapons
   D. Summaries the long biological effects of use of nuclear weapons

3. The scientists engaged in manufacturing destructive weapons are ....
   A. Very few in number
   B. Irresponsible and incompetent
   C. More than half of the total number
   D. Engaged in the armaments industry against their desire

4. According to the passage, the argument on use and manufacture of nuclear weapons
   A. Does not stand the test of legality
   B. Possesses legal strength although it does not have moral standing
   C. Is acceptable only on moral grounds
   D. Becomes stronger if legal and moral considerations are combined

5. The author of the passage seems to be of the view that
   A. Utilization of scientific skills in manufacture of weapons is appropriate.
   B. Manufacture of weapons of death would help eradication of poverty.
   C. Spending money on manufacture of weapons may be justifiable subject to the availability of funds.
   D. Utilization of valuable knowledge for manufacture of lethal weapons is inhuman

6. Which of the following is one of the consequences of nuclear war?
A. Fertility of land will last for a year or so
B. Post-war survivors being very few will have abundant food
C. Lights would be cooler and more comfortable
D. Southern Hemisphere would remain quite safe in the post-war period

7. Which of the following best explains the word devoted, as used in the passage?
A. Dedicated for a good cause
B. Utilized for betterment
C. Abused for destruction
D. Underutilized

8. The biological consequences of nuclear war as given in the passage include all the following, except:
A. Fall in temperature below zero degrees Celsius
B. Ultraviolet radiation
C. High doses of ionizing
D. Abundant food for smaller population

9. It appears from the passage that the use of nuclear weapons is considered against morality by:
A. Only such of those nations who cannot afford to manufacture and sell weapons
B. Almost all the nations of the world
C. Only the superpowers who can afford to manufacture and sell weapon
D. Most of the scientists devote their valuable skills to manufacture nuclear weapons

10. Which of the following statements I, II, III and IV is definitely true in the context of the passage?
I. There is even likelihood of survival of the human species as a consequence of nuclear war.
II. Nuclear war risks and harmful effects are highly exaggerated.
III. The post war survivors would be exposed to the benefits of non-lethal radiation.
IV. Living organisms in the areas which are not directly affected by nuclear war would also suffer.

A. I   B. III
C. II   D. IV

Instructions (Qs. No. 11-15): *Three of the four words given in these questions are spelt wrong. Choose the correct one.*

11. A. Renaissance   B. Renaisance
C. Reneissance   D. Renaisence

12. A. Melaise   B. Melaize
C. Maleise   D. Malaise

13. A. Irrelavant   B. Irelevant
C. Irrelevant   D. Irrellevant

14. A. Survilance   B. Surveillance
C. Survillance   D. Surveilliance

15. A. Gaiety   B. Gaity
C. Geiety   D. Gaitty

Instructions (Qs. No. 16-20): *Given below are a few foreign language phrases that are commonly used. Choose the correct meaning for each of them.*

16. Mala fide
A. In good faith   B. In bad faith
C. Without any faith   D. With full faith

17. Pro rata
A. At the rate of   B. At quoted rate
C. In proportion   D. Beyond all proportion

18. Vice versa
A. In verse   B. Versatile verse
C. In consonance with   D. The other way round

19. Ab initio
A. From the very beginning
B. High initiative
C. Things done later
D. Without initiative

20. Alibi
A. Every where   B. Else where
C. No where   D. Without any excuse

Instructions (Questions 21-25): *Some idioms given below are commonly used. Choose the correct meaning for each of the idioms and shade the appropriate answer.*

21. To give the game away
A. To lose the game
B. To give a walk-over in a game
C. To reveal the secret
D. To play the game badly

22. To cool one's heels
A. To close the chapter
B. To walk on the heels
C. To kick someone with the heels
D. To wait and rest for some time

23. To bury the hatchet
A. To fight with the hatchet
B. To forget the enmity
C. To bury the treasure under ground
D. To pick up enmity

24. Gift of the gab
A. Gift for hard work
B. Gift undeserved
C. Gift of being a good conversationalist
D. Gift from unknown person

25. To smell a rat
A. To suspect a trick
B. To detect a foul smell
C. To behave like a rat
D. To trust blindly

Instructions (Qs. No. 26-35): *Given below are sentences with a blank in each sentence. Choose the right answer to fill in the blank by shading your answer.*

26. Some people believe that in emotional maturity men are inferior .... women.

A. Than B. To
C. From D. Against

27. My father was annoyed .... me.
A. Towards B. Against
C. With D. Upon

28. Some orthodox persons are averse .... drinking liquor.
A. Against B. For
C. Towards D. To

29. The Cinema Hall was on fire and the Cinema owner had to send .... the Fire Brigade.
A. For B. Through
C. Off D. In

30. He was not listening .... I was saying.
A. That B. Which
C. To what D. What

31. Drinking country liquor at marriage is a custom .... certain tribes.
A. In B. Among
C. Between D. With

32. The struggle for justice brings, ... the best of moral qualities of men.
A. Forward B. About
C. In D. Out

33. If he .... a horse he would fly.
A. Was B. Were
C. Is D. Goes

34. Mohan has a bad habit of .... at an odd hour.
A. Turning up B. Turning in
C. Turning over D. Turning off

35. He must refrain .... immoral conducts.
A. Off B. Through
C. From D. Against

Instructions (Qs. No. 36-40): *The constituent sentences of a passage have been jumbled up. Read jumbled sentences carefully and then choose the option which shows the best sequence of sentences of the passage and shade the appropriate answer.*

36. (*i*) The Collector said that the Dams should receive
(*ii*) To ensure uninterrupted
(*iii*) Water up to a particular level
(*iv*) Supply of water for irrigation

The best sequence is:
A. (*ii*), (*i*), (*iv*), (*iii*) B. (*i*), (*iii*), (*ii*), (*iv*)
C. (*iv*), (*i*), (*iii*), (*ii*) D. (*ii*), (*iv*), (*i*), (*iii*)

37. (*i*) He loved to distribute them among small kids
(*ii*) He wore a long, loose shirt with many pockets
(*iii*) And in doing so his eyes brightened
(*iv*) The pockets of his shirt bulged with toffees and chocolates

The best sequence is:
A. (*ii*), (*i*), (*iii*), (*iv*) B. (*i*), (*iv*), (*ii*), (*iii*)
C. (*iv*), (*i*), (*iii*), (*ii*) D. (*ii*), (*iv*), (*i*), (*iii*)

38. (*i*) As we all know, a legislation
(*ii*) Needs the assent of the President
(*iii*) Passed by the Houses of Parliament
(*iv*) To become law

The best sequence is:
A. (*i*), (*iii*), (*ii*), (*iv*) B. (*i*), (*iv*), (*ii*), (*iii*)
C. (*iv*), (*i*), (*iii*), (*ii*) D. (*ii*), (*iv*), (*i*), (*iii*)

39. (*i*) The farmers grow food for the whole country
(*ii*) And therefore it is our duty to improve their lot
(*iii*) Yet these fellows are exploited by the rich
(*iv*) Hence they are the most useful members of the society

The best sequence is:
A. (*ii*), (*i*), (*iv*), (*iii*) B. (*i*), (*iv*), (*ii*), (*iii*)
C. (*i*), (*iv*), (*iii*), (*ii*) D. (*ii*), (*iv*), (*i*), (*iii*)

40. (*i*) The ripples looked enchanting in the light of the Sun.
(*ii*) We went to the pond.
(*iii*) We flung stones to create ripples.
(*iv*) We stood knee-deep in the muddy water of the pond.

The best sequence is:
A. (*ii*), (*i*), (*iv*), (*iii*) B. (*ii*), (*iv*), (*iii*), (*i*)
C. (*iv*), (*i*), (*iii*), (*ii*) D. (*iv*), (*ii*), (*i*), (*iii*)

Section-II : General Knowledge/Current Affairs

41. Capital market means:
A. Mutual Funds
B. Money Market
C. Securities Market
D. Banking Business

42. From which river would the National River Project be started?
A. Yamuna B. Gomti
C. Ganga D. Krishna

43. "The Audacity of Hope" is a book written by:
A. Bill Clinton B. Barack Obama
C. George Bush D. Bill Gates

44. 'WPI' is used as an acronym for:
A. World Price Index
B. World Price Indicators
C. Wholesale Price Index
D. Wholesale Price Indicators

45. If the tax rate increases with the higher level of income, it shall be called:
A. Progressive Tax B. Proportional Tax
C. Lump sum Tax D. Regressive Tax

46. Who is the Director of "Chak De India"?
A. Shimit Amin B. Yash Chopra
C. Shahrukh Khan D. Ram Gopal Verma

47. What is the full form of the scanning technique CAT?
A. Complete Anatomical Trepanning
B. Computerized Automatic Therapy
C. Computerized Axial Tomography
D. Complete Axial Transmission

48. Who got the World Food Prize, 2009?
A. Kofi Annan B. Man Mohan Singh
C. Hillary Clinton D. Robert T. Fraley

49. ISO 9000 is a:
A. Quality Standard Mark
B. Space Project
C. Trade Technique
D. Loan Security

50. What is 'AGMARK'?
A. Name of Brand
B. A Marketing Research Organisation
C. Eggs supplied by Government-run cooperative
D. Agriculture marketing for agro products

51. The Headquarters of Indian Space Research Organisation is at:
A. Trivandrum B. New Delhi
C. Bangalore D. Ahmedabad

52. "Saras" is the name of:
A. An Aircraft B. A Tank
C. A Missile D. A Submarine

53. First woman Prime-Minister in the World was from:
A. Sri Lanka B. Bhutan
C. India D. Nepal

54. Who was felicitated with 'Nishan-e-Pakistan'?
A. Shatrughan Sinha
B. Maulana Azad
C. Morarji Desai
D. Khan Abdul Gaffar Khan

55. Which State provided separate reservation for Muslims and Christians in the State Backward Classes List in 2007?
A. Andhra Pradesh B. Tamil Nadu
C. Bihar D. Kerala

56. Which of the following dances is not a classical dance?
A. Kathakali B. Garba
C. Odissi D. Manipuri

57. Sulabh International is an organisation which provides?
A. Health Services in Rural Areas
B. Good Sanitation at cheap rates
C. Low Cost Accommodation
D. Low Cost Credit

58. Who among the following was honoured with 'Officer of the Legion of Honour' award by French Government in July 2008?
A. Dev Anand B. Yash Chopra
C. B.R. Chopra D. Mrinal Sen

59. The largest gland in the human body is:
A. Liver B. Pancreas
C. Thyroid D. Endocrine

60. The Railway Budget for 2007-2008 has declared the year 2007 as the year of:
A. Cleanliness
B. Passenger Comfort
C. Staff Welfare
D. Computerization of Reservations

61. In the world of Hindi Cinema, who was affectionately called as 'Dada Moni'?
A. Balraj Sahni B. Prithviraj Kapoor
C. Ashok Kumar D. Utpal Dutt

62. Outstanding Parliamentarian Award (2006) was presented in 2007 to:
A. Mani Shankar Aiyar B. Sharad Pawar
C. Sharad Yadav D. Sushma Swaraj

63. World's longest sea bridge has taken shape in 2007 in
A. China B. Japan
C. Singapore D. USA

64. Who among the following became Citigroup's Investment Banking head?
A. L.N. Mittal B. A.K. Subramaniyam
C. Vineet Seth D. Micheal Corbal

65. The Green Revolution in India has been identified with:
A. Dr. Man Mohan Singh
B. Dr. Montek Singh Ahluwalia
C. Mr. Rajendra Singh 'waterman'
D. Dr. M.S. Swaminathan

66. Indian Judge in the UN Law of the Sea Tribunal is:
A. Dr. P.S. Rao
B. Gao Zhiquq
C. Justice Jagannath Rao
D. Justice Rajendra Babu

67. The Ozone Layer thins down as a result of a chain chemical reaction that separates from the layer:
A. Oxygen B. Chlorine
C. Nitrogen D. Hydrogen

68. Joint SAARC University of eight SAARC Nations has been established in:
A. Colombo B. Dhaka
C. Kathmandu D. New Delhi

69. Which country recently produced the world's first cloned rabbit using a biological process that takes cells from a foetus?
A. UK B. China
C. USA D. Germany

70. Which one of the following Vitamins is responsible for blood clotting?
A. Vitamin A B. Vitamin E
C. Vitamin C D. Vitamin K

71. What is the meaning of 'Gilt Edged Market'?
A. Market in Government security
B. Market of smuggled goods
C. Market of auctioned goods
D. Market of Gold products

72. Who is the Central Chief Information Commissioner of India?
A. Prof. Ansari
B. Mrs. Padma Subramanian
C. Ms. Sushma Singh
D. Dr. O.P. Kejariwal

73. The youngest recipient of Padma Shri so far is:
A. Sachin Tendulkar
B. Shobana Chandrakumar
C. Vishwanathan Anand
D. Billy Arjan Singh

74. Who is the Director of the film "Elizabeth : The Golden Age Cast"?
A. Rama Nand Sagar B. Ram Gopal Verma
C. Karan Johar D. Shekhar Kapur

75. The territorial waters of India extend up to:
A. 12 Nautical Miles B. 6 Km
C. 10 Nautical Miles D. 15 Nautical Miles

76. 'Samjhouta Express' runs between the Railway Stations of:
A. New Delhi - Wagah
B. New Delhi - Lahore
C. Amritsar - Lahore
D. New Delhi - Islamabad

77. Blue revolution refers to:
A. Forest Development B. Fishing
C. Poultry Farming D. Horticulture

78. Dr. A.P.J. Abdul Kalam has been appointed as Chancellor of:
A. IIT Mumbai
B. IIT Kanpur
C. IIM Ahmedabad
D. IIST Thiruvananthapuram

79. In which State "Kanya Vidyadhan Yojna" is operational?
A. Andhra Pradesh B. Uttar Pradesh
C. Rajasthan D. Haryana

80. Who emerged the fastest woman of the world at Beijing Olympics?
A. Sheron Simpson B. Keaon Stewart
C. Ann Fraser D. Elina Basiena

81. Savannah grasslands are found in:
A. North America B. Africa
C. Australia D. East Asia

82. Which State has launched the "Aarogya Sri" a health Insurance Scheme for families below poverty line?
A. Andhra Pradesh B. Uttar Pradesh
C. Maharashtra D. Kerala

83. The first nuclear reactor of India is named:
A. Rohini B. Vaishali
C. Apsara D. Kamini

84. In May 2007 Air Sahara acquired by Jet Airways is being operated as a separate airline under the name of:
A. Jet Lite B. Jet Sahara
C. Air Jet Line D. Jet Sahara Lite

85. Suez Canal connects:
A. Mediterranean Sea and Red Sea
B. Mediterranean Sea and Black Sea
C. Baltic Sea and Red Sea
D. Baltic Sea and Black Sea

86. Government has launched E-Passport Scheme and first E-Passport was issued to:
A. Mr. Arjun Singh
B. Mrs. Sonia Gandhi
C. Dr. Man Mohan Singh
D. Mrs. Pratibha Patil

87. The Hindu outfit 'Hindraf has been banned in:
A. Pakistan B. Thailand
C. Malaysia D. Bangladesh

88. Which organization was headed by Indian Environmentalists R.K. Pachauri, a Nobel Laureate?
A. International Environment Panel
B. International Panel on Climate Change
C. International Pollution Control Panel
D. International Panel on Global Warming

89. Kandhamal, the worst affected town by sectarian violence in September-October 2008 is situated in:
A. Odisha B. Gujarat
C. Andhra Pradesh D. Karnataka

90. World "No Tobacco Day" is observed on:
A. January 10 B. June 1
C. May 31 D. March 5

Section-III : Elementary Mathematics (Numerical Ability)

91. The average monthly income of a person in a certain family of 5 members is ₹ 1000. What will be monthly average income of one person in the same family if the income of one person increased by ₹ 12,000 per year?
A. ₹ 1200 B. ₹ 1600
C. ₹ 2000 D. ₹ 3400

92. A dishonest shopkeeper uses a weight of 800 gm for a kg and professes to sell his good at cost price. His profit is:
A. 20% B. 21%
C. 24% D. 25%

93. By selling 11 oranges for a rupee, a man loses 10%. How many oranges for a rupee should he sell to gain 10%?
A. 9 B. 10
C. 8 D. 5

94. A person takes 3 hours to walk a certain distance and riding back. He could walk both ways in 5 hours. How long could it take to ride both ways?
A. 1.5hr B. 1 hr
C. 0.5 hr D. 2 hrs

95. Change 1/8 into percentage:
A. 12.5% B. 15%
C. 8% D. 25%

96. 12.5% of 80 is equal to:
A. 8 B. 20
C. 10 D. 40

97. Fill the blank space to complete the series:

1, 2, 4, 5, 7, 8, 10, 11, ...
A. 12 B. 13
C. 14 D. 15

98. The smallest of the fractions given below:
A. 9/10 B. 11/12
C. 23/28 D. 32/33

99. Three friends shared the cost of a television. If Amit, Bharat and Dinesh paid ₹ 3000, ₹ 1800 and ₹ 1200 respectively, then Dinesh paid what per cent of the total cost?
A. 10% B. 20%
C. 30% D. 40%

100. The average age of 29 boys of a class is equal to 14 years. When the age of the class teacher is included the average becomes 15 years. Find the age of the class teacher.
A. 44 years B. 40 years
C. 52 years D. 66 years

101. It takes 8 people working at equal rates to finish a work in 96 days. How long will 6 workers take for the same work?
A. 92 days B. 128 days
C. 111 days D. 84 days

102. Ram's income is 20% less than Shyam's. How much is Shyam's income more than Ram's in percentage terms?
A. 20% B. 30%
C. 25% D. 15%

103. The monthly salary of A, B and C are in the ratio 2 : 3 : 5. If C's monthly salary is ₹ 1,200 more than that of A, find B's monthly salary.
A. ₹ 2000 B. ₹ 1000
C. ₹ 1500 D. ₹ 1200

104. In a town there are 94500 people. 2/9 of them are foreigners, 6400 are immigrants and the rest are natives. How many are natives?
A. 67100 B. 27400
C. 77600 D. 88100

105. Total salary of three persons A, B and C is ₹ 1,44,000. They spend 80%, 85% and 75% respectively. If their savings are in the ratio 8 : 9 : 20, find C's salary.
A. 48000 B. 64000
C. 40000 D. 32000

106. The population of a town is 155625. For every 1000 males there are 1075 females. If 40% of the males and 24% of the females are literate, find the percentage of literacy in the town.
A. 33.7 B. 32.7
C. 31.7 D. 30.7

107. 10 sheep and 5 pigs were brought for ₹ 6,000. If the average price of a sheep is ₹ 450, find the average price of pig.
A. ₹ 380 B. ₹ 410
C. ₹ 340 D. ₹ 300

108. Ram weighs 25 kg more than Shyam. Their combined weight is 325 kg. How much does Shyam weigh?
A. 150 kg B. 200 kg
C. 125 kg D. 160 kg

109. Find out the wrong number in the series:

3, 8, 15, 24, 34, 48, 63
A. 24 B. 34
C. 15 D. 63

110. What is the place value of 7 in the figure 9872590?
A. 72590 B. 7
C. 70000 D. 7000

Section-IV : Legal Aptitude

111. Which is the oldest Code of Law in India?
A. Naradasmriti B. Manusmriti
C. Vedasmriti D. Prasarsmriti

112. Private international law is also called ....
A. Civil Law B. Local laws
C. Conflict of laws D. Common law

113. A nominal sum given as a token for striking a sale is called:
A. Earnest money B. Advance
C. Interest D. Solatium

114. Joint heirs to a property are called:
A. Co-heirs B. Coparceners
C. Successors D. Joint owners

115. The right of a party to initiate an action and be heard before a Court of law is called:
A. Right in rem B. Right in personam
C. Fundamental right D. Locus standi

116. Indian Parliament is based on the principle of:
A. Bicameralism
B. Universal Adult Franchise
C. Dyarchy
D. Federalism

117. The Supreme Court held that evidence can be recorded by video-conferencing in the case.....
A. State of Maharashtra v. Praful B. Desai
B. Puramjit Kaur v. State of Punjab
C. Pappu Yadav v. State of Bihar
D. Bachan Singh v. State of Punjab

118. When the master is held liable for the wrongful act of his servant, the liability is called:
A. Strict liability B. Vicarious liability
C. Tortous liability D. Absolute liability

119. The act of unlawfully entering into another's property constitutes:
A. Trespass B. Restraint
C. Appropriation D. Encroachment

120. Which Parliamentary Committee in Indian system of democracy is chaired by a member of Opposition Party?
A. Estimates Committee
B. Joint Parliamentary Committee
C. Public Accounts Committee
D. Finance Committee

121. Supreme Court held that Preamble as a basic feature of Constitution cannot be amended in the case of:
A. Golaknath v. State of Punjab
B. Maneka Gandhi v. Union of India
C. S.R. Bommai v. Union of India
D. Kesavananda Bharati v. State of Kerala

122. In the year 2002 the Competition Act was enacted replacing:
A. Trade Marks Act B. Copy Right Act
C. Contract Act D. MRTP Act

123. A right to recover time barred debt is:
A. Universal right B. Perfect right
C. Imperfect right D. Fundamental right

124. The law relating to prisoners of war has been codified by:
A. Geneva Convention B. Vienna Convention
C. Paris Convention D. None of the above

125. Public holidays are declared under:
A. Criminal Procedure Code
B. Civil Procedure Code
C. Constitution of India
D. Negotiable Instruments Act

126. When a person is prosecuted for committing a criminal offence, the burden of proof is on:
A. Accused B. Prosecution
C. Police D. Complainant

127. Offence which can be compromised between the parties is known as:
A. Non-compoundable offence
B. Cognizable offence
C. Compoundable offence
D. Non-cognizable offence

128. Husband and wife have a right to each others company. The right is called:
A. Conjugal right B. Human right
C. Civil right D. Fundamental right

129. A person 'dying intestate' means he
A. Died without legal heirs
B. Died without making a Will
C. Died without any property
D. Died without a son

130. If a witness makes a statement in Court, knowing it to be false, he commits the offence of:
A. Forgery B. Falsehood
C. Perjury D. Breach of trust

131. A child born after father's death is:
A. Posthumous B. Heir
C. Intestate D. Bastard

132. A formal instrument by which one person empowers another to represent him is known as:
A. Affidavit B. Power-of-attorney
C. Will D. Declaration

133. The temporary release of a prisoner is called:
A. Parole B. Amnesty
C. Discharge D. Pardon

134. The offence of inciting disaffection, hatred or contempt against Government is:
A. Perjury B. Forgery
C. Sedition D. Revolt

135. India became the member of United Nations in the Year:
A. 1956 B. 1945
C. 1946 D. 1950

136. A party to the suit is called:
A. Accused B. Plaintiff
C. Litigant D. Complainant

137. Who heads the four member Committee appointed to study the Centre-State relations especially the changes took place since Sarkaria Commission?
A. Justice M.M. Punchi
B. Justice Nanavati
C. Justice Barucha
D. Justice Kuldip Singh

138. No one can be convicted twice for the same offence. This doctrine is called:
A. Burden of proof
B. Double conviction
C. Double jeopardy
D. Corpus delicti

139. A participant in commission of crime is popularly known as:
A. Respondent B. Under-trial
C. Defendant D. Accomplice

140. Which of the following is not payable to Central Government?
A. Land revenue B. Customs duty
C. Income tax D. Wealth tax

141. Where is the National Judicial Academy located?
A. Kolkata B. Bhopal
C. Delhi D. Mumbai

142. Who have constitutional right to audience in all Indian Courts?
A. President
B. Chief Justice of India
C. Attorney General
D. Solicitor General

143. Which of the following is not included in the Preamble to the Constitution?
A. Morality B. Justice
C. Sovereign D. Socialist

144. 'Court of Record' is a Court which?
A. Maintains records
B. Preserves all its records
C. Can punish for its contempt
D. Is competent to issue writs

145. A judge of the Supreme Court can be removed from office only on grounds of:
A. Gross inefficiency
B. Delivering wrong judgments
C. Senility
D. Proven misbehaviour or incapacity

146. Fiduciary relationship means a relationship based on:
A. Trust B. Money
C. Contract D. Blood relation

147. The Chairman of Tehelka Enquiry Commission is:
A. Justice Kripal
B. Justice S.N.Phukan
C. Justice Saharia
D. Justice Liberhan

148. The concept of judicial review has been borrowed from the Constitution of:
A. USSR B. UK
C. USA D. Switzerland

149. Every duty enforceable by law is called:
A. Accountability B. Obligation
C. Burden D. Incidence

150. The killing of a new born child by its parents is:
A. Malfeasance B. Infanticide
C. Abortion D. Foeticide

151. Offence of breaking a divine idol is:
A. Salus populi B. Crime
C. Sacrilege D. Blasphemy

152. A person who goes under ground or evades the jurisdiction of the Court is known as:
A. Offender B. Under-ground
C. Absentee D. Absconder

153. What is a caveat?
A. A warning B. An injunction
C. Writ D. Certiorari

154. Muslim religious foundations are known as:
A. Din B. Wakfs
C. Ulema D. Quzat

155. Beyond what distance from the coast, is the sea known as "High Sea"?
A. 20 miles B. 300 miles
C. 200 miles D. 12 miles

Section-V : Logical Reasoning

Instructions (Qs. No. 156-165): *Each question below consists of one Assertion (A) and one Reason (R). Examine them and shade the correct answers using the Code below*

A. Both A and R are individually true and R is the correct explanation of A.
B. Both A and R are individually true, but R is not the correct explanation of A.
C. A is true, but R is false.
D. A is false, but R is true.

156. Assertion (A): Area along the Equator records the highest temperature throughout the year.

Reason (R): On the equator, days and nights are equal for the largest part of the year.

157. Assertion (A): Commercial fisheries have not developed in tropics.

Reason (R): The demand for marine food from low income population is low in the tropics.

158. Assertion (A): Lightning thunder and heavy rain accompany volcanic activity.

Reason (R): Volcanoes throw water vapour and charged particles in the atmosphere.

159. Assertion (A): Soils in some parts of Punjab, Haryana and Rajasthan are saline.

Reason (R): Evaporation exceeds precipitation.

160. Assertion (A): The monsoons arrive suddenly in India in June.

Reason (R): The monsoonal low pressure trough is well-developed over India.

161. Assertion (A): India built dams and reservoirs to manage water resources.

Reason (R): India had enough experience in canals.

162. Assertion (A): The life expectancy in European countries is very high.

Reason (R): European countries have low mortality rate.

163. Assertion (A): The nomadic herders slaughter their animals for meat.

Reason (R): Animals form the chief source of food and livelihood for nomadic herders.

164. Assertion (A): Exploitation of equatorial rain forest of Amazon basin is not easy.

Reason (R): This region is very rich in several types of deadly animals and insects.

165. Assertion (A): The Sea remains free from ice from British Columbia to Bering Sea.

Reason (R): Air moving off the comparatively warm waters of North Pacific Drill gives the coastal areas of British Columbia a warmer climate.

Instructions (Qs. No. 166-175): *In each question below are given one statement and two assumptions I and II. Examine the statements and choose the correct assumption.*

166. Statement: The patient's condition would improve after operation.

Assumptions: I. The patient can be operated upon in this condition.
II. The patient cannot be operated upon in this condition.

A. If only assumption I is implicit
B. If only assumption II is implicit
C. If either I or II is implicit
D. If neither I nor II is implicit

167. Statement: Detergents should be used to clean clothes.

Assumptions: I. Detergent form more lather.
II. Detergent helps to dislodge grease and dirt.

A. If only assumption I is implicit
B. If only assumption II is implicit
C. If either I or II is implicit
D. If neither I nor II is implicit

168. Statement: "As there is a great demand, every person seeking ticket of the programme will be given only five tickets".

Assumptions: I. The organizers are not keen on selling the tickets.
II. No one is interested in getting more than five tickets.

A. If only assumption I is implicit
B. If only assumption II is implicit
C. If either I or II is implicit
D. If neither I nor II is implicit

169. Statement: Double your money in five months- An advertisement.

Assumptions: I. The assurance is not genuine.
II. People want their money to grow.

A. If only assumption I is implicit
B. If only assumption II is implicit
C. If either I or II is implicit
D. If neither I nor II is implicit

170. Statement: Films have become indispensable for the entertainment of people.

Assumptions: I. Films are the only media of entertainment.
II. People enjoy films.

A. If only assumption I is implicit
B. If only assumption II is implicit
C. If either I or II is implicit
D. If neither I nor II is implicit

171. Statement: 'To keep myself up-to-date, I always listen to 9.00 p.m. news on radio' – A candidate tells the interview board.

Assumptions: I. The candidate does not read newspaper.

II. Broadcast only on radio.

A. If only assumption I is implicit
B. If only assumption II is implicit
C. If either I or II is implicit
D. If neither I nor II is implicit

172. Statement: Never before such a lucid book was available on the topic.

Assumptions: I. Some other books were available on this topic.

II. You can write lucid books on very few topics.

A. If only assumption I is implicit
B. If only assumption II is implicit
C. If either I or II is implicit
D. If neither I nor II is implicit

173. Statement: In case of any difficulty about this case, you may contact our company's lawyer.

Assumptions: I. Each company has a lawyer of its own.

II. The company's lawyer is thoroughly briefed about this case.

A. If only assumption I is implicit
B. If only assumption II is implicit
C. If either I or II is implicit
D. If neither I nor II is implicit

174. Statement: Present day education is in shambles and the country is going to the dogs.

Assumptions: I. A good education system is essential for the well being of a nation.

II. A good education alone is sufficient for the well being of a nation.

D. If only assumption I is implicit
B. If only assumption II is implicit
C. If either I or II is implicit
D. If neither I nor II is implicit

175. Statement: Children are influenced more by their teacher nowadays.

Assumptions: I. The children consider teachers as their models.

II. A large amount of children's time is spent in school.

A. If only assumption I is implicit
B. If only assumption II is implicit
C. If either I or II is implicit
D. If neither I nor II is implicit

Instructions (Qs. No. 176-180): *Each question below contains a statement on relationship and a question regarding relationship based on the statement. Choose the correct option on relationship.*

176. Pointing to a photograph, a lady tells Ram, 'I am the only daughter of this lady and her son is your maternal uncle'. How the speaker is related to Ram's father?

A. sister-in-law B. wife
C. either (a) or (B) D. neither (A) nor (B)

177. Introducing a man, a woman said, 'he is the only son of my mother's mother". How is the woman related to the man?

A. Mother B. Aunt
C. Sister D. Niece

178. Shyam said, 'This girl is the wife of the grandson of my mother'. Who is Shyam to the girl?

A. Father B. Grandfather
C. Husband D. Father-in-law

179. Pointing to a man on the stage, Sunita said, 'He is the brother of the daughter of the wife of my husband'. How is the man on the stage related to Sunita?

A. Son B. Husband
C. Cousin D. Nephew

180. Introducing a man to her husband, a woman said, "His brother's father is the only son of my grandfather". How is the woman related to his man?

A. Mother B. Aunt
C. Sister D. Daughter

Instructions (Qs. No. 181-190): *In each question below two words are paired which have certain relationships.*

181. Legislation : Enactment :: Executive : ?

A. Minister B. Officer
C. Implementation D. Leader

182. UP : Uttarakhand :: Bihar : ?

A. Jharkhand B. Chhattisgarh
C. Madhya Pradesh D. Manipur

183. Gold : Silver :: Cotton : ?

A. Yarn B. Silk
C. Fibre D. Synthetic

184. Botany : Flora :: Zoology : ?

A. Fauna B. Biology
C. Fossils D. Pathology

185. Cold wave : Winter :: Loo : ?

A. Humidity B. Frostbite
C. Summer D. Storm

186. King : Royal :: Saint : ?

A. Religious B. Red
C. Priesthood D. Blue

187. Sculptor : Statue :: Poet : ?

A. Painter B. Singer
C. Poem D. Writer

188. Laugh : Happy :: Cry : ?

A. Sad B. Bickering
C. Frown D. Complain

189. Black : Absence :: White : ?

A. Red
B. Presence
C. Rainbow
D. Crystal

190. Governor : President :: Chief-Minister : ?

A. Commissioner
B. Attorney-General
C. Justice
D. Prime-Minister

Instructions (Qs. No. 191-195): *Each question below contains a Statement and two Courses of Action I and II. Assuming the statement to be true, decide which of the two suggested Course of Action logically follows.*

191. Statement: One of the problems facing the food processing industry is the irregular supply of raw material. The producers of raw materials are not getting a reasonable price.

Courses of Action:

I. The government should regulate the supply of raw material to other industries also.
II. The government should announce an attractive package to ensure regular supply of raw material for food processing industry.

A. If only I follow
B. If only II follow
C. If either I or II follow
D. If neither I nor II follow

192. Statement: The Officer-In-charge of a Company had a hunch that some money was missing from the safe.

Courses of Action:

I. He should get it recounted with the help of the staff and check it with the balance sheet.
II. He should inform the police.

A. If only I follow
B. If only II follow
C. If either I or II follow
D. If neither I nor II follow

193. Statement: If the retired Professors of the same Institutes are also invited to deliberate on restructuring of the organisation, their contribution may be beneficial to the Institute.

Courses of Action:

I. Management may seek opinion of the employees before calling retired Professors.
II. Management should involve experienced people for the systematic restructuring of the organisation.

A. If only I follow
B. If only II follow
C. If either I or II follow
D. If neither I nor II follow

194. Statement: The sale of a particular product has gone down considerably causing great concern to the company.

Courses of Action:

I. The company should make a proper study of rival products in the market.
II. The price of the product should be reduced and quality improved.

A. If only I follow
B. If only II follow
C. If either I or II follow
D. If neither I nor II follow

195. Statement: Mr. X, an active member of the Union, often insults his superiors in the office with his rude behaviour.

Courses of Action:

I. He should be transferred to some other department.
II. The matter should be referred to the Union.

A. If only I follow
B. If only II follow
C. If either I or II follow
D. If neither I nor II follow

Instructions (Qs. No. 196-200): *Each question below contains a Statement and two Arguments I and II. Assume the statement to be true, shade the Argument which is strong.*

196. Statement: Should a total ban be put on trapping wild animals?

Arguments:

I. Yes. Trappers are making a lot of money.
II. No. Bans on hunting and trapping are not effective.

A. If only argument I is strong
B. If only argument II is strong
C. If either argument I or II is strong
D. If neither argument I nor II strong

197. Statement: Should school education be made free in India?

Arguments:

I. Yes. This is the only way to improve the level of literacy.
II. No. It would add to the already heavy burden on the exchequer.

A. If only argument I is strong
B. If only argument II is strong
C. If either argument I or II is strong
D. If neither argument I nor II strong

198. Statement: Should government jobs in rural areas have more incentives?

Arguments:

I. Yes. Incentives are essential for attracting government servants there.
II. No. Rural areas are already cheaper, either and less complex than big. So, why offer extra incentives.

A. Only argument I is strong
B. Only argument II is strong
C. Either argument I or II is strong
D. Neither argument I nor II strong

199. Statement: Should luxury hotels be banned in India?

Arguments:

I. Yes. They are places from where international criminals operate.

II. No. Affluent foreign tourists will have no place to stay.

A. If only argument I is strong
B. If only argument II is strong
C. If either argument I or II is strong
D. If neither argument I nor II strong

200. Statement: Should the political parties be banned?

Arguments:

I. Yes. It is necessary to teach a lesson to the politicians.

II. No. It will lead to an end of democracy.

A. If only argument I is strong
B. If only argument II is strong
C. If either argument I or II is strong
D. If neither argument I nor II strong

ANSWERS

1	**2**	**3**	**4**	**5**	**6**	**7**	**8**	**9**	**10**
A	D	C	A	D	A	C	D	B	D
11	**12**	**13**	**14**	**15**	**16**	**17**	**18**	**19**	**20**
A	D	C	B	A	B	C	D	A	B
21	**22**	**23**	**24**	**25**	**26**	**27**	**28**	**29**	**30**
C	D	B	C	A	B	C	D	A	C
31	**32**	**33**	**34**	**35**	**36**	**37**	**38**	**39**	**40**
B	D	B	A	C	B	D	A	C	B
41	**42**	**43**	**44**	**45**	**46**	**47**	**48**	**49**	**50**
C	C	B	C	A	A	C	D	A	D
51	**52**	**53**	**54**	**55**	**56**	**57**	**58**	**59**	**60**
C	A	A	C	B	B	B	B	A	A
61	**62**	**63**	**64**	**65**	**66**	**67**	**68**	**69**	**70**
C	C	A	D	D	B	B	D	B	D
71	**72**	**73**	**74**	**75**	**76**	**77**	**78**	**79**	**80**
A	C	C	D	A	B	B	D	B	C
81	**82**	**83**	**84**	**85**	**86**	**87**	**88**	**89**	**90**
B	A	C	A	A	D	C	B	A	C
91	**92**	**93**	**94**	**95**	**96**	**97**	**98**	**99**	**100**
A	D	A	B	A	C	B	C	B	A
101	**102**	**103**	**104**	**105**	**106**	**107**	**108**	**109**	**110**
B	C	D	A	B	C	D	A	B	C
111	**112**	**113**	**114**	**115**	**116**	**117**	**118**	**119**	**120**
B	C	A	B	D	A	A	B	A	C
121	**122**	**123**	**124**	**125**	**126**	**127**	**128**	**129**	**130**
D	D	C	A	D	B	C	A	B	C
131	**132**	**133**	**134**	**135**	**136**	**137**	**138**	**139**	**140**
A	B	A	C	B	C	A	C	D	A
141	**142**	**143**	**144**	**145**	**146**	**147**	**148**	**149**	**150**
B	C	A	C	D	A	B	C	B	B
151	**152**	**153**	**154**	**155**	**156**	**157**	**158**	**159**	**160**
C	D	A	B	C	B	C	A	A	A
161	**162**	**163**	**164**	**165**	**166**	**167**	**168**	**169**	**170**
B	B	D	B	A	A	B	D	B	B
171	**172**	**173**	**174**	**175**	**176**	**177**	**178**	**179**	**180**
D	A	B	A	A	B	D	D	A	C
181	**182**	**183**	**184**	**185**	**186**	**187**	**188**	**189**	**190**
C	A	B	A	C	A	C	A	B	D
191	**192**	**193**	**194**	**195**	**196**	**197**	**198**	**199**	**200**
B	A	B	A	D	D	B	A	B	D

EXPLANATORY ANSWERS

91. Sum of the monthly income of 5 members

$= 5 \times 1000$

$= ₹\ 5000$

New sum of the monthly income of 5 members

$= 5000 + \frac{12000}{12}$

$= 5000 + 1000$

$= 6000$

$\therefore$ Required new monthly average

$= \frac{6000}{5}$

$= ₹\ 1200.$

92. Let the cost of 1 kg goods = ₹ 1

Then cost price of goods = ₹ 800

Selling price of goods = ₹ 1000

$$\% \text{ Profit} = \frac{SP - CP}{CP} \times 100$$

$$= \frac{1000 - 800}{800} \times 100$$

$$= \frac{200}{8}$$

$$= 25\%$$

93. Let x oranges should be sold for a rupee to gain 10%

$$\because \quad \frac{SP_1}{100 \pm L/P\%} = \frac{SP_2}{100 \pm L/P\%}$$

$$\frac{\frac{1}{11}}{100 - 10} = \frac{\frac{1}{x}}{100 + 10}$$

$$\frac{1}{11(90)} = \frac{1}{x(110)}$$

$$x = \frac{990}{110}$$

$$= 9.$$

94. 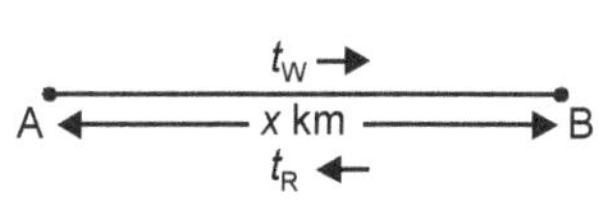

We have,

$t_w + t_R = 3$ hour

$2 \times t_w = 5$ hour

$t_w = 2.5$ hour

$\therefore t_R = 3 - 2.5 = 0.5$ hour

Required times to ride both ways

$= 2 \times 0.5$

$= 1$ hour.

95. $\frac{1}{8} \times 100 = 12.5\%.$

97. 1, 2, 4, 5, 7, 8, 10, 11, **13**

+1, +2, +1, +2, +1, +2, +1, +2

98. $\frac{9}{10} = 0.90,\ \frac{11}{12} = 0.92,\ \frac{23}{28} = 0.82,\ \frac{32}{33} = 0.97$

Hence, smallest fraction $= \frac{23}{28}$

99. Required percentage $= \frac{1200}{3000 + 1800 + 1200} \times 100$

$= \frac{1200}{6000} \times 100$

$= 20\%$

100. Required Age of the teacher $= 15 \times 30 - 14 \times 29$

$= 450 - 406$

$= 44$ years.

101. $\because \quad M_1D_1 = M_2D_2$

$8 \times 96 = 6 \times x$

$\therefore \quad x = \frac{8 \times 96}{6}$

$= 128$ days.

102. Let Shyam's income = ₹ 100

Then Ram's income = ₹ 80 (20% less)

Required percentage $= \frac{100 - 80}{80} \times 100$

$= \frac{20}{80} \times 100$

$= 25\%.$

103. Let monthly salary of A, B and C are ₹ $2x$, ₹ $3x$ and ₹ $5x$ respectively

Then,

$5x - 2x = 1200$

$\Rightarrow \quad 3x = 1200$

$\therefore \quad x = 400$

Then, B's monthly Salary $= 3 \times 400$

$= ₹\ 1200$

104. Number of natives

$$= 94500 - \left(\frac{2}{9} \times 94500 + 6400\right)$$

$$= 94500 - 27400$$

$$= 67100$$

105. Let salary of A, B and C be ₹ a, ₹ b and ₹ c respectively,

Then, $\frac{20}{100} \times a : \frac{15}{100} \times b : \frac{25}{100} \times c = 8 : 9 : 20$

$\Rightarrow 4a : 3b : 5c = 8 : 9 : 20$

$\Rightarrow \quad a : b : c = 2 : 3 : 4$

Thus, C's salary $= \frac{4}{2+3+4} \times 1{,}44{,}000$

= ₹ 64000.

106. Number of males $= \frac{155625}{1000 + 1075} \times 1000$

$$= \frac{155625}{2075} \times 1000$$

$$= 75 \times 1000 = 75000$$

Number of females = 155625 – 75000 = 80625

Number of literate persons

$$= \frac{40}{100} \times 75000 + \frac{24}{100} \times 80625$$

$$= 30{,}000 + 19350 = 49350$$

Required percentage $= \frac{49350}{155625} \times 100 = 31.7\%$

107. Average price of pig

$= \frac{1}{5}$ (₹ 6,000 – 10 × ₹ 450)

$= \frac{1}{5} \times$ ₹ 1500 = ₹ 300.

108. Let weight of Ram and Shyam be $(x + 25)$ kg and x kg respectively, then

$x + 25 + x = 325$

$\Rightarrow \quad 2x = 300$

$\therefore \quad x = 150$

Thus, weight of Shyam = 150 kg.

109. 3 →(+5)→ 8 →(+7)→ 15 →(+9)→ 24 →(+11)→ 34 (35) →(+13)→ 48 →(+15)→ 63

Thus, wrong number = 34

110. Place value of 7 in the figure 9872590 = 70000

9 788194 233626

Printed by Libri Plureos GmbH in Hamburg,
Germany